Tradigital Animate CC

Learn how to bridge the gap between traditional animation principles and digital software.

Tradigital Animate CC: 12 Principles of Animation in Adobe Animate brings the essentials of traditional animation and Adobe Animate together. The early masters of animation created a list of 12 principles which are important for anyone who wants to create interesting and believable animation. Digital animation continues to make incredible technological advancements that give animators the capability to produce visually stunning work. New technology, however, also has a tendency to create an environment where animators are so focused on adapting to the new workflow that they tend to dismiss these fundamental animation principles, which often leads to poor and lifeless character animation. *Tradigital Animate CC* helps you focus on these principles while using the program's wide array of features to create believable animation, consistently.

Tradigital Animate CC joins three other Tradigital books covering Maya, Blender, and 3ds Max. This new volume in the series approaches the topic in a different way, giving readers both a practical look at the software, and providing a theoretical understanding of the genre.

- Learn a new principle in each chapter, the Animate CC tools most related to it, and how to put it all together.

- A plethora of examples demonstrate the good methods that animators should use in Animate CC, how to avoid the bad ones, and ways to create a workflow that works for you.

- An easy-to-follow approach with examples throughout the book that build on each other, showing how the principles act together.

- A companion website (www.rubberonion.com/tradigital-animate) features more examples, downloadable FLA resource files, and video tutorials.

Stephen Brooks is the creator of Rubber Onion Animation, a freelance and virtual studio operation. With ads, cartoon shorts and his character work on games such as Moshi Monsters paying the bills, Stephen has been active in creating his own animated shorts, podcast and tutorial series. With a focus on classical, hand-drawn animation, Stephen has been working in Animate CC (formerly called Flash) for over ten years, bridging the gap between the traditional and digital worlds.

Tradigital Animate CC

12 Principles of Animation in Adobe Animate

Stephen Brooks

CRC Press
Taylor & Francis Group
Boca Raton London New York

CRC Press is an imprint of the
Taylor & Francis Group, an **informa** business

CRC Press
Taylor & Francis Group
6000 Broken Sound Parkway NW, Suite 300
Boca Raton, FL 33487-2742

First issued in hardback 2017

ISBN-13: 978-1-138-01292-9 (pbk)
ISBN-13: 978-1-138-42828-7 (hbk)

Library of Congress Cataloging in Publication Data
Brooks, Stephen, 1983–
Tradigital flash : 12 principles of animation in Adobe Flash / Stephen Brooks.
pages cm
1. Flash (Computer file) 2. Computer animation--Computer programs. I. Title.
TR897.72.F53.B76 2016
006.6'96--dc23
2015024188

Typeset in Xenois Pro
by Servis Filmsetting Ltd, Stockport, Cheshire

Visit the Taylor & Francis Web site at
http://www.taylorandfrancis.com

and the CRC Press Web site at
http://www.crcpress.com

Contents

Acknowledgments

If your name is on this list, you should hear the words THANK YOU ringing in your head!

G

My family

Chris Georgenes

Rob Yulfo

Andrew Kaiko

Alan Becker

Ross Bollinger

Jennifer Adkins Smith

David Stiller

Nathan Quarry

Alexandru Craciun

Ryan Woodward

Adam Phillips

Nathan Viney

Greg Pugh

Tim D Saguinsin

Nathan Kester

Christopher S Murphy

Richard Butler

Dave Johnson

Jules Jammal

Tom Hand

Thank you to all the companies and copyright holders featured in this book, Frank and Ollie for writing theirs, and to all those who I may have missed ... you may yell at me later.

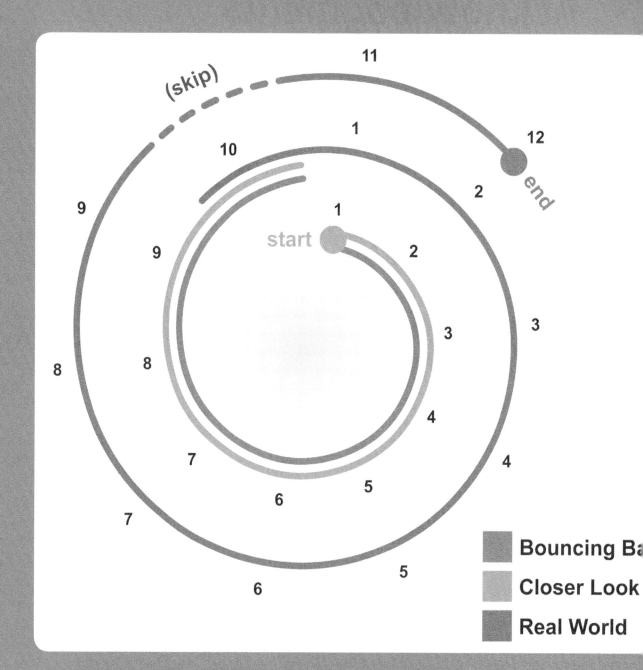

Image 0.0 How to read through the chapters in this book as a beginner.

INTRODUCTION

The mission statement of this book is to bring the traditional principles of animation together with Adobe Animate for anyone, regardless of their previous involvement with either. This teaching guide focuses on becoming well versed in both, together. We will walk step-by-step through each principle as its own chapter and see how to apply it using our digital tools. There will be a simple guided exercise, real-world examples, conceptual explanations, and a reinforcement of the new information you have learned in each chapter. This is not a coffee table book nor a strict instructional; it's a hybrid, like the Tradigital workflow we'll inhabit.

There are two aspects to this book: the 12 Principles of Animation, and the program we know as Animate CC. We will be splitting up the principles and the program into sections to tackle them independently and then merge the concepts and practices together more in depth to really nail it in—including this Intro. Before we go on, though, I did want to mention one very important thing: **cumulative learning**.

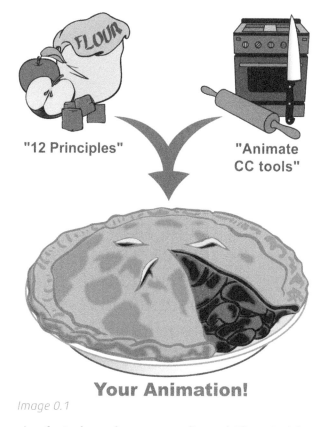

"12 Principles"

"Animate CC tools"

The 12 Principles all build on each other. Animate's features and their uses build on themselves too. Used together, the principles and Animate CC build on top of one another to make endless, wonderful combinations. This layering is at the heart of any animation. To make an apple pie, you need dough, apples, sugar and a few other ingredients. You also need kitchen tools to put these items together such as a rolling pin, knives, oven and so on. The point is, in order to get the desired result of "delicious apple pie" you need these

Your Animation!

Image 0.1

ingredients to be combined in a certain way using the tools you have at your disposal. The principles are your ingredients. The program's features are your tools (*Image 0.1*).

By the end of this book, you will be able to use the principles in your animation and the tools in Animate CC to make them happen in wonderful ways. The interpretations of the principles and the combinations are what make up individual style. In the beginning, everyone copies. But once the concepts sink in and all that practice has been baked into knowing, an individual's style emerges. If you follow chapter by chapter the path in the spiral learning chart at the beginning of this Intro, by the end of this book you will have a command of the program and an understanding of the principles to improve your animation and develop your own sense of artistic style in movement. So let's quickly run through how we'll go about that.

Each chapter is made up of three main activities: the **bouncing ball** exercise, a **closer look** section for it and a **real world example**. We'll start off by getting a conceptual understanding of the principle in the intro by including what it means and when it can be used. The bouncing ball exercise is a classic animation learning technique and will help you get a grasp on pulling the abstract ideas of the principle into actual use, while exposing more of Animate's toolset. In the closer look section, we'll dive a little deeper into what you just did in the bouncing ball exercise. After this, there's a real-world example of the chapter's titular principle at work. And finally the chapter ends with "Final Words."

HOW TO READ THIS BOOK

Notice the spiral learning chart at the beginning of this Intro. It sets out the best path in which to use this book as a beginner to Animate CC, the 12 Principles or both. The bouncing ball is an important learning tool, but it *is* just a ball. Visually it's not all that stimulating. I wanted you, the reader, to see what kind of fruit all the practicing and learning you are doing will bear. The issue of the real world exercises though is that in order to produce it in a Tradigital workflow using the 12 Principles of Animation and Animate's toolset, those two areas first need to be covered. But instead of having the first half of the book only be program screengrabs and images of a bouncing ball while all the "good stuff" of the real world exercises are in solitary confinement in the last half, I opted to lay out this book to have them all together for motivation.

If you're a beginner, you won't be ready for the real world exercises until you've learned the basics of Animate CC and the Principles — that much has already been said. But the beauty of a book is that once you flip a page it doesn't disappear; it's still there for you to go back to. So if you didn't quite understand the spiral learning chart in the intro image here's the path in written form. As a beginner:

- Read Chapters 1–9, do the bouncing ball and closer look sections but *skip the real world exercises*

- Read Chapter 10, complete all exercises within

- *Return* to Chapters 1–9 and complete the real world exercises

- Read Chapters 11 and 12 and complete any exercises within

The book is set up this way for **progressive and reinforced learning**. As you're going through your first pass in Chapters 1–9, feel free to check out the real world exercises for inspiration and motivation. That's why they're there instead of in the back of the book!

If you have experience animating in Animate CC or already understand the 12 Principles, you can choose what you want to read, when and how. There's something in here for everyone. Keep an eye out for "Pro-tips" and "hotkeys" (the ones in bold) in the exercise steps. The next three sections of the Intro will serve as a primer for that chapter format I mentioned. Please *do not skip these*. I will be referring back to the information in the Intro throughout the rest of the chapters.

INTRODUCING: THE PRINCIPLES

The range that the 12 Principles cover is so wide that it encompasses everything from the cold physics of movement to the warm embrace of illustration. Through their exploration, we will have an opportunity to actually use the program at the center of this book to facilitate the animation itself, while exploring those principles. First, though, let's cover a little bit about the 12 Principles of Animation.

I'm assuming that most of you who bought this book have an understanding of what the principles are on at least a surface level (any quick Google search will pop up endless results). Even so, it's important to know what they are and how they originated if we are to understand and use them best. So, where did these coveted 12 Principles of Animation come from? Were they recently uncovered in a long forgotten tomb? Maybe they appeared unto the blade of a legendary sword, only to be wielded by the hand of a righteous man.

In 1981, two of Walt Disney's Nine Old Men (the original masters in the early years of Disney's golden age), Frank Thomas and Ollie Johnston, released a book called *The Illusion of Life: Disney Animation.* In an effort to describe the methods used to create characters that seemed to exist in a physical world, they put the 12 Principles of Animation in public print for the first time. These principles were nailed down over about 50 years at that point, starting with the creation of *Snow White and the Seven Dwarfs* (1937)—the time Disney started going for a more realistic approach to their animation. You can clearly see some of these principles being applied to non-Disney works before that, of course, but that was a very experimental time in animation. Once Walt Disney moved to this new direction of realism, everything changed. It was a renaissance for animated film.

Image 0.2 Ilustration by Rob Yulfo (youtube.com/AnthraxYulfo).

The Nine Old Men were so called (in jest) by Walt in reference to U.S. President Franklin D. Roosevelt's derisive name for the Supreme Court justices during his court-packing campaign after the start of the New Deal. It was the studious nature of these early animators that truly moved the Disney style forward to become ... what it would become: a very cohesive style where everything's playing by the same basic rules. A keen eye can pick out the acting subtleties between these Nine Old Men in the early movies. It was how they combined and played with the principles that made them unique to each other, while still working in the same style.

It's important to note, however, that these principles are not necessarily universal, nor do they all need to be applied in every sequence. A principle is a fundamental basis for a thing. In this case, it's the Disney style. You all know it. But if you're looking to foster a different style, having this base knowledge of Disney's 12 Principles of Animation will still help you understand the fundamentals of motion and design, we'll talk about why they work and when you can break these principles for effect.

INTRODUCING: THE BOUNCING BALL

I'm a big believer in learning-by-doing. Actually, "believer" might be the wrong word here, since what I really am (and any animator, really) is an example. I'm a big example of learning-by-doing, then. Many people, when they start out, have a hard time rectifying what practicing the mechanics of a bouncing ball has to do with animating characters—or anything other than a ball, for that matter. It's not an unfair question. Other than "bumbles" (+10pts if you got the animation reference), what bounces? Everything. I would say "everything that falls" but even that's not accurate. Sure, if you drop something off a building it's going to bounce (… or splat). What if something doesn't fall first? How often am I going to need to animate something falling, anyway? If I'm typing the questions, and you're reading them in the first person, who's "I" and who's "you?" All good questions.

The lesson of the bouncing ball is about timing, squash and stretch, arcs and a myriad of other

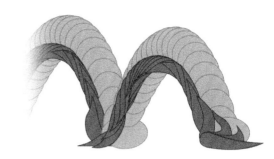

Image 0.3 Bouncing Ball exercise from Chapter 8 "Follow Through and Overlapping Action".

principles that are directly applied to just about every movement you will animate. Mastering the bouncing ball is the quickest way to conceptualizing the principles of animation. While it may seem easy when you start, the complexity will increase throughout the chapters, so it's important to have a solid base (meaning, please follow along from the beginning). Crawl before you walk. Look before you leap. Ball before you … draw? You get my point.

Let's take a grasshopper as an example. The one thing we all know about them is they hop; it's right there in the name. Animating that grasshopper would take into account all the principles I just listed above; ones that you will understand deeply by the time we get to the more complicated and abstract principles like appeal and solid drawing. So on your path to understanding the 12 Principles of Animation, Adobe Animate and how to use them in unison, you will pull them all together by learning how to bounce a ball in various ways. That knowledge can be directly applied to animating that grasshopper … and *everything*.

In one chapter, you will apply a principle to a ball to start it bouncing and then save the file. In the next chapter, a new principle will be *added* to the bouncing ball so that it exhibits both principles simultaneously and a new file will be saved. By the end of the book, you will have many files and a clear path of learning. You will have a bouncing ball exhibiting multiple Principles of Animation simultaneously within Adobe Animate and be ready to put it all together yourself in your own animation!

INTRODUCING: THE PROGRAM

Adobe Animate is a fantastically versatile tool. The thing about versatility is that it can sometimes be a synonym of daunting. In this case, though, the reason that Animate CC has become so popular for budding animators is that it takes a fairly minimalist approach, letting the artists do what they want and largely getting out of their way. Almost everything from the workspaces to the tools to the properties and beyond is customizable, so the program essentially "grows" with the capabilities of the artist. This ability to create with a minimum that can expand with experience makes it very attractive to the average user. And it doesn't hurt that it's affordable. Taking things one principle at a time throughout the bouncing ball exercise allows for a step-by-step look at the tools within the program. But before we get into the specific tools, let's just review what this program actually is.

Adobe Flash is now Adobe Animate

It was announced on November 30, 2015 that Adobe was rebranding its animation program "Flash" to now be called "Animate." Basically, the change is in name only, but as with any version update there are new features in Animate CC that weren't available when it was still called Flash. This brings up the second part of this section, which is that this book was designed to be compatible with all previous versions of the program now known as Animate CC, and that includes Flash versions.

There are two main differences that arose when Adobe Flash became Adobe Animate in name: some user graphics (the way the program looks to you as you use it) and new tools. **To help, there are highlighted sections throughout the**

Image 0.4

book that point out the differences between Flash and Animate CC so that you can follow along no matter which version of either you have. The focus in this book's exercises is the workflow and how to create your own version of a workflow that is best for you and your animation goals. So while there are new features that are addressed, the core of these lessons rests firmly in tools and processes which have been well established in the programs regardless of name or version number.

Vector VS Raster

Animate CC is a *vector* based program (often called a "draw program"). This type of program is in contrast to a *raster* based program, such as Photoshop (often called a "paint program"). If you aren't aware of the differences, it's a fairly simple distinction: vector images can be resized and never get blurry as opposed to a raster image which would look pixelated. Have you ever taken a picture of something and then tried to zoom in really far only to find it getting fuzzy and indecipherable? That effect is because the image is raster—made up of a series of set pixels. A vector image will never fall into that trap because it's instead made up of reference points.

Image 0.5 Zoom view of vector image (left) and raster image (right).

When you draw lines in Animate CC, the program translates those lines into a series of points which the computer itself then draws between. The program basically just takes your drawing and makes it a connect-the-dots/paint-by-numbers type image for the computer. When you stretch it out, the points just get farther apart and the computer simply redraws the lines between them. That's why the image will never get blurry. The user isn't usually aware of the distinction because, functionally, it's the same. You draw and the program does the rest. However, this difference *is* important to note because there are many things you will be able to do with this ability of increasing or decreasing the size of an image and always keeping the same clarity.

Layout

Enough with all these words, let's get into the audience participation! When you first open Animate CC, you're greeted with a dialog box asking you to choose which template you want to use. Don't worry about all these settings right now, simply chose any "ActionScript" version under the "Create New" section (*Image 0.6*). Different versions of Animate CC support varying versions of ActionScript (for instance, Animate CS6 supports both 2.0 and 3.0 while CC only supports 3.0). Now you're in the workspace. Animate CC has multiple versions of this layout

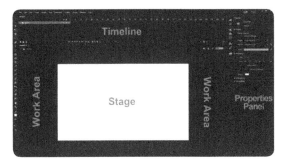

Image 0.6 We're working in the "Classic" Animate CC layout in this book.

built into the program. To make sure we're all on the same page, let's double check we're working in the same workspace. Select the "Classic" layout by going to **Window > Workspace > Classic**.

Right now, you should see a set of tools on the left, the Properties Panel on the right, a timeline on the top and a white rectangle in the middle (*Image 0.7*, overleaf). We will cover the details of these panels throughout the book, but let's take a quick look at what these things actually *are* before we start messing around. The white area in the middle is known as the "stage." There is a gray area around the white, and that is known as the "work area" (also, "pasteboard"). Think of these two things as you would a theater and the area behind the curtains in the theater. Anything on the stage (the white area) is viewable to the audience, anything outside of that is not ... it's backstage. That gray area, the "work area," is cut out of your final video. The work area is where we put notes to ourselves and extra assets, but it also acts as an easy crop to images that are bigger than we actually use. So remember: white area is "on stage" and seen by the audience, the gray area is "offstage" and hidden from them.

Now let's look at the tools to the left of the layout (*Image 0.8*, overleaf). This bar is like a drawer holding your pens, pencils, paint brush and paints, straight-edge, you name it! With these tools, you will be creating and altering images. Let's do something really quick just to see what it feels like to draw in the program. Select the paint brush from the toolbar on the left (pressing the **B** key will do the same). On the stage, draw whatever you want. A squiggle—let's draw a squiggle. Now, say you want to draw something on the bottom-right but want that area centered on screen so you can draw it better. Press-and-hold the **Space Bar** and you'll see a hand replace your cursor. With the space bar still held, click the stage and drag it around as you see fit. When you're happy with the position, release the space bar and continue drawing. The press-and-hold quick selection of some tools is very helpful for speed but there's always a more permanent version of those selections, which in the case of the Hand

Tool you just used is (appropriately) the **H** key. These shortcuts to using the tools through use of your keyboard are called *hotkeys*. You will see these throughout the book in **bold** while Apple OS specific keys will be in green and **PC specific keys will be in blue.** Look back over to the toolbar and hover your cursor over any one of the tools for a second or two. You should see a simple text popup which says the name of the tool plus its hotkey; for instance *Brush Tool (B)* (again, see *Image 0.8*). Learning to use these hot keys early on will really help your workflow and keep things moving, allowing you to focus on the actual act of creating ... which is the whole point!

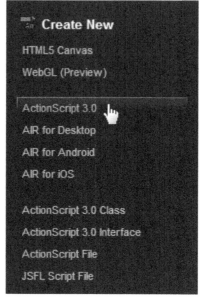

The Properties panel on the right has information which changes contextually based on what is selected. If you still have the Brush Tool (**B**) selected, you will see information such as Fill and Stroke and Smoothing. If you were to switch back to the Selection Tool (**V**) but have

Image 0.7 Opening prompt (Animate CC 2016).

no object actually selected you would see information relevant to the overall project such as the resolution, frame rate, and the stage color which is white, by default (*Image 0.9*). I would like to mention a couple things about these before we move on. Basically, the resolution just says how many pixels the image is wide (number on the left) and how many tall (number on the right). If the resolution is preceded with a larger number than the other, it will make the rectangle be wide (like a movie screen) while the other way around will make it tall (like a standard notebook). For now we will simply be using 1920 × 1080 and for the remainder of this book. Notice that the first number is larger (1920) than the second (1080), so this will be widescreen.

Image 0.8 *Toolbar with hotkeys shown and Brush Tool selected (Animate CC 2016).*

FPS stands for "frames per second," and it's exactly what it sounds like: the amount of frames Animate CC will show during one second. The higher the fps, the more frames will fly by in every second. Film is 24fps, North American TV is 29.97fps (basically 30), and European TV

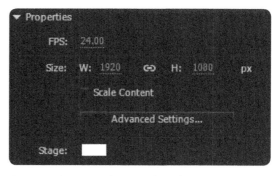

Image 0.9 Properties panel (Animate CC 2016).

is 25fps. We will be working in 24fps because it is easy to work with (it is more easily divisible, and that advantage will become apparent when we talk about "animation math" in Chapter 1). Plus, that is what the classic animation masters were using.

Image 0.10 Timeline (Animate CC 2016).

Frame rate refers to the speed at which the frames are displayed, and those frames are represented in the timeline at the top of the layout (*Image 0.10*). As we work through the bouncing ball exercise we will cover how to work in it, but essentially this area is where you see how many frames you have drawn in and where they are in time. It's just like the timeline of a video player showing you where you are in the video, except each frame cell also shows you which frames actually have information in them. Currently, you're seeing one blank frame (the white box with the dot at the beginning) and the rest are empty frames (a series of ghostly white and gray boxes, looking kind of like piano keys).

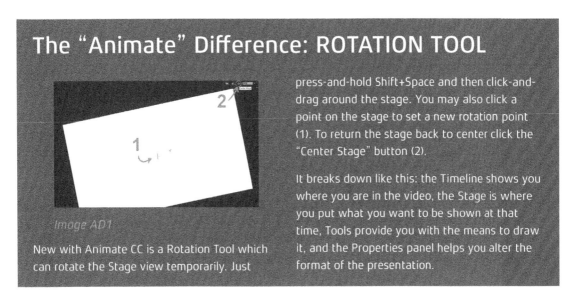

The "Animate" Difference: ROTATION TOOL

Image AD1

New with Animate CC is a Rotation Tool which can rotate the Stage view temporarily. Just press-and-hold Shift+Space and then click-and-drag around the stage. You may also click a point on the stage to set a new rotation point (1). To return the stage back to center click the "Center Stage" button (2).

It breaks down like this: the Timeline shows you where you are in the video, the Stage is where you put what you want to be shown at that time, Tools provide you with the means to draw it, and the Properties panel helps you alter the format of the presentation.

HERE WE GO

Now that some of the housekeeping is out of the way, we can get to the good stuff! It's best to go through this book from front to back, as laid out in the spiral learning graph at the start of the Introduction (*Image 0.0*). I know I've said this, but it bears repeating that one of the great things that the 12 Principles of Animation have in common with Adobe Animate is that every part of them build on each other. To create your animations, you will be using your knowledge of multiple principles at once as well as working with many tools and expertly navigating your timeline. We will work through the simple stuff first and build on them up to the more complicated and abstracts parts. By the end of the book you will have multiple Animate CC files showing progressively more impressive versions of a bouncing ball, a working knowledge of Animate CC and its features, an understanding of the 12 Principles and some experience with chaining these principles and the program features together in real-world scenarios. So ... here we go!

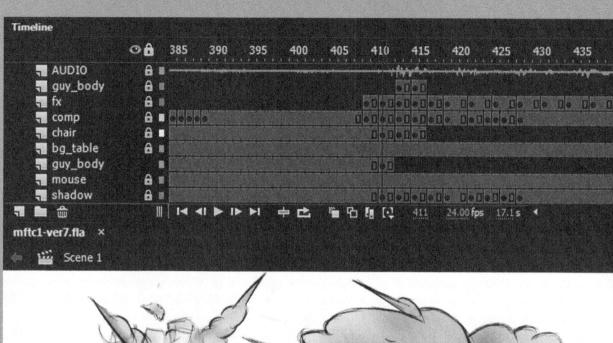

Image 1.0 My Friend the Computer #1: Three, Two, One...
by Stephen Brooks
(RubberOnion.com).

Chapter 1

TIMING

INTRODUCING
Timing

Timing is the very basis of animation.
At its core, to animate is to take something that is not alive and, in the words of Captain Jean-Luc Picard, make it so. We all know that animation is displaying sequential images in time to make them move, but the timing of it all will affect the mood of the action. A batter hitting a baseball at "real-time" speed will evoke a different response from the viewer than watching that same action in "slow-mo." Just as the type of music playing during a scene will change its feeling, so too will Timing.

Think of Timing as the heartbeat of the character. Is it erratic? Calm? Intense? Lazy? It will define what you do. If you have a shot of a boxer being punched in the face with a duration of only 0.5 seconds, think of how the drama of the shot will change if it takes 1 second to elapse or a slow-motion-style 5 seconds. Timing is at the beginning of this book because it should be the first thing on your mind when you start to animate. Ask yourself, "how long should this take to happen?"

In this chapter, we will cover technical terms such as frame rate, tween, as well as get a further look at some aspects of Adobe Animate we covered in the book's Introduction like the shape tools, timeline, and Properties panel. We'll also begin our work with understanding symbols so that you will learn how to draw a simple shape, move it around, and get an understanding of what Timing encompasses and how to use Animate CC to implement this principle in your animation.

A WORD ABOUT
Graphics Tablets

Image 1.1 Wacom Intuos4XL.

There are some of you out there who might not have a graphics tablet for drawing, which I can understand. One of the appeals of Animate CC is its affordability whereas a tablet would be another purchase to add to the list. This book will not force you to draw on a tablet, but I would recommend it for no greater reason than it helps preserve the connection your brain has made between the art you *imagine* and the art you *make.* That connection is deeply rooted in almost everyone, stemming from when you started drawing ducks on your parents' walls with cheap, unwashable, wax crayons.

By working through the bouncing ball exercises using Animate's shape and movement tools, you can connect the concepts of the principles to that animator part of your brain—and then that to the program. Once you feel like you want to move beyond that, try doing the exercises over again by drawing each frame with a graphics tablet. For now, however, let's go step by step through the timing exercise with the bouncing ball and learn some of the program on the way.

BOUNCING BALL Timing

Note: Animate's layout is covered in this book's Introduction. If you are uncertain as to what and where the timeline, tools and stage are, please refer back to the section "Introducing: The Program."

Setting Up

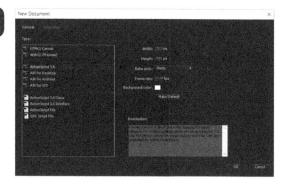

Image BB1.0 Pictured: Flash CS6 when the Oval and Rectangle tools were docked together.

If you haven't already done so, open Animate CC and create a new document (**File > New**). The only things that truly matter right now are the width, height, and frame rate. For our purposes we will use 1920 for the width and 1080 for the height. Anyone who has a hi-def TV out there that says 1080i or 1080p—that's this resolution. As for the frame rate, for the remainder of this book we will be working in 24 frames per second (henceforth known as *fps*). Once you select OK, your document is created. If you made a mistake, not to worry! Locate the Properties panel. If you don't locate this panel for some reason the hotkey combination to bring it up is Cmd**+J** on Mac and **Ctrl+J** on PC. There you can see the size and fps settings which can be altered at any time to get the settings you want. These affect the entire document, meaning there's only one value for each setting in a document such as the one you just created.

Before we get too far, let's save this bad boy right now; we'll be working in it a lot. Choose an obvious name like "bouncing ball 1 – timing." We will be saving a new file for every chapter so that as we progress we won't lose the work from previous chapters. *(Pro tip: select **File > Save As** ... and put a 1 at the end of your file name, and periodically do the same but with increasing numbers to create "mile marker" files. In the event of a computer crash, power outage, cat unplugging cord, you won't lose much work at all. It's helpful on bigger projects.)*

Because of our resolution being so high, some computer monitors may not be seeing the whole stage right now. To show the entire stage, locate the Zoom control drop-down menu on the top-right corner of the stage. It should currently be set at 100%. Select that drop-down menu and click "Show Frame." You should now see the stage surrounded by gray work area. As mentioned in this book's Introduction, only the things inside the stage will appear in the final video that exports. So for the purposes of this bouncing ball exercise, the "ground" will be the bottom of the stage.

Now that we're all set up, it's time to get started with animating!

PART I
"Drawing The Ball"

1. In the toolbar, select the Oval Tool (**O**). If all you see is a square like in Adobe Flash CS6 or below, click and hold on it until a popup appears with subset tools and select the circle. Don't worry about the color right now. *Image BB1.1*

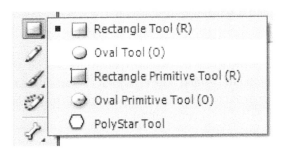

Image BB1.1

2. Click and drag on the stage somewhere in the top left to draw a circle. This shape will be the ball that we will be bouncing ever so wonderfully. *(Pro tip: hold **Shift** as you're dragging to force Animate CC to draw a perfect circle). Image BB1.2*

Image BB1.2

3. Choose the Selection Tool (**V**) from the toolbar and double-click the circle we just drew to highlight all of it.

4. Right-click the now highlighted circle and select **Convert to Symbol ... (F8)**. A popup will appear, asking for some information. Name it "ball," select **Graphic** from the Type drop-down menu, and make sure the Registration point is in the middle. Click OK. *Image BB1.4*

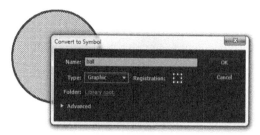

Image BB1.4

Interlude

A quick note: you might be wondering what the difference is between the symbol types in step 4 and why we chose "Graphic." The symbol types will be explained in the closer look section later in this chapter. We won't get into the Registration point until much later, but to satisfy any nagging curiosity, it's basically the default pivot point. But now, let's talk about the ball you just created. Take a look at it. How long do you think it will take to fall to the ground (bottom of the stage)? Whatever answer you just gave to that question has determined how large the ball is. We have drawn one ball of a certain size, and it is already a certain distance from our ground. How long it takes the ball to reach the ground tells us how big the ball is around. For instance, given the size I drew mine (which you can see in the provided *.fla file), if you said "1 second" then it's about the size of a beach ball. If you said "0.5 second," it would be a softball. "3 seconds?" The NYC Times Square New Year's Ball with all the lights and expensiveness—you get the point. Timing affects a great deal in physics; you want to understand why so you can break the rules to the greatest effect.

Image 1.2 Depending on the timing of a fall, the same size circle could represent a range of sizes.

The trick here is to use your brain as a simulator. You drew your bouncing ball already; now close your eyes and imagine it bouncing. Without even thinking about it you have come up with how long it will take the ball to hit the ground and how long it will take to bounce back up. I could tell you to do that with anything. Think of an asteroid. Now close your eyes and make it explode into a magnificent spectacle. Do the same thing with a chipmunk (those unholy creatures who eat the tomatoes right off the vine that *someone* tried very hard to cultivate). That's your imagination at work—the world's greatest render machine. So if you go back to the bouncing ball, the goal is to take that information you created in your imagination and use it in our timing. When I asked you to imagine it bouncing, how long did it take to hit the ground? How high did it bounce afterward? Try tapping the table with the beat of the bounce to help bring the timing out of your imagination and into the real world. Side note: if you've done everything I've just asked of you in the presence of someone else who is not reading these same words, you will look very odd. You're welcome. Step one in becoming an animator: you will look very odd when you work.

Getting back to the exercise, for the upcoming steps you should follow along with the timing I give you, and we will build together. I will be referring to specific timing and other choices made here in the later chapters. If you're already comfortable with the principles and are in this more as a way to learn Animate CC, you can choose your own timing; but be aware that you'll have to compensate mentally for the differences in the ensuing chapters' exercises. To make things easy, I will start out with the bounce taking 1 second.

PART II
"Making It Move"

5. Since we start on frame 1, our frame rate is 24fps, and the duration of the bounce will be 1 second, the end will be on frame 25. Right-click on the empty square at frame 25 and select **Insert Keyframe (F6)**. This last frame will be our end "up" position. More on keyframes later, but for now it should be noted that they are the important frames—the ones where we initiate a computer-generated or a manual change to the shape or position of an image. *Image BB1.5*

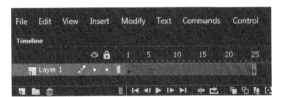

Image BB1.5

6. Now that we have the start and end "up" keyframes, we need the "contact" keyframe where the ball touches the ground. Right now you are seeing a gray bar from frame 1 to 25. This bar is showing you that the computer will display the image on frame 1 as it is until the next keyframe (currently on frame 25). Select frame 13 on the timeline and make another keyframe by hitting the hotkey **F6** on your keyboard. *Image BB1.6*

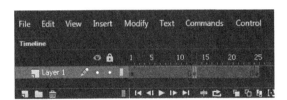

Image BB1.6

7. With the ball highlighted on the stage, hold the down arrow until it reaches the bottom of the stage. *(Pro tip: hold Shift while pressing the down arrow to jump 10 normal increments at a time.)* This keyframe is the "contact" position. *Image BB1.7*

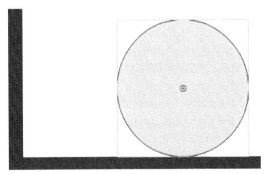

Image BB1.7

8. Time to make this ball move! Right-click on the keyframe on frame 1 and select **Create Classic Tween**. *(Note: "Classic" was added from Flash CS4 on because another type of tween was included. Before this version however, it'll say "Motion" instead.)* The gray area between the two frames will turn blue with an arrow. Hit **Enter** and you'll see the ball drop. *Image BB1.8*

Image BB1.8

9. Repeat step 8 for the keyframe on frame 13 to return the ball back to the top. *Image BB1.9*

Image BB1.9

10. To see your work, select **File > Publish Preview > Animate**, and you'll see a window pop up (if you don't see your ball bouncing very well, right-click in the popup and select **Show All**). The hotkey for this particular Animate CC publishing is Cmd/**Ctrl+Enter**.

It's a simple thing we just made, just a circle moving up and down … and rather stiff at that. But this is just the beginning. There are a few important things to note at this point. If you are new to animation and the program, what you have learned is how to create an image and make it move where you want within the time you want. If you are already familiar with the program but not so much with the principles, this is the essence of Timing. Think about the object or character and what's happening on screen, and through this context you can discover the time frame needed for an action to happen. If you're familiar with this principle and not the program, you may already have a bias against tweening … it's OK, because I honestly did too at first. In part, you feel like you're giving up control to the computer if you're used to drawing every frame. Ultimately, you can still do that in Animate CC. But you will see that through using symbols, tweening, and some of the other features of the program that you'll encounter in this book you will be able to apply the same 12 principles that have worked for traditional animation for almost a century … and faster, at that.

As mentioned in this book's Introduction, the bouncing ball exercise is an excellent way to grasp the fundamentals. Being that this is the first exercise, it doesn't get much more basic than this. The more you learn about a program (its tools, functions, and options), the more you can combine that knowledge together. When writing an email, you may capitalize entire words for EMPHASIS using the caps lock and paste in a web address from your browser … and maybe even draw a heart with a < and a 3. At some point, you had to learn each of those particular features, functionalities, and tricks—and now you can combine them together at will to communicate to someone whatever it is you <3. This ability to flow between tools and techniques to express yourself will happen with Animate CC as well.

You might also guess that this process is exactly what happens with the principles; they can and should be combined together in various and wonderful ways. Think of the principles like muscles: to perform a particular action, certain muscles need to be engaged. Perform a different action, and a different combination of muscles will flex. But there are always those core muscles that will be used in practically everything you do. One of these core muscles (or principles, if you follow my analogy) is Timing. As you learn the principles and the program through the bouncing ball exercise, your ability to combine all of this knowledge together to create great animation will grow. So let's look a little deeper into one very important aspect of the program and see what more we can learn here before moving onto the next principle.

CLOSER LOOK
Graphic Symbol Vs. Movie Clip

The first thing we did in the exercise was to draw a circle and create a symbol out of it. There are three types of symbols you *can* create, but only two types you will use in animation: "Graphic" and "Movie Clip." When a symbol is created, it is saved within the document's Library (**Window > Library**). Symbols are containers for animation. Double-clicking one will show you what's inside: you'll see a timeline just as you do on the main stage. Inside either of these types of symbols, you can create a completely independent animation (such as a character walking in place). You may then take that symbol with the animation playing inside it like a projector and move it around just as we did with the ball (such as across the stage to make a character appear to be running across it). Symbols can also be endlessly repeated on stage. The terminology can sometimes get confusing so I will periodically repeat and reinforce this but when a symbol is on the stage it's actually called an "instance." You can have a hundred *instances* of the bouncing ball symbol on stage but if you edit the *symbol* all of the instances will show that same edit because it is the source.

The interior may look the same, but these two symbols are quite different in function which impacts how you will use them. A Movie Clip will play its internal timeline from its beginning to its end no matter what's happening on the main stage, and in almost all versions of Animate CC/Flash isn't able to be exported to video (a big problem for most animators). A Graphic Symbol's playback, on the other hand, can be controlled and does export to video. There is an added feature since Flash CS3 that Movie Clips bring to the game however, and that is that they can have filters applied to them (such as blur, drop shadow, and glow). So our general use of symbols as animators breaks down like this: Graphic Symbols for animation, Movie Clips for illustration. You will see this for yourself in later chapters but for now, we're just using the mighty Graphic Symbol. Now let's get around inside the symbol to see what we can learn.

"Graphic symbols for animation,
Movie Clips for illustration."

Image 1.3 The midground tree and background trees are Movie Clips with a blur filter. The child is a Graphic symbol with nested animation.

"Editing Inside A Symbol"

1. Locate the Library panel (Cmd/**Ctrl+L**) and double-click on the symbol labeled "ball" (it should be the only one there). If you look at the timeline again, our animation looks like it's gone! It's not, this is the timeline *within* our symbol of the ball as mentioned before. This separate work area is nested inside the ball symbol. *Image CL1.1*

2. Double-click on the ball so that we can change its color. In the toolbar there are two colored boxes: one with a pencil next to it and the other with a paint bucket. These are the Stroke Color and Fill Color options, respectively. They should currently correspond to the colors on the ball (stroke is the outline color, fill is the inside color). *Image CL1.2*

Image CL1.1

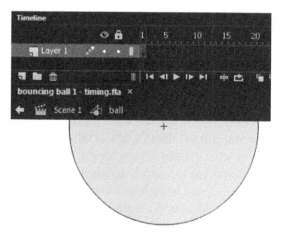

Image CL1.2

3. Click on the Fill Color box in the toolbar and pick any color you desire your bouncing ball to be. *(Pro tip: to select a more specific color, click the color wheel on the top right of the Fill Color box popup. Hue is left-right, Saturation is top-bottom, and Brightness is the extra bar to the right.)* Do the same for the outline using the Stroke Color. I chose different shades of orange. Try that. *Image CL1.3*

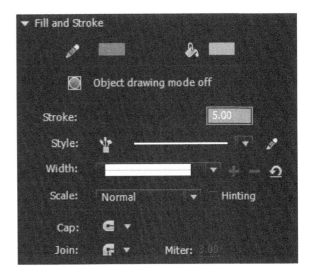

Image CL1.3

4. Locate the Fill and Stroke section in the Properties panel. You'll notice you can change the color and fill here as well (there are many ways to change these colors). Notice the slider-bar labeled "Stroke." This slider changes the thickness of the outline. You can use the slider-bar to change it or simply click the current number there and type in your own. I chose 5 for the size. *Image CL1.4*

Image CL1.4

5. Just above the stage, you'll see text next to a movie clapboard labeled "Scene 1." Next to that will be the title of your "ball" symbol. This is because we're currently *within* the symbol for editing. Click on "Scene 1" to go back to the main stage. *Image CL1.5*

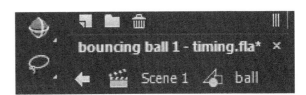

Image CL1.5

6. Press **Enter** on your keyboard and you'll see our newly colored ball bounce just as before! This preview is another way to play your animation quickly within the program without exporting anything (as we did in step 9 of this chapter's main bouncing ball exercise).

Now you can see one of the many benefits of using symbols. Anything within the symbols can be altered without changing what was already done on the main stage. But what if you wanted to change the timing? You have the ball bouncing, and you just think it's a bit too fast. In that case, we just need to add a few extra frames into each movement so that it takes longer. Let's try that.

"Adjusting Keyframe Positions On The Timeline"

7. Click anywhere between frame 1 and 12, right-click, and select **Insert Frame** (F5). You'll notice that didn't just add a frame in between 1 and 12, it actually adds a frame where you click and moves everything *after* it over one frame. Press its corresponding hotkey, **F5**, on your keyboard two more times to see it in action again. *Image CL1.7*

Image CL1.7

8. Now the "contact" (second) keyframe is no longer centered between our two "up" keyframes and that's messing up the timing. To correct this, click anywhere between frame 16 and 27 and press **F5** on your keyboard three times. You've added six total frames to our bouncing ball's timing, so now our one bounce sequence takes 30 frames to elapse (ending on frame 31), six more than when you first created it to take 24 frames. *Image CL1.8*

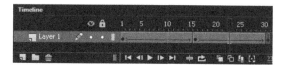

Image CL1.8

9. To adjust it back where it was before you can highlight three frames in the first tween, right-click and select **Remove Frames** and do the same for the second tween. Additionally, and usually easier, you can use the undo

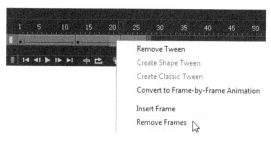

Image CL1.9

function by pressing **Cmd/Ctrl+Z** until you see the frames appear back where you wanted them. The end frame should now be back at 25. *Image CL1.9*

If this were animated frame by frame, changing the timing this way would be decidedly more difficult! These types of changes and alterations are where Animate CC really shines. There's no denying the personal control you feel over drawing each frame by hand, but there's also no escaping the feeling of tedium when a seemingly small change needs to be made (like a ball bouncing 0.5 seconds slower than it was) and you have to redraw everything, or if colors need changing and you have to manually recolor everything. You will see me stress this over and over in this book (as I have already multiple times in the Introduction): Animate CC is simply a *tool* to help you work more efficiently. It's versatile enough to allow for many different workflows (as you will see), but it isn't a magic push-button-and-make-cartoon machine (*image 1.4*). If it were, you probably wouldn't be reading this book. You are still very much in control of the 12 Principles of Animation and how you implement them.

IN CASE OF EMERGENCY

PUSH BUTTON

MAKE CARTOON

Image 1.4

Using Timing With "Animation Math"

Math: it helps. Especially with Timing. Let's take a look at the timeline again. There are some numbers in the border under the timeline which have our frame rate 24.00 fps , the frame number on which the red marker is currently sitting 25 ,

Image 1.5

as well as the time at that point 1.0 s (like a video player, but in seconds). Frame 25 is at exactly 1 second because there is no frame 0—we are starting on frame 1. Remember that our frame rate is 24 frames per second … 1 + 24 = 25. So frame 25 really *is* at exactly 1 second. This is an example of what I like to call "animation math" and it will help in the future when timing things out.

I know what you're saying, "If we can see the seconds under the timeline, why would we ever need math? Math is boring and should be burned with fire." The answer might be found in this challenge. Right now look at the timeline and without using "math," tell me on what frame number the timeline should show the animation ending if the ball bounces one more time and it takes another 3 seconds. Without animation math, you're going to have to use trial-and-error to get the answer. I can tell you what the answer is: frame 97. We already have one bounce taking 1 second, meaning another three means the total time is 4 seconds. With our starting frame being 1 and a frame rate of 24fps … 1 + 24 + 24 + 24 + 24 = 97. Animation math.

Animation often comes down to trying to control the creative chaos in your brain long enough to put it down in physical form ... and then do it hundreds more times until something looks like it's alive for a few seconds. You close your eyes and you can just *see* that goblin falling down the hill in a hilariously bumbling manner. Who wouldn't want to see that? You need to put this down on paper right now! But when you opened your eyes and started to draw you lost it. The magic of the movement is gone somehow—forgotten and shrunken back in the recesses of your brain to entertain only your subconscious.

"Animation often comes down to trying to control the creative chaos in your brain long enough to put it down in physical form ... and then do it hundreds more times until something looks like it's alive for a few seconds."

However, what if you were to close your eyes to *see* the movement, time it out by tapping a pencil to hear the beat with your ears, move your body to the flow of the movement, and feel the hilarity with multiple senses? You could become the action long enough to jot down movement notes like "goblin bounce 0.5 second hard, lots of squash/stretch, bound off edge of cliff, pause 1 second in air, fall FAST" and *then* start drawing. This way, the staying power of the thing you saw when you closed your eyes will be much greater. The timing can be written down for your reference, so you don't forget. Then when you animate—since you have the goals written down and the movement in mind—you'll know when you're on frame 1137 and you're mid-air, Wile E. Coyote-esque pause takes a second you will end it on frame 1161 just as he starts to fall. *That's* where you draw your "oh no" face. Math helps.

REAL-WORLD EXAMPLE
Looking Around

A Word For Beginners

If you check out the chart in this book's Introduction, the recommended way to absorb this book if you are a beginner is to skip these real-world examples in each chapter until you finish Chapter 10's exercises on Solid Drawing. You are absolutely encouraged to check out the Animate CC project files (*.fla*) in the companion website for these examples to see how they are broken up and where everything is headed. However, following along with the steps, since they're "real world," requires that you know a little bit of the terminology and methods; this goes for both the principles and the program. If you work through each chapter's bouncing ball exercises and their closer look sections and read what's written about using the principle within Animate CC you will have all the information you need to work through the real-world examples.

The idea of the book is to not only explain the meaning of the 12 Principles of Animation and then how to bring them into your animation using Animate CC but also be a primer for approaching Tradigital animation as a whole by way of this merging. One way to put this application of information to real-world animation into the book was to add a chapter at the end which would just cover a bunch of examples together. I felt that by forcing everything to the end, it would make the steady learning of the program and principles in each chapter feel longer because there's no real view of what's at the end of the tunnel. By putting these examples within each chapter, we're able to see the principles used in conjunction with others (that might not have been covered yet) as well as a peek into the methods it takes to make them happen without getting overwhelmed. Books are wonderful resources of learning specifically *because* you can flip through them at will, and we're taking advantage of that here.

So if all of this is new information to you, check out what you'll be coming back to after Chapter 10 for inspiration. If you're familiar with Animate CC, let's move on to some real-world examples of the principles and the program at work.

Principles Used

Solid Drawing: As the pupil moves around the eye, keep in mind that the eyeball is a sphere, not a flat circle. The pupil's appearance should change in size and dimension (getting thinner as it turns away from the viewer) when it moves around. Likewise, if making the face turn left or right, the same principle applies.

Slow In and Slow Out: The eyes move *very* quickly which assures the subject can quickly focus on what is being watched. Eyes can move slowly if they're unfocused or if they're focused on something that is moving (which means that they are tracking a slow-moving object). Otherwise, they're quick darts. Take your finger and put it on your eyelid (while open) and look around the room; you'll feel your eye twitching instead of the slow and steady scan you think and *feel* like you're doing when you look around a room. You will choose whether to apply this principle to the eye darts, but head turns will have both slow in (at the start) *and* slow out (at the end) to achieve smooth, organic movement.

Image 1.6

Timing: Use this chapter's principle to determine the acting needs of the character by considering the story point.

Setting Up

Open the file titled "ch1-real_world-looking.fla" provided on the companion website. In it you will see a character looking at you and a timeline which is extended out so that it covers 7 seconds. Right now, if you test the movie, he blinks once … and that's it. The idea of this scene is to have him looking around and blinking from time to time. The story point is that he's bored, so the timing you choose for the blinks and the eyes looking around will be dictated by that.

The specifics of the setup are as follows. The blink animation has already been done in the "character-head-eye-eyelid" so that anytime you want it to play, just put a keyframe on *both* eyelids' layers at the frame where you'd like it to start, with the eyelid symbols selected choose "Play Once" from the Looping section in the Properties panel and set it to start from frame 1. The pupils are symbols, so they can be moved around using classic motion tweens. They are also kept "within" the eyeball area by way of a mask layer.

We'll step through an example of a couple eye movements to show how this setup works, but basically you can mask the eye movement with a blink or dart them around with short, quick bursts. Usually, in real life, when eyes move a long distance (like looking at the right of a room and then over to the left), the eye movement is made with a blink over it. Smaller eye movements (like reading a newspaper) are just short and quick eye darts. Eyes almost never move in slow, controlled motions unless they're following something they're focused on (such as when the optometrist moves his finger in front of your face and asks you to follow it with your eyes). OK, let's look at those eye movements!

"Blink Move"

1. Double-click to enter the "character-head" so that you can see its timeline. There is a layer for each feature (much in the same way as we did/will do in the exercises in Chapter 10 on Solid Drawing). Specifically, notice that there's a unique symbol for each eye.

2. Double-click to enter the *character's* right eye (meaning, the one left of the other on screen) so that you're in "character-head-eye_r." Notice that there are only two layers: eyelid and eye.

3. Double-click to enter the symbol on the eyelid layer which you'll see is called "character-head-eye-eyelid_house." This name helps describe that it's just a housing for an instance of the eyelid symbol ("character-head-eye-eyelid") which has a single blink in it. When we want our character to do a standard blink, we can just tell the symbol to play that nested animation instead of creating the same simple animation over and over.

4. Let's have the eye move around the 2 second mark. We're going to facilitate this movement with a blink. Still inside the "character-head-eye-eyelid_house" symbol, insert a keyframe (**F6**) at frame 50. *Image BM1.4*

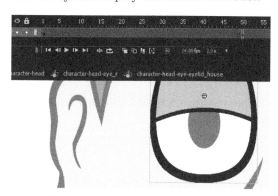

Image BM1.4

5. Click the symbol on the timeline and in the tweening section of the Properties panel set the "Play Once" frame number to 1. If you go

back to the main timeline (click on "Scene 1" above the stage) and hit **Enter** on your keyboard to quick-test the movie, you'll see that *both* eyelids blink. The reason both blink is because there's one eyelid housing symbol, the instance is just flipped horizontally in the character's left eye

to be a mirror image. So when you edit the eyelid instance, it changes the symbol. Because the other eye's eyelid is another instance of the same housing symbol (but flipped), that same change appears in the instance for the other eye. *Image BM1.5*

Image BM1.5

6. We need to move the eye now. Note the frame number where the eyelids are fully closed (frame 53) and double-click the necessary features to re-enter "character-head-eye_r." From there, double-click to enter the eye symbol so that you're in "character-head-eye-eyeball&pupil." You can tell (since there is no direction referenced with a "r" or "l") that this is a master symbol which will reproduce to each eye. The difference this time is that it's not

flipped, so when you move the pupil within this symbol to the left, the other eye's pupil will also move left (instead of right, which is what would happen if it were a mirror image).

7. There are three layers: mask, pupil, and eyeball. Since the "mask" and "pupil" layers are locked the mask is "activated" on stage so that you can see what the outcome will be on export. Unlock the "pupil" layer, and you'll see the mask shape show up. To move the pupil around unobstructed, either hide the mask layer or choose outline mode (both options are boxes to be checked next to the layer name). Which way you choose is a matter of preference. For simple setups like this one, I usually choose the outline mode so that I can see where the edge of the eye is. *Image BM1.7a and BM1.7b*

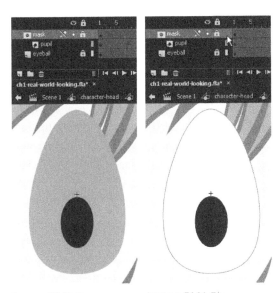

Image BM1.7a   *Image BM1.7b*

8. Insert a keyframe (**F6**) on the "pupil" layer at the frame noted in step 6 and move the pupil to the *character's* right. (*Note: Since you double-clicked to enter the symbols, you can see the rest of the face and how it will look on stage. The obscured view in the background currently shows the scene at frame 1 (most likely) on the main timeline, but you're further down this symbol's internal timeline. It will look like the pupils don't match, but don't worry. You will see that they will match when we get back to the main timeline and everything shows up synched.) Image BM1.8*

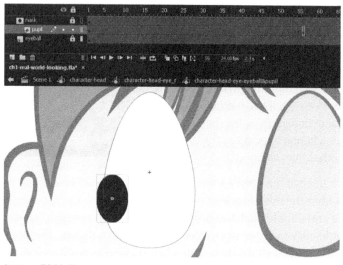

Image BM1.8

9. Test the movie with Cmd/**Ctrl+Enter** to see the result which is the character blinking once and then again 2 seconds later, resulting in his eyes now looking to his right.

This example demonstrates the idea of working with character packs. They can be more or less complicated and you will see many various ones if you work with others, and/or will come up with your own the more you animate within Animate CC. The only animation, per se, was the blink (which was provided for you, but in the real world you would have created it for the scene) which was repeated. By way of the setup using multiple instances of the same symbol, changing something in one symbol changed it on the opposite side as well so that the amount of steps required was kept to a minimum. This process is overkill for just one eye movement, but over the course of 7 seconds for this scene and maybe many more for an entire animated short, this setup saves a *lot* of time. Now that we've hidden the pupil movement with a blink, let's do a couple eye darts without one.

"Eye Dart"

1. In the "character-head-eye-eyeball&pupil" symbol, using the principle of Timing, pick a good frame for our character to look down after he had looked to his right. Remember, he's bored. About 1.5 seconds after the move to the right would probably be good, so insert a keyframe (**F6**) at frame 90 on the "pupil" layer and move the pupil symbol down a bit. *Image ED1.1*

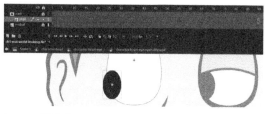

Image ED1.1

2. Being aware of the principle of Solid Drawing, rotate the eye counter-clockwise a little, using the Free Transform Tool (**Q**), to give the effect that the eyeball is a sphere with real volume (just moving the pupil straight down would make the eyeball feel flat). *Image ED1.2*

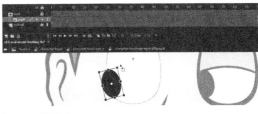

Image ED1.2

3. Since this eye movement isn't hidden by a blink, we must tween it. It will be a quick movement since that's what eyes do (so they can maintain focus). You'll want to put a keyframe (**F6**) two frames before the

Image ED1.3

frame you were working on to create a starting point for your tween. You should now have keyframe at frame 88 which is looking to the character's right (not down). *Image ED1.3*

4. Right-click the keyframe created in step 3, and create a classic tween. There are two ways you can go about the easing. Some animators choose to have no easing (a setting of 0) to emphasize the mechanism of eyes in the way they dart around. Others choose to have a

little bit of a settling into the final position, meaning that it will have a slow out applied to the dart (a setting of 100). I go with the latter, because in my opinion it makes the eye movements feel more organic—but it's purely the prerogative of the animator. *Image ED1.4a and ED1.4b*

Image ED1.4a

Image ED1.4b

5. The eye dart is so called because it's a quick, temporary movement—so we're not going to let it sit here too long. Still on the frame from step 3, copy (**Cmd/Ctrl+C**) the pupil symbol; we're going to move the eye back to this position.

6. Scroll ahead a few frames after the last existing keyframe and Insert Blank Keyframe (**F7**) around frame 98. *Image ED1.6*

Image ED1.6

7. Paste-in-place (**Cmd/Ctrl+Shift+V**) on the keyframe created in step 6 to put the pupil symbol in the exact place he looked to in the previous blink move (looking to his right).

8. Follow the method outlined in steps 3–4 to tween the eye back up. *Image ED1.8*

Image ED1.8

9. Test the movie with **Cmd/Ctrl+Enter** to see the result which is the character blinking once, 2 seconds later looking with a blink to his right, and then glancing (darting) down and up again about a second later.

"Continuing With Timing"

From here, the timing exercise is about using the two methods of moving eyes to create a 7-second scene of our character looking around the stage. It would be good to have him look back at the starting point again, which you can do by copying that first keyframe and pasting it at the end and moving the eye using either a tween or a blink. The great thing about a scene like this in Animate CC is that you can alter the tween and movement timings by simply dragging around frames on the timeline once everything's done. Just keep hitting **Enter** when on the timeline to "quick-test" the movie and see it play out on stage. Use that to adjust the timing as you see fit. It's trial and error but very quick!

Image 1.7 Front.

Now let's say you wanted to have some more movement in the scene. Maybe your character looks far to his right, and it just looks odd that his head doesn't move at all. Since the features of the face are split up into various symbols, it's very easy to move them around the head to get the feeling of small movements like a five-degree head turn. The method for turning the head (which you can see at work in the provided Animate CC project file) is fairly simple:

- **NOTE** ... all the features that need to be repositioned on the face and where you want the head to be in that new arrangement and create keyframes for each feature (on their layers) at that frame.

- **MOVE** ... the features into position using the principle of Solid Drawing to help maintain the sense of volume. For instance, when the head turns to the right in real life, the right eye will get farther away from the viewer since the right part of the face is turning away—so you would want to use the Free Transform Tool (**Q**), to shrink the left eye as well as make it less wide since the perspective is changing.

Image 1.8 Turned.

Image 1.9 Sample Progression: NOTE to MOVE to TWEEN.

- **TWEEN** … create keyframes before the ones just made, then set a classic motion tween in between the two new keyframe sets and apply a slow in/out "S" curve in the Easing Editor (which, if you're not familiar with this yet, will be covered in the next chapter).

- **RETURN** … to get the head back to the original position, just copy/paste the frames of the starting positions for each of the features and tween them back.

This use of Timing is acting. Knowing when to move and when not to is a refined skill that is usually best learned through experience and observation. Try playing around with different variations and combinations of eye and head movements, not only to see what effects they have on the acting, but also to see how easy it is to make these movements and alter them within Animate CC.

In a real-world scenario, having a scene like this where a character is looking around, bored, for 7 seconds is one of those situations where you really have the opportunity to try out variations in near real time. The animation in this example isn't strictly pose to pose nor straight ahead (which are methods in the principle covered in Chapter 7); it is a kind of Tradigital performance through quick trial and error. There is forethought, but it's not necessarily strictly adhered to. Think of this more like an actor working out physical acting choices before a performance.

FINAL WORDS
Timing

What it all comes down to in the end is that more frames between two positions means the movement will be slow/smooth and fewer frames means it'll be fast/hard. Take, for example, a train. You know it's going to be moving from one side of the screen (starting position keyframe) to the other (ending position keyframe). If you want it to slowly traverse the landscape, there will be more frames in between the two keyframes which will make the action take longer to elapse. If you want this to be a bullet train that rocks the socks off the land speed record, you'll use fewer frames between the two keyframes and the action will happen much faster.

There are completed *.fla files provided on the companion website that you are encouraged to look through and dissect at will to support the learning of the principles and the program. If you are new

Image 1.10

Image 1.11 The more space between two keyframes in a tween, the slower something will move. Notice the end frame times for "train_slow" (top) and "train_fast" (bottom). Examples taken from "ch1-examples-trains.fla" on the companion website.

to either the 12 Principles or Animate CC (or both), I suggest that you continue ahead onto the next chapter. If you're looking for a little inspiration, though, feel free to take a peek at the end of the book or the more advanced project files any time you like. It's important to have an inspiring goal to work toward. As long as the actual learning of these basics aren't skipped, a little peeking around can't hurt.

In the next chapter (as with all the rest) we will be building on this principle and newly found knowledge of the program when we talk about Slow In and Slow Out.

Image 2.0 The principle of Slow In and Slow Out is one of spacing.
As a leaf falls and tumbles it moves faster in some parts than others.
Example taken from "ch2-examples-leaf.fla" on the companion website.

Chapter 2
SLOW IN AND SLOW OUT

INTRODUCING
Slow In and Slow Out

One of the things that unites all creatures on Earth is the effect this planet's gravity has on us. It's perceivably constant, both in rate and intensity. An old classroom experiment that you (should) all do in Physics lab shows this wonderfully: take a bowling ball and a golf ball, hold them at the same height from the ground, let them go and watch them hit the ground at the same time. As long as the item isn't light enough to be affected by air resistance, any two objects will fall at the same speed. This experiment demonstrates the constant rate of *acceleration due to gravity* and we'll be using that to apply our next principle: Slow In and Slow Out.

"A Slow In is when something is speeding up, and a Slow Out is something slowing down."

A Slow In is when something is speeding up, and a Slow Out is something slowing down. This process is also called "cushioning" or "easing." This property isn't just for acceleration due to gravity however; it's any type of acceleration. Two other physics terms you may be familiar with are "momentum" and "inertia." When a car takes off from a starting line, it starts off fairly slowly while it overcomes inertia and gets faster and faster. When it slams on its brakes, that car will start screeching its tires and slow down more and more as it tries to overcome its momentum until it ultimately stops. The beginning was an example of Slow In, and the end was Slow Out. This phenomenon gets extended to many different movements but they can exist without each other. For instance, a punch will slow in until a very abrupt stop with no slow out, while a kicked soccer ball (football for my non-USA readers) is launched from the start with no slow in but will slow out as it comes to a stop on its own. Pretty much every organic motion has either Slow In or Slow Out, if not both.

As you work through this next bouncing ball exercise, try to think about all the things in life you can notice that exhibit this trait. Keep in mind that many movements are sandwiched by these two. Watch your own arm while it swings when you walk. It will slow in as it's moving forward, and when it gets there it'll slow out to a stop … unless you're a robot—in which case, I surrender.

BOUNCING BALL Slow In and Slow Out

Setting Up

If you have already worked through the previous chapter ("Timing"), you will be adding to that Animate CC file (*.fla). We named it "bouncing ball 1 – timing." What we'll be doing this time is saving a copy of this animation with a different name so that we can continue working with it without altering what we've already done. As you can imagine, saving progressive files like this is incredibly useful! When working on a certain scene, you may have done some great work animating one character and don't want to lose that when you move onto animating another character in case the power company decides to play musical chairs with your electricity. By periodically using **Save As**, you create a

Name	Date modified	Type	Size
mftc3-cleanup1	12/21/2012 1:02 AM	FLA File	2,894 KB
mftc3-cleanup2	12/21/2012 5:01 PM	FLA File	4,866 KB
mftc3-cleanup3	12/22/2012 6:55 PM	FLA File	4,353 KB
mftc3-cleanup4	12/23/2012 3:29 AM	FLA File	5,295 KB
mftc3-cleanup5	12/23/2012 2:22 PM	FLA File	4,724 KB
mftc3-cleanup6	12/24/2012 4:49 AM	FLA File	6,245 KB
mftc3-cleanup7	1/3/2013 7:21 PM	FLA File	6,718 KB
mftc3-cleanup8	1/3/2013 8:44 PM	FLA File	7,049 KB
mftc3-cleanup9	1/4/2013 7:38 PM	FLA File	7,251 KB
mftc3-cleanup10	1/4/2013 7:47 PM	FLA File	7,273 KB

Image 2.1 Using File > Save As periodically with increasing suffix numbers (as I did here in my own animated short) keeps a progression of work without the fear of overwriting.

protected trail of work to act as a backup so that you never lose too much progress on your latest masterpiece.

With your "bouncing ball 1 – timing" file open, go to **File > Save As** and type in the next obvious title "bouncing ball 2 – slow in out." In this file, we will add to what was previously done and explore this new principle as well as get into some of the more automated parts of Animate's toolset. If you actually have a bouncy ball in real life that you can play with as we go through this chapter that would be very helpful. It's not completely necessary, but live reference is always beneficial. Also, they are nothing if not fun, so you should have one anyway.

The Animate Difference: Onion Skin

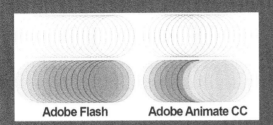

Adobe Flash   **Adobe Animate CC**

In every version of Flash, the onion skin view was made of "ghosted" images. There wasn't any distinguishing feature of the onion skinned frames in the past or future of the selected frame as they were all just varying levels of transparency (left). With the Animate CC update, onion skinning now shows blue tinted images for the past and green tinted images for the future frames (right). It's the same for outline mode with the addition that this time the present frame is represented with a red outline (top). In all cases of the Adobe Flash/Animate program, frames which are farthest from the presently selected frame are more transparent. To help you no matter which version of the program you have, throughout this book the markers which are clearly labeled with blue and green colors in Animate CC will be referred to by their position left or right relative to the currently selected frame since they aren't color coded in Flash versions. Image AD2 shows a tween with onion skin view from the center of the tween span.

PART I
"Onion Skin Mode"

1. Move the playhead so that it's on the "contact" (middle) keyframe. If you're following along exactly, that should be frame 13. *Image BB2.1*

Image BB2.1

2. The first thing we should do is look at our spacing as it is right now. To do that, first we have to locate and toggle the "Onion Skin" option. Directly under the timeline you'll see some icons (play/pause buttons, loop arrow, etc.). Look for the set of three icons with overlapping squares. One set has both squares dark, another with both filled in white—we're focusing on the set with one white square and one dark. Hover your cursor over it and it will read "Onion Skin." Click that icon. *Image BB2.2*

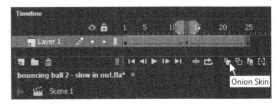

Image BB2.2

3. Two things should've happened: you now see a few green and blue tinted semitransparent images of the ball on the stage and the timeline now has two markers, which look like brackets, on either side of the current frame position. The

Image BB2.4

blue bracket is to the left of the current frame and represents the past frames (and blue tinted images) while the green bracket represents the future frames (and green tinted images). You have turned on "onion skin mode." We can now see the spacing of the ball's movement within the span of the brackets on the timeline.

4. We want to look at the timing for the first half of the bounce (the fall). Grab the left bracket on the timeline and drag it all the way back to the beginning (frame 1). *Image BB2.4*

5. Grab the right bracket and drag it as far to the left as you can. It won't pass the frame you're on so it should stop at frame 13. Right now you should see a trail of blue-tinted, semitransparent bouncy balls getting more and more opaque as it gets closer to the bottom. It looks a little like a slinky (another toy you should own). *Image BB2.5*

Interlude

Notice that all the images are spaced evenly. That means that this movement is going to be very robotic, cold, and uninteresting. To make the animation more interesting we'll need to add some texture to this movement. We'll do that by way of what was mentioned earlier: acceleration due to gravity.

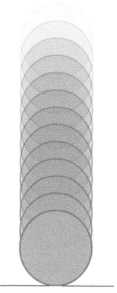

Image BB2.5

When dropping a ball from a height, does it fall fast or slow to start? By the time it hits the ground, will it be moving faster or slower than when it was first dropped? Hopefully you answered slow and then faster, respectively. Asking yourself these questions is a simple way of determining whether it's going to "slow in" or "slow out." Simply, these two concepts are broken down like this:

SLOW IN, starts off slow and gets fast.

SLOW OUT, starts off fast and gets slow.

This concept in practice within Animate CC is a setting called Easing. You will see how to manipulate this setting in Part II of this chapter's bouncing ball exercise. For now just know that, within Animate CC, "ease in" corresponds to "slow in" and is represented with negative numbers. "Ease out" is "slow out" and is represented with positive numbers.

The second half of this exercise will actually apply this principle to the bouncing ball. As you are learning how to adjust the Easing setting and apply varying degrees of slow in and slow out, I encourage you to play around with the amount of easing and adjusting the span of the onion skin markers to see how things change. There's really no better way to learn something than messing around with it. Just remember to Cmd/Ctrl+Z (undo) to get back to whatever you were doing before you went off-road!

> "In Animate CC, "ease in" corresponds to "slow in" and is represented with negative numbers. "Ease out" is "slow out" and is represented with positive numbers."

PART II
"Slow In/Out = Ease In/Out"

6. Put the playhead back to frame 1 (that's your first keyframe). The ball should be in its highest position, and it's called the "up" key (short for keyframe). *Image BB2.6*

Image BB2.6

7. Currently, you should see no extra onion skinned images of the ball because we had set the bracket to not show any frames past the one we're on (and there's nothing before it). Let's change that by dragging the bracket on the right of the frame to frame 13 (meaning just to the right of our middle keyframe). You should now see something similar to what you saw back at step 5, except this time the semitransparent slinky of bouncing ball images is tinted green and the currently selected frame shows the ball at the top. *Image BB2.7*

8. Click on the keyframe at frame 1 and then locate the "Tweening" section of the Properties panel. If you can't find it, you can open the Properties panel with the hotkey with Cmd/Ctrl+F3.

9. Next to the text saying "Ease" is a number (currently at 0). Click and drag the number to the left until it says *–100*. Notice what happened to the arrangement of bouncy ball images. They should now be closer together toward the top and farther apart at the bottom. This change in spacing is because it's not moving very far from itself per frame at the top, but by the time it gets to the "contact" position it's moving more distance per frame. That is to say, this spacing represents what it looks like when something's moving slowly at the top and wicked fast at the bottom. *Image BB2.9a and BB2.9b*

Image BB2.7

10. Test the movie right now (remember: Cmd/**Ctrl+Enter**). You should see it looking quite good in the beginning by accelerating into the fall, but then looking very stiff on the bounce up. This is because we haven't changed the timing for the second half yet. Let's do that next.

11. Click on the middle keyframe again like you did in step 1 (this is frame 13, if you're following along exactly). Right now you should see a whole mess on the stage because the onion skin brackets are spanning the entire length of the animation, so it's showing every frame on the same stage … all 25 of them.

Image BB2.9a

Image BB2.9b

12. Go back to the "Tweening" area of the Properties panel. This time, drag the number all the way to the right until it reads *100*. You'll notice that images showing the ball bounce look the same way they did in step 9 except they're a little darker now. This is because the spacing of the ball on the way down is now the same as on the way up and the ghosted frames are overlapping each other. *Image BB2.12a and BB2.12b*

13. Export a *.swf to see the current movie (Cmd/**Ctrl++Enter**).

Image BB2.12a

Congratulations! Between the previous chapter and this one you have already created a pretty good-looking bouncing ball using Animate CC. And this time the ball is bouncing more in tune with physics. It's accelerating on the way down (gravity), and then when it hits the ground it bounces back up only to slow down until it can't travel any higher (also because of gravity). Hopefully you have that bouncy ball I mentioned in the introduction to this chapter. If you were to drop it you would see what happens in that real motion is exactly what we've simulated in our bouncing ball animation.

Image BB2.12b

However, Slow In and Slow Out is not just about gravity. It's simply that acceleration due to gravity is the easiest way to start understanding the principle in action. Just look at it. The bouncing ball is *so* much more interesting to watch now. Before it was even, cold, robotic, and just plain boring. Now

Images 2.2a and b Since there's less friction on a wooden floor surface (left), a toy train's rolling speed will decrease at a slower rate than on the higher friction carpet (right). Examples taken from "ch2-examples-toy_trains.fla" on the companion website.

the speed varies and the bounce is actually *felt* rather than just seen. This type of change is referred to as "texture." We just added texture to the movement.

One of the things you may be asking yourself now is "what happens if I chose something other than one of the 100s?" ... that's a good question to ask. Take, for example, the beginning of the movement (the fall) where we set our tween to *−100*; you saw the difference in speed in the beginning versus the end when that was done. So, the closer that number is to zero, the less the difference is. If you were to set it right now to *−50*, the start of the fall would already be faster and the difference between the beginning and end velocities wouldn't be as large. The effect of varying levels of easing is important to know because not everything needs a huge acceleration. An example would be something like a child's rolling toy on a carpet being kicked. It will come to a stop so much faster and with less "easing" in the transition from moving to not moving than if it were on a hardwood floor because of the friction. In that case, the Easing setting of the slow out would be something like 30 or 50.

CLOSER LOOK
A Basketball Bounce

In the closer look section of the last chapter, we changed the colors and line thickness of our ball. I chose different shades of orange. And now that we've added Slow In and Slow Out, it looks a little like a basketball, so let's run with that idea. If you know anything about the sport, dribbling is a main part of the game. Basically, it's just bouncing the ball by putting your hand on the top, quickly pushing it to the floor, and then stopping it from bouncing too high when it comes back up. For us animators, this action means that the ball's change in speed is *much* more than it would be if the basketball were just allowed to fall on its own ... and that drastic changes means having a greater slow in than we can get with −100 to 100 scale in the Properties panel. We need a more custom approach—enter the "Custom Easing" feature.

"Custom Easing"

1. Before we do *anything* let's select **File > Save As** (or the hotkey sequence Cmd/**Ctrl+Shift+S**) to duplicate the file so as not to screw up our beautiful bouncing ball with our shenanigans. Just tack on a simple "– closer look" to the name of the file and that should be fine. Moving on ...

2. Click on the keyframe on the first frame of the timeline, and then locate the "Tweening" section of the Properties panel again.

3. Currently, the "Ease" is set at *–100* (in). To the right of that, you will see a pencil. Click that icon to bring up a panel called "Custom Ease In / Ease Out." *Image CL2.3*

Image CL2.3

4. Let's get acquainted with the graph we're looking at in this step. The % value on the left (the y-axis) is the amount of distance traveled in the selected movement; in this case 0% is the ball at the top, 100% is the ball at the bottom. The numbers at the bottom of the graph (x-axis) are labeled "Frames" for the obvious reason that these are the frame numbers corresponding to this tween's span on the timeline. Notice the x-axis spans from 1 to 13 (though is currently only showing even numbers) because that's the length of the first tween (from the "up" position falling to "contact" with the ground).

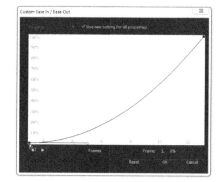

5. The graph right now shows a curve that sags which means this ball will be speeding up. In order to make the ball accelerate faster to the ground (like it's being pushed) we need to make that line sag even more. Click the black dot on the left end of the line, another line will pop up with a white dot at the end of it. This handle edits the curve. *Image CL2.5*

Image CL2.5

6. Click and drag the white dot further to the right (around the halfway point, where frame 7 would be). Already you can see the line graph with a more drastic bowing to it. *Image CL2.6*

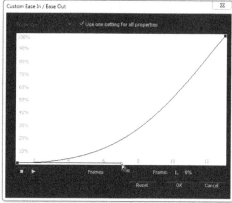

7. Click the black dot at the rightmost end of the line to bring up the Curve Editor (line with the white dot on the end). Click and drag this white dot all the way to the right until it's pointing straight down. *Image CL2.7*

Image CL2.6

8. There's a play button in the bottom right of the "Custom Ease In /Ease Out" popup. Pressing that will play the tween that we're on all the way to the end of the movie. You will see the ball accelerate *very* quickly to the ground but then bounce back up as before. We need to change the second tween now.

9. If you haven't done so already, click OK in the popup to save and exit the Custom Easing panel. Now click on our middle keyframe to select the second tween and then reopen the Custom Easing panel popup (as you did in step 2). Notice that *this* curve is bowed up like you're looking at part of a hill. This curve, of course, means that the ball will be traveling faster in the beginning than it is in the end (slow out) ... but not fast enough for us.

10. Click the black dot on the left of the line graph to open the Curve Editor. We are basically just reversing what we did to the tween before. Click and drag the white dot all the way to the *left* until it's pointing straight *up*. *Image CL2.10*

11. Click the black dot and then click and drag the white dot on the rightmost point of the graph to the left until you reach frame 19. This new graph is exactly like the last one except turned upside-down. You may stand on your head to verify. When you're done, click OK to save and exit out of the Custom Easing panel and test your new movie (Cmd/**Ctrl+Enter**). *Image CL2.11*

Do you see how much harder the ball is hitting the ground now? It's clear that there's a force on it, other than gravity, pushing it down. In our basketball scenario, that would be the player's hand (not shown). All we did was change a little graph. We didn't have to redraw anything or

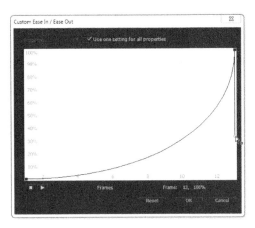

Image CL2.7

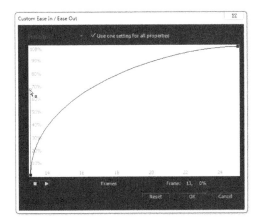

Image CL2.10

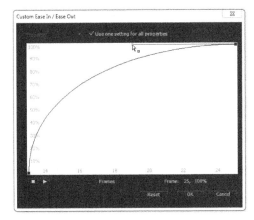

Image CL2.11

reposition our keyframes. This level of control is what we want to have in a program in order to get the results we're after in our use of the 12 Principles of Animation; in this case, Slow In and Slow Out. But as I've said numerous times in this book so far, the whole point is to be able to express multiple principles at the same time, so let's look at how Timing can be brought back in.

Beginning To Act

Currently, for all the animation we've actually done, this ball is pretty inanimate. There's no story it's telling with its movement other than "I fell and bounced back up again." Pretty boring, truth be told. What if the ball was a little scared about hitting the floor? What if this was the first time our little basketball had ever seen a floor and didn't know if it was going to eat him alive? It would just want to *touch* the floor ever so slightly and then retreat back to the safety of inexplicably floating in the air (this is animation after all; we can do anything we want). How might we do that?

Well, we know that it would need to start going to the floor slowly and then slow down again just as it's picking up speed because our little basketball wants to barely touch the scary floor ever so slightly. This motion will require a slow in *and* a slow out before even getting to the bottom of the screen. Then it will dart away as fast as possible back to its starting position; that action is very clearly a slow out but a *very* heavy one. You might be saying, "We can't slow in and out in the same tween ... that's madness! Surely we must add another keyframe in there." Nay, intrepid but weary reader, this feat can be accomplished with a few simple clicks!

Image 2.3 Acrophobic basketball.

"More Custom Easing"

12. Click the first keyframe to select our first tween and open the Custom Easing panel.

13. This span is already a slow in, but we need it to slow out as well. In order to do that, we'll take this ski-jump looking line and turn it into a wave. Click the black dot on the right to bring up the Curve Editor. *Image CL2.13*

14. Click and drag this white dot and bring it all the way to the top-center of the graph (making

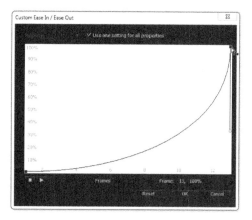

Image CL2.13

its line go from pointing down to pointing left and the graph will get a nice "S" curve in it). *This* curve is what it looks like to have a slow in *and* out in a single tween. *Image CL2.14*

15. Use the play button in the bottom left of the Custom Ease panel to test the outcome. It looks good, but the rebound isn't as drastic yet ... it still looks a little stiff. I bet you know where I'm going with this.

16. If you haven't already, click OK in the Custom Easing panel to apply the easing and close the panel. Click anywhere in the in span of the second tween and open the Custom Easing panel again.

17. To make the slow out already present to be that much more intense, use the Curve Editor of the leftmost point on the graph (the black dot) to increase the arch by dragging the white dot all the way to the top. *Image CL2.17*

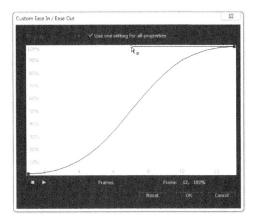

Image CL2.14

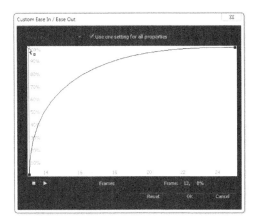

Image CL2.17

Now you can actually feel some emotion out of this bouncing ball. But it still feels a little dry. So far we have brought Timing into this equation by editing our motion graph (that's the thing in the Custom Easing panel) for our classic tween to slow in approaching the halfway point at the 7th frame and then slow out from there to the final position at the 13th frame without adding another keyframe. However that first movement still feels a little fast and the second movement feels slow. Just as we did in the previous chapter's closer look, let's change the timing of the first two keyframes to better reflect the bouncing ball's timidity.

"Keyframe Adjustment"

18. Click and drag the middle keyframe to the right by 5 frames. *Image CL2.18*

"That's it?!" Yes. If you test the movie, as I figure you already have, you'll now very clearly see a ball that approaches the floor cautiously before darting back up to its beginning position, having determined that the ground is not cool ... *not cool!*

I know the results might seem a bit tame right now, but we're just at the beginning. This

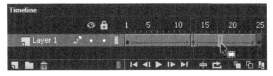

Image CL2.18

is just scratching the surface of what's to come. Changing the timing of a movement will almost always change its meaning. Changing the amount of slow in or slow out in a movement will almost always change the intensity of that meaning. In traditional animation, changing the timing of the keys after inbetweens were already done meant redrawing the whole sequence. In Animate CC, as you just saw, the *program* adjusts the spacing within a tween for you on-the-fly when you change the timing of the keyframes. Animating tradigitally within Animate CC means that we have more tools and opportunity at our disposal now to get our motion right. Conveying meaning through motion is the essence of acting as an animator. What you do matters mostly to the brain but *how* you do it may matter more emotionally.

> **"Conveying meaning through motion is the essence of acting as an animator."**

Using Slow In and Slow Out With "Digital Timing Charts"

There was a moment in the closer look exercise in this chapter that we applied a slow in *and* slow out to the exact same tween. The Custom Ease graph that allowed us to do that is a fantastic tool in Animate CC, and it has its roots (like so many other features) in a classical animation tool. Before we get into that, let's cover a couple of necessary words in traditional animation terminology first. You already know the term *keyframe* (key, for short). They're basically the important drawings ... ones that define what the action is in broad terms. The *inbetweens* are the drawings which fill in the spaces between the keyframes. This is where "tween" gets its name, because when an instance of a symbol is moved from one keyframe to another via this feature, Animate CC is the one "drawing" all of the inbetweens.

Now we can talk about *Timing Charts*. In traditional animation, they are a simple method of showing how the lead animator wants the timing and slow in/out of a span to be handled. You'll usually see them in the top-right corner of key drawings; they look like little rulers. It starts with the drawing of what looks like a capital "I." Usually, the top line is the start keyframe and the bottom is the end (although sometimes it's the reverse); both of which are labeled with their frame numbers. The vertical line between them represents the span of the motion. The basic way the chart works is that the lead animator will place more horizontal lines on the span to represent the inbetweens, and the way they are spaced shows the proportional progression the assistant animator needs to "move" the drawing. Remember what the bouncing ball looked like when you turned on the onion skin mode for the first span of the bounce—the slinky? The balls were close together at the top and far apart at the bottom. That's what the Timing Chart for that span of the motion would look like, except with vertical and numbered horizontal lines.

You may have noticed that the description of Timing Charts seemed familiar in function to the Custom Ease graph, and there's good reason for that. The Custom Ease graph is the Animate CC equivalent to traditional animation's Timing Chart. Think of it as its digital version. They both show the start and end frame numbers in the span (x-axis in the Custom Ease graph). They both use position to represent the percentage of the entire movement (y-axis in the Custom Ease graph) where an object should be by that corresponding frame number. And finally, they are both simple graphical representations of movement—specifically using the principles of Timing and Slow In/Out. While the Timing Chart is laid out like a ruler, the Custom Ease is a line graph. They are both quite simple and very powerful when you know how to read and use them.

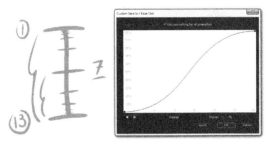

Image 2.4

> ### "The Custom Ease graph is the Animate CC equivalent to traditional animation's Timing Chart."

There is a lot you can do by simply changing the easing between two positions; just look at how much changed when we did the small alterations for the bouncing ball in this chapter. Slow In/Out and Timing work so intimately with one another. Think of a character sitting in a chair, minding his own business. Someone walks by and our character turns his head. Simply by determining how long it takes for that to happen and with what level of easing (the spacing of the drawings), I can already tell the character's emotional state. Think about it; if it happens in a short period of time with minimal slow in or out applied to the movement, how might that be different than a head turn taking longer with very smooth easing?

Timing and Slow In/Out inform each other. While Timing will help you determine the amount of frames between two key drawings, the amount of Slow In/Out will determine *how* you get there. These two principles already help you layout so much of the action in front of you. Look what we've accomplished with the bouncing ball in only these two chapters. Manipulation of the Custom Ease graph is as paramount to applying these principles within Animate CC as the Timing Chart is to traditional animation. If you're going to use tweens, knowledge of the Custom Ease is crucial.

REAL-WORLD EXAMPLE
"Heavy Lifting"

Principles Used

Staging: All of the action must be clearly presented so that the audience can see what is going on. Use negative area (a woman who has a hand on her hip would have negative area in the space enclosed between her arm and her body) and obvious poses/postures to show what is going on even if there was no detail in the form (as in, if you turned it into a silhouette, would it be clear what was happening?).

Timing: *When* something happens is always important, but with pantomime it's crucial. If the character picks up an object that's supposed to be heavy too quickly, it won't feel like that object is actually heavy. There needs to be a struggle.

Solid Drawing: In the crash course in Chapter 10, we cover balance which also mentions the center of mass. As a character picks up a heavy object, the center of mass changes because for all intents and purposes, that character and the object are now acting as one.

Pose to Pose/Straight Ahead: Using the Pose to Pose method to create the most important story sketches when doing the rough animation and Straight Ahead for the moments which feel spontaneous (like how he positions himself under the heavy object) is a good method when applying this principle in shots like the one in this exercise.

Image 2.5

Squash and Stretch: Simplified, when our character is lifting a heavy object it will result in a stretch, and when holding that object it will result in a squash.

Slow In/Out: Use this chapter's principle to enhance the feeling of weight. Heavy objects will have "slower" easing (meaning the slow in/out will be slight and gradual) and lighter objects will be "faster" (which makes their slow in/out harsh, quick and drastic).

Setting Up

Open the project file "ch2-real_world-heavy_lifting.fla" provided on the companion website. You can probably tell from the title what we're going to be doing here. Right off the bat, you can see that the rough animation has been created for you. The keyframes sketched in blue were done using the Pose to Pose method. Then between those sketches are the breakdowns in red. Finally, the rough animation was further broken down in some spots using straight ahead action sketched in green, so some spontaneity could be injected into the scene. Through that rough animation I looked at what the needs of the cleanup would be. With this information, a character was created, its features split up into symbols, and those instances were posed over his first main key (our character assessing the task). From here, we will clean up the rest of the scene.

If there's one area that Slow In and Slow Out are applied most heavily (pun), it's in the presentation of weight. When a character is lifting something heavy, like a boulder, the slow in/out will be much more drastic than if he's just lifting a tennis ball. Even the movement of the body in relation to the heavy object will change based on its weight and configuration. The character is probably not as heavy as the boulder, so as he's able to lift it up using strength and leverage, he's going to need to reposition his body and get under it in order to actually hold it in the air.

In the "looking around" example in the previous chapter, the principles of Solid Drawing, Slow In/Out, and of course Timing, showed up. This time, it's the same collection of principles but with the addition of Staging, Straight Ahead Action, Pose to Pose, and Squash and Stretch. When our character picks up the boulder, it's like he just grew a really big, extremely heavy belly and is trying to deal with this new girth. To sell that idea, all of the principles listed earlier will come into play.

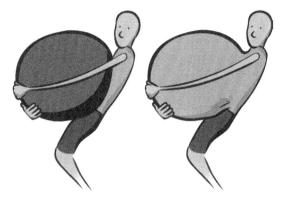

Image 2.6 Positioning for carrying a heavy weight (left) is treating it as part of the character (right).

"Cleanup With The Rig"

1. Visually analyze the needs of the animation and the current "rig." Make mental notes of any time a feature changes perspective (like a hand opening or closing). These special cases will need to be animated frame by frame: we'll call them "problems." Be aware, also, of the times when these complicated features are *not* changing and could easily be tweened into position. Anytime a feature stays relatively the same in makeup and perspective between frames (like most of the arm and leg segments and the feet), these can be tweened: we'll call them "easies." *Image CR2.1*

2. For the keys (blue sketches), insert keyframes (**F6**) on the frames that make up the "easies" for the movement that makes up the sequence and move the body part symbol instances into position over the rough, rotating and squash/stretching as necessary. *Image CR2.2*

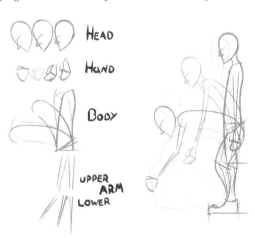

3. Do the same as in step 2 for the breakdown frames. *Image CR2.3*

Image CR2.1

4. If it looks like a feature could be tweened easily from here, do that. Apply any easing that would be needed to make sure the feature lines up with the breakdown position at that frame. *Image CR2.4*

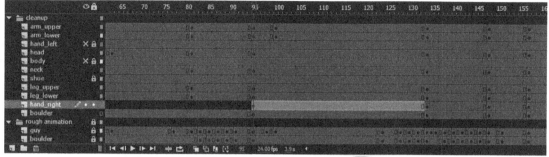

Image CR2.2

5. For any one of the "easies" that didn't line up appropriately with the breakdown position in the rough, insert a keyframe (**F6**) at the breakdown frame and move the symbol instance into position. Adjust the easing for the first and second tweens that have now been created in this span to apply proper slow in and out. *Image CR2.5*

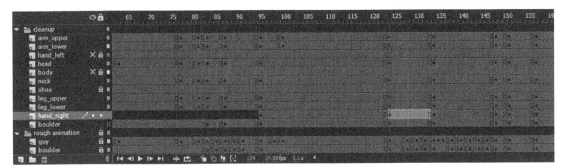

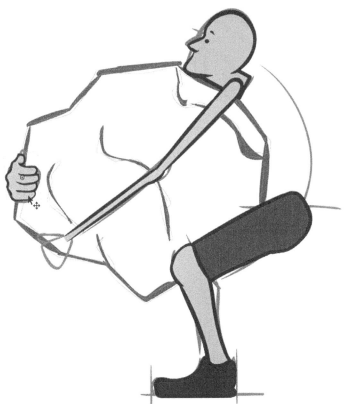

Image CR2.3

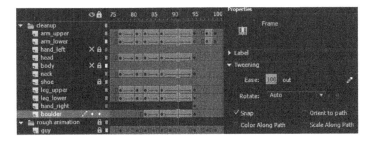

Image CR2.4

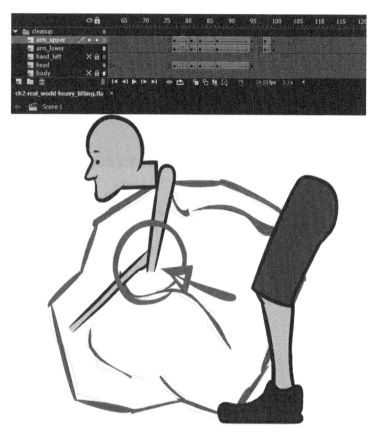

Image CR2.5

6. The "problems" are ... problematic. You need to look at what their specific needs are. For these, we are going to be using symblification (as described in Chapter 8). Where possible, we can use shape tweens (like the body) for our form changes. Others are going to need to be cleaned up frame by frame (like the hands). The following steps will focus on the shape tweening of the body.

7. Right now, the body symbol is set to "Play Once" from frame 1 (and this keyframe is on frame 1, so the timelines, internal and main, will match) and the symbol's internal timeline is extended out to the same number of frames as the main. When a keyframe is created, it will say "Play Once" from whichever frame number it's on. So going forward it's important not to move around these keyframes after they're created, or else the timelines will become misaligned. Insert a keyframe (F6) at the first key (blue) on the "body" layer and move the symbol into position with proper rotation (but without squash/stretch). The part that will anchor our symbol is the waist, so that's what will determine the alignment and rotation. *Image CR2.7*

8. Double-click to enter the body symbol at the keyframe. The marker should be set to the same frame as the main timeline (since they're playing "together"). Insert a keyframe (F6) at that

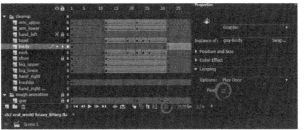

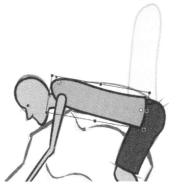

Image CR2.7

frame and alter the body shape as necessary to match the rough sketch. *Image CR2.8*

9. Repeat step 8 for the rest of the keys (blue).

10. Do what we did in steps 3–5 to apply proper classic motion tweens to the body symbol instances. When you're determining if the body symbol is lined up with the breakdown sketch, it's good to use the hip as the reference point.

11. Enter the body symbol by double-clicking at the beginning of each span, insert a keyframe (**F6**) there, and create a shape tween. Use shape hints if necessary (described in Chapter 8) and make sure to account for proper easing. *Image CR2.11*

12. Return to the main timeline to verify if the body shapes are lining up correctly (it doesn't have to be exact, but it should follow a similar arc) throughout the rest of the rough frames. If they aren't aligned, figure out if it's the position or rotation that's the problem or if it's the actual shape of the body. If it's the shape, you'll need to enter the symbol and put another keyframe in the problem span and adjust the shape. Keep adding keyframes until it fits the rough (or you end up just

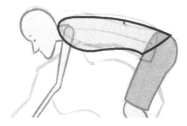

Image CR2.8

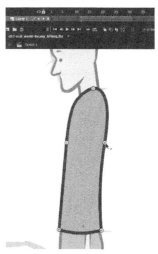

Image CR2.11

frame-by-framing it). Don't forget that you'll need to reapply shape hints in that case if they were applied. If the problem seems to be the position or rotation, you'll insert a keyframe on the main timeline and move/rotate as necessary. Remember to always be aware of the easing values as you hijack a tween (shape or classic motion).

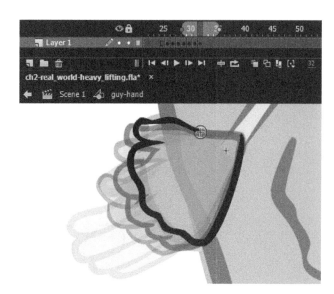

Image CR2.13

13. Anything that needs to be cleaned up frame by frame, you'll be doing the same process as steps 7–12, just without shape tweens. You'll be entering in each frame that needs a new hand shape drawn or where you want a facial expression change and creating it there. Don't forget to insert *blank* keyframes (**F7**) and use onion skin mode when in the symbol's timeline to keep track of the arcs and make sure you're always on model. *Image CR2.13*

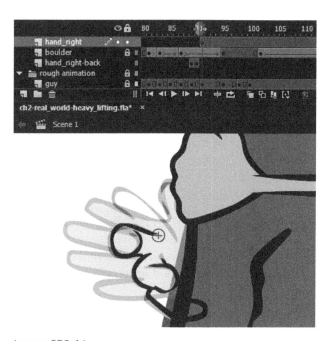

Image CR2.14

14. Sometimes the benefits of symblification's precision will not outweigh the amount of time it would take to replicate the motion you wanted from the rough animation. If it becomes apparent while working through the animation that there is a movement that is just too complicated to clean up using symblification, it would be wise to abandon it and clean that span up using frame-by-frame animation right on the main stage and go back to symblification after the problem point (just remember that when you bring the symbol back into the workflow that the "Play Once" setting has the proper frame number to it). *Image CR2.14*

"Continuing With Slow In/Out"

The amount of slow in and out really determines what amount of weight you're going to show and what proportional strength the "supporter" (the guy lifting the boulder in this case) has. You can see how many principles came into play here, but the one that takes center stage is the slow in or slow out of the character's movements. They're the descriptors of the moment here. Once the cleanup is done, you don't *have* to stick with it if you're still not completely happy. Playing with the easing values to increase, decrease, or add nuance to the slow in/out of a motion is the quickest way to change the feel of a scene apart from timing. If you try new variations, don't forget to **Save As** with an increasing number value or with "exploration_1" added at the end of the file name, for instance, so you don't lose your wonderful work.

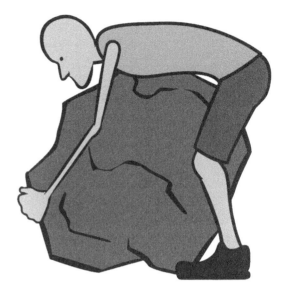

Image 2.7 First Key.

The other thing to note is the use of symblification and our "rig" to clean up the traditional rough animation that was created first. If you have already worked through the book or have an understanding of Animate CC already, this process isn't much of a surprise. It can be summed up thus:

- **ANALYZE** ... the rough animation in terms of each possible moveable feature (upper arm, lower arm, hand, etc.) and when you'll need to break the form. Mentally separate the features into "easies" and "problems."

- **"EASIES"** ... get taken on first, while hiding the rest. Most stiff features (like the forearm) can be done at this stage *(point 2)*.

- **"PROBLEMS"** ... are started just the way the "easies" were, by moving the symbols into position and tweening them *(point 3)*.

- **SYMBLIFY** ... the animation by entering the problem symbols and changing their form

Image 2.8 Last Key.

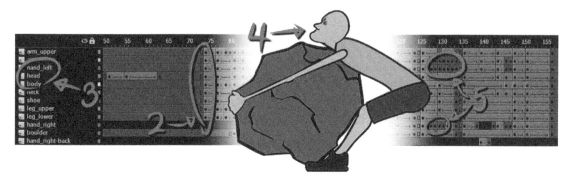

Image 2.9 Though not all are easily seen on the timeline and therefore not all are labeled, each step is in use in this example. Some tweens, some frame by frame, with some both at the same time (symblification).

from within. The body part is *moved* around the stage by classic motion tweens but is *altered in form* through either shape tweens or frame-by-frame animation from within the symbol itself.

- **ABANDON** ... the precision of this method if the problems of a movement are too great to try to replicate using symblification and animate it frame by frame on the main stage *(point 5)*.

In the "real-world," creating an animated scene like this obviously has a lot of parts. Even the original masters at Disney didn't usually do every inbetween and especially didn't ink and paint them. The "big guys" were about the performance, and you probably already have an idea of how many things needed to be figured into those performances—not to mention all of this was done off a blank page! It's an incredible amount of work and a very refined skillset. For us in Tradigital animation, the delegation of the inbetweens and cleanup (coloring/inking) still usually rests back on our shoulders. For these tasks, Animate CC helps lift the weight with tweening, symbols, and broad but precise drawing tools.

Animators always want to break the rules—it's just plain too enticing to see what *shouldn't* be done and go do that; it's one of the great joys and benefits of the medium. Methods, techniques, and set workflows are there to help us stay on track and not get *too* carried away, but sometimes that's just what needs to happen. That last step of "abandoning" the symblification of nested animation and tweening to clean it up using the time-honored technique of frame-by-frame animation is a very important one. Sometimes the movement you have in mind is just not something that the program, any program, would be ready or able to handle. For that, even though it may take longer, you will need to be more traditional than digital in your Tradigital work.

> **"Animators always want to break the rules—it's just plain too enticing to see what *shouldn't* be done and go do that; it's one of the great joys and benefits of the medium."**

FINAL WORDS
Slow In/Out

Realistically, there aren't too many reasons that you won't use this principle in your animation because pretty much everything has at least *some* naturally cushioned movement. Taking away this easing makes things look harsh, mechanical, explosive, and a bunch of other similarly veined adjectives. As with everything, though, knowing when to *not* use a principle can be just as valuable.

As we continue with the chapters, you will see exactly how important a handle on the basics are. You may think that things are moving slowly, but this foundation is imperative to being able to put it all together. Conceptually, a lot of these principles are rather easy; though the use of them gets more complicated as we try to apply them. Animation rarely works in a vacuum as far as the 12 Principles are concerned. So as we continue to layer the principles, your understanding of how these slight alterations can have large effects on the whole will grow.

Image 2.10 Gertie the Dinosaur *by Winsor McCay (1914).*

Slow In and Slow Out is a magnificent principle because it probably does the most to make motion believable. There is a *huge* difference between animation that employs it and that which doesn't. *Gertie the Dinosaur*, by animation pioneer Winsor McCay, while not the *first* animated short is pretty close to it. It was completed in 1914, well before any of these principles had been worked out by the Nine Old Men at Disney. If you've seen it, you'll notice one thing that is largely missing: it has almost no Slow In/Out. There is still a lot of great work in Gertie's acting, specifically within the timing (and arcs, but we'll get to that in a later chapter) for being such a new art form. But think of how much more lifelike it would be if when Gertie picks up her foot it were to have some nice Slow In/Out applied to it (like we did to the first tween of the ball in the closer look section in this chapter). Think of how much larger this enormous dinosaur would *feel* rather than having to already know, be told, or guess based on its size in relation to the ring leader. This principle really adds a lot, and movement just feels empty without it. You can't hold this against Winsor McCay, however, since these accepted principles of motion were just starting to be developed. Now that they have, though, you can use it in *your* animation!

But I can't bury the lead any longer; I know why you're all here. In the next chapter, we're going over the pop-star of the 12 Principles: Squash and Stretch. If you take one thing away from this chapter it should be that while everything starts with Timing, the Slow In/Out gives some much needed realism to the motion. This sense of realism is important because no matter how cartoony something is, there is almost always a need on the part of the viewer to see something relatable. You may not know all the details and physics of why a ball bounces the way that it does, but you know when it looks right. It's the same for the audience. Keep that in mind as we move on to smushing things around in the next chapter.

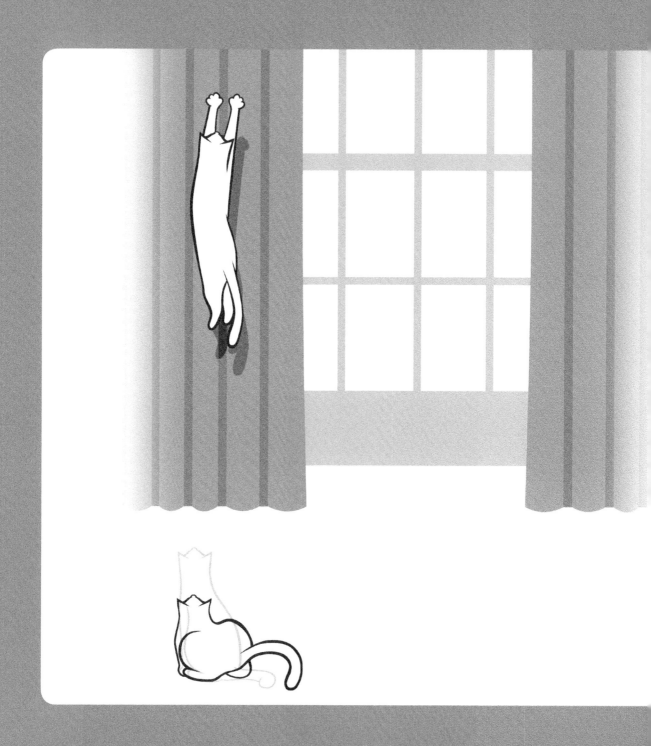

Image 3.0 A cat will crouch (squash) before it leaps (stretch).
Example taken from "ch3-examples-cat.fla"
on the companion website.

Chapter 3
SQUASH AND STRETCH

INTRODUCING
Squash and Stretch

Here we go. Squash and Stretch: the cool uncle of animation. If Timing and Slow In/Out are the meat and potatoes of the 12 Principles, Squash and Stretch is the pizza. It's what you bring to a gathering to officially make it a party. Because of its popularity, tutorials abound on the internet with this principle, and often only this one. It's not the be all and end all but a fantastic tool in your animation. Both of these statements are especially true for a young artist, because when learning these principles it's really the first crazy way you can play within the world of movement. It can be overused, of course (one pizza's great, ten are a bit much), but the variety in which it can be implemented is truly amazing.

So what does this principle mean exactly? Squashing and Stretching an object aids in the illusion of weight and flexibility and helps the audience feel more of the action. Imagine a water balloon. If you set it on a table, you will see it squash. If you pick it up by the tied end, it will stretch. Notice that only the shape of the container changes and not the contents or volume. This idea is important because as we'll be morphing the shape of images the idea isn't to stray too far into the actual "growing" or "shrinking" category à la Hank Pym (he was Ant-Man; I read comic books). Using this principle is a matter of knowing what effect Squashing and Stretching has on an animation and what your intention is with that particular shot.

Take any live-action movie, go to a section with an action scene, and pause. What you'll see is a big, blurry mess. That blur will be in just about any frame that has movement in it. You don't notice this because you have a brain, and that brain has a nifty little software capability known as motion perception. If you're really curious about the science of it, I encourage you to look up the *phi phenomenon* and go get yourself a thaumatrope (I swear these aren't bad sci-fi novels). For now, focusing on the point, why is this blur important to bring up in this chapter? Basically, your brain already knows that something moving fast looks blurry.

Image 3.1 Whether it's stretched (left) or squashed (right), the volume of the balloon stays the same.

Take a pencil, hold it in your hand, and move it back and forth in front of your face faster and faster until all you see is a blur. Your eye can't track it fast enough. It looks like it's a completely different shape now! In animation, we call that image a smear, which is basically just a big ol' stretch. Squash works much the same way but in reverse; it's usually when something comes to a sudden stop or is about to take off.

> "The real magic of animation resides in doing things live-action can't."

In the days before computers, there weren't many ways to show motion blur in animation. Squash and Stretch is a great way of doing just that. It's all about creating the illusion that these images are really moving, so you can suck the audience into the experience. This principle has many more uses than just simulating motion blur however; it can be used to show a wide range of emotions as well. If the character is sad, squash his form a bit to really show the weight of life on his shoulders. If he's happy, stretch him out to show him walking tall. This alteration is more than just posture, we're talking about actually changing the size distribution of your character's features. The real magic of animation resides in doing things live-action can't.

As far as our bouncing ball is concerned, we've already addressed that it'll slow in as it's falling to the ground, get faster and faster until it hits, and then bounce back up slowing out as it reaches the top again. This spacing made

Image 3.2 Something moving fast like this bullet could show up as a blur (top) or we could stretch the bullet and insinuate the blurry trail with rifling spin lines (bottom).

it look *much* better, but it still looks a little uninteresting; a cardinal sin in animation. The physics is good, but boring is boring. What we'll be doing in this chapter's exercise is adding a little flavor to our physics.

BOUNCING BALL Squash and Stretch

Setting Up

When the ball hits the ground there's no real feeling of impact. It just sort of exists. We've got the relative size worked out in our timing and the sense of speed by way of slow in/out, but the bounce still needs something extra. Giving the ball some elasticity will add to the texture of the movement (remember that word from the last chapter). Texture of movement is something that will come up a lot in this book. All that energy the ball is building up while accelerating to the ground has to go somewhere, and in this case it'll go into *squashing* the ball. The motion blur that a real ball would've incurred due to its speed will translate to our *stretching* the ball.

We'll be working off the file created at the end of the last chapter's bouncing ball exercise (*not* the one in the closer look section). The existing title should be "bouncing ball 2 – slow in out." So, naturally, we'll be titling this one "bouncing ball 3 – squash stretch" (by using **File > Save As**). And don't forget that a good practice is saving duplicate files in ascending numbers whenever you do any work you don't want to lose. Don't worry, I'll remind you again mid exercise.

PART I
"Where We Squash"

1. Select the contact key (where the ball is on the ground). Clicking the keyframe selects everything on the frame; in this case, the "ball." We'll be squashing the instance of that symbol.

Image BB3.2a

2. Locate the toolbar and choose the Free Transform Tool (**Q**). You'll see a few little boxes surround our instance of the ball symbol on the stage. These are handles used to transform the shape of the object. The white dot in the middle is the object's center point, but don't mess with that yet. *Image BB3.2a and BB3.2b*

3. We want to squash the ball, and I'm sure you know what that looks like. You can scale the size manually by

Image BB3.2b

dragging the handles. It will take a little practice to keep the same volume while also keeping the ball in its relative position. For now, open the Transform panel (Cmd/**Ctrl+T**) for more precise control. *Image BB3.3*

4. There's a link icon next to the % values. If it's solid, click it to make sure that icon turns into a broken link. Unlinking the values makes sure we can change them independently. *Image BB3.4*

5. Adjust the shape's percentage manually in the Transform panel to 120% horizontal and 80% vertical. *(Note: when attempting to keep the same relative volume, the two numbers need to add up to 200.) Image BB3.5*

6. The previous step moved the ball off the ground a little, so it needs to be repositioned. With the symbol selected, locate the "Align" panel (Cmd/**Ctrl+K**) and make sure the "Align to stage" box is checked. *Image BB3.6*

7. In the "Align" *section* of this panel click the "Align bottom edge" icon all the way to the right. Hovering over the icons will display pop-up text for verification. *Image BB3.7*

Interlude

If you test the movie right now (Cmd/**Ctrl+Enter**), you'll see that it looks very weird. It's squashing *as* it's falling! That's not what we want. Stretch needs to come into the equation first because as the ball's falling, it's accelerating. We want it to stretch to enhance the illusion of speed. Squash and Stretch are complimentary actions and rarely exist separately. It's like Newton's Third Law of Motion if it were more ... animated. So likely where there's a *squash*, so exists an equal and opposite *stretch*.

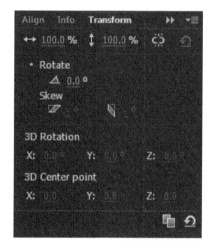

Image BB3.3

Image BB3.4 Top: unlinked; bottom: linked.

Image BB3.5

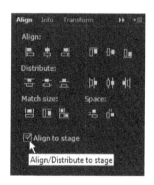

Image BB3.6

BB3.7

8. Up in the timeline, select the frame before contact and create a keyframe (**F6**). You've now essentially hijacked the entire tween *before* it by changing the endpoint. Do what you did for squash now, but opposite values (80% horizontally and 120% vertically). We'll call this frame the "contact stretch." *Image BB3.8*

Image BB3.8

9. Reposition the ball like you did in step 7. Aligning the ball with the bottom edge will assure that the impact is really felt. The ball touches the ground stretched, then is squashed in the very next frame (while still on the floor). *Image BB3.9*

10. We want to apply that same stretch going back up to the top now. To copy it easily, right-click the "contact stretch" from step 8, and select **Copy Frames**.

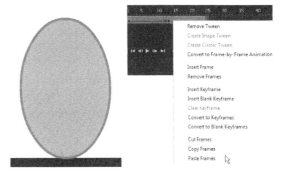

Image BB3.9   *Image BB3.11*

11. Right-click the frame after our "squash" frame and select **Paste Frames**. *Image BB3.11*

Image BB3.12

12. You'll need to reapply the slow-out for the rebound tween (100 on the easing in Properties panel) since step 10 changed its starting keyframe. *Image BB3.12*

13. Right now, there are three contact frames in a row (stretch, squash, and stretch again). To make sure the ball doesn't feel as though it's sticking to the ground before bouncing, move the second stretch key up about half its height so that it's not still touching the ground. We'll call this frame the "rebound stretch." *Image BB3.13*

Image BB3.13

If you test the movie now, you'll see that the ball gradually stretches more and more as it falls and squashes only on impact and then shoots back up with a stretch. The speed has been emphasized by the stretch, the weight has been emphasized by the squash, and the ball's elasticity has been emphasized by both of them. Now a simple bouncing ball is more interesting to watch. We've just scratched the surface of what this principle brings to animation and how Animate CC can make it happen.

What you've added to the previous work on the bouncing ball is the feeling of what the audience would expect to see ... not necessarily what they would see in real life. Frank and Ollie titled their book *The Illusion of Life* for a reason. Complete reality wasn't the goal; realism was. The principles, and everything they did in animation, were about representing life without directly copying every aspect. Any scene with the Seven Dwarfs or Tweedle Dee and Tweedle Dum, the two oft-cited examples of Squash and Stretch use, will show you that. But there's a trick being played on you.

Image 3.3

When watching an animated film, like when watching sci-fi, you know it's not real. It's the ability of people to imagine "well, if it *were* real ..." that allows for these stories to be told and loved. The phrase "suspension of disbelief" comes into play here. You know that Gaston's sidekick, LeFou, is a human character in *Beauty and the Beast*; but you also know he couldn't really move like that if he existed in real life. In a few sequences, it seems like there's no way his head could possibly have a solid skull in it at all. It doesn't matter though because the use of form flexibility is done in support of the acting—so in a way the unreal aspects of this anatomy feel somehow even *more* real than if strict physics were adhered to. Squash and Stretch is this first principle that introduces you to the world of doing something that doesn't actually happen that much in real life to make your animation actually *feel* more real.

One of the brilliant things about animation is that you can break the rules of reality, but one of the needs of humans is to relate. The reason you see faces in inanimate objects around town is the same as why you can look at Daffy Duck and not only know that's a duck who talks but also identify with parts of his personality and can anticipate his reactions to events before they happen. People are putting themselves into the characters they see. You know when you fall out of a tree and hit the ground you feel all squashed up. This great force has compacted you into a little strip of a human being—and it hurts, a lot. The fact is, you didn't actually squash so much anyone could see. But if you were to animate that happening, you might go ahead and add that squash because that's what it *feels* like is happening and that is more important than the reality.

CLOSER LOOK
Supporting The Action

This time we'll be working from the "bouncing ball 2 – slow in out – closer look" file that we created last time. In it, there was a timid ball that starts to approach the ground, afraid of what might happen once it gets there; and once reaching the ground it immediately shoots back up to a floating position of safety and happiness. It looks good, but we can add more life to that action with a little Squash and Stretch. When the ball is approaching, what should it do? Well imagine that a character in a bank is scared to step onto a floor that might set off an alarm. They'll stick out their foot as far away from them as possible and only touch with the end of the toe. Now once that's done and the alarm actually goes off, they'll jump away as fast as possible. Let's do that. Before we continue, though, don't forget to **Save As** the file mentioned above to "bouncing ball 3 – squash stretch – closer look" before we continue.

"Squash and Stretch Acting"

1. You should be seeing three keyframes (on frames 1, 18, and 25). Since we know we want a stretch on the way down, let's make that happen like in step 6 above. Create a keyframe (**F6**) on frame 17, *before* the middle keyframe with the ball in the contact position. *Image CL3.1*

Image CL3.1

2. Either with the Free Transform Tool (**Q**) or by manually imputing % via the Transform panel (Cmd/**Ctrl+T**), create a stretch on the ball. Don't forget to move it back down to touching the ground.

3. Select the contact key (at frame 18) and apply a squash to the ball.

4. Create a keyframe on frame 19. *Image CL3.4*

Image CL3.4

5. Simply copy (Cmd/**Ctrl+C**) the stretched ball from frame 17, **Delete** the ball from frame 19, and paste-in-place (Cmd/**Ctrl+Shift+V**). This does the same as steps 10–11 in this chapter's main bouncing ball exercise. But with these hotkeys and a little practice, this will be the faster method for copy/paste.

Notice that we did not move the last stretch key up so that it wasn't a contact frame as we did in the main exercise. We're keeping it in contact with the ground in this case because our newly anthropomorphic ball is pushing off the ground, so it makes sense that it would be still touching the ground in the beginning of the last tween. It's no longer a rebound; it's now a push.

Remember what happened earlier in this chapter during the main bouncing ball exercise: placing a keyframe in the middle of a tween doesn't change the easing value *before* it, but it does create a different one *after* it. For example, click on the "squash" keyframe (18) and look at the Custom Easing graph. You'll see the same hard slow-out curve that we applied to this part in the last chapter's closer look section. If you select our newly created key on frame 19 and look at the Easing Editor for that, you'll see a different graph. We want to replace the tween on key 19 with the one currently on 18.

"Copying Motion And Changing Frames"

6. Right-click frame 18 and select **Copy Motion**.

7. Right-click the key on frame 19 and select **Paste Motion**. *Image CL3.7*

8. A new keyframe has been created on frame 19 and pushed the existing key forward one frame. Right-click that key on frame 20 and select **Clear Keyframe** to remove it. *(Note: NOT clear frames ... that would just delete everything on that frame.) Image CL3.8*

Image CL3.7   *Image CL3.8*

9. To make the "push" read better and shorten the time it takes for the ball to get back to its top position, click and drag to highlight both keys on frames 18 and 19. With those two frames highlighted, click and drag them one frame to the right so they now inhabit frames 19 and 20. *Image CL3.9*

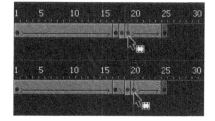

Image CL3.9 Progression is shown top to bottom.

Keeping Things Clean

You can alter the tween on frame 17 to your heart's content, though currently it should already be slowing-out, and that's the way I would keep it. Another thing to note is that there is still a tween applied to frame 19 though there are no frames inbe*tween* that and the next keyframe, so it effectively does nothing. I will bring this topic of "legacy tweens" up later in the book, but if you would like to keep things clean (like I do) you can right-click that keyframe and select **Remove Tween** to bring it back to just a normal, single image. It won't hurt being there, but if you're a clean freak in real life this will keep you sane.

Pencil Tests And Changes

If you test the movie now, you'll get more of a sense on how this effect is coming together. Traditional animators reading this passage will agree that one of the things that was important but also cumbersome in the time before computers was testing out an animation. The "pencil test" is pretty famous now among young, aspiring animators to see what is essentially the raw vision of their favorite animator's work. Viewing a pencil test involved taking a picture of each frame and playing it back at their selected frame rate on the closest TV they had. Even that sentence masks the frustration this process often caused, but the test was necessary to see how the animation was coming along. The real punchline, though, was that if a mistake was found, you'd better hope it wasn't in the timing because that would often mean redoing work. Simply shifting frames around wouldn't change the outcome of the *other* principles that were applied to the sequence. In this regard, with Animate CC things have become *much* easier.

Our current acting chops shown off in this iteration of the bouncing ball has it timidly approaching the ground, stretching out along the way out of fear, squashing to build up the power necessary to jump and stretch its way back to the starting position. The concept is great, we have some well-done Slow In/Out and you have just applied that wonderful Squash and Stretch. The problem currently lies in the timing. The ball approaches the ground a bit too fast to really sell that idea of fear. Because our "character" here has no face or other anthropomorphized features, it's all down to the movement, so we really need to be particular. As I said in the previous paragraph, because

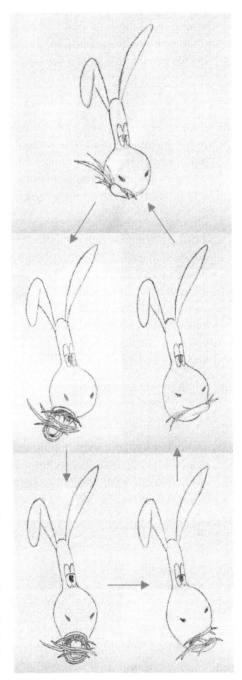

Image 3.4 "Donkey Chew Cycle" (reads counter-clockwise).

the ball is stretching on its way down, finding any mistakes in the timing would normally result in having to redraw the entire span of frames to adjust its spacing *and* amount of incremental stretch applied to each drawing. Let's see how easy it is with Animate CC.

"Adjusting The Timing"

10. Before we do anything, close your eyes and time how long you feel it should take for the ball to hit the ground. This time estimate will serve as the blueprint for our changes. Currently, going up to frame 17, the "approaching" tween is 0.7 seconds long (remember it says so right under the timeline). You can choose whatever timing you like, but for sake of following along I will be doubling the approach time, meaning it'll be 1.5 seconds now.

11. Click anywhere in the tween between the first and second keyframes. Hold down **F5** to create extra frames and push everything in front of that point forward until the next keyframe is at the 37th frame. *(Pro-tip: remember "animation math"? At a frame rate of 24fps, 1.5 seconds would be 36 frames ... multiplication. Since we're starting on frame 1, the ending keyframe of this tween will be on 37 ... addition). Image CL3.11*

Image CL3.11

12. **Cmd**/**Ctrl+Enter** to test the movie. You can see that now the ball's approach looks much more timid, but the loop makes it hard to see the acting properly. Let's change that.

13. Again, closing your eyes, timing out the shot and deciding where you would like the movie to stop is pretty essential. When I did it, I arrived at 3 seconds as a good complete time. My animation math tells me that should be on the 73rd frame, so go out to that frame, click on the gray box, and hit **F5** one time to extend our timeline out to that point. *Image CL3.13*

Image CL3.13

14. Follow step 12 again and, if you'd like, step 13 again until you have a happy loop. This loop right now is just for you, but ultimately this process will help you with timing out how long a scene should be by putting yourself in the audience's position.

As you moved around the keyframes, the tween adjusted to accommodate. We didn't mess with a single thing on the main stage, only the timeline. You will see this helpful little feature come up further in later chapters and in a *huge* way on your own work; tweens help in more ways than one. Tweens aren't just about saving you time in the initial drawing of inbetween frames but in the *redrawing* of those frames if you need to change your timing.

Our squash and stretch was preserved throughout this alteration in the intuitive way you would expect. So far, the only thing we have drawn is a ball. The Free Transform Tool has allowed us to give new qualities to the drawing to either emphasize the real-world physics of a movement (as in the main bouncing ball exercise) or add feeling to the acting on a shot (as in this closer look).

During this closer look, we have applied Squash and Stretch, copied and preserved Slow In/Out, and adjusted our Timing all to service the acting. All of these tools and hotkeys are layering onto one another in our work as are the principles we've covered. Now we're rolling (pun, intended)!

> "Tweens aren't just about saving you time in the initial drawing of inbetween frames but in the *redrawing* of those frames if you need to change your timing."

Using Squash and Stretch with "Real-World Reference"

You can already see that Squash and Stretch is a hugely versatile principle. Remember the grasshopper example from the Introduction? Translating a real jump into an "illusion of life" jump means seeing certain positions and actions in terms of the 12 Principles. For instance, as it's about to take off with its legs folded up next to its body, that's a squash. Right after jumping with its legs extended, that's a stretch.

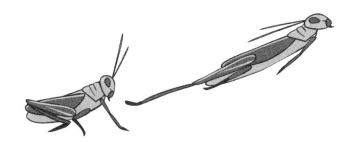

Image 3.5

So in order to express these actions within animation, take the squash moment and actually add some squash (and likewise for the stretch moment). With life as our reference point we can **interpret, infuse,** and **implement**. Interpret the action using the 12 Principles, infuse this interpretation into the planning for the animation, and implement it into our work

Let's take another example. You're in a creepy old building's boiler room. You think you're alone. It's dark, quiet, and musty. You could swear that you heard something behind you, but when you look back nothing can be seen. Your senses might be playing tricks on you. Suddenly, you feel hot breath on your neck. What would you do? First thing that would happen is you would probably grit your teeth, squint your eyes, and duck your head down into your shoulders; you'd flinch. But immediately after that, you straighten up like a board and freeze. Your neck stretches out like a weak attempt at fleeing, but every bit of you is tense and wide-eyed. Act it out. The flinch is a squash, while your freeze moment will be met with a stretch. When animating, you'll use Squash and Stretch to accentuate those moments.

Every time you watch cartoons from now on you will be seeing Squash and Stretch. It's ubiquitous. Running, jumping, falling, cowering, celebrating, yelling, pointing, fighting, sleeping ... all the ,ing's really—they can and usually do use some form of this incredibly flexible (I am *killing* it with these puns) principle. Accentuating a squash can easily be done with a good stretch before it. We all know the "movement" principles (Timing and Slow In/Out) impact just about everything in the animation. But the other fairly unique characteristic about this particular principle is that even though it's more on the "look" side instead of the "movement" side of the spectrum (meaning its work is done on the image rather than the timeline, like timing), it too pairs well with other principles. It's in these pairings that Squash and Stretch really shows its effectiveness. We've already seen how it's paired up with the likes of Slow In/Out (or vice versa), but in next chapter's Anticipation or the later chapters like Exaggeration you'll really see Squash and Stretch shine.

REAL-WORLD EXAMPLE
"Bite and Chew"

Principles Used

Overlapping Action: Features rarely move at the same time, even (and especially) when linked. Since the jaw is the main part of the action, that will move first and the rest of the features will follow.

Slow In/Out: Chomping down on something means that you are compacting it under pressure, which will mean a quick slow in when closing but a longer slow out as the jaw really shuts. When the jaw releases for another bite, all that pressure is released and is really easy to open, which means that the easing is opposite—slight slow in but a drastic slow out.

Solid Drawing: The features of the head/face are full of volume and specific arrangements. To sell the idea that something has entered our character's mouth and he is chewing on it, care needs to be taken to present the volume and construct of his head and their features at all times.

Image 3.6

Anticipation: Before the bite (down) there needs to be an anticipatory beat (an up) that precedes it. This setup makes the bite itself more intense as well as leading the viewer to a quick visual payoff.

Squash and Stretch: This principle is what really gives that visceral feeling to the chewing motion. Structural (mouth opening and closing) and exaggerated (head squashing and stretching back up) versions of the application of this principle are being used to best sell the flexing of the features.

Setting Up

Open the project file "ch3-real_world-chew. fla" provided on the companion website. Just as in the "Heavy Lifting" real world example in Chapter 2, the rough animation is already done. What we're going to be doing isn't much different than that example either, workflow-wise, but as the squash and stretch was used mostly in the body, in this example we're using this principle in the structural makeup of the face. An example of a structural squash and stretch is a folded and unfolded umbrella *(Image 3.7)*. When biting down, the cheeks will bloat out and the chin will pull up further into the head; these will reverse when the mouth "opens" during the chew. These are structural squashes and stretches, but we want to go further than that. Every facial feature will squash and stretch together to really exaggerate the size of the bite our character has taken.

In Chapter 2's real-world example, there were more principles at work in an obvious way than this one. I say "obvious" because, really, there are more principles at play in this example than I specifically listed. Timing, for instance, is in every sequence. Appeal is something you should always consider. Arcs are a constant need while animating and as a double-check. But certain principles are more integral than others in any given animation sequence, and those are the ones we're focusing on in this example: Slow In/Out, Solid Drawing, Anticipation, Pose to Pose/ Straight Ahead, and Squash And Stretch (which takes center stage). One thing to note before we

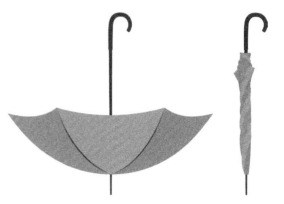

Image 3.7 "Squash" (left) and "stretch" (right).

Image 3.8 Frame layer visible (left) and frame layer hidden (right).

continue is the layer above the rest named "frame." In Animate CC, as you know, even though only the stage is exported to video (and not the gray work area) you can still see everything which expands outside of that area. Sometimes it helps to see what will be visible in the final export without actually exporting it, that's where the "frame" shape comes in. Unhide this layer if you ever want to cover up what won't ultimately be seen on export *(Image 3.8)*.

"The Bite"

1. The only feature which requires symblification is the head, so that's what we'll focus on first. The interior of the "head" symbol is already extended out the full length of the main timeline, it's set to Play Once from frame 1 and cleaned up using the first key of the rough so we're all set to work. Still on the main timeline, hide all layers except for the two "head" layers (the one in "cleanup" and the other in "rough animation") so that we can focus the work on this feature without clutter. *Image BC3.1*

Image BC3.1

2. Scroll ahead to the first moment where the mouth is open (frame 15), place a keyframe (**F6**) on the cleanup "head" layer, move the head instance up to the rough, and double-click to enter the symbol on that frame. *Image BC3.2*

3. Insert keyframes (**F6**) for all layers on the frame you entered into in the previous step (frame 15) and then hide everything except the "mouth" layer. We'll tackle this one first.

4. Because of the complexity, the mouth opening motion is best animated frame by frame. The first key has already been done for you so you can delete what's on the "mouth" layer on the keyframe created in step 3 and clean up the mouth design I've sketched in the rough, which you can see ghosted on the stage. *Image BC3.4*

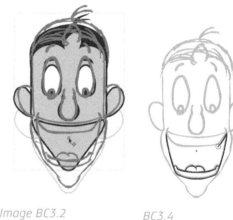

Image BC3.2   *BC3.4*

5. Insert a new layer, name it "rough." The mouth opening motion will be a fast action and the one which leads the other features (that will follow via subtle overlapping action). Create three blank keyframes (**F7**) on the newly created "rough" layer on frames 12–14 and use onion skin mode to sketch those three inbetween frames. These are best to complete using straight ahead action. *Image BC3.5*

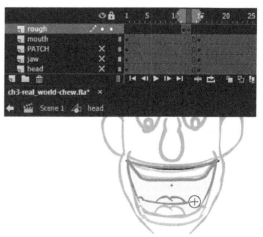

Image BC3.5

6. Return to the "mouth" layer and clean up the inbetweens you created in the previous step. To call this particular part of the cleanup done and move on to others, lock and select outline view for the "mouth" layer and then guide and hide the "rough" layer.

7. One by one unhide and cleanup the "easies" of the face (eyes, ears, cheek lines, nose, and head) on frame 15 using classic tweens for the symbols and shape tweens for everything else (the level of easing is up to you). Then lock and select the outline view for each of those layers as well. *Image BC3.7*

Interlude

There is a layer in the head symbol called "PATCH" right above the "jaw" layer. If you unhide the jaw layer and *then* the patch layer you'll see what purpose the patch layer serves. It covers up the top line segment of the jaw shape. In Animate CC, a shape needs to either have no outline or be fully outlined in order for a shape tween to work correctly. This means that in the case of our character's jaw we can't delete the top line which runs through his face if we also want to shape tween it. There are a couple workarounds for this and the one we're using here is a "patch." Simply stated, a patch covers up unwanted artifacts that come

Image BC3.7

up during animation. In this case, we want to shape tween the jaw and to not see the line currently running ear to ear so the patch's only function is to hide that line. The patch itself is nothing more than a flesh-colored shape with no outline which overlaps the jaw shape in just the right way to cover what we don't want the audience to see. Since it's on its own layer, this shape can and will be moved and shape tweened whenever it's needed in order to cover up the problem line on the jaw shape.

8. With only the "jaw" layer visible, on the keyframe created in step 3 (on frame 15) alter the jaw shape to match the rough key using the Selection Tool (**V**) by dragging the vector points and curves around stage (the same method used in Chapter 8's bouncing ball exercise, steps 9–11). Try to move the points to similar corresponding positions so that Animate CC, will have an easier time with the shape tween. *(Note: if it's hard to see what you're doing with the flesh-colored fill in the shape, click and delete the fill (the way I did in the corresponding image) to make the alterations, then use the Eyedropper Tool (**I**) to select the color from the previous keyframe and refill this one with the Paint Bucket Tool (**K**).) Image BC3.8*

Image BC3.8

9. We've determined that the beginning of this mouth opening animation is frame 12 (in step 5) so the entire motion will be four total frames. Insert a keyframe (**F6**) at frame 12 on the jaw layer and apply a shape tween. Use shape hints if the shape tween gives unwanted results.

10. Repeat step 9 for the patch layer.
    Image BC3.10

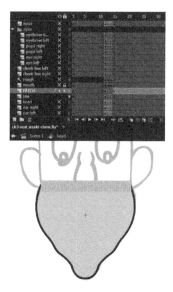

11. Still inside the "head" symbol, unhide and deselect outline view for all layers so you can see everything except the rough and hit **Enter** to test the animation to see if it's performing the way you want. *(Pro-tip: select the loop feature from the icon under the timeline and drag the markers the way you would in onion skin view to select the loop region.) Image BC3.11*

Image BC3.10

Image BC3.11

12. Repeat steps 2–11 for the rough key on frame 26 (which will hereafter be referred to in these steps as *mouth closed – squash*). Remember that step 2 starts on the main stage. *(Note: the precision we get from Animate's tweens is well used in a loop (which is what we're creating next). So to make the tweening easier, be sure the facial features such as the closed eyes and the eyebrows are simple shapes and that the mouth is represented with a line created using the Line Tool (N).) Image BC3.12*

Interlude

At this point in the scene, our character chews a few times so we're going to create a separate looping symbol for that. So far, it's been important to use "Play Once" in the instance looping options on the Properties panel to lock the main and symbol timeline's playback together. For a loop, these two timelines will be independent of one another so it's important to keep an eye on

Image BC3.12

symbol instance names and looping options as we progress onward from here. You'll notice I wrote "LOOP 1" in the top-right of the key on frame 26. There are four total loop labels in top-right of the rough animation so this chew sequence we're about to do will loop four times. The first loop is from frames 26–37 (we don't include the key on frame 38 in our first loop since that's the starting frame of the *next* loop). This means our chew cycle is 12 total frames because,

Image 3.9

remembering "animation math," we have to add the starting frame to the difference between the frame numbers. This information is necessary to determine how to actually create a loop that fits the needs of our scene.

"Creating The Loop"

13. On the main timeline at frame 26, right-click the "head" symbol and select **Duplicate Symbol**. Name this something easy to remember such as "head-chew_loop." With the instance of the "head-chew_loop" symbol you just created, set it to "Loop" from frame 1 in the looping section of the Properties panel. You'll notice the image displayed on stage has reverted to our first key; we'll fix that in the next step. *Image BC3.13*

14. Double-click the "head-chew_loop" instance on stage, highlight everything on the timeline from frame 1–25, and **Remove Frames**. Go ahead and delete the "rough" layer too. This should leave you with the third rough key's mouth closed design on frame 1 inside this symbol. *Image BC3.14*

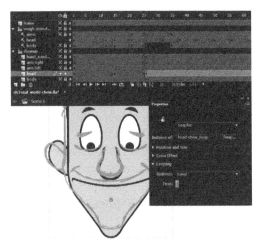

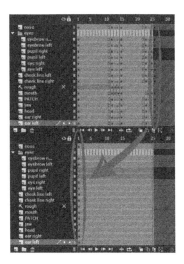

Image BC3.13   *Image BC3.14*

15. Return to the main stage, insert a keyframe (**F6**) at the next rough key, which is on frame 32 (we'll cleverly refer to this design as *mouth closed – stretch* in the following steps), move the head into position over the rough (I've placed the registration point at the spot where the next would attach to the back of the head so you can use this to approximate where "into position" is) and double-click the instance to re-enter the "head-chew_loop" symbol. *Image BC3.15*

16. Notice that you are *not* on frame 32 within the symbol. You are on frame 7. As we saw in step 13, the "head-chew_loop" instance is now looping internally starting on frame 1 but beginning that loop on the *main timeline's* frame 26. So since we scrolled ahead six frames to frame 32 on the *main timeline*, that corresponds to scrolling ahead six frames (starting from frame 1) on "head-chew_loop"'s own *internal timeline* to frame 7. Knowing that, clean up this *mouth closed – stretch* frame using the same process as we cleaned up the others before it. *Image BC3.16a and BC3.16b*

Image BC3.15

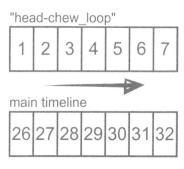

Image BC3.16a

Image BC3.16b

17. Return to the main timeline, scroll ahead the next key (mouth closed – squash) on frame 38 but this time do *not* create a keyframe. Instead, we're using this to time out the perfect loop. Double-click to re-enter the "head-chew_loop" symbol here and you should be on the symbol's internal timeline at frame 13. As mentioned in the interlude right before this section, this is the starting frame of the *next* loop. Highlight all frames from 13 until the end of the timeline in use (which should stop at frame 56), right-click and **Remove Frames**.

18. Somewhere between frames 1 and 7, click and drag to highlight one frame from each layer and then drag and drop the highlighted frames over to frame 12 all at once. This clicking and

dragging of already highlighted frames essentially does a copy/paste of those highlighted frames onto the new frame they were dragged to (frame 12), creating keyframes for them in the process. The cleaned up image on frames 1 and 12 now are the same. When this loops on the main timeline, this *mouth closed – squash* design will be shown for two frames as it finishes on frame 12 and reverts back to frame 1 to repeat the loop. That's OK for our purposes because it will sell the "chomping" part of the bite more. *Image BC3.18*

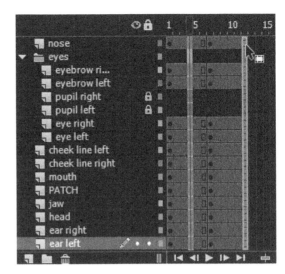

Image BC3.18

19. Use tweens to finish cleaning up this looping animation. You'll want to apply a slow in to slow out for the span between the squash (1 and 12) and stretch (7) keyframes. Since there's no Easing Editor for shape tweens, you can do this by creating a tween with 0 easing, insert a keyframe (**F6**) as close to halfway through the span as you can (splitting the one tween into two) and then go back to set the first tween to slow in with a value of −100 and the second to slow out with 100. Use shape hints as necessary. *(Note: to keep your timeline even cleaner, since the eyes are closed in this loop you're free to delete the pupil layers as I did (notice their absence in this step's image versus the previous).) Image BC3.19*

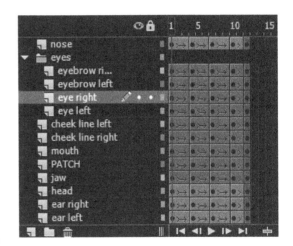

Image BC3.19

"Swallowing"

20. Back on the main timeline, insert a keyframe (**F6**) at the second to last rough key (frame 74) and drag the instance of our "head-chew_loop" symbol up to the position indicated on the rough animation.

21. Right-click on the instance of the head symbol, select **Swap Symbol**, and choose "head." This is the symbol we started with. The reason for this is because we want to return to the first

frame and this symbol also has the design for the *mouth closed – squash*, which is what should be showing on the frame we're currently on. *Image BC3.21*

22. Set this symbol instance to "Play Once" (it should already be set to start from frame 1). Then right-click the head, **Duplicate Symbol** and name it "head-swallow."

Image BC3.21 Image showing after Swap Symbol action.

23. Double-click on the instance to enter the newly created "head-swallow" symbol. We want only the first and last key designs, so highlight all frames between them (that would be everything on frames 2–25), right-click and select **Clear Keyframe**. *Image BC3.23*

Image BC3.23

24. Since we're returning to the first key, we want to switch their order on the timeline. Right-click anywhere on the timeline and **Select All Frames**. Right-click again and **Reverse Frames**. *Image BC3.24*

25. The timing is still messed up though, so return to the main timeline, insert keyframe (**F6**) at the last rough key (frame 81) which happens to be the last frame of the timeline in use.

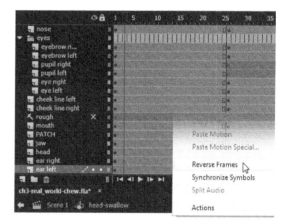

26. Double-click on the instance of "head-swallow" to enter the symbol. You should now be on frame 8 of the symbols internal timeline. *(Note: remember this frame number as you'll need to know it a few steps from now.)* Bring the second set of keyframes on the timeline back to this frame number so there is a set of keyframes at frame 1 (*mouth closed – squash*) and another at frame 8 (the design we started with). *Image BC3.26*

Image BC3.24

Image BC3.26

27. Clean up the animation as we did previously and take into account what's happening in this action overall in order to know where to start the span. I chose to start the return animation

at frame 5 of the internal timeline, which would make the entire span last four total frames (5, 6, 7, and 8).

28. We still have to return the instance of this symbol on the main stage back down to the starting position. Return to the main timeline, right-click the keyframe on frame 1 of the "head" layer and **Copy Frames**. Right-click on the last keyframe (81) on the "head" layer and **Paste Frames**.

29. While the previous step put an instance in the correct spot, it also replaced the existing instance so the one there now is representing the wrong symbol. So right-click the head instance on this frame and **Swap Symbol** with "head-swallow."

30. With the instance of the "head-swallow" symbol still selected, set it to "Play Once" from the frame you made a note of in step 26 (hint: it's frame 8).

31. Now that the symblified animation of the head is complete, return to the main timeline and clean up the character's other features by unhiding the layer of the feature you want to focus on, inserting keyframes (**F6**) at each rough key and moving them into position. Use the Free Transform Tool (**Q**) and be mindful of size, rotation, and distortion. *Image BC3.31*

32. Finally, decide what timing you want for each span, insert keyframes (**F6**) where necessary and apply classic tweens to the spans. *Image BC3.32*

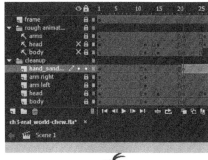

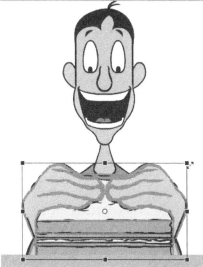

Image BC3.31

Image BC3.32

33. You can play around with what easing you would like for the movements, but I chose an "S" curve for all of them to apply a slow in and out in the same span which will make this sequence feel more wobbly and oscillating.

"Continuing With Squash And Stretch"

The main timeline (as long as you're not moving around keyframes on the "head" layer) is simpler to follow. For instance, I decided that I wanted the character to slowly drop his hands a bit while chewing. So all I did to make that happen was to insert keyframes toward the end of the animation

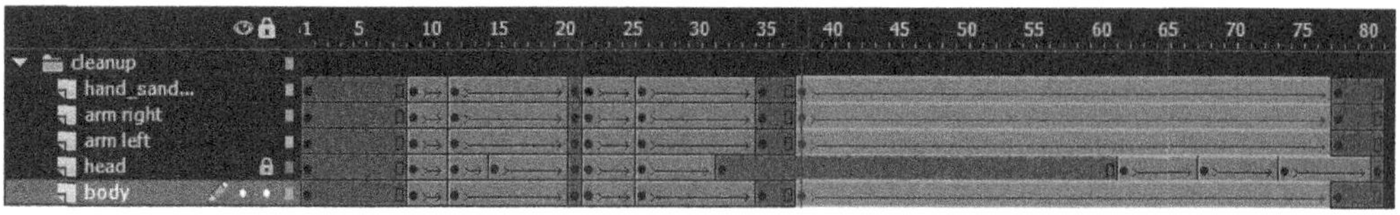

Image 3.10a

on the arm, hand, and body layers (to preserve the position) and then returned to where he first brings his sandwich down after taking a bite and adjusted *those* layers to make him not bring it down as far. Then it was a matter of applying another tween between those keyframes with a long, slow "S" curve in the Easing Editor to bring them back down to the starting point *(Image 3.10a)*. I also added a bit more squash or stretch to the head in some parts that I thought could use some more exaggeration *(Image 3.10b)* and enlarged the instance of the head symbol a bit when he takes the bite, which added more dimension to the scene by making it feel he was leaning forward more *(Image 3.10c)*. You can add extra bits of movement like these with very little effort or risk. Try it out!

In this example there was more work with symblification and straight ahead frame-by-frame cleanup animation to complete the scene. Tradigital animation needs to jump back and forth between these methods seamlessly to work properly. It's not hard to see what features need to be animated frame by frame, which can be shape tweened, and which need to have a combination of both and motion tweening to get the proper and precise results. Though there was less attention on the full body, like in Chapter 2, the fact the face is taking up most of the entire screen means that greater attention needs to be paid to the finer details.

Image 3.10b

The squash and stretch in the scene is an exaggeration of life, but almost all animation will be exaggerated in some way. You will rarely be done with a scene on the first pass, especially not the more complicated scenes which display multiple features in movement and distortions (like this scene). Take a break and then come back at it with fresh eyes to see if it can be improved in some way. And don't forget to check out the finalized scene that has been provided on the companion website to deconstruct it and see if something more can be learned about the setup.

Image 3.10c

FINAL WORDS
Squash and Stretch

So far, we have gone through three chapters and three different principles. The bouncing ball exercise now reflects each of these, and you have learned how to create a ball, turn it into a symbol, adjust it, tween it, ease it, and now squash and stretch it. In the closer look areas of these chapters, you have learned how to take these tools and properties (no matter your previous knowledge of either) and take an inanimate object like a ball and apply some acting to it, overlapping your knowledge of the principles and tools.

I've been where you are now, and I know you *still* may not feel like it's getting you anywhere. Believe me, I understand. Truth is, you're probably not going to feel satisfied until you've animated a full shot from start to finish; I know I didn't. When you're learning, it can feel like everything is going so slowly. But somewhere down the line, after you have a good grasp of the basics, everything will just click and the creativity in your head and that which you can actually create will finally start to match! In the words of Kaa, "trusssssst ... in meeeee."

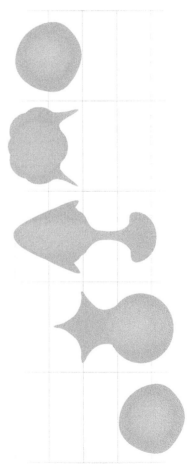

Squash and Stretch, in a lot of ways, is emblematic of animation as a whole. It's all about a heightened sense of movement—more interpretive than actual. It can be subtle or extreme, and both are equally valid. There are no real strict terms or rules for its application. Actions in real life can be seen in terms of these two complimentary concepts and so can feelings. In animation terms, to squash or stretch something is usually that which goes beyond its standard form. A hard blink can have a squash to it, for instance, if the eyelids are spread out a bit more than anatomy would actually allow in order to punctuate the intensity of the act. All of these principles live and die on their use; it's up to you to decide if the movement needs it and to what amount. That simply takes practice—practice and observation.

I was going to make a joke about anticipating the next chapter on Anticipation, but I couldn't come up with a good one ... so I settled on this self-referential sentence. Next chapter!

Image 3.11 Squash and Stretch is the foundation of this amebic blob's entire locomotion. Example taken from "ch3-examples-blob.fla" on the companion website.

Image 4.0 The more that time passes on a long shot of a guy at his most vulnerable the more anticipation is built. My Friend the Toilet #3: Surprise Guest *by Stephen Brooks (RubberOnion.com).*

Chapter 4

ANTICIPATION

INTRODUCING
Anticipation

If you were to look up "anticipation" in the dictionary, you would find this: the action of anticipating something. Helpful. But if you look up "anticipate" in that same dictionary you'd find its synonyms: expect, await, look forward to, and be prepared for. So now that we have covered some principles on the physics of movement (Chapters 1 and 2) and the interpretation of motion (Chapter 3), this principle is our first exposure to one of the 12 Principles of Animation which focuses on the storytelling aspect of our medium: Anticipation.

Try to imagine a world of storytelling *without* anticipation; that impression should illuminate just how important it is. What would a storm really be without the calm before it? In animation terms, Anticipation is about guiding the audience through the actions. Sometimes it's to lead into a reveal, which is as simple as someone looking at something off screen before seeing what's there. Other times it is used to accentuate an action. When a person is attempting something difficult, like lifting an abnormally heavy bag of laundry, the sense of weight is greatly intensified if, before the difficult lift, our intrepid character prepares for it intently ... fearfully. That little beat of anticipation serves to prop up the audience's focus on the importance of what comes next.

We will be making a little detour with this chapter's bouncing ball exercise. It's still building on our previous work, but the purpose of the shot will change. Up till now the intent of our exercise was to have this ball starting from a height drop and bounce back up by the force of its own momentum being redirected. There was no discernible start and no end. This time, instead of an endless loop, we will create an actual beginning to this action.

BOUNCING BALL Anticipation

Setting Up

Our good friend **File > Save As** comes back to save us from the perils of overwriting work. Saving from the last file (bouncing ball 3 – squash stretch) we're moving one up and naming this "bouncing ball 4 – anticipation." The goal of this particular exercise is to take what we've done and turn it into a scene. The ball will start in the "contact" position and slowly squash until it looks like it can't anymore and enough potential energy has built up (anticipation) to allow it to shoot up off the ground and into the air. Then it will bounce once before coming back to the starting position (which Animate CC will loop for us when exported to SWF).

Part I, here, will essentially be more setting up than this actual "Setting Up" section. You'll notice, too, that I'm not spending as much time clarifying the steps, as many of them we've been over multiple times in previous chapters. In some I give new ways of doing the same things. This varying level and type of step description is all built to help you become accustomed to the versatility Animate CC offers. Let's go.

PART I
"Positioning Keys"

Image BB4.1

1. On the timeline click and drag the full length of the movie from frame 1 to 25 to highlight all work done so far. *Image BB4.1*

2. Right-click on this highlighted portion and select **Copy Frames.**

Image BB4.3

3. Right-click on the final keyframe (frame 25) and select **Paste Frames.** *Image BB4.3*

4. Using the "Go to first frame" button on the timeline (vertical line followed by a back arrow) and then the "Play" button (obvious) check out what you did in steps 1–3. Everything has copied over: every tween value, every symbol position. You

Image BB4.4

even replaced the last keyframe with the first (even though they were in the exact same position anyway). With an extra bounce in there, now we can create our new start and end frames. *Image BB4.4*

5. Right-click the key on frame 12 (the "contact stretch") and select **Clear Keyframe.** We won't need that because ... *Image BB4.5*

6. We'll be starting on the ground. Click the key on frame 1; as you know, that will select the ball on that frame. "Align bottom edge" from the Align panel (Cmd/**Ctrl+K**). *Image BB4.6*

7. With our starting position created, let's make the ending. When it lands on the ground we want some squash/stretch to cushion the impact. So we'll need the three frames which make up the bounce earlier, as well as the "up" key. Click and drag to highlight frames 25 to 38. *Image BB4.7*

8. Right-click the highlighted area and select **Copy Frames.**

9. Right-click on frame 49 (currently the last keyframe) and select **Paste Frames.** The keen observer will notice that leaves us with a stretched key as the last frame. Good eye! We're not yet completed with our end frame. *Image BB4.9*

10. We're going to copy the first key and paste to one frame *after* the current end. You already know how to copy and paste with right-clicks. Alternatively, you can click frame 1 and copy with Cmd/**Ctrl+C**, select the empty box at frame 64 and hit **F7** to "Insert Blank Keyframe" (which can also be done with a right-click), and use the hotkey sequence Cmd/**Ctrl+Shift+V** on that same frame to paste in place. This is a commonly used approach, and you'd be amazed how fast it is when you get used to it. *Image BB4.10*

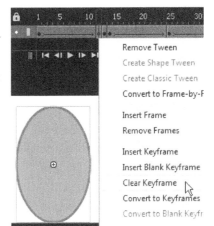

Image BB4.5

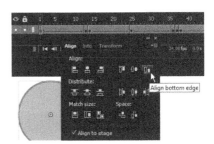

Image BB4.6

Image BB4.7

Image BB4.9

Image BB4.10

Interlude

As we mentioned, the goal is to have the ball slowly squash until it's built up enough energy to jump, shoot up in the air, bounce once, and then come back down to the starting position. Play the timeline. What's missing so far? "Until it's built up enough energy to jump" for starters. I'm not convinced there's enough energy buildup the way it is now, are you? Also, when it comes back down to the ground, the squash and stretch is much too fast—the timing there needs to be adjusted. Finally, there's something strange about the way it's bouncing in the air. It feels like the ball shouldn't be bouncing as high the second time. Actually, there's a physical reason for this. It's called "decreasing max height," and it simply means that each time a ball bounces, it loses some of the energy it had before crashing into the ground. That's why a bouncing ball won't bounce forever when it's dropped. Otherwise there would be stray bouncing balls everywhere, taking over our cities. Let's fix these issues in Part II.

PART II
"Improving The Action"

11. First fix is going to be the final squash and stretch; it's too fast. Let's give it some breathing room to come to a full stop by putting an extra frame in the last tween by using **F5** once at frame 61. The final key should now be on frame 65. *Image BB4.11*

Image BB4.11

12. Next up is the actual anticipation, the reason we're here! That first tween, where the ball is slowly squashing, needs more time to develop, and it needs a nice slow in *and* out. Use **F5** again to extend it. Around 1.5 seconds would work, so push the squash key out to frame 40 just to make things easy (meaning the *final* frame of the whole movie would now be at 92). *Image BB4.12*

Image BB4.12

13. If you test the movie right now, it clearly looks better this way, but to really drive home the anticipation we need a beat after the ball is fully squashed before it jumps. Insert five frames (**F5**) at frame 40 to add about one-quarter of a second between the squashed and stretched keyframes. *Image BB4.13*

Image BB4.13

14. If you're following along exactly, you'll notice that even though it wasn't doing anything there was a tween applied to the keyframe on frame 40, and now there's a horrible tween from the squash to stretched state before our jump (if you cleaned that up earlier, good work! You already did this step). Right-click the tween between frame 40 and 46 and select **Remove Tween**. If you test the movie now, you can see the anticipation is *much* stronger with this extra beat. *Image BB4.14*

Image BB4.14

15. With the first tween selected, open the Easing Editor. You should see that right now it's a slow in (–100) and looks like a ski jump. We're going to give this tween a hard slow in and out like we did in the closer look "More Custom Easing" in Chapter 2. Remember that it looks like an "S." *Image BB4.15*

16. Click the first edit point (remember the black dot, lower left) to get the handle. Move that white dot on the end until it's about two-thirds of the way to the right and the handle is perfectly horizontal on the bottom. *Image BB4.16*

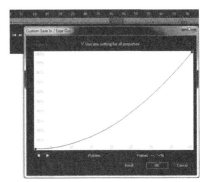

Image BB4.15

17. For the end edit point (top right), do the same in the opposite direction, and then click OK to save this new tween. *Image BB4.17*

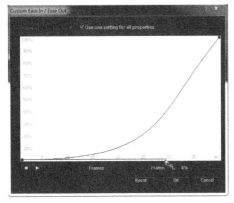

Image BB4.16

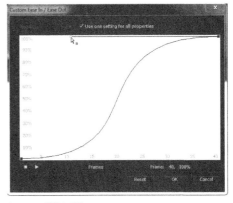

Image BB4.17

Interlude

There's not a lot to say here; just thought you might want a break. What we're going to do next is deal with the "decreasing max height" issue. Addressing this issue may not seem like it fits in a chapter about Anticipation, but it does. Decreasing max height builds Anticipation in its own way. "What's going to happen when it gets to the bottom?" In this case, we don't allow it to play out to the full extent of physical law. We're animators after all, and that's our prerogative. What we're doing is creating anticipation for the first jump (with the squash) and anticipation for the final rest (with a decreasing max height), which in turn is the anticipation for the buildup. That's the way this principle works. Anticipation, at its core, is about stringing events together in a visually meaningful way. There's the setup and the payoff.

I think you all understand that the decreasing max height of a bouncing ball is owed to the ball losing energy due to friction every time it hits the ground. For this same reason, the amount of squash and stretch added to the ball will be decreasing proportionally (we'll "guesstimate" on the amount). Losing, decreasing ... these "changing" words are a sign of building expectation. Sometimes in storytelling you'll want to pay off those expectations with their natural conclusions; other times it would be best to do something *un*expected. The more you create anticipation and pay it off with expected conclusions, the more effective an unexpected result will be. As much as I hate jump-scares in horror movies, they're pretty effective for this reason. Back to the exercise. Remember, we're going to deal with the height, the levels of squash and stretch, and some timing alteration.

> "Anticipation, at its core, is about stringing events together in a visually meaningful way."

PART III
"Decreasing Max Height"

18. The first height is fine, but we need to make the second up position lower. Locate its keyframe (hint: it's frame 81). Move the ball straight down until the ball is about one-third its own height lower. *Image BB4.18*

19. Now that the ball bounces lower, it shouldn't be in the air as long—so the timing must be adjusted. Just take three frames out of each tween in the second bounce sequence (tween spans from frames 70–81 and 81–92). You should be comfortable performing this action by now (highlight the amount of frames, right-click, and **Remove Frames**). After the timing

Image BB4.18

is adjusted like this, the movie will end on frame 91. *Image BB4.19*

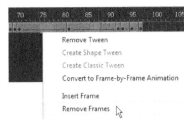

Image BB4.19

20. Let's adjust some of these squashes and stretches, starting with the first squash on frame 40. If we really want to create anticipation, the ball should have more squash on it. It should look like a balloon almost ready to pop. Select that frame and give the ball slightly more squash. I used the Transform panel with values of H:125% and V:75%. Realign to the ground. *Image BB4.20*

21. One final alteration before we continue with the squash/stretch changes. With this new, more intense squash, the slow out applied to the first "jump" should be more intense as well. Click that tween (between frame 46 and 57) and open the Easing Editor. Drag the left edit point's handle all the way to the left so that it's pointing straight up and extend it to reach around 80%. You can see the curve change as you drag. *The more vertical the beginning part of the curve is, the more speed the tween will have at the start. Image BB4.21*

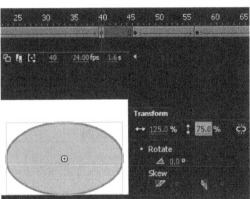

Image BB4.20

22. Do the same as you did for the squash in step 20 for the next keyframe's stretch (H:75%, V:125%) on frame 46. *Image BB4.22*

23. Skipping the next bounce's squash and stretch, move onto the final set of keyframes. Adjust these to have less of each. For instance, the

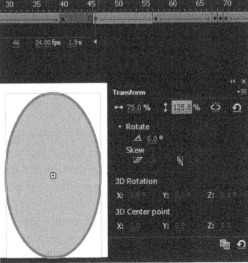

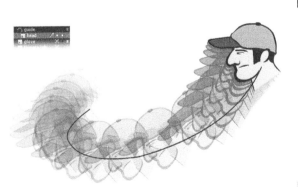

Image BB4.21

Image BB4.22

stretch on frame 86 should still be 80/120 horizontal/vertical. We want to change these settings to something less stretched like 85/115. To *really* get the sense that the bouncing is coming to a stop, each successive squash/stretch should be less. So if that stretch was 85/115, the next *squash* should be 110/90 followed by the final stretch at 95/105. But feel free to play around with it! And finally, don't forget to realign it. *Image BB4.23a, BB4.23b, and BB4.23c*

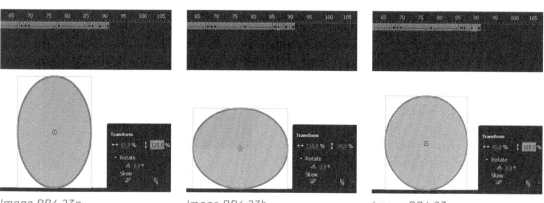

Image BB4.23a   Image BB4.23b   Image BB4.23c

I know that was a long one, but you'll definitely want to be testing this movie. Look what's been created. Now we're on a roll! This single, 3.5-second, looping video incorporates the four principles we've covered so far (Timing, Slow In/Out, Squash and Stretch, and Anticipation) as well as a myriad of tools and functions in Animate CC and multiple ways to use them ... *with* hotkeys! We created new keyframes, copied some over, and altered almost all of them to fit our needs. Now might be a good time to go back to your folder and one by one open up and view each SWF created in this main exercise for each chapter. See how they compare. This movie is vastly different than what we started with, and we're still working from the exact same ball! It's just one symbol; we haven't even altered it from Chapter 1. If you're following along with the bouncing ball exercises, skipping the real-world examples for now, and itching to finally draw something more than a circle, don't worry. We will get into drawing (obviously, since one of the 12 Principles is literally called "Solid Drawing") in the later chapters.

The held squash before the jump in our bouncing ball in this chapter adds a lot to the following action. Before it happens, you know what's to likely happen. How anticlimactic would it be if after intensely squashing like that, the ball just sort of went back to its normal position? There are really only two options your brain wants: either jump or explode, because either way that energy has to go somewhere. If it doesn't, it'll just feel wrong. Breaking this rule to surprise your audience is effective but if you don't do it in the right way they will feel tricked and robbed of a proper payoff (see horror movie jump scares comment from the previous interlude). Anticipation is like a promise to the viewer, "this is what's coming next." It's been used on the stage for centuries. When playing up to an audience in the back of the theater, actors would need to make their actions readable.

Inserting anticipation into their movements was one way to help convey the following action better for everyone watching.

One of my favorite examples of anticipation used in acting is basically every punch thrown by Harrison Ford in any movie. He's a master of acting in action. When Indiana Jones is fighting the big, bald mechanic by the plane in *Raiders of the Lost Ark*, every punch is preceded by a huge windup. Each time, Indy leans back and brings his fist up next to his head while lifting his elbow high. If you were to take a picture of that moment, what else could possibly be coming next? He's not answering a phone. In real life, obviously a punch like that would never land because you would see it coming from a mile away. It's the very definition of telegraphing a punch. But on stage, film, and in animation, this anticipation sets up our audience for an emotional reaction, one way or the other. When the promise is kept there's a feeling of jubilation, for our hero has landed a solid shot. When the promise is stifled, either by missing or the punch's apparent ineffectiveness due to the iron chin of his villain, the emotion shifts to distress. Anticipation has taken the fight scene and upped the emotional ante.

"Anticipation is like a promise to the viewer, 'this is what's coming next.'"

Image 4.1

CLOSER LOOK
Advanced Easing Editor

You have learned so much about the layout, terms, and movement tools in Animate CC. These are usually what people have the hardest time learning when first starting. Everyone knows what something called the "Pencil Tool" does, but not many know about the "Easing panel." There's a level of intimidation with this new stuff which can stilt creativity. By focusing on the movement aspects first, we have covered a whole area around what it takes to make things move in Animate CC. and how it can help. You're one-third of the way to the end of the book and things will, of course, get more involved from here. But as the concepts and execution get more detailed, the tools are more intuitive after this point.

What we'll do in this section is look at what more can be done with the Easing panel. So far we've been able to adjust the curve of a simple slow in or slow out to be more intense (obviously you can do the opposite as well), and we've also created an "S" curve to apply a slow in *and* out to the same tween (as in the case of the closer look section of Chapter 2). We've also compared the Custom Ease graph to Timing Charts in traditional animation. But there's something we can do with the Easing panel that can't be replicated on a single Timing Chart.

You've seen that there is an edit point at the bottom-left of the graph (start) and the top-right (end). This time, we'll be creating new points along the line to make a more sophisticated easing graph and create a "quivering" look to the ball during the anticipatory squash. Don't forget to **Save As** your file. This time, since we're exploring two ways of doing the same thing, save it with a "- closer look – method 1" suffix on it so that we don't lose any work we've done.

"Quiver, Method 1: Tween"

1. Open the Easing Editor for the first tween in order to cause a quivering effect, it's a "two steps forward, one step back" kind of situation. In this case, we want the ball to squash a little, then unsquash a little less, and continue that until reaching the end. Keep in mind going forward that Cmd/**Ctrl+Z** *does* work to undo any mistake you make in here. *Image CL4.1*

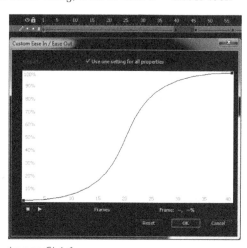

Image CL4.1

2. The quiver shouldn't start until the slow out since that's the moment of most tension, so click on the graph after the halfway point to create a new edit point. I chose just before the 25th frame. *(Pro-tip: If you need to delete a point, hold **Alt** and click the point you want to delete.) Image CL4.2*

3. Now we want to create a few more points to the right of this last one. These will be our "anchor points" on the original tween. Try making the "anchor points" spaced in a slow in and out fashion. In other words, they should get denser in the middle of the grouping than the beginning and end. I put seven more points in this way (spaced wide, spaced narrow, and then wide again). *Image CL4.3*

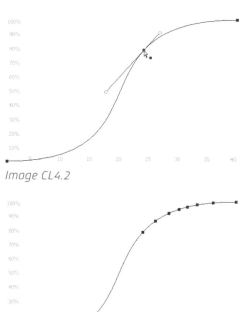

Image CL4.2

4. Now we need "quiver points" where we take a step back before returning to the next "anchor point." Click and drag down a point inbetween the first two "anchor points" to de-squash

Image CL4.3

the ball a little. So if you click a point on the 25th frame position which should be around 80%, drag that down to around 70% so that it's lower than our previous point (which should be around 75ish). *Image CL4.4*

5. Do the same as you did in step 4 to create "quiver points" between each of the "anchor points" you created in step 3. Try to also do these in a slow in/out fashion proportional to the amount they're pulled down. *Image CL4.5*

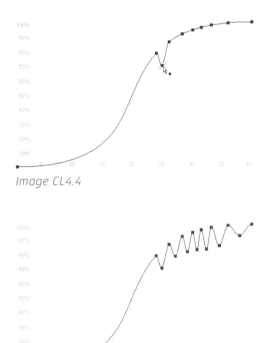

Image CL4.4

6. You should now have something that looks like a small earthquake went off on the last half of our tween. You can press the play button in the Easing Editor now to see what it looks like. You can adjust to your heart's content, and when you're satisfied click **OK** to save the tween.

This kind of special manipulation of the Easing Editor in Animate CC is what makes it so valuable. There's one line on the graph to deal with, any point you create you can undo or delete, each point is editable in both position and curve that comes before and after

Image CL4.5

it ... this is the type of functionality we want from programs. It only gets more complicated as we add more features to our own project. It's directly scalable in this way to the user's skill level.

Even though the ability is there, you don't have to do this kind of graph manipulation at all. What you will see next is how to make similar adjustments by moving the keyframes around instead. This method won't allow for the kind of flexibility that the Easing Editor does, but it is a bit more tangible (if I can use that term in a book on digital animation) and straight forward in understanding. Many animators I know, including myself, actually still use this method from time to time because in

certain situations it can be a hair faster to get an expected result. Before doing anything, **Save As** and add the suffix "- method 2."

"Quiver, Method 2: Manual"

7. First, let's undo what we did in this section so far. Open the Easing Editor for the first tween again, and press the **Reset** button. You should see our beautiful, but slightly complicated, graph turn back to a single, ramp-like line. Click **OK**. *Image CL4.7*

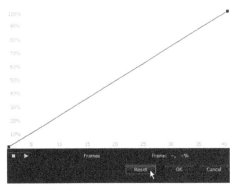

Image CL4.7

8. Our tween's easing is set back to 0. We still want the first half of the squash span to slow in.

Image CL4.8

Click a frame halfway down the tween (about frame 21) and create a keyframe. *Image CL4.8*

9. Select the newly sectioned first tween and apply a slow in (ease of −100). *Image CL4.9*

10. Do the same as step 3 for the second tween (between frame 21 and 40) but this time with a slow out. *Image CL4.10*

Image CL4.9

11. What we want to do now is make each one of these frames along the slow out portion of the tween, a keyframe. Click and drag from frame 21 to frame 39 (*not* keyframe 40) to highlight all 19 frames and press **F6**. The tween is now broken up into a keyframe for every frame. *Image CL4.11*

Image CL4.10

Image CL4.11

12. Each frame still has a tween applied to it. These legacy tweens will get confusing if we don't remove that, so with all the 19 frames still selected from step 5 right-click and select **Remove Tween**. *Image CL4.12*

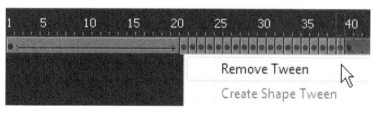

Image CL4.12

13. With these frames, we'll apply the "step forward, step back" pattern literally. But first we need to create a little space. Select frame 25 and press **F5** to insert a frame (we'll remove this later). *Image CL4.13*

14. For sake of clarity, let's call the frame directly to the right of the space our "base" keyframe.

Image CL4.13

Currently it's on frame 27. Now take the frame to the *right* of that base keyframe (that would be frame 28) and click-and-drag it back into the space (frame 26). *Image CL4.14*

Image CL4.14

15. Repeat the process in step 8 down the line until you get to a couple frames before the end (moving key 38 to frame 36 is a good place to stop). *Image CL4.15*

Image CL4.15

16. Right-click on the space and select **Remove Frames**. *Image CL4.16*

Now when you test the movie, you can see what effect it had on the final. It looks almost identical,

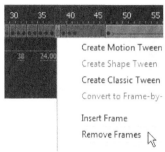

though "method 2" probably has a more subtle quiver effect to it. A lot of people (myself included) find this method easier to understand on a visceral level. The real benefit to this method is if you have a longer tween where you want a shutter like this, you can get right in there and make it happen. The Easing Editor window doesn't get any bigger or smaller (as of the writing of this book), so if you need the frequency of the quiver to be high, then it's probably easier just to move the individual frames than try to get the edit points on the   *Image CL4.16*

graph close enough together to get you the effect that you want. Conversely, the biggest benefit to "method 1" is its ability to easily control and edit the amount of the quiver.

As with all things, both methods clearly have their benefits and their weaknesses, and it's up to you to decide which one should be employed at any given moment. A lot of traditional animation was about manipulating the spacing of keyframes. Even the original masters of animation, like Ollie Johnston, would manipulate the spacing of frames often when blocking out a shot, apparently much to the chagrin of the animation assistant responsible for deciphering the scarcely legible frame numbers on each sheet and applying the inbetweens according to the Timing Chart. If you notice the comparison here, Animate CC is our assistant animator. At least we don't hear complaints from the program for changing things around and all of the numbers are perfectly readable.

A big part of this book is exposing you to different workflows, not just the simple tools. Workflows are kind of like the unseen signature of artists, and you'll often hear animators talk about how they accomplish the exact same thing. Everyone has their tricks of the trade and methods that help them cut those unnecessary corners to get right to the creative core of their work. Which corners an animator decides are unnecessary is what makes them unique. Everyone has a different focus in their work and, not that it's reading tea leaves or anything, but you can tell a lot about a person by the way they animate. You will increasingly find that as you progress with bringing these traditional principles into the digital world of creation, the goals you have will ultimately result in adopting certain methods and rejecting others. This progression all culminates in creating a workflow that's very "you."

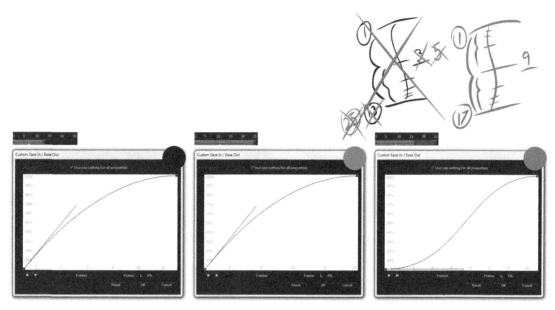

Image 4.2 Two alterations to timing and one of them with changes in spacing could make for a messy Timing Chart (top right), which is hard for an assistant animator to follow. These same changes (below, left to right) are altered by Animate CC in real time with no complaints.

"You can tell a lot about a person by the way they animate."

Using Anticipation by "Knowing Your Purpose"

If you have the opportunity, watch some Olympic fencing and then compare and contrast with Inigo Montoya fighting the Dread Pirate Roberts in *The Princess Bride* (1987). You'll see some drastic differences. The major one is that real fencing is all about "economy of motion." The fencer wants to be quick and efficient, which directly leads to their effectiveness. It's completely the opposite in movies. First and foremost, you want to tell a story. Second, there needs to be an emotional reaction to the fight as it progresses. Finally, it needs to be clearly understood by the majority of the non-fencing audience. One thing you'll notice is not on this list: whether or not it would actually work in a real-life sword fight. That's not important at all ... not even a little.

What if in *Peter Pan* (1953) those great Disney animators were worried about the economy of motion in Peter's fight with Captain Hook? There would be no flare, no fun, we would have absolutely no idea what was happening during that scene nor would we probably care. He also could've just flown over Captain Hook with a big net and then delivered the old codfish to Tick-Tock the Croc—done and done. But that wouldn't be an entertaining climax either. Each sword thrust, slash, and attempted death-by-hook attack had a wonderful anticipatory action in front of it. This made everything readable to the audience so that they could be invested in the story. I understand that Disney didn't write the original play (J. M. Barrie did), but in both the play and the Disney animated film, anticipation was used to heighten the emotional connection of the audience to the action played out in front of them.

Let's look at one more film reference. This one is from even earlier: the 1925 silent film masterpiece *The Phantom of the Opera*, with the great Lon Cheney as the Phantom. The famous unmasking scene is one with almost unparalleled anticipation and ultimate payoff. As Christine Daae, played by Mary Philbin, very slowly approaches the Phantom from behind as he's distracted playing the organ, there's a look of equal parts fear and delight on her face. She's intensely curious about what is under that mask. The camera shows a profile two-shot of Christine and the Phantom (the disconnected observer view) as her hands get close to the mask. First time she's close to the mask she pulls her hands back in a moment of trepidation but then goes back to pursuing this desire to satisfy her curiosity. The anticipation is extremely high in those moments. What will he look like under there? What will he do when she rips it off? When the moment finally comes and Christine lifts the mask off the Phantom, the camera immediately cuts to a shot from the front of Phantom, now fully unmasked. It's an incredibly up-close and personal view and a terrifying reveal to the audience. But there's another layer of anticipation because Christine is shown still standing behind him. We, the audience, have seen what horrors lie beneath the mask and how angry he is about being revealed, but Christine hasn't yet. That moment lasts a full 3 seconds as he quickly stands up and turns around, now out of frame, with Christine taking the full attention on screen and recoiling in terror. We get anticipation, payoff, more anticipation, and more payoff—all in the same brilliant scene.

> ## "Anticipation is like salt in cooking; it intensifies the flavor that's there."

Each of these examples has taken us back through the decades of film all the way to the silent era. Because it was so prevalent in theater, the closer you get to the beginning of film the more obvious the use of Anticipation is to see. It makes sense for silent films because they lived and died on pantomime. Charlie Chaplin is a perfect case, but even contemporaries like Rowan Atkinson's *Mr. Bean* use the same methods. In order to use this principle properly, you must know the purpose of the scene. If it is to highlight the sword-fighting skill of your hero, you'll want those special moves to be anticipated before they happen. In the event you want to scare your audience, make them worry about what might happen next (but don't forget to make the pay-off actually

Image 4.3 The Phantom of the Opera *(1925)* *unmasking scene, progression order top to bottom.*

satisfying). At its core, Anticipation is all about leading the audience into predicting a following action, whatever that may be, to better sell the impact when it does (or does not) happen. Anticipation is like salt in cooking; it intensifies the flavor that's there. This principle may take different forms, but it always plays that same roll.

REAL-WORLD EXAMPLE
"Pitching A Bomb"

Principles Used

Timing: Though this principle is the lynchpin to many scenes, it plays a big part in anything which also employs Anticipation. The timing of how long it takes for the bomb's wick to run out, the windup sequence to elapse, and when the bomb finally goes off will make or break the scene. For this scene, it will enhance the anticipation and make the payoff more enjoyable.

Staging: To clearly see the pitcher, what's he's doing and what's in his hand, proper staging is needed. The size difference between him and the bomb is a large one, so we have to make sure that the focus is on what's in his hand and the fact his eyes/brain don't notice it. Then when the windup for the pitch comes, we need to see the whole action, so this final lead-up to the payoff doesn't become muddy when everything before it was so clear.

Solid Drawing: This principle is mostly needed in a big way for the windup to the pitch. There are perspective changes in the pitcher's form, so in order to make sure he doesn't seem flat and the illusion isn't destroyed before the final joke, solid drawing will take care of maintaining the volume and strength of form of the character.

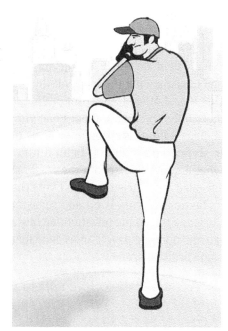

Image 4.4

Arcs: Again, the windup sequence will need to follow arcs to clearly follow what's happening. Arcs also reinforce the living, organic nature of the character which emphasizes the illusion of life ... before a cartoon bomb explodes in his face.

Pose to Pose/Straight Ahead: To finish the rough animation of the windup, employing both Pose to Pose and Straight Ahead action will be needed. The keys are already sketched out in blue, which is the bulk of the pose to pose work, and a couple breakdowns in red on your part couldn't hurt. The Straight Ahead work will be most useful between these frames.

Anticipation: The namesake of this chapter comes into play in two ways—story and movement. The anticipation present in the story is the audience waiting and watching the wick burn closer to the end, while reversing the forward movement and adding an anticipatory beat in the windup help the audience follow and expect the movement, leading to a better payoff.

Setting Up

Open the project file "ch4-real_world-pitcher.fla" provided on the companion website. There are three main parts to this scene: the ball being replaced by the bomb, the windup, and the explosion. I have provided rough animation for the windup sequence ("on twos," which means I drew one image for every two frames) for you to follow along so you may focus on how to do cleanup on a more complicated shot than you may be used to up till now. There's a lot going on here, and a lot of animation principles to keep in mind. Working out the timing between the shots will be a lot like what we worked through in Chapter 1's real-world example, "Looking Around." The process of working through the windup sequence will be a lot like that in

Image 4.5 The rough animation for the "windup" sequence is provided for you. (Note: Screengrab from Flash CS6 to show separate frames with colors as they are.)

Chapter 2's real-world example, "Heavy Lifting." And the wick burning and explosion employ loops like in Chapter 3's "Chewing" example.

As mentioned in the previous chapter, there are technically more principles at work than the ones listed—these are just the major players in the scene. You'll notice other principles being brought up in the steps, because they need to be considered. As always, remember that as you move through the steps there are many ways to do the same thing. This example is another step forward to show the Tradigital animation workflow: using symbols and tweening within Animate CC to aid in precision and reduce the workload, and calling for frame-by-frame animation with digital drawing tools for the more complicated movements. Animate CC is acting 100 percent as a tool for the creation of "hand-drawn" animation. Tradigital "hand-drawn" animation is the slight update to *traditional* methods and techniques which results from the use of *digital* tools that aid in illustration and movement. From now on, there will be even less explanation of each step. Follow the cleanup methods from the previous chapters' real-world examples to finish the scene outlined in the rough.

> "Tradigital 'hand-drawn' animation is the slight update to *traditional* methods and techniques which results from the use of *digital* tools that aid in illustration and movement."

"The Switch"

1. The pitcher's first pose has been created for you, so you will animate the mysterious hand which comes out and replaces the baseball for a bomb. There are mainly just key drawings (in blue) in the rough animation for this sequence (some breakdowns in red) so there's a lot of room for experimentation in how you clean this up. I opted to create a symbol for the arm ("mystery_arm"), and inside that create another symbol for the hand ("mystery_arm-hand") with the registration point at the wrist on a layer above the arm. The hand symbol's internal timeline is extended a few seconds and set to "Play Once" starting from frame 1. This will allow a range of motion for the hand to express, demonstrate overlapping action, and be able to hold objects while the instance of the whole arm (including hand) will be tweened on stage. *Image PB4.1*

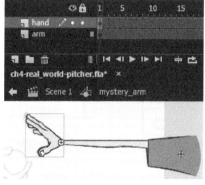

Image PB4.1

2. Back on the main stage, drag an instance of the "mystery_arm" symbol onto a new layer you create in the cleanup folder called "mystery arm." The layer is best positioned at the top of the folder. On the first frame, make sure it's set to "Play Once" from frame 1, and then using keyframes (**F6**), Free Transform Tool (**Q**), and classic tweens apply its movement across the stage as presented in the rough animation. Use appropriate easing. We'll address the hand animation in the following steps. *Image PB4.2*

Image PB4.2

3. First we'll deal with the differing hand designs. At frame 60, you should see that the once open hand of the mystery arm closes around the baseball in the pitcher's hand. Double click the mystery arm's hand until you're inside the "mystery_arm-hand" instance, insert a blank keyframe (**F7**) and clean up the design as shown in the rough. *Image PB4.3*

4. Still in the "mystery_arm-hand" symbol, create a new layer below the one with the hand and insert blank keyframe (**F7**) on the same frame (60). Drag the baseball from the library

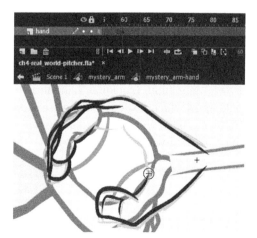

Image PB4.3

90

here and line it up with the one you can see the pitcher holding ghosted on the main stage. This is the first handoff point.

5. Look back at the main timeline and determine where the mystery arm is out of view to the audience (I chose frame 70) and where the second handoff happens (frame 76). Where the arm is out of view to audience, back in the "mystery_arm-hand" symbol insert a keyframe (**F6**) on the baseball layer at this frame and **Swap Symbol** with the "bomb." Then insert a blank keyframe (**F7**) on frame 77 so it's *after* the handoff, since at this point in the scene the bomb should be in the pitcher's hand. A frame or two will be enough to animate the hand from closed around the bomb to open again. *Image PB4.5*

Image PB4.5

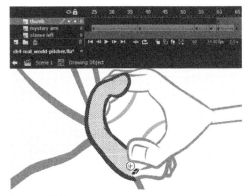

Image PB4.6

6. We want some overlap of the hands during the handoffs to sell the idea that they're interacting. On the main timeline, create a new layer above the mystery arm and name it "thumb" since that's all we'll need to sell the illusion. Copy and paste in place the pitcher's hand to the thumb layer to a blank keyframe (**F7**) at the first handoff (frame 60). With the instance highlighted, Break Apart (**Cmd/Ctrl+B**) the hand symbol and delete everything but the object with the thumb. Turn on outline view on the thumb layer and use the Eraser Tool (**E**) to remove everything covering up the mystery arm's thumb but *not* the baseball. *Image PB4.6*

Image PB4.7

7. Create a keyframe (**F6**) at the next handoff frame (76) so it will serve the same function there and then insert blank keyframes (**F7**) on the frames immediately after the handoffs (61 and 77). *Image PB4.7*

8. Finalize the mystery arm animation by rotating the hand and tweening where appropriate in the "mystery_arm" symbol itself to add some acting and overlapping action to this mostly hidden character.

9. To complete the switch, you'll need to enter the pitcher's "hand" symbol at the moment where the mystery arm gives the bomb to the pitcher (frame 76), insert a keyframe (**F6**) and **Swap Symbol** of the "baseball" for the "bomb." And finally, still in the "hand" symbol, you'll need to insert a blank keyframe (**F7**) on the "ball/bomb" layer at the moment the mystery arm

takes the baseball away from the pitcher (frame 60). *Image PB4.9*

"Wick Burning"

10. The bomb and spark symbols have been provided for you, now you need to animate the wick burning. We will be using motion guides (if you're following the suggested reading path as outlined in this book's Introduction, these guides are described in Chapter 5's closer look section). Enter the "bomb" symbol by double-clicking it in the library and you'll see two layers: bomb and wick. The wick is a simple, curved line.

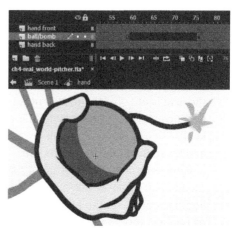

Image PB4.9

11. The "bomb_spark" symbol is an FX loop of the sparks flying off the wick as it burns—it will travel along a guide which hasn't been set yet. Create a new layer in between the bomb and wick layers, name it "spark," and drag the "bomb_spark" symbol from the library onto the stage on that layer. Make sure it's set to loop from frame 1.

12. Since the wick is just a single line and that's what we want the spark to travel down, this can act as the guide. Create a new layer above the "spark" layer and name it "guide." Copy the line on the wick layer, paste in place on the guide layer, and drag the spark symbol so that it connects with the end of the wick (make sure Snap to Objects is on and the transform point should lock onto the line tip). *Image PB4.12*

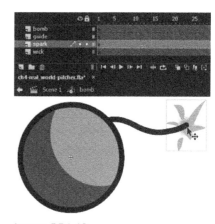

Image PB4.12

13. We want to create a good anticipation buildup as the spark travels down the wick and timing will help us determine the length needed for the span to do that. I used 4.5 seconds. Create a keyframe there on the "spark" layer, drag the instance of the spark symbol down to the base of the wick until it connects like in the previous step. It might help to momentarily hide the "bomb" layer while doing this. *Image PB4.13*

14. Knowing that the mystery arm will be holding the bomb for a few frames, apply a classic motion tween

Image PB4.13

with no slow in or out (easing setting of 0) starting a few frames in (I chose to start the span at frame 10). *(Note: because the spark animation is rather random looking and the handoff happens so quickly, it was not important to match the internal timeline of the bomb symbols between the mystery arm and the pitcher's hand. The only thing at risk of being an obvious jump to the viewer would be the spark traveling down the wick. This is why we left these few frames as a buffer for that motion.)*

15. Guide the "guide" layer (you probably saw that step coming) and drag the "spark" layer into it until it becomes parented to the guide. Hit **Enter** on your keyboard to quick test this tween span and make sure the spark is following the path.

16. We want the wick to burn away. Hide every layer except "wick" and create a layer above it called "mask" (because of the order of your actions, this layer and "wick" should be the only two visible layers). On this layer, draw a rectangle which covers the entire wick line but stops just at the right-most edge. *(Pro-tip: it's best to create masks using a fill color with some Alpha, like 50%, so that you can see through them. Whatever the mask covers is what will be shown when everything is locked, so to work with them it's good to have this x-ray vision to know what it is exactly that you will be showing). Image PB4.16*

Image PB4.16

17. Insert a keyframe (**F6**) on the "mask" layer at the end of the timeline and manipulate the existing rectangle so that it is now only covering the left-most portion of the wick. Insert a keyframe at the beginning of the span chosen in step 14 (I chose frame 10) and apply a shape tween between the two keyframes with no slow in or out. *Image PB4.17*

Image PB4.17

18. Turn the layer we named "mask" into an actual mask layer and drag the "wick" layer into it until one parents the other. Lock all layers and make sure they're all visible except for "guide." Now if the timing ends up being wrong, all you need to fix it is add or remove frames in this timeline and the tweens will do the rest. *Image PB4.18*

Image PB4.18 After parenting and locking the mask, you should see the spark burn away the wick like this (left to right).

The "Animate" Difference: Paint Brush Tool

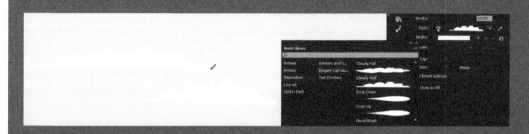

There's a new tool in Animate CC called the Paint Brush Tool (**Y**), bot to be confused with the Brush Tool (**B**). If you've used Adobe Flash in the past, the easiest way to think of the Paint Brush is that it is an enhanced Pencil Tool (**Shift+Y**). With the Paint Brush, you can draw with "Art Brushes" directly on the Stage. If you've used Adobe Illustrator you will be familiar with Art Brushes, which are essentially images that can be drawn in as lines (like the clouds shown in Image AD3). The big benefit of these Art Brushes is that they are treated as normal vector lines, which means that they are easily adjusted and tweened. Any vector line can also have an Art Brush applied to it after it's drawn, no matter which tool created it (such as the Pencil or Line tools). Art Brushes are found in the Brush Library by clicking its icon next to "Style" in the Fill and Stroke area of the Properties Panel. *Note: The hotkey Y in Adobe Flash brought up the Pencil Tool, but it brings up the Paint Brush Tool in Adobe Animate. Since this book was designed to work with any version of Adobe Flash/Animate, we will be using the Pencil Tool whose hotkey in Animate CC is Shift +Y. So if you're a Flash user, anytime you see Shift +Y simply press Y instead to bring up the Pencil Tool.*

Interlude

The windup is a bit more complicated of a cleanup process than previously seen in this book because of the way the pitcher character is designed. In Chapter 2's "Heavy Lifting," for example, all the features were relatively simple Graphic Symbols except for the design of the hands. Because of that, we were able to apply classic tweens to almost all the action. There were some shape tweens symblified in the body symbol but the only feature that needed a frame-by-frame, hand-drawn approach was the hands themselves. With this pitcher character, the body is drawn with the Brush Tool to let the shirt have creases, folds, and weighted (thick-to-thin) lines. This type of body design *can* be set up to be cleaned up with a series of shape tweens inside a symbol that would be classically tweened on stage, but the windup shot is just a hair under 1 second in length so it would be more time efficient to clean it up by hand, frame-by-frame, with the Brush Tool. There are a couple of changes of perspective for the rest of the features, such as the thigh, glove hand, and upper arm.

We will use the other methods we've gone over so far like swapping symbols, symblification, and shape tweens to make these transitions happen smoothly.

"Windup"

19. Looking at the rough animation, we need to determine in which order we're going to clean up each feature. Since the head doesn't change (it's an "easy") and looks like it's traveling in the most interesting arc, we'll let this guide the cleanup. To achieve its movement we'll use a motion guide. But first we need to find the correct arc. Use the arc double-check method described at the end of Chapter 5's bouncing ball section (that is, go frame by frame through the rough animation and put a dot at each head position on a newly created layer). *(Note: if you click on the "head" symbol in the library you'll see the registration point is at the base of the jaw, so you'll use that point to track the arc.) Image PB4.19*

Image PB4.19 (Note: Screengrab from Flash CS6 to show separate frames with different color as they are)

20. Create a new layer above the "head" layer in the cleanup folder, name it "guide," and insert a blank keyframe (**F7**) at the start of the windup sequence (frame 161). Use the Line Tool (**N**) to create a line and then manipulate it by using the Selection Tool (**V**) to pull at the curves and holding Cmd/**Ctrl** to drag out new vector points (as demonstrated in Chapter 8's closer look section, steps 8–12) to match the arc which became apparent through dots on the previous step.

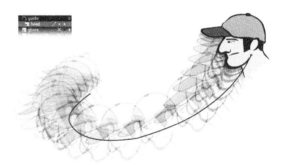

Image PB4.21

21. Turn the "guide" into an actual guide layer, parent it with the "head" layer below, and insert keyframes and apply tweens as necessary to achieve the proper timing and slow in and out as demonstrated in the rough animation. *Image PB4.21*

22. The next thing I like to work on is the feet (they are "easies"). You'll notice the right foot doesn't move, it stays planted. The left, however, is picked up after pushing off so the pitcher can balance on the right. Focus on matching the animation for the left foot demonstrated in the rough with classic tweens and whatever easing is necessary.

23. The next set of easy features are the right shin and thigh and the left shin. Match the animation as shown in the rough using classic tweens.

24. If you compare the first and last keys in the rough animation for the windup sequence you'll notice that the designs of the left thigh are different. Scrolling through the rough, though, you'll see that the transition between designs happens in just a couple of frames as the leg is lifted. We'll clean up this animation by swapping symbols but first we need a symbol for the end design. Insert a blank keyframe (**F7**) at the end of the sequence (frame 183) and using the Brush Tool (**B**), clean up the end left thigh design. *(Pro-tip: to get the thigh shape to be filled with the color of the pants, use the Line Tool (**N**) to close off the shape at the hip and knee areas, fill with the pants color using the Paint Bucket Tool (**K**) and then delete the lines.)*

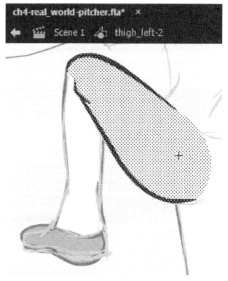

Image PB4.25

25. Turn the left thigh image you drew in the previous step into a Graphic Symbol named "thigh_left-2" (since the existing symbol was named "thigh_left") and then move the pivot point which is visible with the Free Transform Tool (Q) to the hip. *(Note: once created, you may enter the symbol, move the image so the registration point is at the hip, return to the main timeline and realign as I did. But because it's the end of the scene, this is the only time this symbol will be used. So for our purposes, as long as the pivot point is in the correct place it doesn't matter where the registration point is.) Image PB4.25*

26. The transition between thigh designs should happen in the moment where the feature is covering the greatest space, which in this case is when the left leg is being lifted (frames 175–177). Insert a keyframe (**F6**) at frame 175 and position the "thigh_left" instance to align with the rough.

27. Insert a blank keyframe (**F7**) at frame 177, copy/paste in place the "thigh_left-2" instance created in step 25 here, and position it to align with the rough.

28. Insert a blank keyframe (**F7**) at frame 176, hide every layer except "thigh left," turn on onion skin and adjust the span to only view one frame before and after and then draw an inbetween frame for the left thigh to transition between the two designs. *Image PB4.28*

29. Now that the "problem" area of the sequence for the left thigh is taken care of, clean up the spans before and after it with keyframes and tweens.

30. Clean up the left arm (not the glove, yet). Use shape tweens for the sleeve and classic tweens for the bicep and forearm. *(Note: depending on how you want to achieve the end pose, you could draw a different image for the end bicep design and apply the tween the same way as we did for the left thigh.)*

31. There are three different designs sketched in the rough animation for the glove hand. You can see them on frames 175, 177, and 181. Clean the last two designs up the same way you did

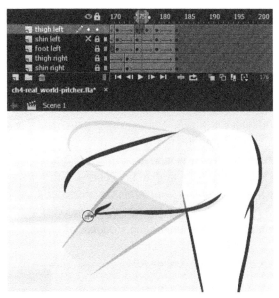

Image PB4.28

with the left thigh (naming the symbols you create glove-2 and 3 in the order they appear on the timeline). *Image PB4.31*

Image PB4.31

32. Inbetweening these designs with new hand-drawn images isn't entirely necessary because the glove is moving fast enough across the stage that an implied transition will fool the eye. So to save time, using the same method keyframe and onion skin setup as we did for the thigh, we will use the Free Transform Tool (Q) on the transition frames (176 and 180) to squash, stretch, and/or skew the symbol instance on those frames to get as close to an inbetween as possible. *(Note: you may want to keyframe and position the "glove-2" instance to the rough on frame 179 to complete the second of the two transition frames.) Image PB4.32*

33. Finish the cleanup of the glove hand using classic tweens. Use frame-by-frame dragging of the symbol into position where necessary if it comes off the arc shown in the rough animation (such as when it's being picked up from the knee to the head).

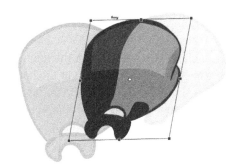

Image PB4.32

34. Now we've arrived at the body animation. This is best cleaned up using good, old-fashioned, traditional, frame-by-frame, hand-drawn animation using the Brush Tool (**B**). First, lock every layer except for "body," turn outline view on for everything except the "body" layer and the rough animation folder, and finally drag the entire rough animation folder below the cleanup folder. Now you can use onion skin mode and reference the rough animation as needed. But while I did the rough animation on twos (one drawing for every two frames) you will need the cleanup to be on ones (one drawing for every frame). *(Note: I cleaned this sequence up myself by working on the key (blue) and breakdown (red) frames from the rough and then mostly animating straight-ahead between them (using my own inbetweens from the rough, drawn in green, as a reference).) Image PB4.34*

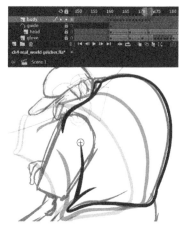

Image PB4.34

35. The last things left for cleanup are the features making up the right arm. The sleeve and arm are only in view for a short time so it will be easy to clean those up. Use shape tweens for the sleeve and classic tweens for the forearm.

36. The hand is currently on a layer above the body but needs to disappear behind the body. Insert a new layer below everything except the left sleeve and forearm and name it "hand-BACK." Clean up the hand animation as normal (keyframe and classic tween) and when the move from front to back needs to happen, copy/paste in place the "hand" instance from its existing layer to this new one (don't delete anything though, this is an overlapping moment). Frame 165 is the perfect place for a transition like that because it's not covering up or being covered by anything. *Image PB4.36*

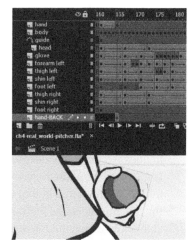

Image PB4.36

37. At the very next frame (167) on the layer we're transitioning *from* (the layer labeled "hand"), insert a blank keyframe (**F7**) so the hand disappears from the "hand" layer in front of the body and continues to be shown on the "hand-BACK" layer which is behind the body. The transition should be seamless. Continue with the cleanup of the hand symbol until complete. *Image PB4.37*

Image PB4.37

Explosions fall under a specialty in animation: effects (FX) animation. They're pretty hard to do even for experienced character animators. When creating animated scenes or entire shorts by yourself, there can only be so many specializations you endeavor to work through before hitting one that causes an artistic problem for you. We're going to treat this explosion as one of them and trick the shot by going with a Wile E. Coyote-style large explosion. The effect is like this, a flashy series of multicolored shapes to represent the actual explosion for about 1 second, and when it quickly dissipates it reveals the ashed-over remains of the character (comically, of course).

"Payoff"

38. At the explosion rough key (frame 218), insert a layer called "explosion" and create a blank keyframe (**F7**). Draw a jagged, star-like shape with the Pencil Tool (**Shift+Y**). Repeat this process over and over until there are many of these inside the one you drew as well as outside (containing it) and they obscure the entire screen. *Image PB4.38*

39. Use the Paint Bucket Tool (**K**) to fill in the shapes with various "explosion-like" colors.

40. Draw one line through all the shapes with the Pencil Tool (**Shift+Y**) so that all the lines are now connected, double-click a line with the Selection Tool (**V**) or Quick Selection (holding down Cmd/**Ctrl** from any other tool) which should select all the lines on the stage and **Delete**. Now all you are left with are the fill colors. *Image PB4.40*

41. Select the explosion frame you've created and turn it into a Graphic Symbol (**F8**) called "fx-explosion." And on its internal timeline, repeat the previous three steps to create three more images, one frame after the other. These frames should create a flashing loop of colored, star-like explosions.

42. Back on the main timeline, drag the playhead forward about 0.5 seconds, insert a keyframe (**F6**) on the explosion layer. With the instance of "fx-explosion" highlighted on stage, locate the Color Effect drop-down menu in the Properties panel and select **Alpha.** Set it to 0% so the instance looks to disappear on stage.

Image PB4.38

Image PB4.40

43. Insert a keyframe (**F6**) halfway between the existing two keyframes on the "explosion" layer and apply a classic tween between this new keyframe and the one created in the previous step. If you quick test the footage you'll see the explosion appear suddenly and then quickly fade away.

44. Finally, drag back to the beginning of the explosion (frame 218) and hide the explosion layer. We're going to be replacing our existing character with an "exploded" version. Insert a blank keyframe (**F7**) on every layer of the pitcher's cleanup at this frame and insert a layer above them all called "pitcher boom" (because why not?). Turn on onion skin and unlock the cleanup layers so you can see your character from the previous frame and draw a version of him like Wile E. Coyote after an Acme explosion. This image will be completely still for comedic effect, so only one drawing needs to be created. *Image PB4.44*

Image PB4.44

45. For added effects, you can create a looping animation showing smoke coming off of the character, nest it in a Graphic Symbol (like the chewing loop from Chapter 3's real-world exercise) and copy it to a couple of places on the body. You may also add a nod (from the pitcher to the catcher off-screen) during the wick burning sequence and/or a settling tween after the windup and before the explosion (to do that you'll have to make the last body image a symbol to tween it. I did this in the completed file which you can find on the companion website). *Image PB4.45*

Image PB4.45

The big anticipation moment came into play in the moments before the windup while the wick was slowly burning down. Without it, the scene just wouldn't work. You can try it. Remove all the frames from every layer during the moment where we see the wick burning down and you'll see just how flat, boring, and completely unnecessary the scene is as a whole. You could've done all that work of animating for nothing, just because the anticipation of the moment wasn't established and the animation wasn't pre-empted with a short bit to let the audience know to pay attention to what they were about to see. Sometimes it's difficult to

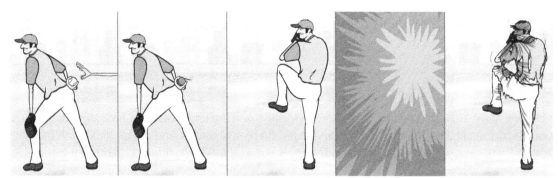

Image 4.6 Scene progression for this real-world exercise is shown left to right and displays setup, anticipation, and payoff.

maintain focus on your animation in terms of what is best for the scene, but it's always easy to think in terms of what's best for you and your time. And really, what's the purpose of animating something like this if it doesn't work for the scene? It's just wasted time, then.

In the case that you have spent all this time animating something like this scene and find out that the timing is wrong and it's affecting the feeling of anticipation, you can see how Animate CC can really help to salvage the work you've already done. Frame-by-frame work will always need to be redrawn, but in the case of the holding moment with the wick burning, the speed at which the sparks travel down the wick, the amount of animation in the spark loop itself, and the time we spend looking at that moment as a whole, Animate CC can help you adjust the timing to your liking since it can redraw its own tweens on the fly. Knowing this strength is really key in being able to use this program effectively in your work. Editing your work is just a fact of life—rarely does someone get it right the first time. If you can save time on the editing, it can make you more confident in the choice to take more time in the preparation and initial execution of the scene. This approach is the best way to think about the benefit to this workflow because there's nothing more valuable than taking care the first time around. It's the fear that you spend so long working on something and have to scrap it all and redo it because some tiny little thing was wrong that made traditional, hand-drawn, frame-by-frame animation so intimidating to many. If even half of this fear can be taken away, it makes the whole process less headache inducing. Notice I said *less*—you're doing animation after all.

FINAL WORDS
Anticipation

This principle is used for readability (looking off screen before showing what's there), intensifying interest in a following action (squashing the ball down before it bounds up in the air), and tension in horror (*Phantom*), comedy (*Mr. Bean*), action (*Indiana Jones*), and drama ("will-they, won't-they?"). You'll find that the more you think about the 12 Principles of Animation, the more you'll start to see their live-action equivalents in film and interpret them yourself from everyday life.

"A well-constructed scene is made up of a setup, payoff, and follow-through."

Let's say some kids are playing kickball. A ball rolls toward a boy. Boy kicks ball. What happened *right* before he kicked the ball? Did he just stand there straight up and down, and when the ball approached, his foot just shoots forward from this static, standing position? Is this boy a robot? Did Skynet become self-aware already? Obviously, he must have wound up his kicking power in some way first—either by leaning back to prepare for shifting his weight forward or by literally swinging his entire leg back before letting the kick loose like a golf swing. When blocking out the shot, you should know that the movement was anticipated by a pre-kick posture. The kick will slow in before contact and slow out after, and the foot will travel in a smooth, pendulous arc.

Arcs! That's the next chapter. Before we move on, though, remember that a well-constructed scene is made up of a setup, payoff, and follow-through. Anticipation is the setup. Most jokes won't be very funny if you say the punchline and nothing else. So remember to use Anticipation. Remember Harrison Ford's punches. They are glorious.

Image 5.0 While every feature on the character follows a different path they're all clearly representable with smooth arcs. Even the relative difference in the two characters' motions can be seen through their arcs. Zombie Cage Fighter by Stephen Brooks (RubberOnion.com), Creator and Executive Producer Nathan Quarry (www.ZombieCageFighter.com).

Chapter 5
ARCS

INTRODUCING
Arcs

The swing of an ax, a home-run hit, the sun across the sky ... these all travel in arcs. A businessman putting his briefcase on the table, a barista pouring coffee and the mechanic putting a tire on your car all also follow arcs. In animation terms, an Arc is a smooth path. It really seems quite obvious when you think about it—or rather, act it out. Do pretty much any singular motion (meaning something from "point A to point B") like bringing a burger up to your mouth. Going step by step through the motion and acting out what would be the frames, you'll see that there isn't one moment where on the way up to your mouth that delicious burger suddenly ends up way off path. Nor does your head veer off course as it's going to take a bite. Tracing the path works with practically any action. Think of how odd it would look picking something up to put it on a table only to suddenly jitter to the left for one-tenth of a second and come back to your previous trajectory. Living creatures mostly move in nice, smooth arcs. Arcs will make your animation flow.

Image 5.1

105

Readability is very important in animation. I briefly mentioned it at the end of the last chapter. We'll go over it much more in the next chapter ("Staging"), but let me expand on it a little bit here. It's exactly what it sounds like: the ability of the viewer to clearly follow what is happening. Implementing readability can be accomplished in many ways (strong silhouettes, clear layout, clever timing), but chief among them is movement through smooth arcs. In the chapter on Anticipation we talked about the setup leading to a payoff to fulfill an expectation; the same idea applies during the movement itself. There's a kind of superpower that pretty much everyone has, and that's the ability to predict motion's trajectory. This ability is what allows you to play catch. In the air, a ball is constantly moving and changing its size relative to your field of view because it's getting closer—but you can catch it. Or maybe *you* can't, I don't know you, but "people" can. Having basic life experience of periodically seeing things thrown in the air (to you, near you, or at you), your mind can now accurately see the current path an object in a free-fall is taking and predict the final position. In animation, we replicate these trajectories, paths, and routes with arcs.

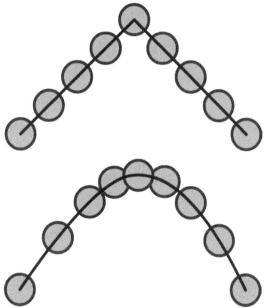

For our bouncing ball exercise, arcs relate in the most obvious way. Instead of making the ball bounce up and down, we're going to have it bounce across the stage. If you close your eyes and picture it, you already you know what it'll look like. But if you want another way to illuminate the importance of arcs, imagine what it would look like if the ball follows a straight line from the contact position to the up position and back down again while it's moving left to right. These lines would make a triangle shape and would look very stiff, wouldn't they? The paths on the way up and down need to be connected into one smooth arc.

Image 5.2 A ball bouncing across a room will have smooth arcs (below), not straight lines (above).

"In animation terms, an arc is a smooth path."

BOUNCING BALL Arcs

Setting Up

This time we're basically going to be skipping the last chapter and working off our FLA (Animate CC project file) from Chapter 3 on Squash and Stretch. So before we do anything, open "bouncing ball

3 – squash stretch" and **Save As** to rename it "bouncing ball 5 – arcs." It's important to familiarize yourself with what was done at this time in the exercises to know what is going to come next. In Chapter 3, we had already picked out our timing, applied slow in/out and some squash and stretch. Our work so far has resulted in a nice 25-frame loop.

The goal of this chapter's exercise is to take that bouncing loop and make it move across the stage in a convincing way. But this time we're going to work a little differently. We're essentially working backward on the principle, meaning that we will do the animation and then use our understanding of arcs to verify the quality of the path. In truth, this type of verification happens in traditional animation all the time. Strangely, the principle of Arcs often plays more of a checks and balances roll. We can do our best to plot out a smooth arc most of the time, but frequently its value is truly seen after we've done our best and need an impartial judge.

Since we're building on what came before, we will be nesting our animation inside another symbol to keep it separate. Nesting is a method by which we take animation and put it inside a symbol which can then be moved around the stage as one unit. This technique is valuable for so many reasons, the bulk of which we will see in later chapters. But even by the end of this exercise, your concept of what is possible within Animate CC will expand with this introduction of nested animation.

Like so many of these principles, there are a few methods of applying arcs to movement within Animate CC, and they each have their strong suits. There will be another exercise in this chapter exploring a tool seemingly designed specifically for this principle (I'm sure there are a lot of you who already know what this tool will be: motion guides). That tool has its place, but not in what we want to do within this first goal of bouncing the ball across the stage, and we will see why after this exercise is done.

> "Nesting is a method by which we take animation and put it inside a symbol which can then be moved around the stage as one unit."

PART I
"Nesting The Animation"

1. Highlight all 25 frames of animation on the main stage. (*Pro-tip: clicking on the layer name, in this case "Layer 1," to the left of the timeline will select all frames on that layer.*) *Image BB5.1*

Image BB5.1

2. Right-click the highlighted section and select **Copy Frames**. *Image BB5.2*

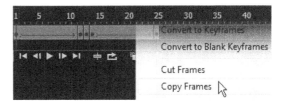

Image BB5.2

3. In the Library panel (Cmd/**Ctrl+L**) click the icon at the lower left that looks like a piece

of paper with one corner folded up to create a **New Symbol** (alternatively, the hotkey is Cmd/**Ctrl+F8**. Intuitive, right?). We want this new symbol to be a Graphic Symbol that will hold our bouncing ball animation. Since you already have a symbol named "ball," let's call this one "ball-bouncing" (object-action). *Image BB5.3*

4. As we know from Chapter 1, you are now inside the symbol. Right-click the first empty frame here and select **Paste Frames**.

5. If you can't see anything, select "Show All" from the Zoom drop-down menu. Now you see that the bouncing ball from the main timeline has been copied into this symbol. *Image BB5.5*

6. Above the stage, you see two clickable icons saying "Scene 1" and "ball-bouncing." Since we're inside the symbol, click "Scene 1" to go back to the main timeline. *Image BB5.6*

7. We've now *created* the new bouncing ball Graphic Symbol with the nested animation, but still need to place an instance of it on stage. At the bottom left of the timeline, under the layer names there is another icon which looks like the one in step 3. Click this icon to create a **New Layer** (you can also create a new layer by right-clicking on a layer name and selecting **Insert Layer** from the drop-down). *Image BB5.7*

8. Make sure frame 1 of this new layer ("Layer 2") is highlighted, then drag and drop "ball-bouncing" from the library onto the stage. *Image BB5.8*

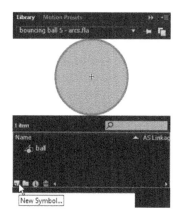

Image BB5.3

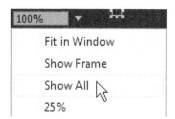

Image BB5.5

Image BB5.6

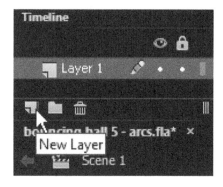

Image BB5.7

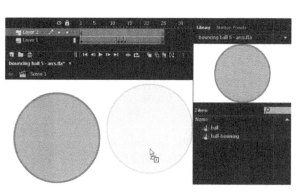

Image BB5.8

9. Drag the instance of the "ball-bouncing" symbol to the same position as the "ball" instance. If you ever lose track of which instance is which, you can see its symbol's name in the Properties panel next to "Instance of." *(Pro-tip: in the toolbar, make sure the magnet at the bottom is selected. This modifier is the "Snap to Objects" feature, and it'll make one object lock onto another object's position). Image BB5.9a and BB5.9b*

Image BB5.9a

Image BB5.9b

10. Right-click on "Layer 1" and select **Delete Layers**. We don't need this layer anymore. As you can see, the animation that was on the main timeline has been replanted into this new symbol. *Image BB5.10*

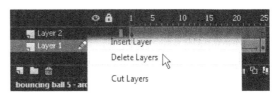

Image BB5.10

11. Now let's make the ball move. I think three bounces will be enough, so extend the timeline to frame 75. *Image BB5.11*

Image BB5.11

12. We want the ball to bounce in from the left and then leave to the right. Hold **Shift** while you click and drag the symbol to the left until the ball is off the stage (white area) and onto the work area (gray). Holding Shift while dragging constrains your movement along a straight path so that it doesn't get out of line. *Image BB5.12*

13. To make our end position, turn frame 75 into a keyframe (**F6**) and repeat as in step 12 to the right until the ball is off stage. *Image BB5.13a and BB5.13b*

Image BB5.13a

14. Create a tween between these two keys.

Interlude

It looks pretty good. But if you look closer, there are a couple of missing details. The obvious issue is that there is no decreasing max height; the ball just keeps bouncing *ad infinitum*. That's fine if the ball is alive and pushing off the ground, but in this case a ball is just a ball. Another aspect

Image BB5.12

Image BB5.13b

that feels off is the stretch. The ball is still stretching directly downward when it's actually falling at an angle (it's moving left to right). Because of this misaligned stretch, the ball doesn't feel like it's bouncing as much as doing a sort of a float/glide combo ... and it's weird. These sorts of observations and applications take a sequence from being something like motion graphics to full-blown animation.

PART II
"Continuing The Bounce"

15. Make sure the timeline's playhead is on one of the keyframes and double-click the ball (you can also double-click the symbol in the library, but we'll want to be able to see the stage for reference on where the ground is).

16. Now that we're inside the "ball-bouncing" symbol, let's make the bounce repeat three times. Highlight the animation, **Copy Frames**, and **Paste Frames** on the last keyframe twice to replace that "end" key with your copied sequence's "start" key. The symbol's timeline now ends on 73. *Image BB5.16*

17. First, we'll deal with the decreasing max height just like in the last chapter. The ball has four "up" position keyframes separated evenly on the timeline at frames 1, 25, 49, and 73. Decreasing max height should decelerate a little over time. This means that the difference between the max height of the first and second bounces will be greater than the difference between the second and third, and so on. So for instance, with a zoom level of 50 percent, if you **Shift+down-arrow** the ball on frame 25 five times, you should do it only four *more* than that for frame 49 and an additional three on frame 73. In effect, the "up" keys are slowing out as they decrease their height. *Image BB5.17*

Image BB5.16

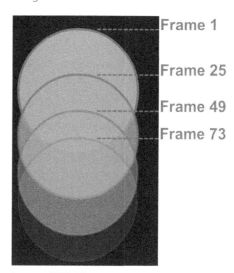

Frame 1

Frame 25

Frame 49

Frame 73

18. Since the ball isn't bouncing as high in each sequential bounce, remove frames to readjust the timing proportionally just like in the last chapter. From contact to contact position is one sequence. Remove one frame from each tween in a sequence, and one additional from the next. And don't forget to remove (three) frames from the last tween (because it's the first half of a sequence). *Image BB5.18*

Image BB5.17

Insert Frame
Remove Frames

Image BB5.18

19. Let's take this opportunity to readjust the timing for the symbol on the main stage. Look at where our nested animation timeline ends (hint: it's frame 64) and then click "Scene 1" to return to the main timeline.

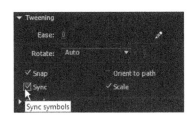

Image BB5.20

20. Since the main timeline ends at 75 and we want it back on 64, animation math says we need to remove 11 frames. Highlight any 11 frames (no keys) in the tween and **Remove Frames**. The timeline should now end on frame 64, the same as inside our Graphic Symbol. *Image BB5.20*

21. Click the tween and in the Tweening area of the Properties panel, make sure the box for "Sync" is selected. *Image BB5.21*

Image BB5.21

Interlude

"Uh, what was that?" I can actually hear this through time and space as I write these words. There is a lot going on right now and I don't think it's wise to dive too far into the workings of these two timelines and what "sync" does. We'll definitely go over this option in more detail later in the book. The quick answer is that you have the option in Animate CC to select which frame you would like the Graphic Symbol to display. You can even set it to play its nested timeline once or loop. The control over which frame within a Graphic Symbol plays on the main timeline (and how) is an extremely valuable feature. However, because the Graphic Symbol's timeline *isn't* locked to the main timeline, when we move around the keyframe of a Graphic Symbol instance that's already playing like we did above, it can move some of the timing out of sync. Clicking the Sync box synchronizes the Graphic Symbol instances along a span to play uninterrupted. By doing that in step 20, frame 64 on the main timeline now shows frame 64 in the symbol. Don't worry if you don't completely understand it yet because almost the entirety of Chapter 9 on Secondary Action will be on nested symbols and how to use them. Now that we've adjusted our decreasing max height and the timing in the symbol's tweens as well as back on the main timeline, it's time to fix the keys with stretch on them.

PART III
"Skewing The Stretch"

22. Re-enter the "ball-bouncing" symbol by double-clicking its instance on the main stage. This is known as "Edit in Place" mode. It allows us to see the stage while we edit, which will help on step 27.

23. Frame 12 is our first "contact stretch" key. Click on it and use the Free Transform Tool (**Q**) to slightly skew the ball so that the bottom is just right of the top. You can get the skew function

by hovering over the sides until the cursor turns into an icon that looks like an equals sign with arrows on it. In our case, you'll skew from the top or bottom of the symbol (with the registration point still in the center of the ball). The easiest way to adjust these is simple trial and error as there's not a lot of precision needed here. *Image BB5.23*

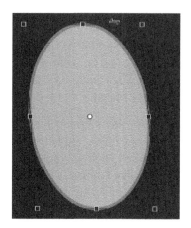

Image BB5.23

24. Do the same as step 21 for the "rebound stretch" on frame 14. Except this time you'll be skewing it so that the bottom is left of the top. You don't need much for these. If you look at the Transform window (Cmd/**Ctrl+T**), the horizontal skew should be labeled somewhere between 4 and 5 (minus goes the other way as in step 22). *Image BB5.24*

25. Repeat for all the stretch keys (34, 36, 54, and 56).

26. Finally, we'll adjust the amount of squash and stretch on the ball to match the decreasing max height just as we did in Part III of the previous chapter's bouncing ball exercise. For each of the last two groupings of squash and stretch (34–36, 54–56), decrease the amount of each through the Transform window by adjusting the percentage (85/115 and 90/110, respectively, would work well here).

27. For the contact stretch, reposition the ball back down to touching the "ground." *(Note: you cannot use the Align panel here because there is no stage inside the symbol, you may use the arrow keys to manually adjust the height and the onion skin tool to compare the bottom line with a previous contact key.) Image BB5.27*

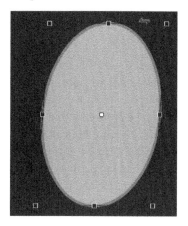

Image BB5.24

28. For the rebound stretch frames, adjust their heights to decrease with each bounce since they're effectively losing energy to the bounce itself. Using **Shift+down-arrow** once for the second rebound stretch and twice for the third would do nicely.

That was a lot more steps than we're used to. If you feel unsure, you can compare what you've done with the progress files I've provided on the companion website. So, let's review what we just did. There were a number of new concepts and features in this chapter (nested timelines, layers, sync, skew) as well as the fact that we used almost everything we have covered in the previous four chapters. It may seem like overkill for a simple bouncing ball to go from one side of the screen to the other. That's not really so though, because you could've called it done after Part I of the exercise. It looked pretty good. But this book isn't about just making

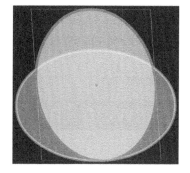

Image BB5.27

something move; it's about bringing the 12 Principles of Animation into the world of digital animation with Animate CC, Tradigital animation aims for something better than just "pretty good."

If you have never animated on paper, you should now have a healthy appreciation for what it took to make great classical animation. All of these tools and steps are really just an external representation of what goes on inside the head of a traditional animator. Timing, Slow In/Out, Squash and Stretch, and Arcs are all things that need to be running through their head while drawing and plotting out every frame. Since each position had to be drawn individually, if you were a fully traditional animator you would have had to know exactly what you wanted to accomplish with each individual frame (and how it would impact the next). In Animate CC, with its toolset designed for delegation, you can build your scene up from the bottom. We do the same work, except instead of doing it all in our heads and all at once, we can sometimes apply the principles one at a time. It's like long division vs. using a calculator. The calculator is a tool to make your life easier. But if you input the wrong numbers, you're going to get a bad result either way.

It's important to note that you have still only drawn a single circle in this main exercise. With that one image, we have created a couple of animated shots while simultaneously learning the program. Think of working in Animate CC, like sculpting from stone. You chip away at the stone until the general form is achieved. Then you remove more and more stone to reveal increasing levels of detail until ultimately you have your finished sculpture. You start with the biggest tool and knock away the biggest chunks of stone and by the end you're using some sandpaper to just polish off little specks to make it more refined. When animating in Animate CC with a Tradigital workflow, you also start with a basic form of movement with the most general tools. Then with each succeeding step you change the basic movement into a more refined one by removing the moveless and stiff parts of the overall sequence. Each time you enter a symbol and edit a nested animation, it's like you're chipping away at a block of lifeless stone to reveal how lifelike it can really be.

If I were to ask you to make this ball bounce exactly as in this chapter from a blank Animate CC file, could you do it? Do you feel confident that you can make a symbol of a circle, block out the shot on the timeline using your knowledge of timing, apply some slow in/out and squash/stretch, give it a decreasing max height and bounce interval for realism, copy/paste that whole animation into a symbol, and tween it

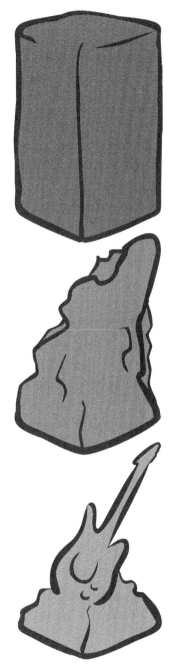

Image 5.3 Creating and refining a sculpture is a lot like the cleanup process in Tradigital animation.

across the stage with constant velocity? If you had read that exact sentence four chapters ago, would you have thrown a conniption? I bet the answer is "yes" to both of those. But now you are ready to see the deeper realms of what Animate CC has to offer.

"All of these tools and steps are really just an external representation of what goes on inside the head of a traditional animator."

Checking Your Arcs

There's one more thing that's important to do: double-check our work. I can tell you that there won't be any arc problems because of the way they were made. But this double-check method will come up in later chapters, so it's important to see how it works now. It's quite simple:

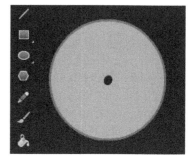

Image AC5.2

1. On the main timeline, create a **New Layer**. You might also want to lock all the other layers now to prevent mistakenly drawing on them instead of the one just created.

2. Starting at frame 1, use the Brush Tool (**B**) to draw a dot on this new layer in the center of the symbol whose arc you're testing. *Image AC5.2*

3. The < and > keys (also where the "," and "." are located respectively) functions to step one frame backward or forward. Step forward one frame and repeat your action in step 2. *Image AC5.3*

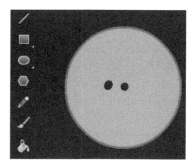

Image AC5.3

4. Repeat steps 2 and 3 until you reach the end of the movement which you're testing. *Image AC5.4*

5. Draw a smooth curvy line through all the dots. If any dots are out of that line, there's the problem frame. *Image AC5.5*

6. Adjust the problem frames to fit the curve.

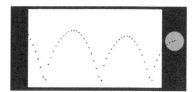

Image AC5.4

This process will come in handy when you're doing character animation ... *very* handy! For the type of motion in this bouncing ball you can also see the arcs fairly clearly by turning on onion skin mode and dragging the markers so that they cover the area of the arcs you want to see. Both of these methods of double-checking your arcs will be increasingly valuable to you the more animation you do.

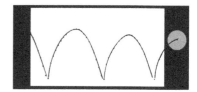

Image AC5.5

We're breaking all the conventions in this chapter because we're going to be creating two brand new FLAs to look at two new areas of our program: motion guides and the pivot point. First up, we'll be tackling motion guides by making a Sun move across the sky. Set up by creating a new file (same resolution as before, 1920 x 1080) and naming it "ch5 – closer look – sun".

"Motion Guiding The Sun"

1. On the stage, draw a sun. Many of you might already know how to illustrate in Animate CC, but if not, a simple way to make a sun is to pick two shades of yellow to represent the outline and the fill and use the Oval Tool (**O**) as you did in Chapter 1 (I've used a 50% alpha setting for the outline to get a corona effect). You may also draw a sun using the Brush Tool (**B**). *Image CL5.1*

2. Highlight this new image and make it into a Graphic Symbol. *(Pro-tip: holding down* Cmd*/***Ctrl*** will turn the cursor into the Selection Tool arrow for as long as it is depressed.)* Name this symbol "sun" and make sure that the registration point is in the center. The default in Animate CC is top left. *Image CL5.2*

3. Create a keyframe (**F6**) somewhere ahead on the timeline. Use your knowledge of timing to decide how long you want this shot of a sun moving across the sky to take. I'm using around 8 seconds, so my next key is at frame 200.

4. Create a new layer.

5. Use the Line Tool (**N**) to make a line spanning horizontally beyond the width of the stage about one-third of the way up from the bottom. *(Note: you might want to change the color of your line to black with 100% alpha setting so you can see it better.) Image CL5.5*

6. With the Selection Tool (try using the pro-tip on step 2 for this—holding down Cmd/**Ctrl** while the

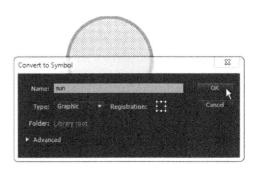

Image CL5.1

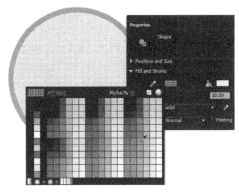

Image CL5.2

Image CL5.5

Line Tool is still selected from step 5), click and drag the center of the line up to about one-third from the top so that it looks like a hill. This curve is our motion guide, the path the sun will follow. *Image CL5.6*

7. Create a tween between the two keys on Layer 1.

8. For the next steps we need to make sure of two conditions: first that the "Snap to Objects" is on (as we did in this chapter's bouncing ball exercise, step 9) and second that the sun's pivot point is lined up with its registration point. To check the pivot point, click the instance of the sun symbol and select the Free Transform Tool (Q). There's a white dot that shows up in the middle of the Transform box around the symbol—that's the "pivot point." It's what the motion guide will snap to. Make sure that it is sitting on the registration point, which is the + symbol. *(Note: in some versions of Animate CC, the pivot point covers up the registration point when aligned, so if you can't see the registration point it's possible that the pivot point is already sitting on it, as is showing in the image accompanying this step). Image CL5.7*

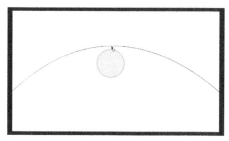

Image CL5.6

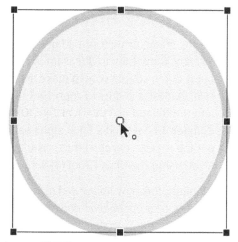

Image CL5.7

9. We have a path and we have set up two keys with a tween. Now we just need to tell the computer to use these together. Right-click on Layer 2 to the left of the timeline with the motion guide and select **Guide**. You'll see the icon next to the layer title turn into a straight-edge ruler.

10. To attach Layer 1 (sun) to Layer 2 (guide), click and drag Layer 1 into the guide layer above. In most versions of Animate CC, you will see Layer 2's icon change into a dotted line arc and Layer 1 is indented under it. These changes indicate that the previously unassigned guide Layer 2 now is set as a guide for Layer 1 to follow. *Image CL5.10*

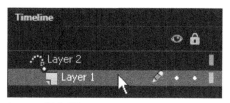

Image CL5.10

11. On the first key, drag the sun symbol to the left until it's at the beginning of the guide-line—it will snap into place. Do the same for the second key to the right (for this key, make sure the pivot point is snapped to the end of the line). *Image CL5.11*

Image CL5.11

Guiding motion is what guide-lines on guide-layers do. They're guides. These are incredibly useful, albeit admittedly in a small selection of cases. Just like the bouncing ball exercise, nested animation can be used with motion guides as well. In the FLA provided, you'll see that I have animated a loop of rays coming out from the sun which plays as it's traversing the sky. Comets, satellites, and other space travelers are obviously benefited by guides, but so are creatures like fish, flies, and other small flying insects and effects such as snowflakes drifting down from the sky wherein the path can be a wavy or squiggly line. A line doesn't need to be a single curve in Flash to work as a guide, it just needs to be unbroken. Also something like a skateboard rolling its way down a ramp all by its lonesome and up a little the other side can follow a guide. Why, then, did we not use it for our bouncing ball?

We didn't use a motion guide for the bouncing ball because of the constant horizontal velocity. Remember that the ball is moving at a steady rate in one direction, nothing's really stopping that. The only part of that movement with slow in and out is the up-and-down motion of the bounce; that's because gravity is always trying to stop the ball from getting away from the Earth. If you were to take an instance of the ball right now, draw a couple of arcs the way we did in the closer look "Motion Guiding the Sun" section's step 6 (which will get you the correct arc the ball should follow, incidentally) and then tween it with a motion guide, you'd see that there's no amount of easing that will make it look right. If the easing is set at 0, the bounce will look

Image 5.4 Motion guides come in very handy for objects like snowflakes.

like it did in Chapter 1 with no accounting for acceleration due to gravity. If the easing is set with a slow out on the way up and a slow in on the way down as we did in Chapter 2, it will change the speed our ball is traveling across the stage. This would make it look like a car that revs forward every second or two, going fast then slow then fast then slow.

You'll notice that our sun's movement looks a lot like a pendulum, just upside down. We can absolutely use a motion guide to create a pendulum (like a grandfather clock or a wrecking ball). But as physics tells us, the path would be part of a perfect circle because the radius is constant. In this case, it would be better to simply animate the symbol pivoting around a point at the origin. Introducing ... the pivot point. First, open a new file and name it "ch5 – closer look – pendulum."

> "A line doesn't need to be a single curve in Animate CC to work as a guide, it just needs to be unbroken."

"Pendulum By Pivot Point"

12. Draw something to be the end of our pendulum. I'm going with a wrecking ball. To create the wrecking ball, I selected the Oval Tool (**O**) and then used the "Fill and Stroke" area of the

Properties panel to select a stroke size of 15 and a gray outline with the alpha set to 75%. Then I went to the Color panel (**Alt+Shift+F9**), clicked the paint bucket there and selected **Radial gradient** from the drop-down menu. Then it was just a matter of swapping the black and white pointers' positions, changing the white to a light gray, and then drawing the circle on the stage. Sound like a lot? If you followed along great, if not ... I bet you can't *wait* until Chapter 10! We'll go over all this stroke and fill stuff there. For now, a simple circle will work just fine. *Image CL5.12a and CL5.12b*

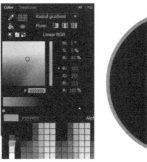

Image CL5.12a   *Image CL5.12b*

13. Change the line alpha back to 100% and, using the Line Tool (**N**), draw a line straight up from the center of our object. This will be what our object is swinging from (in my case, the cable holding the wrecking ball). If you want the line to stop at the outline of the object but you drew it into the center, click on the part you want removed to highlight it and just press **Delete** or **Backspace** on the keyboard. Simple. *Image CL5.13*

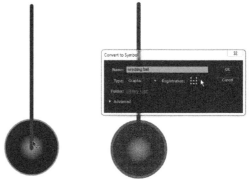

Image CL5.13   *Image CL5.14*

14. Highlight the whole graphic and turn it into a symbol. This time, put the registration point on the top-center so that we can easily snap our pivot point to it later. I named mine "wrecking ball." *Image CL5.14*

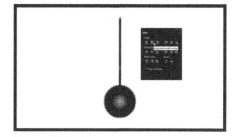

15. Use the Align panel (**Cmd/Ctrl+K**) to center the ball on the stage. Remember that the "Align to stage" box must be checked, and then click the "Align horizontal center" icon. *Image CL5.15*

Image CL5.15

16. If needed, move the symbol straight down so that it's close to the bottom of the stage (simply to see it swing). You may also use the "Align vertical center" button.

17. Use the Free Transform Tool (**Q**) to drag the pivot point (white circle) up to the Registration point (+) which should be at the top of the line we drew in step 2. Animate CC will tween any rotation around this point. *Image CL5.17*

Image CL5.17

18. Still using the Free Transform Tool, hover the cursor just outside one of the corners (bottom ones will be easiest here) until you see the pointer turn into a rotation arrow. Rotate the pendulum to the left about 45 degrees. *(Pro-tip: holding **Shift** while rotating will lock the positions to 45-degree intervals.)* This position will be the starting point. *Image CL5.18*

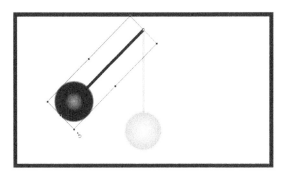

Image CL5.18

19. Using what you know about timing, create a keyframe ahead on the timeline. Since I'm using a wrecking ball, I went with 2 seconds (animation math means that's on frame 49). Knowing

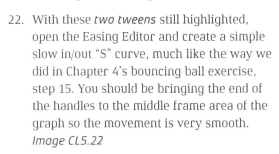

Image CL5.19

that we want the ball to come back to the starting position, let's create another keyframe further down the timeline by the same amount of time while we're at it (for my wrecking ball that would be frame 97). *Image CL5.19*

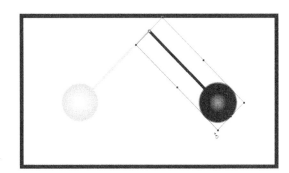

20. On the middle keyframe, adjust the rotation using the Free Transform Tool the way you did on step 7; this time rotate it 45 degrees to the right. *Image CL5.20*

Image CL5.20

21. Click and drag to highlight both the areas between all three keyframes, then right-click and create a classic tween. This should create two tweens spanning between the three keyframes. *Image CL5.21*

Image CL5.21

22. With these *two tweens* still highlighted, open the Easing Editor and create a simple slow in/out "S" curve, much like the way we did in Chapter 4's bouncing ball exercise, step 15. You should be bringing the end of the handles to the middle frame area of the graph so the movement is very smooth. *Image CL5.22*

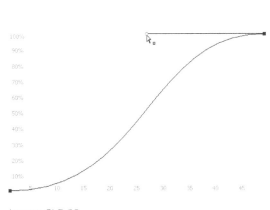

Image CL5.22

We've just created a pendulum by way of tweening around the pivot point. We don't need to get into the physics of it all here but for simple pendulum swings the period (time it takes to complete one full swing) doesn't change based on the starting height (meaning the height of the initial drop to start the swing), but the period will decrease (complete its swing faster) the closer it is to the pivot point. So something like a necklace pendant or a pocket-watch will swing faster than a tether ball, but only because the strings they're swinging from aren't the same length. If you wanted the pendulum to be a water balloon on a string you could even use nested animation to apply some stretch as it approaches the bottom of its swing and comes back to normal at the end (just as long as you put the string and the balloon on different layers). As it stretches it will do funny things to the timing of the swing, but I think that's best learned by doing. Just don't fill the balloon up too much because it'll rip open (something you'd also learn by doing).

You should now be seeing Animate's ultimate strong suits: tweening and nested animation. With these two features, a universe of possibilities opens up in front of you. The more intimately you get to know Animate CC, the more you'll make combinations of your own. In this chapter, you've seen three different ways to animate on a clean arc: layering nested animation, motion guides, and tweening around a pivot point.

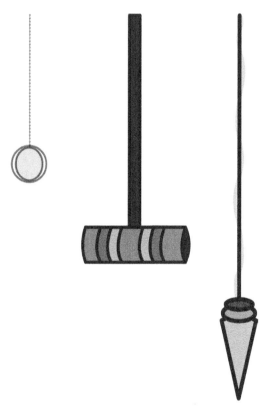

Image 5.5 The closer the weight of the pendulum is to the pivot point, the faster it will swing (from left to right: fastest to slowest swing).

In each of these examples, the arcs are so smooth and clearly readable because you input the information Animate CC needs to do the inbetweening work for you. Communicating the details of an arc was sometimes a hard thing to get across to an animation assistant because while it's fairly easy to draw a simple halfway point between two keys it's not always as easy to draw one on an arc unless it's explicitly pointed out. Animate CC has many ways to help avoid this problem area. For instance, this chapter's bouncing ball exercise was all about delegating the workload. We wanted it to bounce up and down at one rate of easing but also across the stage at another. So we put the up/down motion into a symbol and moved the instance of that symbol around as we wanted. This combination gave us our picture perfect arcs. In the closer look section, we saw the obvious benefit of the motion guide as an easy way to dictate an exact path. It can be simple like the slight curve we gave to our sun's path in the example or more irregular like a curvy line for the path of a snowflake (see ch5-examples-snowflake.fla on the companion website). But motion guides would fail to be of use in our bouncing ball example because symbol instances can only travel along that path using one tween at a time (which means only one easing value at a time). Also in the closer look section, the pivot point gave us yet another method of achieving a smooth arc but only along a perfect circle (since the very definition of a pivot point is the center point of a circular, rotational path), like our pendulous wrecking ball.

As we look deeper into the principle, keep in mind that even though there are all these tools and excellent ways of creating and/or verifying arcs in Animate CC, there are *loads* of people out there who either don't know about them, don't take advantage of them, or both. I'm going to say it again, the whole point of this book is about bringing the 12 Principles together with the program to *improve* your animation. Animate CC won't do everything for you, but it can help you to not have to do everything the long way. Use its toolset well, and you'll have wonderful arcs; and in the event that you check your work and something's off, Animate CC will make it easy to adjust it back on track without having to redo a metric ton of work.

USING ARCS By "Plotting And Checking"

You've read these terms in this book already, but I would like to clarify the exact differences here. A "span" is an animation from one extreme keyframe (which denotes a change of direction) to the next. For sake of simplicity, it's a single tween. A "sequence" is a series

Image 5.6 A "span" is one tween (above). A "sequence" is a series of tweens (below).

of spans that makes up one cohesive movement for either single use or a loop (such as a walk cycle). Spans usually need a smooth arc, while a sequence can have harsh end points as those spans' arcs are chained together. An example might look something like the way a child draws ocean water, looking like many "U"s connected together. In that example, each "U" would be a span and an entire connected line of them would be the sequence (*Image 5.7*). So here's the idea with arcs; if you have an object's span fully animated and play connect-the-dots with the position of that object on every frame (the arc double-check method mentioned in this chapter), would that line be a nice flowy curve? If not, one or more of those frames are out of position. In that case, the movement will look jittery.

Image 5.7

If you have the opportunity, I encourage you to use the arc double-check method to plot out some span of movement from any Disney animated movie. You could probably very easily do this by taping a piece of paper to your monitor and going step by step through a sequence, making dots on the position of Goofy's hand, for instance, as he winds up for a pitch (bonus points if you can name the animated short I'm thinking of here without looking it up). You will see wonderful flowing curves … unless a character is shivering, or something, and then it'll be purposefully very jagged. Not everything needs to be smooth all the time; it all comes down to the purpose of the animation.

A large part of animation is control. Plotting out your intended arcs ahead of time can help, but usually it's most beneficial to sketch a small thumbnail image of what you feel the arc should look like after you're finished. Then use the double-check method. It's a little like in science, having a hypothesis, using that to predict a result, testing, and then verifying. In this analogy, the hypothesis is the animation you envision, the prediction is the thumbnail of the arc, testing is animating, and the verification is your double-check method. This workflow helps keep things loose but also on a course to completion.

Image 5.8 Arcs show simple and compound movements. Example taken from Three's Horrible: Part I by Stephen Brooks (RubberOnion.com).

These principles are here to help you achieve a sense that this art exists in a semi-realistic and believable world and that your characters are alive and organic. Complete believability may not always be what you want. Everyone knows that Wile E. Coyote couldn't defy gravity or take punishment the way he does in every Road Runner short in real life. Chuck Jones wasn't going for that type of realism. But when the character moves, each limb has wonderful arcs in it. This natural motion intuitively tells the audience that Wile is alive, and incidentally those same arcs make all his crazy movements clearly readable. If you want to make something seem mechanical, removing arcs from just about any motion or keeping them very basic such as a simple pivot can help with that. Looking at the transformation scenes in any *Transformers* (1984) episode is evidence of that. But not all robots need to seem that way. The Iron Giant, Rodney Copperbottom from *Robots,* and even Wall-E have a great amount of fluidity and organic complexity to their arcs of movement. Using those types of arcs was a clear decision to make them seem more human, organic, and relatable. Arcs have that kind of power. Plotting mentally or physically how you want them to be (i.e. smooth, jagged, squiggly, wave-like) and checking to make sure they were applied correctly are the two not-so-secret secrets to using arcs.

REAL-WORLD EXAMPLE
"Swing Set"

Principles Used

Slow In/Out: A swing is a pendulum, and as such, it speeds up on the way down and slows down on the way up. Every other motion that helps in the swing will have slow in and out.

Secondary Action: The actual swinging is the primary action; the secondary action is the pumping to keep the swing going. Leaning back/forward and throwing the feet back/forward are complements to the main action of the swing's pendulum.

Overlapping Action: The secondary action actually is also overlapping action. Every motion happens in succession—a chain reaction. At the top of the swing, the legs start to kick out, and then the body leans back as the swing starts moving downward and so on. The pigtails will also be exhibiting overlapping action. Follow through will be applied to the momentary hold at the top of the arcs.

Arcs: There should be little doubt that the main principle at play in animating a pendulous swing is Arcs. The feet that pump travel in arcs, the head as it leans back will travel in an arc, and all of this action will travel together in one big arc as the whole body swings back and forth on the swing set.

Setting Up

When you open the file "ch5-real_world-swingset. fla" provided on the companion website you'll notice one thing right off the bat; there is no rough animation at all this time. The only things that are provided are a character design on the left, the swing in the middle, and a thumbnail (small) storyboard

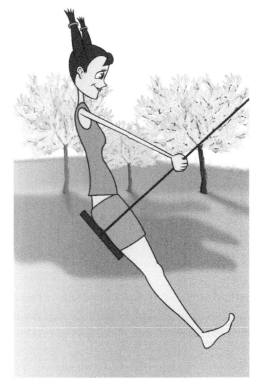

Image 5.9

drawing on the top right. It is up to you to take this information and turn it into an animated looping shot. The storyboard is there to give you the feeling of what we're envisioning. The designs have already been done, and you are the animator who is going to run it through the finish line.

There are a couple of things that are going on when this girl is swinging on the swing set. Her entire character and the seat she's sitting on are going to be moving back and forth in a pendulous arc. During the swinging, she's also going to be pumping her legs and leaning back or forward to get more energy into her swing. All of these various actions happening in concert means that some planning needs to be done. As always, it's best to start with doing rough animation of the entire shot. When the rough animation is done, you'll be putting the character into her own symbol and replicating the same animation inside of that as it's moving. When you nest the animation in a symbol you can look at *just* the symbol (when it's not moving around on stage), see how the animation looks by itself, and fix any arc issues that may have arisen from trying to keep track of all the different types of movement at play. Then you move back to checking your work with the symbol moving and edit as necessary. This built-in double-checking makes the cleanup process easier since you have essentially treated it as a whole, then individually, and then as a whole again. It's like looking left-right-left when you cross the street (or right-left-right if you drive on the left side of the road).

There will be four parts to this example: roughing the whole, character animation tiedown, symblified tiedown, and symblified cleanup. By introducing another facet to the rough animation in "tiedown"

Images 5.10a and b The arcs in the symblified "swing" container are simple and direct (left), but when this once stationary character swings on stage the arcs will blossom into more elaborate and organic paths (right).

and symblifying it, we will be able to address an issue which will arise—namely that since the character's pose changes are essentially overlapping action to the movement of the swing as a whole, the key frames are offset. It is easier to address the swing and character animation separately which plays right into symblification's strengths. Chained movements like this are made much easier in Tradigital animation within Animate CC. A final word before we get into the exercise: I've included a background JPG for you to drop on stage (on its own layer under everything of course) if you want to add a little scenery once you're done.

"Roughing The Whole"

1. Since the whole character will be tweened in a pendulous arc like the wrecking ball in the closer look section earlier, we're going to start by working out the timing with the swing symbol in that same way. To make our animation process easier, frame 1's keyframe will remain in the "down" position. The timing I worked out was frames 1, 33, and 65 are the "down" positions and frames 17 and 49 are the front and back "up" positions (respectively). To make the swing more energetic I chose the "up" positions to be rotated at 65 degrees either way. Insert keyframes (**F6**), use the Free Transform Tool (**Q**) to rotate and tween with proper easing to get the swinging moving within our timing with good slow in and out. *Image SS5.1*

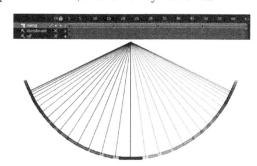

Image SS5.1 (Note: Motion and spacing shown with overlapping images of all frames.)

2. Now we're going to work on the rough animation. Lock the "swing" layer, insert a new

layer above it, and name it "rough." We'll need to address what the keyframes on the swing layer represent right now. Frames 1 and 65 are in the down position and moving forward, so we'll call them the *down-forward* keys from here on out. They are the beginning and end of the loop so they're identical. You can probably figure out now that frame 33 is in the down position and moving backward, so it'll be called *down-backward*. Since the up positions are where the character changes directions, frame 17 is *up-backward* and 49 is *up-forward*.

3. Insert blank keyframes (**F7**) where necessary on the "rough" layer and very loosely sketch the swinging positions for the down positions (that would be frames 1, 33, and 65—and frames 1 and 65 are the same). You'll see in the image accompanying this step that I'm not focusing on anything other than the pose and the general proportions of the character. We will refine this more later. *(Note: though they're not in the lowest point of the arc in the storyboard, those are the backward and forward poses.) Image SS5.3*

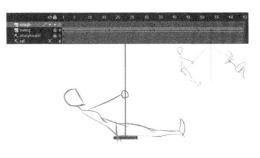

Image SS5.3

4. We're going to have to pause for a second and acknowledge what happens at the top of the swing. This is the transition moment between backward and forward poses so the character will not be in one or the other but changing between them. Therefore, we need to include the breakdown positions of the swing in our rough. They are the halfway points between the existing keyframes, so insert blank keyframes on the "rough" layer at frames 9, 25, 42, and 57. *Image SS5.4*

Image SS5.4

5. The swing's breakdown positions are actually the key positions for our character (which will become clear soon), meaning that they will have the same forward or backward pose we've already drawn. Which one it will be depends on if the swing is moving forward or backward at the time. If it is moving forward (as on frame 9) then the pose will come from the previous key (making it the outstretched pose from the *down-forward* key on frame 1). If it's moving backward (as on frame 25), the pose will come from the *next* key (making it the compact pose from the *down-backward* key on frame 33). You may copy/paste the rough poses you drew and simply move and rotate them into position using the Free Transform Tool (**Q**). Continue like this for the other two blank keyframes inserted from the previous step. *Image SS5.5*

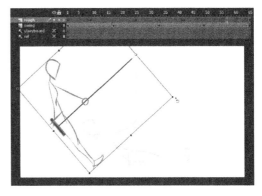

Image SS5.5

6. Now that we have our down keys and some breakdown/not-so-breakdown frames completed in the rough, we're going to insert blank keyframes and sketch in the poses at the swing's up position keyframes (17 and 49). These are essentially the *character's* breakdown frames so we'll treat them as such. If our character is moving from leaning backward to leaning forward as in frame 17, insert a blank keyframe on the "rough" layer and sketch in a pose with that in mind. Do the opposite for frame 49. *(Pro-tip: you can insert keyframes in the frame before and after the breakdown with the keyframe poses you're breaking down. Align them with the swing position on the frame you're drawing the breakdown, then use onion skin mode to draw your breakdown as normal. See accompanying image as an example. Don't forget to clear the two helper keyframes created before you move on.)* Image SS5.6

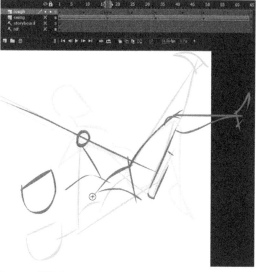

"Character Animation Tiedown"

Image SS5.6

7. In this section you'll be using straight ahead action and the very rough keys and breakdowns you created in the previous section to draw in more accurate proportions and add in some overlapping action of the features such as the foot and head as well as the pigtails. Refining a rough animation in traditional animation is sometimes called a tiedown. Though we're not going to be drawing in that kind of detail here, we'll borrow the term for this section. Let's start by inserting a new layer above the rest called "tiedown" and draw the pose from the rough animation on frame 1, adding in some other details like a flexed foot and trailing pigtails. *Image SS5.7*

Image SS5.7

8. Insert a keyframe (**F6**) at the next frame which has a keyframe on the rough layer (that would be frame 9). We inserted a keyframe and not a *blank* keyframe because we know this is the same pose as before. For the sake of expediency, use the Free Transform Tool (**Q**) to rotate the image into position.

9. Insert a blank keyframe (**F7**) on the "tiedown" layer at the next frame with a keyframe on the "rough" layer (making it frame 17) and draw the pose as represented in the rough animation

but with more character detail as we did before. *Image SS5.9*

10. Repeat the last three steps for the next six keyframes. The accompanying image shows the six keyframes of the entire tiedown swinging sequence thus far shown together. *Image SS5.10*

11. We're going to want some more visual information in the tiedown as we continue. You should guide, hide, and lock the "rough" layer at this point so your≈work doesn't become confusing. Back on the "tiedown" layer, insert a keyframe or blank keyframe halfway between each of the keyframes created in this tiedown section so far. Either draw their inbetween positions or simply rotate a pose from a previous keyframe— whatever the situation calls for. Remember to use the swing as the reference for *where* the character should be at any given time. *Image SS5.11*

12. Go over all the keyframes created in this tiedown section so far and refine their poses or animation as necessary.

Image SS5.9

Image SS5.10

Image SS5.11

"Symblified Tiedown"

13. Click on the tiedown layer to select its entire used timeline, right-click those highlighted frames and choose **Copy Frames** and then lock this layer too.

14. Unlock the "swing" layer and double-click on the swing instance on the stage at frame 1 to enter the swing symbol. Insert a new layer above "swing," right-click on frame 1 and **Paste Frames**. You will have noticed that it extended the timeline but not for the "swing" layer which already existed. Help it out and use **F5** to extend its layers timeline to meet up with the tiedown layer (whose name was pasted in with the frames). *Image SS5.14*

15. As seen in Chapter 8's closer look section (if you're following along as recommended

Image SS5.14

in this book's Introduction) we need to realign the images pasted into the new tiedown layer to the swing. Use the Free Transform Tool (**Q**) to rotate and align each frame so it plays ahead as the character leaning forward and backward on the swing (as seen in the accompanying image to this step). Use the ghosted image of the tiedown at frame 1, which you can currently see on the main stage, as a reference point. The alignment doesn't need to be absolutely perfect since our tiedown wasn't, but it needs to be close enough so the images don't distractingly jump around. *Image SS5.15*

Image SS5.15

16. Return to the main timeline, guide and hide the tiedown layer. Highlight all the tween spans on the "swing" layer, select "sync" from the tweening area of the Properties panel, and hit **Enter** to quickly test how the new symblified tiedown looks in the swing symbol as it's tweened. Obviously it'll look a little choppy but we're looking for obvious position issues here. Make note of any time you think her pose should be altered, specifically if it should be pushed more or less in any direction (for instance tucking her legs in less, leaning the head back more, etc.). Re-enter the "swing"

symbol, but this time through the library by double-clicking its icon there so we can edit in isolation. *Image SS5.16*

Image SS5.16

17. Make any changes to the poses you noted in the previous step and repeat that previous step to check that it's what you wanted. Repeat as necessary until you're happy with the poses and how they help "sell" the swinging motion.

18. Back in the "swing" symbol, use the arc double-check method to verify that the arcs for any endpoint (meaning extremities like hands and feet or joints like the elbow) are smooth. Notice in the accompanying image that while the arc for the ankle is good, there is one point (which I highlighted in red) on the elbow and head arcs which is off path. With this information, adjust the tiedown as necessary. Delete the arc layers when you're done with them. *Image SS5.18*

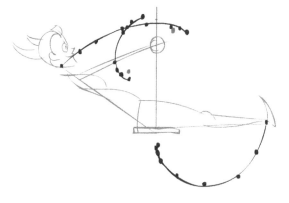

Image SS5.18

Interlude

If you've been following along with the real-world examples in each chapter so far you'll be able to complete the steps by remembering what was done in those previous examples. If you feel you're up to the task of moving on more independently, consider the rest of this paragraph a refresher in the steps. You'll need to analyze the tiedown animation and determine which features are the "easies" and which are the problems. There are so many ways to clean up an animation like this. You may drag in the "girl-reference_model" symbol from the library onto a new layer in the swing symbol you're currently in and break it apart (Cmd/**Ctrl+B**). From here you can turn whatever features you want to classic tween into Graphic Symbols and place them on their own layers. Any features you want to shape tween (including the patches I have included in my design) go on their own layers. But if you feel like that's too much at this point, I have included a helper symbol named "girl_swinging" in the library. There's also a folder named "girl_swinging-symbols" which contains all of the symbols which are used in this helper. This is so that if you *do* decide to go ahead and create your own character pack from the reference, any symbol you name won't be confused with the ones used in this helper since they're collected away in a folder. In that case, you may skip ahead to step 21 and see how I completed the animation by working on larger sections of features and narrowing them down to the smaller or chained movements. Otherwise you should continue ahead step-by-step using the "girl_swinging" symbol I have provided.

"Symblified Cleanup"

19. In the "swing" symbol, guide and hide the tiedown layer, insert a new layer (no need to name it), drag the "girl_swinging" symbol from the library onto it, and line up the swings. *Image SS5.19*

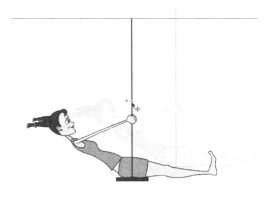

Image SS5.19

20. Break Apart (Cmd/**Ctrl+B**) the "girl_swinging" instance, right-click the resulting highlighted objects and symbols, and **Distribute to Layers**. You should now have a series of named and unnamed layers on the timeline in the "swing" symbol which make up the design of the girl character. The named layers are symbols and the unnamed layers are objects (shapes). Take a moment to familiarize yourself with the setup and name any unnamed layers for your own benefit. You should also delete the "swing" layer which was already there before you

Image SS5.20

did these last two steps since the swing is built into the "girl_swinging" design layout anyway. There is a leftover blank layer from all of this as well which you may delete. *Image SS5.20*

21. There are a lot of moving parts here so it's best to break up the bigger sections and chop away at them individually, starting with the upper body. The head, body, and upper arm are all in one symbol so it will look strange after you complete this step but we will then enter the symbol and work on the other features' cleanup. So right now on the "swing" symbol's timeline, insert keyframes and rotate the body symbol (actually named "girl-body_head_arm") before applying classic tweens with the required easing to match the *basic* movements in the tiedown. To do this, hide whatever layer needs hiding and unhide those that need to be seen (like the body and tiedown layers). *Image SS5.21*

Image SS5.21

22. At each keyframe on the body's layer of the "swing" timeline, enter the symbol, insert keyframes, and move the symbol instances or morph the shapes into position of any feature which needs it according to the tiedown. Tween as necessary. Use shape hints as necessary. We'll come back to the overlapping action of the head (and the pigtail on it) later. *(Note: sometimes for rotation tweens over 180 degrees, Animate CC will rotate in the direction of the closest position. This is just to say that if something like the upper arm (bicep) instance doesn't rotate the correct way, you can change its rotation from Auto to CW (clockwise) or CCW (counter-clockwise) in the Tweening area of the Properties panel. The number of times should be set to 0 as we don't intend for it to ever rotate all the way around.) Image SS5.22*

Image SS5.22

23. Now is a good time to start moving from the upper to lower half of the character's movements so we'll start at the shape tweening of the shorts and the classic tweening of the waist. Shape hints will most likely be necessary for the tweening of the shorts. If they aren't working for you, rotate them clockwise like musical chairs and keep testing until it works. Sometimes Animate CC just likes a different arrangement of shape hints. The waist's classic tweens should be easy. *Image SS5.23*

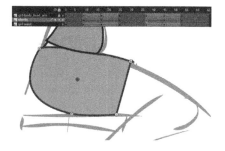

Image SS5.23

24. The reason we haven't animated the forearm yet is because we wanted to make sure that the upper body's animation worked as it is and that would be determined by animating the hips (shorts and belly/back). If adjustments need to be made to the overall motion of the upper body or the symblified animation nested within, make them now because ...

25. ... we need to finalize the major upper body movement by tweening the forearm to match the upper arm movements. The arcs are going to be hard to follow using simple classic tweens and keyframes evenly spaced so whenever they don't you'll need to line up the forearm symbol frame by frame.

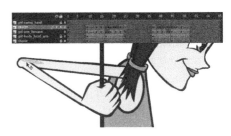

Image SS5.26

26. Shape tween the patch above the forearm to cover up the seams presented in the previous step, frame by frame where necessary. The upper body (aside from the overlapping action of the pigtails) should now be done. *Image SS5.26*

27. The legs are split up into two parts: the thigh is a shape and the shin and foot are packed in one "girl-leg_lower" symbol (this symblification allows for the shin to be shape tweened and the foot to be classic tweened but move together inside this master symbol). Start by animating the lower leg symbol as a whole to match the tiedown (don't worry if the design of the shin doesn't match up perfectly just yet).

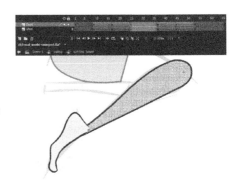

Image SS5.28

28. Now that the major position changes are accounted for, enter the lower leg symbol at each keyframe, insert keyframes on the shin and foot layers, and then alter the shin shape and move/rotate the foot to match the tiedown. Apply shape and classic tweens as needed with appropriate easing. Use shape hints if necessary. *Image SS5.28*

29. The thigh needs to flex and distort just as the shin did so shape tweening is optimal here. Use shape tweens and hints to complete the thigh animation as well as the patch above the lower leg layer. If it looks like the thigh design is distorted too far in any particular position you may adjust the shin's position relative to the thigh in order to reduce the need for that amount of distortion. *Image SS5.29*

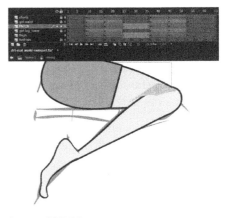

Image SS5.29

30. Now it's time to revisit the features and apply some overlapping action, starting with the foot. Testing the overall animation, the only places where any overlapping action of the foot would really be visible would be the beginning and end of the loop (meaning where the foot is pulled backward). Enter the "girl-leg_lower" symbol and move the first keyframe in the first tween span on the foot layer forward a few frames so the movement starts later than the shin. Then drag the last keyframe on the foot layer forward until it reaches the end of the timeline (frame 65). Make sure that the foot is lined up appropriately with the shin's shape tweens at all times as these changes may have taken them out of alignment. *Image SS5.30*

Image SS5.30

31. Now we will focus on the animation for the pigtails. At each keyframe of the "head" layer enter its symbol, insert keyframes on the two pigtail layers, and position them to line up with the tiedown. Now it's a matter of adjusting the timing inside the head symbol. To nail down the motion, you'll need a little trial and error. Apply classic tweens and test the video export via Cmd/**Ctrl+Enter** to see if all is well (guide the tiedown layer if it's showing up and distracting you on export). If it's not, move the keyframes around and/or adjust the rotational position of the pigtails to match the movement you're going for. I ended up with the keys at 21, 45, and 65 (corresponding to the pigtails being back, front, and then back again) and breakdowns at 33 and 55 (which were the pigtails sticking straight "up"). *(Note: even once the animation looks good, the pigtails can look a little stiff. In that case, you can get the best of both worlds by supplementing the simple classic tweens of the pigtail instances with nested hand-drawn, frame-by-frame animation inside the pigtail symbol where needed to make them seem more flexible.) Image SS5.31*

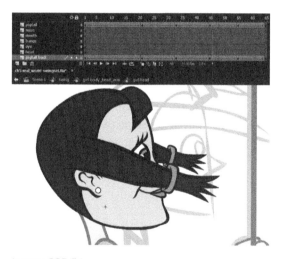

Image SS5.31

32. Complete the animation by adding in any settling tweens that may smooth out the sequence. For instance, from frames 25–37 in the "swing" symbol it would be good to see her moving forward even more instead of sitting in the same position. This means that every feature will move and/or distort. It's best to start with the key position at frame 37, re-pose it, and then tween where necessary. This is also where you should address the overlapping action of the head since after she leans forward and ends in that position at frame 25 the head should keep going a bit. This phase is often called "sweetening" because we're just making the

motions a bit more refined and giving extra life to the overall sequence. *Image SS5.32*

At this point, you might feel as though the swing feels a little stiff because there's not much visible dimension. You can only see one leg/foot and one arm/hand … not to mention that the rope doesn't bend at all, which could make it feel more like a metal rod (although some swings are designed this way so that might be fine). These can all be rectified easily. You can duplicate the layers of the leg features, offset their positions so that you can see them, and then just animate them a bit differently (like increasing/decreasing the slow in/out, the actual distance it travels, and/or offsetting some of the keyframes during the swing so that the movements aren't exact). The same process can be done for the arm as well.

As for animating the rope, it may seem like a complicated thing to endeavor to do, but it's actually fairly straightforward. Think of it this way: when the girl leans back, she's pulling on the rope with her hands, so that's the point where it would bend. We know that the rope's pivot point (the top) shouldn't move in the "girl" symbol because that would throw the pendulum motion out of whack. So if it's going to bend at the point where the hand is and the top has to remain at the same point, that must mean that the girl must move. Knowing this, all you'd need to do is put the girl animation inside another Graphic Symbol (but leave the hand in its layer above the rope), drag it back into the "girl" symbol on a new layer above the folder, line it up with the existing image in the folder so it overlaps, delete the folder, and then drag the pivot point to the center of the hand. From there, you can animate her leaning back or forward and shape tween the rope line to match her movements. That may sound like a lot of steps but in reality it would only take a matter of minutes. It needs to be stated again that in traditional animation, this change would mean

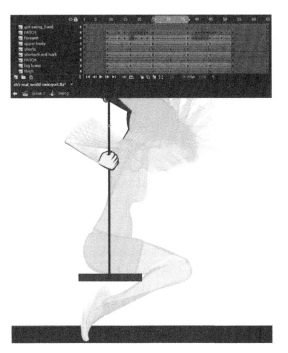

Image SS5.32

Image 5.11 The result of the extra dimension applied and the supplied background added.

a complete redrawing of the frames. The Tradigital workflow of symblifying the animation nested into various symbols that influence each other means that you can focus on one at a time and make changes that will cascade down the line and ultimately on the main stage.

FINAL WORDS
Arcs

Animation is movement. Movement travels in paths. Those paths can either be straight or curved. The straighter the path, the more rigid it is. Rigid movement can be used to show three main things about an object. One, it can emphasize the mechanical nature of something—industrial machines, insects, etc. Two, it can hint at the object's size since immense objects alter their paths so rarely that the arcs will be so slight they're practically non-existent. And finally, three is showing speed and power through straight paths, such as bullets, a character shivering, or Superman flying faster than the previously stated speeding bullet. The more curved a path is, the more organic and soft. This smooth movement supports the feeling of vitality and comfort in a character. This concept of smooth vs. rigid is more readily obvious in design where it can be used to accentuate a character's traits. In *Teenage Mutant Ninja Turtles*, Splinter's long, flowing kimono (smooth arcs) is a welcome alternative to Shredder's stiff, sharp-edged battle armor (no or rigid arcs). We will explore this concept better in the "Solid Drawing" and "Appeal" chapters but it's worth introducing now to help show the unity of meaning between movement and design.

Readability is very important in animation, as you'll continually see illustrated in the next chapter on Staging. The principle of Arcs is very important to the readability of movement for the sole reason that it is easier to follow movement through a well-defined, smooth path than through one which changes direction harshly and suddenly. It's always important to know what you want to

Image 5.12 Arcs can be as simple or complex as needed, and each of them tells a different story.

accomplish with your animation, but if no one can see it clearly it might not matter. As mentioned earlier in this chapter, many times the most useful method of applying Arcs as a principle is by a check to the work you've already done. It can be incredibly difficult to perfectly plot out paths for every part of animation, especially as your scene becomes more complicated. Character animation has a lot of moving parts, but as you're seeing, Animate CC is there to make things easy on you in case a change needs to be made.

Image 6.0 Bully Story by *Stephen Brooks (RubberOnion.com).*

Chapter 6
STAGING

INTRODUCING
Staging

Magicians use a technique called misdirection to get a spectator looking away from something they don't want seen. This technique is essential to tricking the mind into thinking the performer could have supernatural powers. The principle at the heart of this chapter is similar in the way that we want to control our audience's attention. Staging is the presentation of an idea so that it's absolutely clear to the viewer. One example of this could be as obvious as placing trees on the edges of the frame to bring attention to a clearing in the center or as abstract as using bright colors in a scene that needs to seem "happy." It's about getting someone to think or feel what you want them to through a clever direction of elements.

A story often told to illuminate the discovery of this particular principle comes from the days when animation was exclusively in black and white. A character such as Mickey Mouse, with his solid black body color, was difficult to pose for clarity. For instance, whenever his arms were in front of his body or ears there was no way to tell what was happening because they just blended into one another like a panther in the night (which may be the coolest phrase ever typed by human hands). Because of this problem, Walt Disney told his animators to pose all of their characters with a clear silhouette in mind so that no matter what problems with color contrast existed, the body positions would always be readable. Case in point, Mickey Mouse's ears are always next to each other – even when he turns his head to the side, they never overlap. If they did, it would look like Mickey had only one ear and his iconic silhouette would be ruined. Not many people notice that little anatomical inaccuracy because ... magic.

This principle covers such a wide variety of aspects in the art of animation that it's hard to pinpoint specific exercises to work on. But the most obvious and useful of these skills, as well as the one that even experienced animators usually need to brush up on, is animating in perspective. A character doing a little dance is fairly complicated to do. Take that same sequence and animate it in perspective (meaning dancing into the distance and back again) and things get decidedly more complicated. Now that this thought is running through your head, take a moment to reflect on the fact that James Baxter animated Belle and the Beast dancing a waltz in a giant ballroom ... by hand ... as the camera angle is constantly changing. Take another moment.

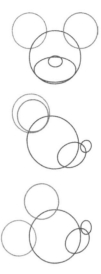

Image 6.1 We see the iconic design from the front (top), how the ear shapes would overlap in profile view if turned in 3D space (middle), and the profile design staged to allow the iconic design to remain after the turn (bottom).

This is an area in which our brothers and sisters in CG animation are sitting pretty. Whereas they have a virtual camera to work with in a 3D plane, we in the 2D must fake this effect by way of staging the perspective of our environment and adhering to that with changes in image size. That's what we'll be doing in the next bouncing ball exercise. The idea is to create a perspective grid to represent the ground fading off into the distance and to bounce the ball back into the horizon like Shane (from the movie *Shane*). Consequently, Westerns are a great reference for the use of perspective in staging.

> "Staging is the presentation of an idea so that it's absolutely clear to the viewer."

BOUNCING BALL Staging

Setting Up

In the previous chapter, we made our wonderfully timed, eased, and squashed/stretched ball bounce across the stage in exquisite arcs. This time, we're giving some depth to our stage. The trick to animating back into perspective is knowing what size the object or character would be at various points throughout the layout. To accomplish this, we're going to draw a perspective grid. After that, we're going to complete our bouncing ball so that it comes to a natural stop. Finally, we will combine these two and use Animate's tweening and our knowledge of slow in/out to effectively accomplish the illusion of depth. Open the main bouncing ball exercise from the last chapter ("bouncing ball 5 – arcs") and **Save As** to rename it "bouncing ball 6 – staging." Also, make sure that the **Snap to Objects** option is toggled (remember, it's the magnet icon in the toolbar) for the start of this exercise.

Hopefully, you are aware of the basics of perspective and know what one-, two-, and three-point perspectives are. If you do, you've probably also created a one-point perspective layout grid before (it looks like a tiled floor); in which case, now you get to see how to do that efficiently within Animate CC. If not, I encourage you to search out any number of excellent resources on drawing in perspective. That just isn't something we can cover fully in this book without getting really off track. We're working in one-point perspective here, so let me define some of the terms just so that we're on the same page for now.

Image 6.2 One-point perspective view is what you see looking straight down a city street. All depth lines converge to the same point.

One-point perspective (1pp for short) is what you see when you look straight down a city street. All the lines showing depth (going away from you, like the sides of the street) converge to a single point in the distance. This is called the vanishing point. That point sits dead center on something called the horizon line, which effectively is your eyeline. To draw our grid on paper, there is another point (called the diagonal vanishing point) that you have to use. Then you can create a series of tiles by way of working your way down other measuring points that have been drawn. It's a fairly tedious job that you will not have to do at all in Animate CC because we have something called the Free Transform Tool.

The "Animate" Difference: Object Draw

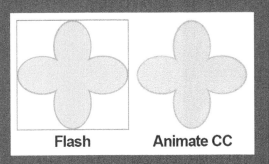

Flash   Animate CC

With the Animate CC update, drawing objects now have what's called an "enhanced bounding box" shown around them when selected. A bounding box basically just shows us what is being selected and in Flash versions it is rectangular (left). Animate CC now shows us the selection as an outline (right). This is a visual improvement as it now helps to quickly and easily distinguish drawing objects from groups or symbol instances.

1. Create a new layer. Refer to the last chapter if you don't remember how *(hint: there are icon and right-click options)*. This time, let's double-click this layer's name and rename it to something helpful like "perspective." And while you're at it, name the one with the bouncing ball on it "ball." *Image BB6.1*

Image BB6.1

2. In the layer name section, there are two icons at the top: one is an eye and the other is a padlock. These two functions are fairly self-explanatory, so toggling off the eye hides the layer and enabling the padlock prevents editing on it. On the "ball" layer, click the dot under the Hide Layer (eye icon) column so that we can work without clutter on our other layer. *Image BB6.2*

Image BB6.2

3. Back on the "perspective" layer, use the Line Tool (**N**) to draw a red horizon line across the stage about one-third from the top. Remember, holding **Shift** while you drag out the line will lock it straight. *Image BB6.3*

Image BB6.3

4. I'm going to introduce you now to my favorite feature of Animate CC: Object Drawing (**J**). In the toolbar, with a drawing tool (like the Line Tool) selected, you'll see an icon that looks like a circle with a box around it next to the Snap to Objects icon (the magnet). Click that or use the hotkey **J** to toggle it on, if it's not already. *Image BB6.4*

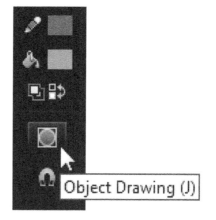

Image BB6.4

5. Object Drawing takes every stroke you draw and keeps it in its own self-contained object so that it doesn't affect other strokes. This can be very confusing if you don't know how to use it but incredibly useful

if you do. In this case, we want to create a center vanishing point for our horizon line and Object Drawing will let us do this quickly and more accurately. First, draw a small vertical line somewhere on the stage.

6. Drag this line up so that its bottom point touches the horizon line. *(Pro-tip: it bears repeating, holding Cmd/Ctrl on any tool will toggle the Selection Tool until you release.)* Use the Align window to set it to "Align horizontal center." The point where this line meets the horizon line is our vanishing point for our 1pp layout. *Image BB6.6*

7. Now that we have the horizon line and vanishing point, we can draw our measuring tiles (the squares of the grid). First, we should create another layer above the rest to keep this separate and easy to work with. Name this new layer "grid." *Image BB6.7*

8. The squares in our grid will be used as reference measurements for our ball. For instance, if the ball has a one-foot diameter, it would sit pretty inside one square foot (1 foot by 1 foot). Unhide the ball layer by clicking the X under the Hide Layer column (the one with the eye icon) so we can match the size of the square to the size of the ball.

9. With the "grid" layer selected on frame 1 and Object Draw (J) still on, use the Rectangle Tool (R), select no fill and black for the line color and draw a perfect square the way you did a perfect circle before (by holding **Shift**) around the bouncing ball to get its size right. If the square doesn't fit the ball perfectly on the first try, use the Free Transform Tool (Q) to adjust it. *Image BB6.9a and BB6.9b*

Image BB6.6

Image BB6.7

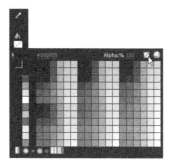

Image BB6.9a

Image BB6.9b

10. Re-hide the "ball" and "perspective" layers again to keep things visually organized as we work. We're going to copy/paste this box next to itself in one move. With the Selection Tool (**V**) in use and the square highlighted, hold Option/**Alt** while you click and drag it to one side until there are two boxes connected next to each other. *Image BB6.10*

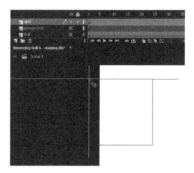

Image BB6.10

11. Repeat the previous step until you have ten perfect squares connected next to each other. You might have to zoom out to see more of the work area to do this. *(Pro-tip: whenever you open Animate CC, get in the habit of clicking the magnifying glass in the toolbar and selecting the zoom out by default. When hitting the hotkey **Z** you can easily get the Zoom Tool and zoom out immediately. If you want to zoom in, a simple click-and-drag to select the area you want Animate CC to zoom into works perfectly and quickly.) Image BB6.11*

Image BB6.11

12. Highlight the line of squares from step 11 and use the dragging copy/paste method in step 10 to get two of these groupings on top of one another and repeat until you have a 10 x 10 grid. *Image BB6.12*

Image BB6.12

13. Click the "grid" layer to highlight all of the squares created in the last couple of steps and create a group out of them by pressing Cmd/**Ctrl+G**. They're similar to Objects but Groups are more protected (e.g. their features can't be edited from anywhere but inside). They're functionally halfway between symbols and objects.

14. Align to the stage's perfect center by using both "Align horizontal center" and "Align bottom edge." *Image BB6.14*

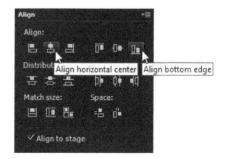

Image BB6.14 (Note: this image is edited to highlight the two align buttons needed.)

15. With the 10 x 10 grid group still selected, hit Cmd/**Ctrl+B** a couple times to Break Apart everything down to lines. The result of this will show all the lines highlighted, like in the accompanying image. *Image BB6.15*

Image BB6.15

16. Use the Free Transform Tool (**Q**) to squash the grid down until the top line is in the center of the stage. In the most recent versions of Animate CC this will squash evenly around the pivot point centered in the image by default. To get around this, you can hold Option/**Alt** as you squash the image or put the transformation point at the bottom of the grid first. Zoom back in using the Show All setting in the zoom drop-down under the timeline. *Image BB6.16*

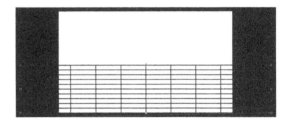

Image BB6.16

17. With Object Draw (**J**) still selected, unhide the "perspective" layer and draw a red line from the bottom-left corner of the grid to the vanishing point on that layer. Repeat for the other side so that you make an upside down V. *Image BB6.17*

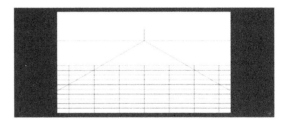

Image BB6.17

18. Select the "grid" layer and the Free Transform Tool (**Q**). Select the Distort option. The icon looks like a square with one corner pulled apart. Remember that rolling over icons will tell you what they are through popup. *Image BB6.18*

19. Click on the top-left transform point and **Shift**-drag it (which moves both sides at the same time) straight to the right until it meets the red diagonal line you drew in step 17. *(Note: do NOT deselect the grid in this process. Once you start distorting an image through this method, if you click away you will not get the same options. All*

Image BB6.18

transform points will reset into a rectangle.)
Image BB6.19

20. Unhide all the layers by clicking on the eye icon, click and drag the "ball" layer to be on top. *Image BB6.20*

Interlude

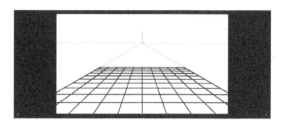

Image BB6.19

As I mentioned, some of you will recognize this and some won't. This is our perspective grid. We have used the Rectangle Tool, snapping, distortion, objects, and groups in order to efficiently create something that would have to be done with a ruler on paper. You also learned how to copy/paste objects, groups, and symbols all in one move by holding **Option/Alt** while dragging with the Selection Tool. This would

Image BB6.20

normally take much longer on paper as each line needed to be drawn and measured out proportionally using a ruler and a completely different vanishing point.

I actually keep a collection of grids (5 x 5, 10 x 10, 15 x 15 and so on) at the ready in an FLA, so I can do these pretty much on the fly (*Image 6.3*). It takes about one minute to make a grid. I know it may seem like a lot more to you right now, but think about it. Draw a horizon line and make a point in the center of it (vanishing point). Make a grid (or drag it from another library, in my case), put it where you want, and draw two diagonal guide-lines to the outside of the grid. Then distort the image, and you're done. That setup saves so much time in trial and error when doing what comes next: throwing the ball into the distance—aka animating in perspective.

Right now, we only have three bounces. We need to complete the bouncing so that it comes to a stop. You could follow what you had done in the last chapter to do this, but since we want to control the full bounce sequence to an ultimate stopping point ourselves, we're going to repurpose the existing bounce into some new timing.

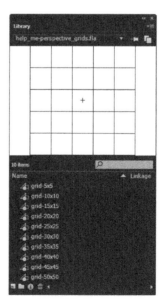

Image 6.3 Library view of a grid collection ranging from 5 x 5 to 50 x 50. Taken from "help_me-perspective-grids.fla" on the companion website.

PART II
"Finishing The Bounce"

21. Enter the "ball-bouncing" symbol and create new layer named "ref" (stands for *reference*) and turn it into a guide layer. *Image BB6.21*

Image BB6.21

22. Copy and paste in place the ball from frame one of the other layer in this symbol to the first frame of our new "ref" layer, and then move it straight up so that the top of the ball is level with the top of the stage. *Image BB6.22*

Image BB6.22

23. Insert a keyframe (**F6**) at frame 101 and **Shift**+drag the ball so that the bottom of the ball is level with the bottom of the stage. *Image BB6.23*

24. Create a classic motion tween between the two keyframes on the "ref" layer with an easing value of +50, a slight slow out. This is going to serve as our reference for

Image BB6.23

Image BB6.24

how high the max height should be at the "up" point of each bounce. We have already determined by step 23 that we want this ball to come to a natural stop after about 4 seconds of bouncing. You may lock the "ref" layer if you like (or just be careful not to move it in the coming steps). *Image BB6.24*

25. Back on frame 1, drag the ball on the other layer (named "Layer 1" by default) up to the ball on the reference layer as we did in step 22. *Image BB6.25*

26. Now that we are starting from a higher position, we want the drop to take longer. Insert two frames (**F5**) within that first span. The second keyframe (contact stretch) should now be at frame 14. *Image BB6.26*

Image BB6.25

Special Note

Because of step 26, now there are 13 frames between the first "up" keyframe and its follow-up "squash" keyframe instead of 11. When we started, each span (between an "up" key to a "squash" or vice versa) decreased by one frame. So the pattern (starting with an "up" to "squash" span) was:

11, 10, 10, 9, 9, and 8 (ending on a "squash" to "up" span.)

Knowing that the ball will approach the ground faster in the beginning than the end (because of our slow out applied to the reference ball in step 24), we want to do the same thing with the spans. Ultimately, we want the pattern to look something like this:

13, 10, 10, 8, 8, 6, 6, 5, 5, 4, 4, 3, 2, 1 ...

Image BB6.26

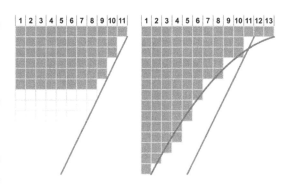

Image 6.4 A visual representation on the pattern of decreasing frame difference in tween spans which we've had up to now (left) and what we want to change it to (right).

... and the rest of the bounces will be tiny, with no frames between the extremes of up and down. So the idea going forward is to change the current spans to fit with their equivalents in our new ideal and then to complete the new pattern with a new set of spans. I attempted to visually represent this change in *Image BB6.4*. Each square in that image represents a frame and each row of squares is a different tween span (first bounce is at the top, last bounce at the bottom). Notice the best fit line in blue for the pattern we had is straight (no deceleration) and the best fit line in red for the new pattern we will implement is curved (decelerating). The blue line shows that the spans we will change to in the following steps are slowing out like the reference ball in step 24.

27. Remove one frame from each span after the second "squash" (to make eight frames between the "up" and "squash" extremes instead of nine), and then remove *two* frames from the last span (so that it has six frames between the "squash" and "up" extremes). *Image BB6.27*

Image BB6.27

28. We now want to complete the next spans. First we'll put a keyframe (**F6**) ahead on the timeline so that there are six frames between the last two keyframes (the keyframe you insert should be on frame 69 if you're following along exactly). Next we want to drag it back down to the bottom of the stage. *Image BB6.28*

Image BB6.28

29. Repeat the previous step but this time for the next "up" (with five frames in between the keyframes). You can place a blank keyframe (**F7**) on frame 75 and then copy/paste in place the ball from the previous "up" key (which was frame 62). We will adjust its height to the reference ball later. *Image BB6.29*

Image BB6.29

30. Repeat steps 28 and 29 in the pattern shown in the Special Note (13, 10, 10, 8, 8, 6, 6, 5, 5, 4, 4, 3, 2, 1 ...) until you reach the last frame (101), which also gets a keyframe. *Image BB6.30*

Image BB6.30

31. Go back through all the "up" keyframes (26, 46, 75, 86, 95, and 100) and **Shift**+drag the ball to match the height of the reference ball.

32. We have fixed the height and the spans, now we'll see how to create reference for the proportional decrease in each squash. Create a reference layer like we did in step 21, copy/paste in place the first "squash" ball on the same frame as the one on the layer with the bouncing ball (frame 15). Do the same with the ball on the second-to-last down keyframe (frame 98) which should have *no squash*, and apply a tween between these two keyframes with an easing of +50 (same as step 24). *Image BB6.32a and BB6.32b*

Image BB6.32a

33. At each one of the "squash" points on the bouncing ball layer, insert a keyframe (**F6**) on the corresponding frames on our new squash reference layer (within the existing tween). Then delete

Image BB6.32b

all the existing squashes on the bouncing ball layer and copy/paste in place those from the reference squashes. *Image BB6.33*

Image BB6.33

34. To do the same for the rebound stretches, you'll be making a reference layer similar to step 32. Create a new reference layer, copy/paste in place the first rebound stretch on the bouncing ball layer to the same frame on the new reference layer, place a keyframe and a ball with no stretch on frame 98 (since this marks the end of the spans which include a stretch), and finally tween with an easing value of +50. *Image BB6.34*

Image BB6.34

35. Repeat step 33 for the stretch rebound. *Image BB6.35a and BB6.35b*

Image BB6.35a

Image BB6.35b

36. Now that you know the workflow, do steps 34 and 35 again but this time for the "contact stretch" keys. *Image BB6.36a and BB6.36b*

37. Now that all the keyframes are in place, create classic motion tweens between the spans which need tweening and make

Image BB6.36a

Image BB6.36b

sure the easing is set to –100 for when the ball is falling and +100 for when it's rising. *Image BB6.37*

Image BB6.37

38. We want one more tiny bounce so that it doesn't look like the ball just stopped suddenly, so add two more keyframes at the end of the sequence (making the end now at frame 103). With the ball selected on the second-to-last keyframe (frame 102), hit the up-arrow on your keyboard once. *Image BB6.38*

Image BB6.38

PART III
"Bounce In Perspective"

39. The sequence should end at frame 103 now, so go back to the main timeline and expand it out that far. The final keyframe for the bouncing ball should end on the same frame as the bounce stops in the symbol now. In some versions of Animate CC, using the Sync feature on the tween will make sure the final keyframe is on the

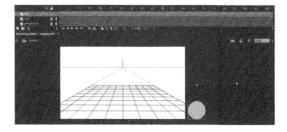

Image BB6.39

right internal frame. If that doesn't work on your version, adjust manually using the Looping area of the Properties panel. *Image BB6.39*

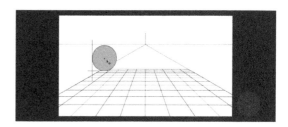

Image BB6.41

40. On the main stage, you should now see the ball bouncing across the front of the grid. Using this as measurement, you know that it travels across what should be all ten squares. This is important to know because we need to count back how far *across* it traveled so we can match it with the size of the square in the back.

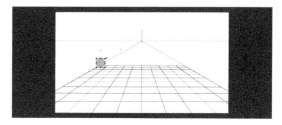

Image BB6.42

41. Turn off Snap to Objects for this next part as it's easier without it. Drag the ball from the last keyframe of the bouncing ball tween (frame 103) until it's sitting inside the last square in the top left of the grid. *Image BB6.41*

42. Without changing the pivot point, use the Free Transform Tool (**Q**) to shrink the ball down to fit inside the square's size. We've already seen that holding **Shift** as you drag one of the transform box's corners will change the size in perfect proportion. We've also seen that holding **Option/Alt** will ignore the pivot/transformation point's position and allow you to edit relative to the overall position of the image being transformed. So to shrink the instance of the bouncing ball's symbol in perfect proportion without moving the bottom of the ball shape "off the ground," hold **Shift+Option/Alt** while dragging the top right or left corner of the transform box. The ball should now look like it's sitting inside the box's area (for reference to your own work, the Transform window says I ended up with the symbol being 35.5% of its previous size). *Image BB6.42*

43. Since the ball is bouncing away from us, we need to add slow out to its movement. Give the tween on the main timeline an easing of 100.

44. If you test right now, you'll see that it looks good but slows too fast at the end. That's because we ended on a bounce and we need it to actually roll a little to a stop. To do this, make sure the first keyframe is set to "Play Once" from frame 1 in the looping area of the Properties

Image BB6.44

panel and that the last keyframe follows suit ("Play Once" from frame 103). Extend the tween and timeline by about seven more frames so that it ends on frame 110. Now the ball should roll to a nice rest at the end. *Image BB6.44*

45. Turn the "perspective" layer into a guide layer (right-click > Guide), locking it and hiding it from our view. Lastly, highlight the grid on the "grid" layer and give the solid black lines an Alpha (transparency) level of 30% in the Color panel. Now test the movie and behold the perspective goodness! *Image BB6.45*

Image BB6.45

This is the exact process you'll be able to use to make a character walk back into the distance or reverse it for an approach. It's not always needed, however. There are going to be many times that you can simply "eye it." But when it's needed, it's invaluable. For instance, obviously drawing backgrounds benefits from this quick layout guide. When you do that, keeping the perspective guide with the horizon line and vanishing point as well as the grid itself hidden on guide layers is good practice so you have them for size reference when it comes time to animate. Say you've drawn a wonderful alley in Pamplona with impeccable perspective, but if you don't follow the same guide when animating a character running down that alley away from a hoard of bulls, it'll just look silly (bull running, aside). Using guide layers for references is a helpful technique because they're hidden when exporting to video but in full view while you work within Animate CC. Just think "guide to hide."

What was just done in this exercise is not all that easy by hand. If you're just starting out with animation in this book, you could have just created a better bouncing ball exhibiting five (arguably six) of the 12 Principles of Animation than you could have done by hand given the same amount of study. This shouldn't be taken as a testimonial that animation in Animate CC is better than on paper, but rather there are some things that come easier. The arcs didn't need to be planned for this bounce, for instance, only double-checked that they were right after the fact. The inbetweens of the stretch approaching and leaving the ground on each bounce have been done for you by the program.

Image 6.5

Basically, you have given Animate CC the parameters by which to make this ball do what you want and have adjusted where necessary. When it comes to character animation, things aren't exactly this easy, but they are similar in that many movements can be delegated to the program to interpolate through tweening without *looking* like that's what you're doing. Many head movements, a backpack on a child, and solid objects like swords, hockey sticks, and pencils all can get the tweening treatment easily without giving away the secret. We're not hiding from the "Flashiness" out of shame; it's to preserve the illusion. Animators have always tried to conceal the answer to "how'd they *do* that?" It takes the audience out of the experience to even ask the question to themselves in the first place. That's part of the reason the 12 Principles exist: preservation of the illusion.

CLOSER LOOK
Improving The Stage

Speaking of preserving the illusion, in this section we're going to improve the look of this scene by essentially rounding off the rough edges. There are three glaring issues here, as far as a completed shot goes. One, you can see the reference grid, and it's distracting to a viewer. Two, if we take away the reference grid, there will be nothing but white space; we'll fix that with a gradient. Three, there's no shadow. Barring the idea that we're animating a vampire bouncing ball, it needs to have a shadow.

"Creating A Shadow"

1. The "perspective" layer is already a guide layer, hidden from our view and locked. Before we give some more depth to this scene with gradients and a shadow, let's turn the "grid" layer into a guide layer and lock it so it can't be altered.

2. Now we need something to suggest depth in the shot. First, create another layer and name it "bg" (stands for background ... you'll want to start using abbreviations like this if you don't already). Place it on the bottom of the layer list so that the references and the bouncing ball itself are on top. Make sure *not* to attach it to one of the guide layers. If you do accidentally, it's OK—to detach it, just pull the new layer down and away to the left until you see it *pop* out of the indent. *Image CL6.2*

Image CL6.2

3. Go to the Color panel **(Cmd/Ctrl+Shift+F9)**. With the paint bucket (which represents fill color) selected, choose "Linear gradient" from the drop-down menu. Double-click on the black pointer, and choose a subtle color to change to white. I chose the lightest gray in the presets. *Image CL6.3*

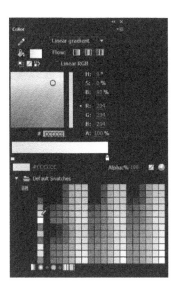

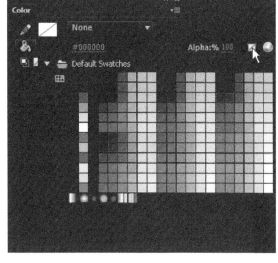

Image CL6.3   Image CL6.4

4. We don't want a line around this rectangle, so when selecting the stroke color, look for a box with a red line diagonally through it in the top-right corner of the color presets. This is the "no stroke" option (for future reference, you can select the same thing for fill). *Image CL6.4*

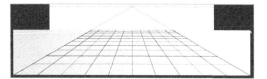

Image CL6.5

5. Use the Rectangle Tool (**R**) to cover the same area as the grid (from the bottom to the middle of the stage). *Image CL6.5*

Image CL6.6

6. Pick the Gradient Transform Tool (**F**). It hides in the same place as the Free Transform Tool in the toolbar. This is the transformation "drawer" of the toolbar, and it functions in much the same way as the Rectangle and Oval Tools being housed together. *Image CL6.6*

7. With the Gradient Transform Tool selected, click on the rectangle we drew in step 4. You will see some points pop up. The white circle at the corner is to rotate the gradient. The box with the arrow in it on the side is to expand or shrink it. The

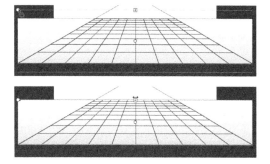

Images 6.7a and b Rotate the gradient to fade north/south (top, Image CL6.7a) and pull center tab down to keep the gradient within the box (bottom, Image CL6.7b).

dot in the middle is to change its position. Click and drag the white circle at the corner to rotate the gradient so that the dark area is at the bottom. Use the box handle to shrink the gradient inside the shape if necessary. You should now see a nice gradient from gray at the bottom of the screen to white in the middle. *Image CL6.7a and CL6.7b*

Image CL6.8

8. Let's create a shadow. Double-click the bouncing ball to get into the "ball-bouncing" symbol. Create a new layer, put it under everything, and name it "shadow." Actually now's a good time to name the ball layer "ball." *Image CL6.8*

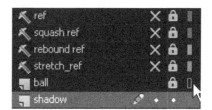

Image CL6.9

9. Lock all the layers except "shadow." Now click the colored box next to "ball" to turn on outline mode for that layer. Now we can see its position without the ball obstructing our view of the "shadow" layer below it, since that's where we will be working. *Image CL6.9*

10. In the Library panel (Cmd/Ctrl+L), right-click the symbol "ball-bouncing" and select **Duplicate Symbol**. Name it "ball_shadow-bouncing." *Image CL6.10*

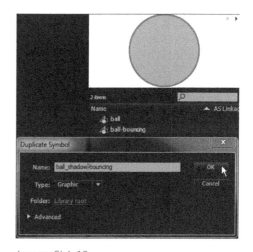

Image CL6.10

11. Drag and drop an instance of this duplicated symbol on the first frame of the "shadow" layer and line it up exactly with the symbol on the "ball" layer so they overlap.

12. Go to the *final frame* (frame 103) so that the bouncing ball is in the contact position with the "ground" at rest and use the Free Transform Tool (Q) to squash and skew the ball's shape, so it looks as though it is being cast like a shadow. Remember that you can do this by holding the **Option/Alt** key as you click and drag the transformation points so the bottom of the ball images never leave contact with each other. Alternatively, you could move the transformation/pivot point to the bottom of the ball (as I did in the accompanying image) in order to transform around this point. *Image CL6.12*

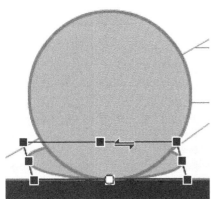

Image CL6.12

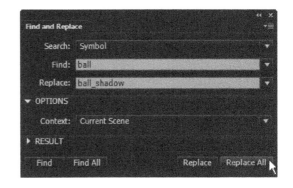

Image CL6.14

13. The movement of the shadow should look good, but it's still colored. We need to turn it black. Back in the library, right-click the "ball" symbol and **Duplicate Symbol**. Name it "ball_shadow."

14. Inside the newly created "ball_shadow" symbol, highlight the ball image and from the Color panel turn the fill to black with no outline (by clicking the no stroke icon, as in step 4 in this very closer look section). Return to the symbol "ball_shadow-bouncing" by double-clicking it in the library. *Image CL6.14*

15. Enter the "ball_shadow-bouncing" symbol and then open **Edit > Find and Replace (Cmd/Ctrl+F)**. To replace all the colored "ball" symbols in this timeline and *only* this timeline (meaning, not on the main stage or in any of the other symbols' nested animations) with the recently created "ball_shadow" we're going to use a specific setting in the following step.

16. In the Find and Replace panel, there are a series of drop-down menus. The provided image is what you see in Adobe Animate, for previous versions it will look different but the general method is the same. The first thing of note is in the "Options" subsection where the "Context" value is set to **Current Scene**. This will find-and-replace within whatever timeline you currently have open. In our case, it's the timeline nested with the "ball_shadow-bouncing" symbol we're currently in.

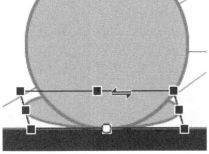

17. For the other values, we're searching for a **Symbol**. We want to "Find" **ball** and "Replace" it with **ball_shadow**. *Image CL6.17*

Image CL6.17

18. This part is easy. Click "Replace All."

19. Now you have a great shadow with corresponding movement, but it shouldn't be as dark. Back in the "ball-bouncing" symbol, click on the shadow and find the Color Effect area of the Properties panel. From the "Style" drop-down menu, choose **Alpha** and set it as you like. I chose 30%. *Image CL6.19*

Image CL6.19

USING STAGING With "The Story Point"

What's the point of animating something wonderfully if no one can see or understand it? That's the essence and purpose of Staging. In Disney's *The Jungle Book* there is a scene where Shanti, the human girl, is singing "My Own Home." She is wearing a subtle pink dress—not formal, but not tattered. There's a container with her as she kneels by a strip of land peeking out into the still water. No one has accompanied her to this watering hole, but a long dirt path carved into the jungle stretches behind her to right of the screen. The sky back there shows no dense trees, and the vegetation seems to get lighter the farther back with the path it goes. Mowgli is watching from a tree to the left of the screen, on all fours like a panther with his orange loin cloth being the only covering. At the point where he sits, the branch is angled directly toward Shanti, almost pointing her out to us in the scene. The jungle Mowgli has just crawled out from to get this closer look is dark and dense. Everything about this shot is clearly laid out in a way to tell you the relative social situations of these two characters, what they're doing, and where they are in relation to each other and their surroundings. It's not just about the perspective as Shanti walks toward us and Mowgli crawls away. It's the colors, arrangement

Image 6.6 "My Own Home" musical number from Disney's The Jungle Book *(1967).*

of background elements, clothing, conditions—everything works together to tell you what you need to know without saying a word.

Staging is so much more than just working in perspective. For proper staging to occur, the artist must know the "story point" of the scene. That is to say, the thing which is most important to the overall story as represented in this scene. Every element has to work together to get you where they want you to go emotionally. That's what makes this principle, while not hard to write about, hard to sum up. It's kind of like this principle exists to remind you to be aware of your story and what your purpose is in the scene. Staging is trying to remind you to not forget the planning when it comes to this shot you're approaching.

> "For proper staging to occur, the artist must know the "story point" of the scene."

In our bouncing ball example, the goal was to have a ball bounce into the distance. Believe it or not, there was a story decision made in this scene, albeit a small one: whether it would come to a stop or keep bouncing to the horizon. The story point, then, would be that this one lonely bouncing ball comes to a stop. The plain white environment, the trajectory hugging one side of the frame while leaving most of it completely empty, and the shadow cast away from the empty space, all give weight to the "lonely bouncing ball comes to a stop." How would that have been different if it were in the middle? Would it have the same feeling if the room were red? It's not a complicated scene, but every element still impacts the projection of the story point in one way or the other.

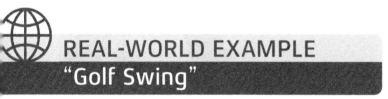

REAL-WORLD EXAMPLE
"Golf Swing"

Principles Used

Arcs: This seems obvious, a golf swing is a pendulous one, so it (and the motions that make up the whole) will travel in obvious and smooth arcs.

Slow In/Out: As with most organic movement, there's an acceleration and deceleration to each. The severity you choose for these during the swing will determine a lot about the feeling of the motion.

Anticipation: Before the swing, there's a small reverse motion before swinging forward—like a tiny windup. Because the golf swing is more about grace, if this anticipatory motion is quick, the swing will feel muscled. If it is slow and smooth, the swing will feel more calculated.

Overlapping Action: There are three joints to consider on the arm alone—shoulder, elbow, and wrist. The chest can move independently of the hip at the top of the legs, which also have knees and ankles. All these joints will start moving at different times and, when they do, they'll move at different rates. The golf club plays follow the leader to the rest of the body's "leader" status and, though the primary action, is the overlapping action. The follow-through will actually be the similarly named motion in professional sports—after the body has turned in full to the swing and come to a stop, the arms and club continue to a stop.

Pose to Pose/Straight Ahead: Which method you use to complete the rough animation will mostly determine if this is a professional's golf swing or an amateur's. Using pose to pose, you can analyze footage of golfers or step-by-step guides in a golfing magazine and sketch the perfect swing. Using straight ahead action, you'll get more spontaneity from the swing and it will probably be out of position at parts, making it feel like the kind of swing you would see someone making at a course for the first time after work with some buddies.

Staging: The contact position of the swing which actually shows the golf club hitting the ball when the character is facing the camera is an almost ambiguous pose. There's very little negative area which really says what you're looking at with a quick glance. This is why the staging of every surrounding key is so important. It's the flow which will really sell the motion to the audience.

Setting Up

Open the "ch6-real_world-golf_swing.fla" file provided on the companion website, and you'll notice that the character you've been given this time around isn't much more than a glorified

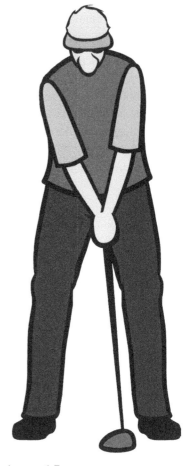

Image 6.7

puppet. I named him "puppet." You may use the pose to pose method or straight ahead action for the rough animation. Quickly explained, using the pose to pose method you will rough sketch only the key frame positions, keeping the staging of each pose in mind, and then clean up by arranging the simple puppet into position for each key and tweening between them to get a smooth swing. When using straight ahead action for the rough animation, you will be sketching many more frames to complete the swing because of the unpredictability inherent in the method. The cleanup process is similar to what I explained for the pose to pose method. The main difference is that while the pose to pose method shows us the most important (key) drawings by design, you will need to analyze your straight ahead rough animation to determine what its key drawings are and use those for the cleanup.

For the sake of simplicity I will be using the pose to pose method in the step descriptions. I encourage you to follow the steps in this fashion first and then return after the exercise is done to redo it using straight ahead action for the rough animation. Look to the *"Note"* sections in the steps for help on working with straight ahead action. Ultimately, the point of this exercise is that no matter which method is employed for the rough animation, after the cleanup is done you'll use the "Color Effect" section of the properties panel to turn the puppet symbol instance into a silhouette in order to analyze the staging and adjust it if necessary. There won't be a lot of steps in this example, since by this point the methods have already been covered. So let's just get started!

"Creating The Swing"

1. Start by tracing the puppet's design in a form you can keep consistent for your rough animation on a new layer above the rest. *Image GS6.1*

2. Complete the rest of the rough animation for the golf swing using the pose to pose method. The sketch you made in the previous step is your first key. There should be three more key drawings: the golf club pulled back in a windup, making contact with the ball, and then up in its resting position after the swing (the contact key could arguably be considered a breakdown because it's between two extremes but nomenclature is not as important as function). *(Note: if you are working through this exercise a second time with straight ahead action, you will need to analyze your rough animation for points on the timeline where a feature changes direction or spacing as that is where a keyframe will be needed on the timeline. Experience alone will improve your ability to determine these points.) Image GS6.2*

3. Lock the rough animation layer and enter the puppet symbol to analyze its design. The "body" (upper body) and "legs" (lower body) are each their own symbols on their own layers. The only other layer in the puppet symbol is one for the "feet," which is locked since they won't move. In the "body" symbol there are three layers: head, arms, and body shape. The head is a symbol and will be classic tweened, the body is a shape and will be shape tweened, and the arms are symblified containing the sleeves, forearms, and golf club (all of which will have classic tweens). Finally the legs symbol is made up of the thighs, shins, and a waist which are all instances to be tweened. *(Note: the feet are symbols, however,*

Image GS6.1

Image GS6.2

*and can be tweened but only one instance
can be tweened at a time. So if your straight
ahead action rough animation had the
golfer's feet moving, you'll need to separate
the feet layer into two, one for each foot,
and animate them individually.) Image GS6.3*

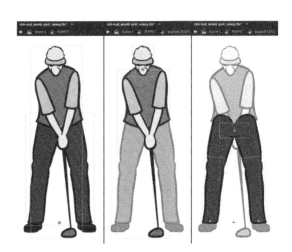

4. On the main timeline, scroll ahead to the
   first key (the windup which for me was
   drawn on frame 13) and enter the puppet
   instance there. Insert a keyframe (**F6**) on
   the body layer and move the instance up
   a few spaces until the bottom of the shirt
   better lines up with the one in the rough.

Image GS6.3

5. Enter the body instance and insert keyframes
   on each of the layers at this frame (still on the windup key
   from the previous step). Position the head and alter the body
   shape to fit the design in the rough. *Image GS6.5*

6. Rotate the arms instance so the near shoulder
   approximately matches the rough. Though the pivot point
   is at the neck, the near shoulder rotational position will
   be used as a reference for how far the arms instance will
   be rotated. This will keep the amount of features which
   need to be rotated *within* the arms symbol to a minimum.
   Image GS6.6

7. Enter the arms symbol on the same frame we've been on
   since step 4 and insert keyframes at this frame across all
   layers. Position the features to match the rough. You might
   need to rotate, squash, stretch, and/or skew the symbols to
   make this happen. *Image GS6.7*

Image GS6.5

8. Repeat steps 4–7 for the next two rough keys (contact and
   resting positions). Keep in mind that for the action you'll repeat
   from step 4, you may need to move the body instance left or
   right on stage as well depending on how you drew the rough
   animation. The goal there is to line up the center of the shirt's
   bottom edge in the symbol to the corresponding position on the
   rough. *Image GS6.8*

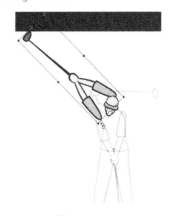

9. You should now have keyframes which need tweening on the
   body layer in the puppet symbol, all three layers in the body

Image GS6.6

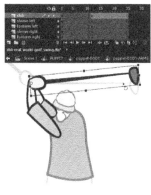

Image GS6.7

Image GS6.8

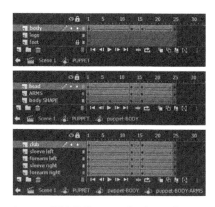

Image GS6.9 Puppet, body and arms symbols after tween (top to bottom).

symbol, and all layers in the arms symbol. Apply these tweens with appropriate easing. Remembering that the image on the body layer in the "puppet-BODY" symbol is a shape, you'll need to use shape tweens and possibly shape hints to complete this inbetween. *(Note: if the body shape becomes out of position at any point revealing the arms to be disconnected from the body, you may need to insert a keyframe along the tween span to adjust its shape, as I did on frame 7 in the accompanying image.) Image GS6.9*

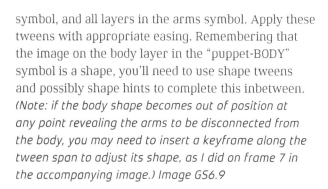

10. In my rough animation there was a little forward lean during the swing so I will be skewing the leg instance forward at the moment of contact. But before that, the body twists as the club is wound up before the swing and so do the legs slightly. So at the windup key in the rough on the main stage (which again is frame 13 on the rough animation I did), enter the puppet instance, insert a keyframe on the legs layer, and then enter the legs instance.

11. Insert a keyframe across all layers in the leg symbol and adjust the instance positions as needed to replicate the legs' positions shown in the rough.

12. Repeat steps 10 and 11 for the *last* key in the rough (the resting position, which for me was on frame 25).

13. In the "puppet-LEGS" symbol, apply a classic tween across all three keyframes on all layers with an "S"

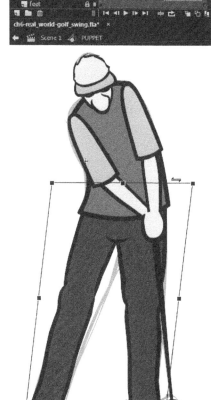

Image GS6.14

curve in the Easing Editor to get smooth slow in and slow out spacing for those movements.

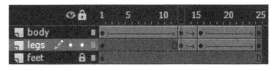

Image GS6.15

14. Return to the "PUPPET" symbol, insert a keyframe on the legs layer at the contact key frame (this will be on the same frame as the one created on the body layer, which for me was frame 16), and skew the legs symbol instance forward until it looks like it's connected to the body. *Image GS6.14*

15. Apply classic tweens to the last three keyframes on the legs layer with whatever easing is appropriate for the action. Make sure that the legs and body don't look detached on any frame along the tween spans. *Image GS6.15*

Interlude

You should now have a complete golf swing animation. The character puppet is rather simplistic in design but it gets the idea across—or at least it should. This is where we test how visually readable the form is as it changes throughout the course of the swing. We will be using the "silhouette test." What we are looking for here is that the overall form is readable throughout the sequence even though there's no color variation or surface detail. Negative area in the form (such as gaps through which you can see the stage, like between the arms) is especially helpful to communicate the content of a pose when all other visual information (like shirt color) is removed except what the form can obstruct (like the background). You'll notice that there are only two steps in this next part. I think this best illustrates how easy it is to implement this quick review into your Tradigital workflow; so let's do just that!

"Silhouette Test"

16. On the main timeline, highlight the puppet symbol instance on stage and locate the Color Effect area of the Properties panel. Choose "Brightness" from the Style drop-down menu and drag the slider down to −100%. You should now see the puppet instance which used to have color variation in its design become an all-black silhouette. *Image GS6.16*

17. Use quick play (hitting Enter on the timeline) to test the animation and see if it is still clear in this silhouetted form.

Image GS6.16

You may also drag the marker across the timeline or step frame by frame through the animation using the < and > keys (which are also the "," and "." respectively) to determine if there are any problem poses ... ones that don't communicate the purpose effectively. If everything looks great, you've confirmed that the action is readable in its most basic representation and you can set the Style drop-down in the Color Effect area of the Properties panel back to "None" and call this golf swing animation done. If any pose(s) seems ambiguous in silhouette and the readability of the golf swing is muddied as a result, enter the instance holding the form in question and edit as necessary. *Image GS6.17*

Image GS6.17 (Note: Shown are each frame overlapped -- you'll want to look at each image individually.)

One of the super benefits to animating by symblification in Animate CC is that when the final animation is nested within a symbol, you can very easily do this silhouette test. It's a quick way of noticing any staging problems with the poses you've chosen. Of course, staging should be considered in the rough animation, but sometimes it's hard to notice problems until the form is completely filled in and the negative area really pops out at you. This is how you truly see the effect and importance of negative area on the form. And if you're not used to considering this particular facet in your work yet, this silhouette test is a quick and easy way to double-check the readability of your work without adding many more steps.

FINAL WORDS
Staging

This is a fairly vague principle, but that should be comforting in a way. Remember that these principles are not to tell you what to do; they're to help you stay on track and improve your animation to create a cohesive look. In much the same way that Animate CC is a tool to help you do what you want to do in your art, the 12 Principles of Animation seek to remind you that what you're doing *is* art—and art needs as much feeling as it does careful consideration. Staging is a nexus zone between those two. You have to know what you want the audience to get out of what they're seeing, and then use all your knowledge of illustrative draftsmanship and cinematography to make that happen. It's not something that can be taught in a few paragraphs.

"For staging, success or failure mostly comes from deciding where and how to put things on the screen."

That's actually why it *should* be comforting. Art is about growth, and animation is no different. You will always learn more about staging, no matter how skilled you become. Just do the best you can, and do it honestly with consideration and the essence will come through. For staging, success or failure mostly comes from deciding where and how to put things on the screen. Get a handle on that, and you're a long way into applying this principle. Perspective gives depth, which will help your audience suspend their disbelief more readily. But sometimes you don't want to engross an audience; you may want something to hit dry, to let them see the moment from the outside. Take a look at any top-ten best of *The Simpsons* lists, and any episode therein is a good place to start in the economy of moving between depth to bring audiences in and flat staging to let them stand back and laugh. The flow from one to the other isn't easy to keep seamless, but I'm sure this homework will come in handy ... as painful as it might be.

You should now be feeling more comfortable with the program as well as how it merges with the 12 Principles. In the next chapter, we're going to explore the two animation methods referenced in the principle's title. Everything we've gone over up to this point will be used. If you have a graphics tablet and have been itching to use it more, now's your chance. In Straight Ahead Action and Pose to Pose, we're going to work some frame-by-frame magic!

Image 6.8 Three's Horrible: Part I *by Stephen Brooks (RubberOnion.com).*

Image 7.0 This scene from Animator vs. Animation IV by Alan Becker was animated using the pose to pose method and depicts on-screen characters animating with straight ahead action (www.AlanBecker.net).

Chapter 7

STRAIGHT AHEAD ACTION AND POSE TO POSE

INTRODUCING
Straight Ahead Action and Pose To Pose

This chapter could easily be called "animation methods" because that's what this principle really is. Straight Ahead Action and Pose to Pose are two ways of approaching animation at different ends of the productivity spectrum. Straight Ahead is an unplanned technique where the artist starts with a certain image and then just animates frame by frame (fbf) until the end of the scene. Pose to Pose is a planned process by which the most important visual beats (key frames) of the story are created first, and then the spaces are filled with inbetweens. Both have their merits and deficiencies, as opposites often do. Knowing those failings and how to combine the two processes to maximize their benefits have allowed generations of animators to use these two animation techniques to better service their visual storytelling.

With Animate CC, you have additional features that weren't easily available when drawing on paper though ... if at all. The ability to use symbols, tween them around, set precise sizes and transformations, and easily alter just about anything off an existing drawing without having to redo it completely are all immense time savers. When sketching out a drawing, if you don't like the position of something, a quick selection and movement or transformation can usually fix the problem. You do have an Erase Tool (**E**), and a good graphics tablet will have an eraser function on the other side of the pen. But sometimes you want an arm you just drew to be a *little* bit to the left, which can be done by selecting the feature and either dragging it or moving it using arrow keys. It is in these quick, on-the-fly alterations where Tradigital work shines.

"Rough animation is made up of relatively quickly sketched drawings that are used to specify position and pose."

It's around now it should be mentioned that what we're talking about when referring to the animation you'll be doing using straight ahead or pose to pose is "rough animation." Rough animation is made up of relatively quickly sketched drawings that are used to specify position and pose. These rough sketches can be very fragmented images or even just simple stick-figures, so in traditional animation there's usually a process called a "tiedown" after the rough animation where those rough sketches are tightened up by drawing over them to get a better sense of the line economy (best use of lines in the figure). Finally, there's "cleanup." This process is where the forms' lines are nailed down and great care is taken to refine each image. In the traditional (classical) style of animation, every frame with animation on it had to be worked over several times before completion. In this chapter after working through the rough animation, you'll see what the quick cleanup in Animate CC can be like!

Image 7.1 Rough animation (top), tiedown pass (middle), and cleanup (bottom).

A WORD ABOUT
Traditional Methods

This chapter is unique in that this principle is about the actual processes used in traditional animation. If you want to hand-draw everything in Animate CC, you absolutely can! All you ever needed for hand-drawn animation, really, was a way to draw (like the Brush Tool, **B**) and create multiple sequential frames (insert keyframe **F6**, or **F7** for a blank one). In this way, you'll probably feel very at home in the first parts of this chapter's bouncing ball exercise because that's exactly what we're doing. So far, we have made all of our movements in Animate CC without drawing much more than a simple circle. The reason for this simplicity was so that you could get accustomed to the movement tools within the program before really addressing workflows as this chapter does. Now that we're on the other side of the hill, so to speak, the last half of this book is going to involve much more drawing, frame-by-frame animation techniques, and actually putting all this stuff to work.

"Drawing is where everything begins."

Frankly, just about anyone can draw something sequentially to make animation; it doesn't make it good, but it can be done. The same can be said for tweening a symbol around a stage. It's the merging of these two basic abilities and the application of the 12 Principles of Animation with them where skill and dedication meet and payoff. Animation can be approached from an academic or trade angle, and both are equally valid and effective. But just like straight ahead and pose to pose, it's best to combine the two. It's great to have a conceptual knowledge when learning, but if it can't be implemented then it becomes rather useless. Learning by doing

Image 7.2 Depiction of animation paper with Acme-style peg bar holes.

is clearly invaluable. However, if that's your sole manner of learning either traditional animation techniques or Animate's vast toolset, you might miss out on the experience of the great animators who came before you. It's easy to overlook their wisdom when you get caught up in the wave of excitement that comes from making your own progress. We haven't jumped into roughing animation by hand or illustrating characters to move for that exact reason: it's too tempting to stop there.

As argued in the Introduction to this book, learning by doing can't be *understated* and is huge to progressing in just about everything. Even though we really haven't drawn anything so far while learning half of the principles and a bunch of the program, I cannot *overstate* how immensely important drawing is to animation as a whole. Drawing is where everything begins. That is the first time in the process that the concepts and ideas in your head get translated to a visual form. It doesn't need to be pretty; it just needs to be honest. The whole reason a workflow exists is to help you get something done incrementally and efficiently. If you could make perfectly drafted illustrations while keeping all the animation principles needed in play *and* act for the character being animated straight from your head to the page with no need for cleanup, you would be a nigh unparalleled artistic genius (or Milt Kahl ... same thing). You will usually start with ugly drawings and work your way up, which is what we'll be doing here.

"Animation can be approached from an academic or trade angle, and both are equally valid and effective."

A FINAL WORD TO THOSE
Without Graphics Tablets

If you don't have a graphics tablet and plan to draw with a mouse, this chapter's bouncing ball exercise might be a little hard for you to follow. In that case, you can drag the "ball" symbol around the stage into position on each keyframe instead. Every time in the steps you see us drawing *specifically* with the Brush Tool, just mentally replace that with dragging the "ball" symbol into a new position. That being said, the rest of the book from this point forward will be using this chapter's methods of rough animation to plot out all the action. It *is* possible to draw with a mouse, but I wouldn't recommend it if it can be helped. If you absolutely cannot get a graphics tablet, draw on paper! A very cheap way to keep all pages lined up with one another is to use thin (read: cheap) printer paper and hole-punch it so that you can put the stack in a three-ring binder. Animating on paper is really the best way to learn animation anyway.

Image 7.3 Some printer paper stacked in a three-ring binder is a cheap and portable solution to a starter animation table. Some binders are even translucent, which would give a light-table effect.

BOUNCING BALL Straight Ahead Action And Pose To Pose

Setting Up

You're going to be working more independently in this series of exercises. There isn't any way you can draw wrongly right now; it's just step one in a longer process. You might feel overwhelmed at some point if this is your first time animating frame by frame, but don't give up. Everything can be worked on and cleaned up, and don't forget to check out the work files provided on the companion website to see more of how they should look.

For these exercises, we're not saving from a previous FLA, but instead creating a brand new one. This file will have the same naming scheme. We'll be splitting up the two principles into different work files, so this first one will be named "bouncing ball 7 – straight ahead." In Chapter 6, we created a simple environment with depth. Here, we're creating an environment with no depth but an uneven, 2D terrain. This background will serve as the setting for our ball to bounce, and the randomness of the surface will show the differences between the methods better than a flat one.

"Setting the Stage"

1. Select the Pencil Tool (**Shift+Y**) and select **Ink** from the options area of the toolbar. This setting will have Animate CC read each tiny move of the pencil instead of smoothing it out in some way. It doesn't matter which color you choose so I just opted for black to keep things simple. Draw an uneven terrain roughly in the shape of a "V" with high walls on either side of the frame so the ball can't bounce out. *Image BB7.1*

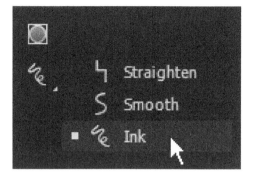

Image BB7.1

2. To give this ground some color, we have to close off the shape. Making sure to only draw in the gray work area, make a line or lines to connect (overlapping counts as connecting because they cross) with the left and right side of the one drawn in the previous step. *(Pro-tip: hold **Shift** while drawing to make a straight vertical or horizontal line.) Image BB7.2*

Image BB7.2

3. Choose a fill color for the ground (I chose a light gray) and with the Paint Bucket Tool (**K**) selected, click on the interior of the shape created in the previous step to fill it. *Image BB7.3*

4. Name this layer "ground."

5. Create a new layer and name it "reference ball." *Image BB7.5*

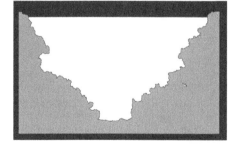

Image BB7.3

6. Open one of the previous work files like "bouncing ball 1 – timing" so that there are two project files open at the same time within Animate CC. You'll see the names of both files on tabs above the stage.

Image BB7.5

7. Click on the tab which has the project file we were working in before ("bouncing ball 7 – straight ahead") to return to it. *Image BB7.7*

Image BB7.7

8. In the library, there is a drop-down menu at the top which has the names of both project files open right now. Chose the previous work file ("bouncing ball 1 – timing") from that menu so that you can see its contents. *Image BB7.8*

Image BB7.8

9. Drag and drop the "ball" symbol from the library onto the upper-middle part of the main stage of the focused file which should be "bouncing ball 7 – straight ahead" and close the older work file ("... timing") by clicking the "X" on its tab. *Image BB7.9*

10. Choose the size you would like your ball to be relative to the environment on stage and resize it. You'll want enough room to play around with the bounces so I recommend making the ball 50% of its default size. *Image BB7.10*

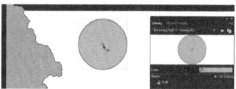

Image BB7.9

11. Create a new layer, and name this "ball rough." This layer is where you'll be drawing.

12. We need to pick a good amount of time for our sequence to play through. Around 4.5 seconds is enough, so extend the timeline out to frame 110. *Image BB7.12*

Image BB7.10

13. Chose the Brush Tool (**B**) and a good rough animating color like blue. *Image BB7.13*

Image BB7.12

14. Lock every layer except "ball rough" and turn the "reference ball" layer into a guide. You're ready to animate. *Image BB7.14*

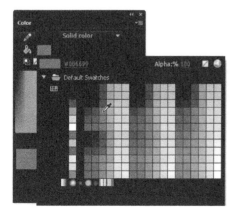

Image BB7.13

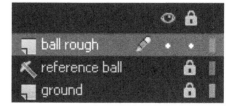

Image BB7.14

Now that we have our setting, what are we going to be doing with it? Two things … namely working through the animation using the two methods in this principle. We're starting with Straight Ahead Action. As mentioned in the Introduction, this method (out of the two present in the principle) is all about being dynamic and flowing from one part to another with no premeditation as to what exactly will happen, or how. There could be two obvious problems with this method. One, it's very easy to get carried away animating based solely on the frame before each one drawn that the

Image 7.4 In this visual example, the ball has seemingly shrunk in size from the first to the final bounce (compare the red highlighted sketches).

sequence can turn into a runaway game of telephone. To fix that, we keep a story point in our heads to remind us why we're animating this scene in the first place: "what's its purpose?" In our case, it's that the ball is bouncing around wildly and hectically on the rough terrain and ultimately comes to a natural rest. The second problem is that we can wander "off model." Wandering off model basically just means that the design (model) we start with doesn't match what we end with—like if our ball ends up inexplicably two sizes larger or smaller by the end of our sequence (a common problem). To stay on model we keep an instance of the ball symbol on stage for our reference—the one on the "reference ball" layer. We could've easily kept the instance of the ball in the work area offstage, but it's good to have it centered and still out of the way while we animate so that the reference is always clearly visible to us.

Unlike previously, we will not have any future keyframes to work toward. Don't get discouraged if the result isn't as smooth and perfect as you want. This first part is just a rough animation to work off. If you're attempting traditional, frame-by-frame-style animation for the first time, it may be an awkward experience. But we will clean up the rough animation you create using knowledge of principles covered so far in this book and the Animate CC tools at our disposal. What you want to focus on in this straight ahead rough animation is just putting what you have in your head down on screen as soon as you can. We've already set the stage, so here's a quick list of things to keep in mind about the other principles we've covered as you draw:

- **Timing:** how long it takes for the ball to complete its current bounce and how that relates to the other bounce that came before it (or might come after it).

- **Slow In/Out:** vertical movement will slow in on the way down and out on the way up; here, varying bouncing angles will change spacing in interesting ways and add texture.

- **Squash and Stretch:** stretch as the ball approaches, making contact right before the squash, and slow out a stretch on the rebound.

- **Anticipation:** some bounces are fast, others are slow; having a fast bounce followed by a long, high bounce can give the viewer time to anticipate what comes next.

- **Arcs:** each frame in a span should follow a smooth arc.

(Note: For those of you not drawing the following steps on a graphics tablet and moving around the "ball" symbol instead, don't worry about squash and stretch on the approaching frames, only on contact.)

15. First, make sure you turn on onion skinning and have it span three frames behind and three frames in front so that you'll be able to see how the images you'll be drawing relate to one another. *Image BB7.15*

Image BB7.15

16. Pick a spot to drop the ball on the left side of the stage. To really have fun, try to pick a spot that when it hits will bounce the ball hard to the right. We're going to draw the ball dropping straight down on this spot to start.

17. *Back on frame 1*, begin off frame directly above the spot you've picked to hit and quickly sketch the ball the same size as the ball on our reference layer. *Image BB7.17*

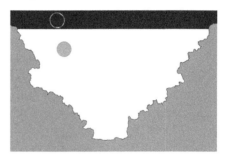

Image BB7.17

18. Hit **F7** on your keyboard to create a blank keyframe after the one you're on and shift the playhead on the timeline so that you're now on the new blank keyframe (which in this case should be on frame 2). *Image BB7.18*

Image BB7.18

19. Sketch the ball again. Considering that it's slowing while approaching the ground, make it lower than the previous one, and repeat the previous step. *Image BB7.19*

20. Continue in this way (sketch, **F7**) until you have made contact via squash with the surface of the ground. Remember that the fall is going to slow in and you should also gradually draw in a stretch to the ball as it approaches. *(Note: the terrain you drew may be different than mine so it may take longer or shorter for your sketch of the bouncing ball to reach the ground.)* *Image BB7.20*

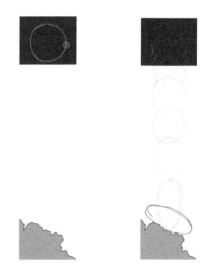

Image BB7.19   *Image BB7.20*

21. Now that the first drop is done, the rest of the animation can continue. Sketch a stretched out ball in the angle and distance from the squash that you want in order to leave the ground and start the next bounce span. *(Pro-tip: the more it angles to the right, the faster its horizontal velocity and the less the slope of the arc. Remember the ball is a projectile, so whatever horizontal velocity it starts with it must continue until changed by contact with something else.) Image BB7.21*

22. Using your knowledge of Timing, Slow In/Out, Squash and Stretch, and Arcs, continue roughing out the animation straight ahead until the ball comes to a natural stop. Each bounce will lose energy, so there shouldn't be much more than a few bounces. Visually test your timing after each sequence is roughed by quick-playing the timeline within Animate CC (**Enter**).

Image BB7.21

23. When this is done, check your arcs. A quick verification can be done with the onion skin mode covering the entire animation (or a selection of spans like in the accompanying image if it looks too cluttered to make out the arcs as one full image) and seeing if the arcs look smooth and well-spaced and have a convincing overall path. If there are any large size discrepancies in the ball from frame to frame, adjust where necessary. *Image BB7.23*

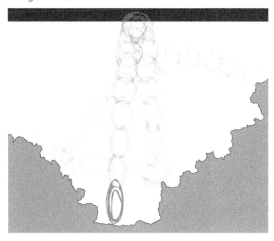

Image BB7.23

What most likely happened here after the logical progression of bounces you animated is that the ball came to a stop in the hole at the bottom of our valley. One of the products of straight ahead animation is that objects with no mind of their own and whose movements are only dictated by simple laws of physics (gravity, momentum, etc.) progress toward an end which seems obvious, even if the path wasn't. It's like if you were to actually drop a ball on a terrain like this, the smart bet would be that it would end up at the bottom of the valley, right? Basic life experience would tell us that. This is the *opposite* when dealing with conscious things, because the animator is choosing what will happen next on a frame-by-frame basis—playing the part of the animated thing's own mind.

Take a dance sequence, for example. While planning out the choreography pose to pose will give a more nuanced and specific performance, straight ahead action can flow and often lead to places and decisions even the animator didn't foresee. Similarly, this applies to certain other action scenes like a foot chase, fight, or even just fumbling around to pick up papers on a windy day. You will come up with new ideas as you progress through a scene when animating this way. It's spontaneous and dynamic and can give wonderfully fresh results in your movement. Animating straight ahead is a bit of a fly-by-the-seat-of-your-pants approach, though. Because of that unpredictability, one of Straight Ahead Action's main weaknesses is the inability to account for specificity, like perspective, a changing background element, or the need for precisely timed character acting. For these cases, we use the pose to pose method.

In this next section, we're going to be starting over and re-animating the ball bouncing around. However, this time we will choose an end point for our ball to rest on—one that would be very improbable if the ball actually was bouncing around randomly. We are choosing a specific ending and will be plotting out the way that it gets there.

Setting Up (Again)

We want to be able to explore this other technique without destroying the work we've already done so that later it will be easy to compare and contrast the two. By now, you know what to do. **Save As** another filename; this time "bouncing ball 7 – pose to pose." Rename the "ball rough" layer into "ball rough straight ahead," and then guide it and lock it. Finally, create another layer and call it "ball rough p2p" (p2p obviously referring to pose to pose).

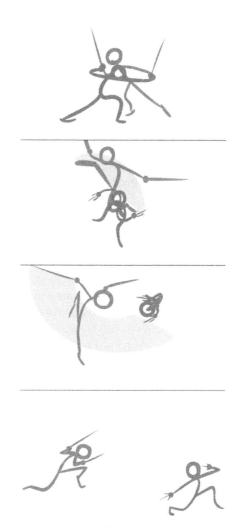

Image 7.5 Excerpts from the straight ahead rough animation of a martial arts fight (sequence progresses from top to bottom).

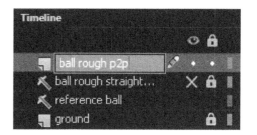

Image 7.6

24. We're going off from the same starting spot, so you can copy/paste in place the first frame from the "ball rough straight ahead" if you like (which would require unlocking momentarily in order to copy the image) or simply redraw it on frame 1. After this, make sure the "ball rough straight ahead" layer is locked and hidden (it should already be a guide layer since you did that in the setup right before this step).

25. Insert a blank keyframe (**F7**) at the end of our timeline on frame 110. *Image BB7.25*

Image BB7.25

26. Pick a spot for the ball to come to a rest and sketch a quick image of the ball there. I chose a nice little ledge on the right I had randomly drawn. This spot doesn't look like an obvious location for the ball to come to a rest, which will be visually interesting to see. *Image BB7.26*

Image BB7.26

27. Determine where you want the "contact squash" key which starts the last bounce. It's best to think of the last two bounces since it has to lose some horizontal velocity by hitting at a slight angle to land on our ledge just right.

28. Use timing and animation math to decide which frame it should go on (this can be adjusted later). I drew it at frame 104, which gives one-quarter of a second for the final little bounce. Use **F7** there and sketch in an appropriately squashed ball to the amount of energy needed to get the ball through the last bounce. *Image BB7.28*

Image BB7.28

29. On that same frame, plot the arc the ball should take. It doesn't need to be perfect, it's just a loose plan for now to get the height of the up position and a visual feel for the path. You can do this with the Line (**N**) or Brush (**B**) Tool; it's your choice. *(Pro-tip: the top of the arc has two paths away from it, these should be "leaving" the arc at the same angle.)* Image BB7.29

Image BB7.29

30. Do the same as in steps 27–29 to plot the second-to-last bounce. I chose nine frames back (to frame 95). *Image BB7.30*

Image BB7.30

31. *Back at the beginning* and on through, plot your contact frames with sketched arcs to ultimately connect the start sequence with the end. Use your mind as a simulator to imagine how the animation will play out as a whole and each bounce individually. Tapping to the beats of the bounces helps to get the timing out of your head for the approaching bounces. We will move the last couple bounce frames in the next step. *Image BB7.31*

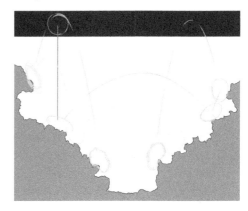

32. According to the timing you've chosen, at the moment the bounces should connect. Drag the last three keyframes back to match that timing. *Image BB7.32*

Image BB7.31

33. Now that all the contact keys and arcs are plotted, use the onion skin mode (as in step 23) to verify how your arcs connect and that they look good as a whole.

Image BB7.32

34. Use quick-play (**Enter** on the timeline) as a sort of digital pencil test to see how the timing you applied works out with what you had wanted and adjust the keyframes where necessary.

Interlude

Right now, we have a series of mapped-out arcs and contact keys. This moment is when illuminating a few terms in traditional animation will help make sense of the next steps.

- Extremes: frames where there is a significant change in direction.

- Breakdown: the transition point between extremes.

- Inbetween: the "fill in" frames between the rest.

The contact keys we have are extremes. But we're missing the "up" extreme. We're also missing the breakdowns. While in character animation breakdown frames are not always centered between extremes on the timeline, projectiles like our bouncing ball often are. In other words, if your starting contact is on frame 1 and your up frame is on 5, the breakdown will be on frame 3. If there's no perfect middle, pick one—this animation is just a planned rough, after all. The actual drawings on stage would be spaced according to slow in/out. Finally, we're obviously missing the inbetweens that connect these all together. To be honest, these aren't technically needed to clean up what we have right now. If you have the arc plotted out, it's just a matter of placing the ball on that line with a constant horizontal velocity. But (and this is a big "but"), the entire benefit of the pose to pose method is that the planning involved increases accuracy in your work and decreases the likelihood of making a mistake too far down the line. "Too far" in this case would be the cleanup phase. The arcs may look good right now, but if you jump to cleanup too fast it might become obvious only then that the arcs didn't play well with each other as a whole or a couple of contact positions were too far away, etc. Because it's a relatively simple object, not a lot of work would need to be redone to fix those kinds of problems in a bouncing ball. But in character animation, trying to rework an entire sequence of arcs and the timing of them would be disastrous.

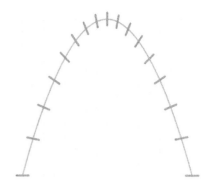

Image 7.7 The orange hatch lines on the blue arc show the ball's position on that path from frame to frame. The light grid in the background shows constant horizontal velocity and slow in/out vertically via line spacing.

Let's move forward with the pose to pose method in full. Keep in mind that if the ball lands higher than where it started, the up frame will be closer to the second contact on the timeline; the opposite is true for landing lower. To keep your timing and slow in/out on track, mentally work it out as if the arc started and ended on the same level. Hatch in some lines throughout the arc to represent the slow in/out of the ball if needed. Finally, as you work through each step, use onion skinning (adjust the span as necessary) and test and retest the animation to see how it's looking. There's no shame in not getting it perfect the first time—few do.

PART III
"Pose To Pose: Breakdowns and Inbetweens"

35. Working forward from the first bounce sequence (after the initial fall) and in a different color (I chose gray), we're going to place the "up" extreme between each "contact" extreme currently on the timeline. Remember, if the end position is higher, the "up" keyframe will be closer to that end contact frame on the timeline (and vice versa). *Image BB7.35*

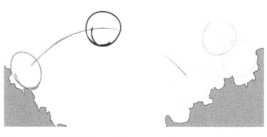

Image BB7.35 (Note: Screengrabs up to BB7.37 are from Flash CS6 to show separate frames with different colors as they are.)

36. With all the extremes on the stage, draw in the breakdowns. For "unconscious

movement" like projectiles, they are centered between the extremes on the timeline (meaning, they are separated by the same number of frames). Accounting for slow in/out in the bouncing ball, the breakdown will always be *drawn* closer to the up position (unless the arc is essentially flat in which case it'll be more centered). *Image BB7.36*

Image BB7.36

37. Now are the inbetweens. Rough one span to completion at a time, and use onion skinning to help account for slow in/out. Draw an inbetween halfway between the existing frames; then draw one again between those frames and so on. Continue in this fashion until all that is left is to inbetween the inbetweens. Because there can only ever be spans with an odd or

Image BB7.37

even number of frames; you'll never need to "straight ahead" more than two inbetweens, which keeps things relatively manageable. *Image BB7.37*

38. Animate straight-ahead for the final little bounces. These are just the little vibration-like jumps as the ball is losing its last bit of kinetic energy.

If you have never done inbetweening before, those steps were probably frustratingly few. There is a reason for simplifying the steps, though. Going step by step through a program's features or the conceptual learning of a principle of movement requires a lot of explanation, while working through an animation method involves more personal discovery. You should now have an understanding of what makes these two approaches different, and what the benefits are to each. There is no best method between the two in general, but there can be on a shot-by-shot basis. Straight ahead is excellent when you want something wacky, chaotic, or just a feel of being unplanned and spontaneous. Pose to pose is what is needed for a more subtle and calculated touch.

People will have slightly different reasons for why they choose more of one or the other. Not to oversimplify, but many people who just want to see their images move will wander into a more straight ahead approach while those looking for refinement will usually lean more toward a pose-to-pose-heavy method. Too much adherence to either method will result in the animation looking repetitive, stiff, or both. To discover what works best for you and in which cases, you're just going to have to animate ... a lot! There's not much difference between what you just did and animating on paper—a couple of efficiency hotkeys and the ability to undo (Cmd/**Ctrl+Z**), really. What this book is about, though, is the merging of the principles with Animate CC; so if the methods haven't changed much so far, what else is brought to the table? Cleanup.

CLOSER LOOK
Cleanup

Cleanup animation is exactly what it sounds like. This process is where we take the rough drawings and turn them into final frame-by-frame illustrations. Animate CC; helps a great deal not only in making it easy for us to maintain our character on model, but also by giving us the means by which to adjust every detail of the frame if need be. If you have drawn a nose, eyes, and mouth as separate objects, they can be slightly nudged around to achieve subtle facial animation. If those features are symbols, they could even be tweened and resized to make a difficult move into a precise, seemingly multi-dimensional head turn. If you're following along as described in this book's Introduction and haven't worked through the real-world sections yet, you will see an example of this at the end of Chapter 1.

In the case of our bouncing ball example, we have a symbol that we'll mostly be moving around stage by hand. The rough animation that we've done using both methods will serve as the blueprint for where we'll put the ball and how it needs to be transformed. You have already tested the timing and placement, adjusted for slow in/out and squash and stretch, and verified your arcs using rough animation. Now it's a matter of refining this animation even further using symbol tweens, perfect line tool arcs for reference, and the transformation panel to make sure we don't deviate from the model too far.

We're going to clean up both roughs. Since we'll wind up with one file by the time we're finished, you will have more layers on one timeline than we've had before (in the bouncing ball exercises). It's about time to start getting used to working with an increasing number of layers; we'll be using layers a lot more down the road. First, we'll clean up the straight ahead roughs. Save the current document as "bouncing ball 7 – straight ahead – cleanup." Create a new layer, name it "ball cleanup straight ahead," and copy/paste the symbol from the "reference ball" layer to it. This is the first time that the bouncing ball exercises have shown that multiple instances of a symbol can be on stage at any given time, which makes everything from bookshelves to crowd scenes so much more manageable. Everything except the "ground," "ball rough straight ahead," and "ball cleanup straight ahead" layers should be guided, locked, and hid. Of the three layers, "ground" should be the only one that is locked. Now let's get to work.

Image 7.8 Multiple symbol instances on stage helps create a tiled wall. Grouping tile instances into a larger symbol, also seen here, makes it even easier.

> "Multiple instances of a symbol can be on stage at any given time, which makes everything from bookshelves to crowdscenes so much more manageable."

"Cleanup: Straight Ahead"

1. We'll start out with a tween—the first drop. Move the ball you put on the "ball cleanup straight ahead" layer to the first "up" position you sketched on the "ball rough straight ahead," insert a keyframe at the frame with the "contact stretch" rough you drew, match the ball and stretch with the "ball" symbol, and then tween that span. Make sure to have the span slow in (easing value of −100). *Image CL7.1*

2. Insert a keyframe after the "contact stretch" and create the squash needed as indicated by your rough. Keep an eye on the proportions in the Transformation panel. Keep in mind that in order to keep the same volume, the two percentages should add up to 100 (since we started by shrinking the ball to half its size in step 10 in "setting the stage"). *Image CL7.2*

3. Insert another layer and name it "horizontal velocity ref." What we do with this layer in the following steps will act as our simple reference to keep each bounce traveling across the stage at a constant horizontal speed.

4. Insert yet another layer and name it "arc." We'll be making all the refined arcs here.

5. Using the Line Tool (**N**), draw a horizontal line starting from the center of the squashed ball but on the layer "arc". *Image CL7.5*

6. Scroll ahead in the timeline until you see the contact stretch frame which ends the first bounce sequence.

7. Press **Cmd/Ctrl** to get the Quick Selection Tool so that you can click and drag the other end of the line created in step 5 to meet the middle of the contact stretch found in step 6. *Image CL7.7*

8. Scroll back in the timeline to the "up" position in this sequence.

9. Click and drag (using selection) from anywhere and pull up and left/right as needed until the top

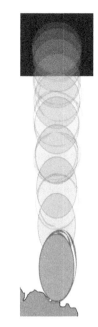

Image CL7.1

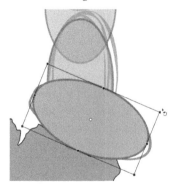

Image CL7.2

Image CL7.5

Image CL7.7

of the arc is centered in the ball from step 8. *Image CL7.9*

10. Use onion skin mode to check your reference arc with the one you made using straight ahead. How did you do? Turn off onion skin when you're done for the next step. *Image CL7.10*

11. Back on the squash frame in this sequence, create a blank keyframe (**F7**) on the "horizontal velocity ref" layer and copy/paste in place the squashed ball from the "ball cleanup straight ahead" layer to it.

12. Skip ahead to the stretch key referred to in step 6 and create a keyframe (**F6**) on the "horizontal velocity ref" layer.

13. Drag the ball over to the "contact stretch" and line the two centers together. *Image CL7.13*

14. Create a tween on "horizontal velocity ref" with no easing so that it is moving at a constant speed from left to right. *Image CL7.14*

15. Lock every layer except "ball cleanup straight ahead" and make sure that the "Snap to Objects" feature is enabled in the toolbar.

16. Momentarily hide the "horizontal velocity ref" layer, create a keyframe (**F6**) after the squash frame on "ball cleanup straight ahead," and apply stretch and rotation to the ball symbol appropriately. Unhide the "horizontal velocity ref" layer before moving on to the next step. *Image CL7.16*

17. Click and drag the newly stretched symbol to the right until it lines up vertically with

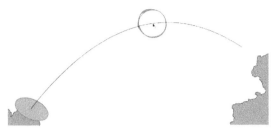

Image CL7.9

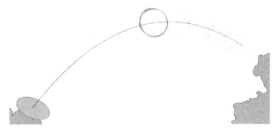

Image CL7.10

Image CL7.13

Image CL7.14

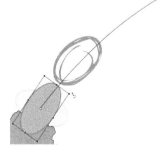

Image CL7.16

the ball's position on the "horizontal velocity ref" layer and it also is snapped to the arc at the center. *Image CL7.17*

18. Hit **F6** again (creating another keyframe on the "ball cleanup straight ahead" layer), reduce the amount of stretch, and repeat step 17. *Image CL7.18*

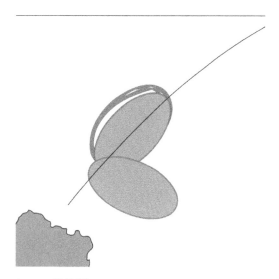

Image CL7.17

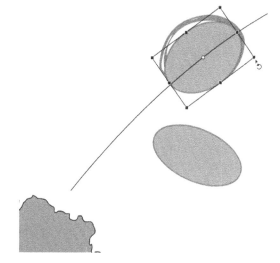

Image CL7.18

19. Continue in this fashion (steps 5–18) until the rest of the span is complete. *Image CL7.19*

20. Now that you're at the next squash frame, insert a blank keyframe (**F7**) on the "arc" and "horizontal velocity ref" layers (since the new bounce will need a new arc and horizontal movement references), then insert a keyframe (**F6**) on the cleanup layer and match the squash you sketched in the straight ahead rough. *Image CL7.20*

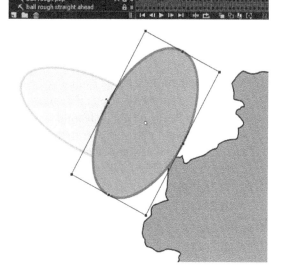

Image CL7.19

Image CL7.20

21. Repeat steps 5–20 for all the following bounces until the animation is complete. *Image CL7.21*

22. When you get to the final small bounces, use your knowledge of principles thus far and use straight ahead action for the cleanup by dragging the ball around to jitter to a stop.

23. Guide the "arc" and "horizontal velocity ref" layers (so they won't show up upon export).

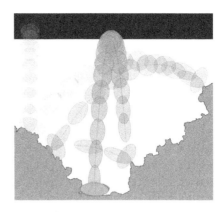

Image CL7.21

That's cleanup, according to the needs and specifications given to us by this scene. You could go another mile in accuracy and allow Animate CC to do the easing on your squash and stretch as well. To set it up for Animate CC to do that, you would apply this principle to three keyframes (rebound stretch, "up," and contact stretch), include rotation, tween with appropriate easing between them, then turn the entire tween to keyframes, remove tween on those frames, and complete step 17 as written for each of those keyframes. There are so many ways to clean up animation within Animate CC. It's all about knowing the tools and their abilities to put them to proper use. But we haven't yet done the cleanup for the pose to pose rough. **Save As** "bouncing ball 7 – pose to pose – cleanup," create a new layer and name it "ball cleanup p2p," and make sure everything except the "ground," "ball rough p2p," and "ball cleanup p2p" layers are guided, locked, and hidden.

"Cleanup: Pose To Pose"

24. Follow steps 1–23 in "Cleanup: Straight Ahead," and adjust for layer names. Optionally, use the squash and stretch reference tween method described in the preceding paragraph. *Image CL7.24*

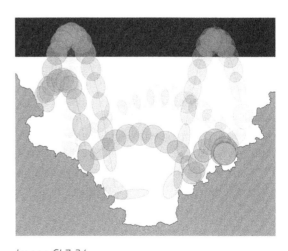

Image CL7.24

The needs of the scene dictate how we clean up in Animate CC. What we're dealing with here is a ball that bounces according to simple laws of motion, and for that animation all that was really needed was the path, distance traveled, and duration. The rough animation was used as a way to map these out. But it was also a teaching moment to get used to the feeling of rough animation in Animate CC by using its tools and hotkeys. Character animation is the ultimate goal here, and for that we need to know how to manipulate symbols, use the timeline, and sketch roughs and paths confidently within the program. All of that needs to happen while also taking into account a multitude of principles.

Drawing out a rough for something that could've just been animated right after plotting a few arcs around a stage may seem redundant, and for this particular scenario you would be correct. But let's take the common walk-cycle as an example. A lot of a character's personality can be infused into their walk-cycle. Walking is a conscious, deliberate series of movements and which *type* of walk a character employs requires a consideration of its personality and performance. That being said, much of what happens *within* a walk is done with unconscious, inanimate-like movements. Swinging of the arms, dragging the feet forward, a loose spike of hair flopping up and down with every step—these all can be easily plotted and virtually finished with symbols without so much as a single rough, using much the same process as we did in the cleanup phase in this closer look section. As a matter of fact, almost every facet of a walk seems like an involuntary motion only existing because of it being chained to another. But to separate and remove these "mindless" movements from each other and animating them as such would take away the soul of the overall walk.

Image 7.9 This walk-cycle is cleaned up with a combination of frame-by-frame animation and symbol tweening (instances are highlighted in the bottom frame).

Even though a walk can be broken up into its parts, there is an emergent property when addressing it as a whole: personality. This is where being able to rough out movement as complicated as a walk in its entirety is so valuable. Believe it or not, having the ability to hand animate a ball bouncing around on stage when all these tools are at your disposal is the exact ability that will allow you to infuse personality into your animation. Helping you develop this ability is one of the many reasons the bouncing ball exercise exists in the first place, and why in this book we started with the tools to animate. Now you know what is possible with the tools, know how the layered movement can be used to create a completely different motion, and are beginning to put it together with hand animating. The question of "why draw everything if Animate can tween?" is being answered now.

Using Straight Ahead Action and Pose to Pose With "Compartmentalization"

Character animation shouldn't be split up into its parts when initially roughing out the scene; that's true. The risk of losing the spirit of the movement to the minutia of physics is too great. But that's not to discourage you from separating a larger movement into smaller, more manageable chunks, though, only to highlight when the appropriate time for this distribution is. For instance, usually storyboards are done before animation starts. These are images that map out the visual story beats. After that, they get turned into an animatic, which looks a bit like a motion comic where the storyboards are displayed and often moved around on screen in time. The goals of both the storyboard and animatic are very close, but they focus on different things: visual representation of a theme or concept and the display of that information in time (respectively). The trick is to start with the most generalized goal and whittle down through each process in the workflow until the last step is fine tuning the smallest details in your animation.

So what would be an appropriate workflow when actually animating? A quick rundown of the steps would look like this: thumbnails, rough, tiedown, and finally cleanup. Thumbnails are tiny sketches drawn to help work out what you want to do in your animation. They are small so that you don't get caught up in detail but can address the overall gesture and silhouette of the form. Because they're so quickly drawn, there is no fear on the part of the creator to immediately throw away any images that aren't working to support the scene. You already know the rough, tiedown, and cleanup terms as they came up previously in this chapter. The rough basically takes the thumbnails, draws them bigger with a bit more detail in form, and fills in some more of the essential frames; the tiedown tightens up those drawings; and the cleanup finalizes them. Each step is about improving the look and content of the previous one. This incremental process is the compartmentalization of a workflow.

Image 7.10 Sequential storyboards can be very loosely sketched on sticky notes which I call "stickyboarding" (top), detailed drawings on paper (bottom), or anything in between.

You want to start with acting as a whole within rough animation and then work down to the finer details. How to do either or both of those steps is where the battle between the Straight Ahead vs. Pose to Pose crowd comes in. Some feel that it's better to use straight ahead action in a scene first to get the instant feel of the acting, while others like to start with pose to pose so that all the beats which need to be hit are accounted for first. Whichever method you use, when the acting is worked out, the specifics of the movement can be finetuned. A walk-cycle can technically be addressed by animating the legs first and then roughing the body, arms, and finally the head—but why? How much acting will you be able to accomplish this way? In pose to pose, if those main poses (keys) are ironed in first, by the time you get to the breakdowns there is enough visual information there to work back over the details of the arcs, slow in/out, etc., in order to finish the rough with correctly applied movement principles. Likewise, straight ahead can lay the groundwork for fantastically uninhibited acting which can be maintained while fixing some mistakes in the motions that make up the whole without changing it. You will discover which works best for you, but both are usually utilized in some form or another in the same scene (i.e. keys/extremes via pose to pose, then straight ahead between them). The best workflow will address the whole, then refine and return back to verify that the entire scene maintained its original story and acting goals.

REAL-WORLD EXAMPLE
"Toilet Paper Shoe"

Principles Used

Overlapping Action: This principle could be the star of the show which is why it's listed first—it's obvious. Our character walks into screen with a line of toilet paper stuck to his shoe. Every time he moves his leg, the toilet paper flaps about with overlapping action.

Secondary Action: As the character tries to remove the unwanted item from his shoe, he's not completely efficient with it; if he were, it wouldn't be funny or interesting. As he's wiggling his foot to shake the toilet paper off, the secondary action you choose will communicate to the audience if he is nervous, annoyed, angry, or whatever else you might think of.

Solid Drawing: Stiff movements result in mostly cold feelings. To get a vibrant reaction from the audience, the movement should look the part. When our character moves about, keeping him on model lets the viewer get sucked in to the world.

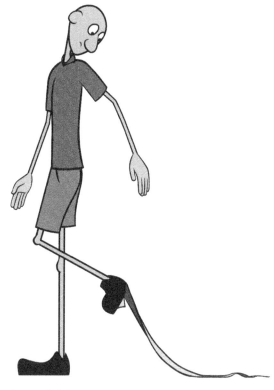

Image 7.11

Timing: Specifically, we're talking about comedic timing. During the rough animation phase, doing quick tests will be essential to nailing the timing of the keys down.

Staging: It's safe to say that any pantomimed action needs to be staged well in order to work. The poses for the hop-kick will need to be clear because a lot will be going on. The toilet paper shouldn't get too bunched up for very long throughout the scene for the same reason.

Pose to Pose/Straight Ahead: The reason this principle is highlighted here is that it's a perfect example of the strengths between these two methods. Most of the character's movements will be pose to pose, if not all—while the toilet paper will be animated straight ahead. They are connected, and both aid in the storytelling of the scene but are best animated in different ways because of their features.

Setting Up

Open the project file provided on the companion website titled "ch7-real_world-tp_shoe.fla" and have a look around. You'll find a turnaround model sheet provided for you which is actually made up of the different frames in the character pack. The turnaround model sheet (or just "turnaround" for short) shows you the various angled views of the character as it makes a 360-degree spin and the proportionate dimensions of the features. This is in the work area off-stage at all times and will be used to stay on model during the rough as you animate your character sometimes rotating in perspective. The character pack which makes up the turnaround is there for you to use as a starting place for your cleanup frames. Essentially, the work to be done during cleanup will be a combination of the "Golf Swing" from Chapter 6 and the "Pitching a Bomb" from Chapter 4. The visual information of the character is provided, as well as a collection of features in different perspectives.

Another thing you might have already noticed is that there are no numbered steps in this example. You have all the information needed to complete this scene without a step-by-step walk-through, so what we'll be doing this time is looking at it in broader terms … not in technical terms. If you have any difficulty following along, the work has already been done in the different stages and put onto the companion website for your reference and ease of exploration. First, we'll take a moment and explore the character pack.

"The Character Pack"

When you first double-click into the character pack symbol, you'll notice that there are eight frames and that these are the turnaround poses: front, 3/4 left, profile left, 5/4 left, back, 5/4 right, profile right and 3/4 right (*Image TP7.1*). The features of the character are distributed across named layers (with a * preceding the name for each feature which is a symbol that can be classically tweened). Some frames on various layers have nothing on them because the features change their arrangement of what's in front and in back of other features during the turnaround.

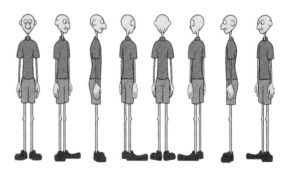

Image TP7.1

If you enter any one of those symbols, you'll notice that it's set up much the same way as the character as a whole: one frame for each angle of the turnaround. The head, hand, and foot symbols display this most obviously. So in the character pack we have these differently angled views of features nested within symbols the same way as we've nested animation thus far which allows us to switch between angled views of features independently of the angled view of another. Using nesting in this way means that if you need reference for a pose where the body is facing front and the head is turned at 3/4, you can essentially "make" it by breaking the front view (frame 1) of the character pack apart and then changing the frame number of the head instance to frame 2 (which is the 3/4 view).

For complicated movements, character packs like this one are mostly best used as references— but for simpler movements, especially those which don't change perspective much, these can be used to expedite the cleanup process by tweening the features around like we did to the puppet in Chapter 6's real-world section (such as will be the case for the initial walk-cycle). TV shows utilize character packs in their pipelines to keep everyone on the same page. You might be asking, "If I can use the character pack as a turnaround reference, why does the turnaround model sheet layer even need to be there?" The turnaround model sheet layer is for your quick reference when sketching in the rough animation. It is faster when you are drawing everything by hand to have each angled pose right there at your fingertips without having to change frames or enter any symbols in order to view them. This process is the way it has been done for decades in traditional animation, and the technique is just as sound as always. When it comes time to clean up the animation, being able to basically take the turnaround model sheet information and actually pose it around on stage as I mentioned in the previous paragraph can speed up the process, since accuracy and precision are important at the cleanup phase.

"Roughing The Walk"

There is no shortage of information out there on animating a walk-cycle. It is one of the most common first steps for a character animator, and because it's a loop it's easy to make great progress quickly— that's appealing to beginners. Because of this flood of information, it can be seen as just a beginner's exercise. But the fact is that an amazing amount of information can be communicated through a walk. It's not just about getting from point "a" to point "b." It's about having a quiet opportunity to reinforce to your audience what the character is thinking and feeling consciously or subconsciously. The method for animating a standard walk, off which you can branch any walk, isn't much different than the way you animate a bouncing ball using the pose to pose method.

- **Contact (key)**: for the bouncing ball, this key was the "contact stretch." For a walk, it's the moment the lead foot *just* touches the ground.

- **Passing (key)**: similar to the bouncing ball's "up," the passing key is the uppermost position where one foot is directly under the character and the other is swinging from behind the body to the front ... it's passing by.

- **Cushion**: the "squash" for the bouncing ball plays this part. For the body, this "squash" is shown as overlapping action acting as a cushion for the impact. After the heel makes contact with the ground, the toe is in the air and the knee is still basically straight; the following frame (or couple) needs to exhibit a cushion where the foot finally lays flat and the knee bends slightly to absorb the impact.

- **Breakdowns**: self-explanatory, these are the halfway points on the timeline and are demonstrating Slow In/Out, Arcs, and Overlapping Action in the roughs.

Sketch in the rough animation of the character walking on stage using pose to pose. Don't worry about the toilet paper. We'll do that later. Most importantly we want to have a normal walk where our character is unaware of any stowaway on his shoe until he reaches the middle of the stage. Start with the contact position just off screen and repeat that pose ahead a couple times on new keyframes while connecting the feet positions like a chain until our character is around center stage (*Image TP7.2a*). Space these keyframes out evenly with the timing you chose for the walk. Halfway between the contact keys goes the passing key (*Image TP7.2b*). You now have the skeleton of the walk. I would wait until later to finish the rough for the walking sequence because we want to add some secondary action to this walk.

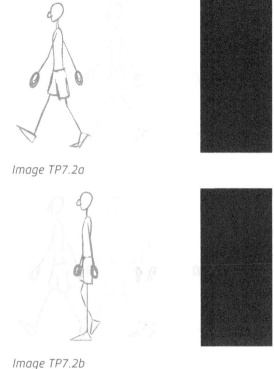

Image TP7.2a

Image TP7.2b

"The Double Take"

A classic! The double take is a time-honored method of showing comedic surprise. We'll be implementing it as a secondary action during the walk which makes him stop his strut and turn the primary action of moving across the stage to trying to kick off the toilet paper. First we're going to set up the reason for the look down in the first place. Let's assume he's walking out of the restroom and there wasn't enough paper towels so he's going to dry off one of his hands by wiping it up and down his shirt. He will have just finished by the last step so we start by sketching the arm with its secondary action across all the steps currently shown. On a new layer or using Object Draw (J), rough in this wiping motion with the character's left hand over the course of the steps it took to get to the last contact position. Erase the left arm roughs you had drawn earlier since this new secondary action we're adding is replacing them (*Image TP7.3a*).

Now we'll address the double take and the final "I see toilet paper on my shoe" pose. Since the last contact pose the character is back to stride, the contact before that is where he leans over to

Image TP7.3a

Image TP7.3b

finish wiping his hand and turns his head to look at the result. I leaned his head toward the camera at a 3/4 view for this pose. To complete the look, I have him looking down from the front view on the last passing position (after the contact we just edited). The final contact pose is where he's returned his head looking in the direction he's walking but the right arm is obscured by the body instead of swung back as it should be because of his left arm's position and where we want the final pose to end up. This final pose is *after* the last contact key and it depicts him looking directly at the toilet paper he thought he saw last time (*Image TP7.3b*). This pose will also serve as an anticipatory beat.

"Hop-Kick"

Now that our character is about halfway across the stage and has noticed the toilet paper on his left shoe (not yet applied in the rough animation), we want him to turn around and hop-kick himself off screen while he's trying to remove it. The weight is on the front foot now, so he'll be pivoting on that while kicking the toilet-papered foot away. Ultimately we need to be in a high-kick pose while hopping off the ground. From here, you just need to create one hop-kick animation ending at the same high-kick pose in order to create a loop to move backward off-stage.

Remember that solid drawing is very important in these actions to show not only dimension, but also weight. This hop-kick motion he's doing backward while moving off screen can be achieved very well with straight ahead action. If you absolutely know what you want to do and need a certain amount of control to dictate each movement, you'll need pose to pose. But to keep the action spontaneous and "zany," straight ahead action is the way to go. He should do approximately the same number of hops as he did steps—so about three or four. The whole scene I ended up with was a little less than 6 seconds which you can see in the FLA on the companion website to this book.

Image TP7.4a and b First couple of kicks are weak and provide an opportunity to pivot (top). The hop-kick loop is more intense and allows us to tween the final looping symbol backward off-stage (bottom).

"Toilet Paper"

Finally, let's add the toilet paper. It's best to do this part on another layer in another color. If you did rough animation in blue, using red for the overlapping action is a good and clear choice. There's not much to say about this rough animation that wouldn't be repeating. You'll be roughing the action out straight ahead following arcs and

Image TP7.5 Rough pass (left) treats the toilet paper like a string to nail down movement. Tiedown pass (right) adds dimension to the movement.

subjecting the overlapping action and follow through (covered in the next chapter, if you are working through the real-world examples linearly) to slow in and out. Remember that the toilet paper is so thin that it's seemingly 2D. A good way to approach this sequence is to first animate the toilet paper as though it were a string to get the movement and flow to a place that's working for you.

When you have the general movement roughed in, return to your character rough and complete it further to give more information to your toilet paper animation sequence. Further completing the character rough would be adding in the cushion and breakdown poses for the walk we skipped earlier and inbetweening some of the frames between the hop-kicks. With this done, you can then add believability to the sequence by applying the principle of Solid Drawing to the toilet paper and show it twisting from time to time. That solid drawing pass could be considered the toilet paper's tiedown pass since you are redrawing it with a focus on nailing down the motion better, with more detail to the form.

"Cleanup"

As mentioned, this cleanup phase will be a combination of the work done in the real-world examples of Chapters 4 and 6. The walk is cleaned up quite well using the method outlined in Chapter 6 with the puppet this time using the character pack, while the "hop-kick" is best finished the way we did in Chapter 4 in which "easies" are tweened and "problems" are frame-by-frame. The character pack can and should be used whenever possible and appropriate to help keep you on model throughout the frame-by-frame work. Clean up the character animation first and then make another cleanup pass for the toilet paper. When all is said and done, check your staging with the silhouette test you did in Chapter 6. Again, looking at the completed FLA on the companion website can help give you an idea of how to complete your own.

Image TP7.6 Some features are symbols and ready to be tweened while others need shape tweens or frame-by-frame animation.

On Making Our Lives Easier

There are so many ways a scene like this can be approached from an acting standpoint. You, as the animator, choose the one that makes sense for the character and help it to act on the paper. You're a director, an acting coach, and when necessary a critic to the character. You give it life, but it's the one that is acting directly for the audience. At its core, a character animator's responsibility is to tell the character what to do, when, and how. Pose to pose allows for specific acting and subtle connections to be made with the audience, while straight ahead keeps things unexpected when they need to be. We're building a world for the characters, not for us. So when you choose to use one of these methods, it's not always motivated by making things easy on the animator but by what the needed result is for the character animation in this moment: specificity or spontaneity.

FINAL WORDS
Straight Ahead Action and Pose to Pose

Any way you slice it, character animation should start with drawings. They don't have to be beautiful; they have to be functional. And really, unless you're working at a studio or as part of a group where someone will be using your roughs for cleanup, they only have to be functional to *you*. You might be surprised how many animators will rough out a movement using glorified stick figures before anything else. Stripping away the pretense of design just leaves the raw movement to use in acting. Too much animation seems to be reliant on facial acting—which is to say, "dialog." Animators often call this "talking head" animation because there isn't a lot of acting happening on the part of the gestures or movement, just a lot of talking. It saves money but doesn't do much visually. When using straight ahead and pose to pose within Animate CC, it should be done with sketching.

Up to this point, we have started with an idea of what motion we wanted and went right on to making that happen with absolutely no rough animation. First of all, we could jump right in because the animation was that of a simple projectile, the bouncing ball. Through it, you learned the tools and features of Animate CC, as well as the concept behind the principles of movement. But now that this knowledge has been acquired, rough animation utilizing the two methods in this chapter's principle should be used. We will start by applying this principle to the workflow of the bouncing ball in the next chapter on Follow Through and Overlapping Action.

Image 8.0 From left to right, the first couple of images
show the cape with Overlapping
Action while the last exhibits Follow Through.

Chapter 8

FOLLOW THROUGH AND OVERLAPPING ACTION

INTRODUCING
Follow Through and Overlapping Action

Slow In and Slow Out, Squash and Stretch, and last chapter's Straight Ahead Action and Pose to Pose all have something in common; they are complimentary opposites. In each case, these dual principles can be considered bookends to each other. Actually, one-third of all the principles of animation are actually made up of pairings. But of these, Follow Through and Overlapping Action are the most confused with one another. Many animators use them interchangeably or even mix them up with the subject of the next chapter, Secondary Action. This confusion is because unlike something like Squash and Stretch, which are very clearly opposites, Follow Through and Overlapping Action are more like variations on a theme.

To clarify their meaning, it's probably easiest to explain what overlapping action is first since it informs what a follow through is. Overlapping Action is when two movements on the same body happen at different rates, and Follow Through is where something continues to move after a body has come to a stop. An example of overlapping would be long hair starting to fall a couple of frames after a head does because they're paired together but move semi-independently of one another. Follow through would be a trench coat continuing to flow forward before coming back to a natural position after a man stops running. The effects are based on Newton's first law of motion where an object in motion tends to stay that way (momentum), and likewise for rest (inertia).

> "Overlapping Action is when two movements on the same body happen at different rates, and Follow Through is where something continues to move after a body has come to a stop."

In this chapter, we're going to be applying last chapter's principle to doing rough animation for an addition to our bouncing ball. We're adding a tail. The most common way you will encounter overlapping in your day-to-day animation will be in hair, clothing, and extremities (arms, legs, what have you ...). The same items to have overlapping action applied to them in one scene will be the ones to have a follow through applied to them when the whole comes to a rest. This sequence of events will be exemplified in our tail for the bouncing ball exercise; it will be plotted through rough sketches first and then cleaned up. Think of this chapter's principle as being the one that's mainly applied to the supporting features of a body's movement. So while we have a good handle on bouncing a ball (the main body), we will now apply the same principles *plus* this one for the tail (supporting feature).

BOUNCING BALL
Follow Through And Overlapping Action

Setting Up

Image 8.1

The overall goal of the exercise in this chapter is to make a tail drag behind our bouncing ball for a couple of bounces until the ball comes to a sudden stop, whipping the tail around in front of it. We will be using pose to pose for the normal overlapping rough animation for the tail during the bounces and straight ahead for when the tail follows through with its momentum after the ball comes to a stop.

The best place to continue from would be our "bouncing ball 5 – arcs" project. **Save As** "bouncing ball 8 – overlapping," since that's the first part of this principle that we will cover. On the main timeline, create a new layer called "tail rough," name the one with the bouncing ball on it "ball" and lock it. Click and drag the "tail rough" layer so that it's below the "ball" layer. Remember that for the rough animation, it's best if you use the Brush Tool (**B**) for that natural feel, but you *can* use the Pencil Tool (**Shift+Y**).

Overlapping action of items that are not attached to the body (coats, skirt, etc.) are often roughed in red in traditional animation to keep them visually different than the blue usually associated with character roughs. You will often see this color scheme applied in Animate CC as well, but it's simply a carryover from traditional, pencil/paper animation and not a rule that needs to be followed. You could rough in purple, forest green, fuchsia … it doesn't much matter as long as it can be seen and isn't too overpowering so that when it comes time to clean up you can visually tune out the rough when need be without having to actually hide the layer. The color change is about speed and efficiency, not necessity.

PART I
"Overlapping Action—Rough Pose to Pose"

1. Working on the "tail rough" layer, scroll ahead on the timeline to the first "contact stretch" you see on the stage, insert a keyframe (**F6**), and sketch a tail stretched out at the angle of approach (diagonal) to the ground. As the ball was falling, it was dragging the tail with it. This is the moment of highest speed, so it's the most stretched out. *Image BB8.1*

2. Create a keyframe (**F6**) for the next "contact stretch" and either **Shift+arrow** or **Shift+drag** to reconnect the tail with the ball's new position. *Image BB8.2*

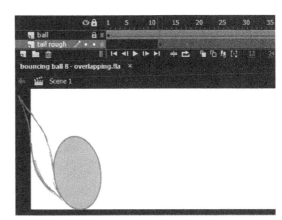

Image BB8.1

3. At the "rebound stretch" frame after the first contact (frame 14), insert a blank keyframe (**F7**) and draw the tail flat on the ground with the base of the tail very slightly curved up a bit to meet the ball. This frame is the first time you clearly see the overlapping action in this exercise. The tail was dragged behind the ball in step 2, and here it is contacting (squashing, if you like) the ground after the ball is already leaving … always trailing behind when the ball is in constant forward motion. *(Note: I made the contact with the "ground" higher*

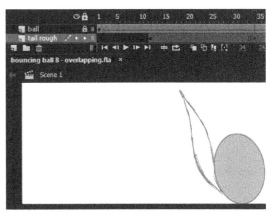

Image BB8.2

for the tail than the ball to give the illusion that the tail is farther back into perspective.) Image BB8.3

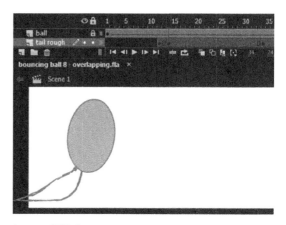

4. Repeat step 2 for the sketch drawn in step 3 for the corresponding frame and position.

5. Insert a blank keyframe on the "tail rough" layer at the "up" position and draw the tail as though it had just been dragged up to the top at an angle. Remember, the base of the tail will be higher because it's connected to the ball. The tip of the tail is dragging behind it, so it will be curved down, pointing at the contact point the ball made with the ground at its "squash" frame. You can use onion skin mode to help draw the correct position. *Image BB8.5*

Image BB8.3

6. To get a proper arc for the next steps, we need to draw one more defining key for our overlapping action. Insert a blank keyframe on the frame *after* the ball's "rebound stretch" and sketch the tail following the ball on the way up. The tail should be long enough where even though

Image BB8.5 (Note: Screengrabs up to Bb8.12 are using Flash CS6 onion skin mode to show each frame in its own color.)

Image BB8.6

the ball is off the ground, the tip of the tail isn't. Since the end tip is being dragged forward due to the ball's horizontal velocity, the whole tail will be a bit "S" shaped. *Image BB8.6*

7. Repeat step 2 for the sketch drawn in step 6 for the corresponding frame and position.

8. Create another layer and name it "tail arc." Scrolling through the roughs, put a dot at the end tip of the tail on this new layer (without adding new keyframes). *(Note: to make things easier on you, skip making a dot for the first "contact stretch." Start at the frame where the tail is flat on the ground, since this frame is its "down" position.) Image BB8.8*

Image BB8.8

9. The one piece of info you don't have in these dots is the highest point the tip of the tail will get to. Go to the "up" frame and draw a little horizontal line at the point where the base of the tail connects to the ball. *Image BB8.9*

10. Hide every layer but "tail arc," and play connect the dots by making an arc from the first lowest dot to the highest point (line in step 9) and back down to the last dot. By making a smooth arc, it should look like half a heart (where it has been tipped on its right side). *Image BB8.10*

Image BB8.9

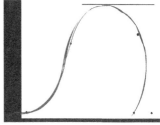

Image BB8.10

11. Unhide every layer and make sure that "ball" and "tail arc" are locked to work back on "tail rough."

12. Create blank keyframes at the two breakdown positions (halfway between the "contact stretch" and "up" keys) and sketch the tails so that the tip follows the arc and the base follows the ball. The first should look like one open quote mark, and the second should look like an eyebrow (I drew them in blue so that you can distinguish them in the image). *Image BB8.12*

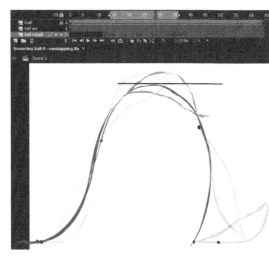

Image BB8.12

13. The final rough needed for our purposes before cleanup is an inbetween at the ball's "squash" key. To get the right path for the tail tip, copy the arc drawn in step 10 and move it back so that the start and end points connect on the "tail arc" layer. Use the Free Transform Tool (Q) with **Shift** to adjust the size of the arc proportionally until the height reaches the first "up" frame's height (the one like in step 9). *Image BB8.13*

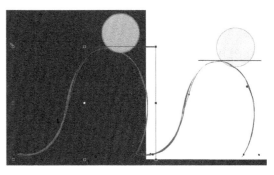

Image BB8.13

14. Back on "tail rough" draw the inbetween at the ball's "squash" key. Remember that the base of the tail is already pulled down to contact the ground but the tip is trailing behind. It will look like the bottom half of a "C" in that way. You may want to turn on outline view for the 'ball' layer to better see the surrounding tail frames. *Image BB8.14*

Image BB8.14

15. Repeat step 2 for the sketch drawn in step 14 for the corresponding frame and position. Because the arc is slightly different for each bounce, the corresponding tail positions might not line up with the arc exactly. You can adjust it slightly with the Free Transform Tool (**Q**) to line it up. *Image BB8.15*

16. The first "up" frames and the breakdown between that and the first "contact stretch" are missing. Repeat step 2 for these two corresponding frames.

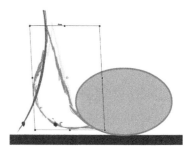

Image BB8.15

17. To make things pretty on playback, insert a blank keyframe (**F7**) after every keyframe already created. Adding blank keyframes will make the tail appear to "flash" on and off on playback but is important to do so that the tail is never standing still while the ball moves onward. This flashing is also called "strobing." And don't forget to guide the "tail arc" layer. *Image BB8.17*

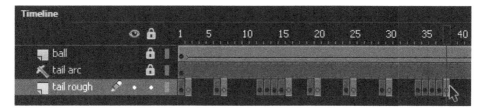

Image BB8.17

Interlude

That part of the exercise was a pose-to-pose rough of a tail trailing a bouncing ball with some overlapping action through one bounce. We'll clean this rough up later and in that process will complete the tail's movement with the ball through the next bounce as well. For now, we're not done with our rough work on the tail. The next step is the rough of the tail's follow through where it whips around in front when the ball comes to an abrupt stop. We'll be using straight ahead this time because of the spontaneity desired in this particular movement. Before moving ahead, make sure you **Save As** "bouncing ball 8 – follow through." Finally, create a new layer called "tail rough front" and make sure it's above everything.

18. We want to end on the third bounce, so double-click to enter the "ball-bouncing" symbol, right-click the last "rebound stretch" keyframe and **Clear Keyframe**. *Image BB8.18*

Image BB8.18

19. Drag the last keyframe (which should be the "up" key) back to about three frames in front of the "squash" key. *Image BB8.19*

Image BB8.19

20. Reposition the ball so that it is back on the ground (which can still be seen because we double-clicked into the symbol from the stage). There's probably already a tween assigned to this last span unless you cleaned it up earlier. If there isn't one, give it a classic tween with a slow out. You should now see the ball come to a flexible stop. *Image BB8.20*

Image BB8.20

21. Returning to the main timeline by clicking "Scene 1" above the stage, find the frame with the final "stretch" (frame 55) and insert keyframe (**F6**) in the existing tween on the "ball" layer at that frame. *(Note: because the tween had no easing (value of 0), inserting a keyframe here does not affect the ball's movement.)* *Image BB8.21*

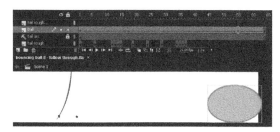

Image BB8.21

22. Right-click the keyframe created in step 21 and **Remove Tween**. *Image BB8.22*

Image BB8.22

23. Right-click the last keyframe on the "ball" layer of the timeline and **Clear Keyframe**. Now the ball bounces a couple times and comes to a squishy-squashy stop at the end of the third bounce. *Image BB8.23*

Image BB8.23

24. We need to add one final element before animating our follow through ending for the tail. On the "contact stretch" keyframe (which should now be one frame before the last keyframe), place a keyframe on the "tail rough" layer and copy/paste in place the corresponding sketch from earlier in the timeline, adjusting its position to the right so that it lines back up with the ball.

25. Insert a blank keyframe (**F7**) after the key in step 24 and then *another* on the same frame (after step 24) on the "tail rough front" layer. *Image BB8.25*

Image BB8.25

26. With onion skin mode on, animate straight ahead the tail falling in front of the ball as it comes to a stop. Remember that since the ball's horizontal velocity is coming to a sudden stop, the tail continues forward. Ultimately, the tail will be pointing ahead of the ball having wrapped around in front of it. Four frames (on the "tail rough front" layer) is enough for the tail to come to a rest. *Image BB8.26*

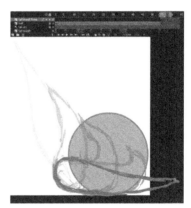

Image BB8.26

For this exercise, you used every principle covered in this book so far. The two that might not be readily apparent are Anticipation and Staging. Though we didn't specifically aim for this, there's a subtle anticipatory beat at the top of the arc where the tail seems to hang longer than the ball. This extra moment is the result of the overlapping action rounding the top of the arc and the stretch applied as the ball gets to the bottom of its arc. Because of these factors, there's much more whipping action happening to the tail. As far as staging, everything can clearly be seen in the shapes of the ball and its tail such that if you were to turn it completely black, the silhouette would still show what's happening on each frame very effectively—there's no fuzzy misunderstandings of what you're looking at (*Image 8.2*). Our application of Overlapping Action and Follow Through seems rather self-explanatory on reflection, but it's a very important principle. Basically, the animation isn't different than anything else you'll do but for the fact whatever motion is overlapping is usually being dragged, and follow through is simply a continuation of motion through a stopping point.

If you test the movie now, you'll see the ball cleaned up while its tail is still in a strobing rough animation form, flickering between visible and invisible. The movement is still readable even with the missing frames though. In traditional animation we would call a video showing the rough animation a "pencil test," but here it's more common to just say "test" (Cmd/**Ctrl+Enter**) or "quick test" (**Enter** or

Play Button on the timeline). This constant ability to see the progress of the movie is fantastic and a real timesaver in the long run. It will help solidify the movement you want to achieve better and faster because there exists this accessible loop between the idea in your head, progress through drawing, and immediate feedback by way of testing. You could continue ahead and rough out the rest of the frames in the tail's animation and then

Image 8.2 The tail trailing behind the bouncing ball with overlapping action in profile view exhibits naturally good staging.

clean them up frame by frame with the Brush (**B**) or Pencil (**Shift+Y**) Tools, but we'll be progressing ahead with more precision tools in Animate's arsenal for our cleanup.

Our Tradigital workflow makes use of traditional principles and concepts in the digital world with its tools and features to allow for a cohesive combination of the two. As you've already seen, these can be combined in many ways. Our previous exercises using Animate's tools and features only represent the technical aspects; however, something needs to be said for style. Style is a result of the merging between artistic sense, tools, methods, and the chosen medium. In this case, it's safe to assume that by reading this book, you've already chosen digital vector art (what Animate CC creates) as the medium and the 12 Principles with Animate CC to make up your tools and methods. But the goals you have for your animation will change the approach. These goals are the result of the design and movement choices in your artistic sense. The style in the animation thus far is a result not only of the medium, tools, and methods, but the choices that I, as the author, make in the movement—which results in the use of those tools and the creation and implementation of those methods.

The bottom line is that in order to learn, you almost *need* to copy … style and all. Progression will mean the slow formation of your own style and methods using the information learned here. Even though the major choices so far are mine, the goal of this book is to show *how* we arrived at these choices and what it took to implement them. Ultimately, you will learn to use Animate CC differently than others as your understanding of the toolset sharpens. Your continued experience animating in Animate CC will culminate in a style uniquely your own but built on the knowledge and experience of others, the way every great artist who came before you has done.

"Style is a result of the merging between artistic sense, tools, methods, and the chosen medium."

CLOSER LOOK
Cleanup of Follow Through and Overlapping Action on Tail

In this section, we'll be cleaning up the rough animation created in this chapter's bouncing ball exercise. To do the cleanup, we'll be using different types of tweens and simple vector art techniques. It will become apparent why certain choices were made and what their benefits are. There is a lot to take in here, so it's been split up into smaller bite-sized pieces of work. I encourage you to reflect on what was done in each of these subsections and how you might be able to apply any previous knowledge to it.

Essentially, the workflow breaks down like this: clean up the rough images for the looped animation (bouncing tail) into a more final form, align all the cleanup images together to be attached at the same place, copy/paste these into a symbol, put an instance of the resulting symbol on the bouncing ball, tween that instance up and down with it, and finally trace the rough images for the final self-contained, follow through animation on the main stage. Already, you might be asking why we need to put the tail inside a symbol if we already drew it on stage. "Isn't that redundant?" The action may seem that way, but here's what's happening. The tail is going to be moving around in relation to *itself* at a different rate than it goes around the *stage*. Those different rates mean that while the tail is still rounding the top of the arc at a steady pace, it will also be straightening out *and* increasing its downward velocity as it's being dragged down by the ball's weight. You can animate this frame by frame. But what we're doing is letting Animate CC inbetween some of the tail extension and contraction movements using shape tweens at one rate while moving the entire tail at the same rate up/down and left/right that the ball does (since they're connected).

Image 8.3 This preview progression shows (left to right) cleanup on stage, aligning cleanup to a single point in its own symbol, tweening that symbol up/down with the bouncing ball, and cleanup of the tail's final follow through on stage.

To get the result we're looking for, we're using a method that I call, for lack of a better existing term, "symblifying" (sounds like *simplify* but with a *symbol* twist). Symblifying is the layering of nested animation within symbols multiple times to result in one complicated movement out of many simpler ones. We actually already did some simple symblification in the Arcs chapter. We put an instance of a symbol, which had nested animation of the ball bouncing up/down with slow in and out, inside another symbol so that we could move *that* symbol left-to-right on stage at a constant rate. That matryoshka doll setup is what ultimately gave us the wonderfully smooth arcs.

That "arc" bouncing ball animation is the one we're using in this chapter, but this time we're adding a tail. The symblify method is the same but with an added level of depth. For the tail to move with the arc of the ball, it still needs a constant horizontal velocity and to slow in/out just like the ball. But this time it will be changing the orientation of its own shape (changing its curves and direction of the tip, for instance) unlike the ball, which despite squashing and stretching is still the same basic shape. Since the horizontal velocity is already accomplished by the ball-bounce symbol across the stage, we'll put an instance of the tail symbol inside that (which we'll animate up/down with the ball) and the shape changes nested inside the tail symbol itself. You'll want to resave your "bouncing ball 8 – follow through" file as "bouncing ball 8 – cleanup." And if there was ever a chapter's exercise to periodically save with incremental numbers added onto the end of the filename so that you don't lose much work if something goes wrong, it's this one.

> "Symblifying is the layering of nested animation within symbols multiple times to result in one complicated movement out of many simpler ones."

"Drawing With The Pencil Tool"

1. Create a new layer on the main timeline called "tail cleanup" and lock everything but that layer. *Image CL8.1*

2. Choose a good color for the stroke and fill for the tail as well as stroke size. I chose dark brown, a lighter brown, and 5 respectively. *Image CL8.2*

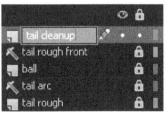

Image CL8.1

3. We're going to quickly clean up the series of frames starting at the first "squash." Create a blank keyframe at the first of those frames and select the Pencil Tool (**Shift+Y**), and make sure that "smooth" is selected in the options area of the toolbar. The tail can be thought of as two strokes: the top of the tail and the bottom. When lines overlap, they can be easily deleted later, so use the rough image as a reference to draw one curve for

Image CL8.2

the top of the tail and another for the bottom, crisscrossing at their ends. *Image CL8.3*

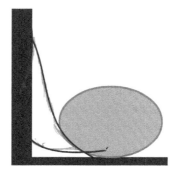

4. Select the two extra lines sticking out both ends created in step 3 and **Delete** them. *Image CL8.4*

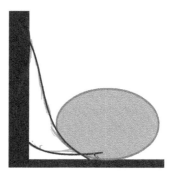

Image CL8.3   Image CL8.4

5. Use the Paint Bucket Tool (**K**) to fill in this new shape. *Image CL8.5*

6. Repeat steps 3–5 for the next frame ("rebound stretch"). *Image CL8.6*

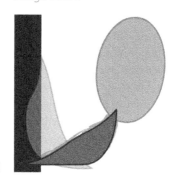

"Drawing With The Rectangle Tool"

7. The previous steps were drawing to clean up. Now we're going to use a shape tool. Using a shape tool limits the amount of vector points which makes shape tweens easier. Select the Rectangle Tool (**R**). *Image CL8.7*

Image CL8.5   Image CL8.6

Image CL8.7

8. Insert a blank keyframe (**F7**) for the frame after "rebound stretch." This keyframe is the last rough drawn for a few frames, and we're going to make Animate CC inbetween it for us. First draw a small rectangle over the sketched image of the tail so that you can clearly see the image under it. *Image CL8.8*

9. Using the Selection Tool (**V** or holding **Cmd/Ctrl**), drag two corners of the rectangle until they meet the ends of the tail. *Image CL8.9*

10. Drag the other two corners to points along the lines of the tail on opposite

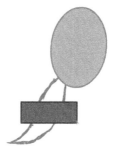

Image CL8.8   Image CL8.9

sides. Where you put these points depends on the curve you're ultimately trying to emulate. Try visualizing the "S" curve as two separate "U"-shaped lines and drag the corner points of the rectangle where they would meet. Choosing where to bring the points to will take a little practice, but it becomes clearer when you see what effect the placement of these points has (as you will in the next step). *Image CL8.10*

11. Click somewhere along the middle on any of the four lines and drag them up or down like we did for the guide-line for the sun in Chapter 5 to match the curve of the sketched tail. You can freely move the two middle points' positions from step 10 around to get them in the spot that allows you to create the correct curves to get the right shape of the tail as indicated in the rough sketch. *Image CL8.11*

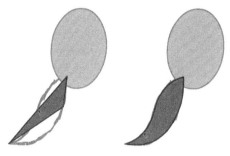

Image CL8.10   *Image CL8.11*

12. Repeat steps 8–11 for the next four rough images. Those should be the first breakdown, "up," second breakdown, and "contact stretch" keys. *Image CL8.12*

"'Symblify' It"

13. Hide every layer except "tail cleanup."

14. Using onion skin mode, drag every frame down so that the point where the tail connects with the ball are all in the same spot. On playback, you should see the tail flapping about from a stationary point. We align the tails' connection point so we can put all of these images in a symbol and treat it as one object to move around with the arc of the ball. If the tail looks like it's changing sizes; you may fix that using the Free Transform Tool (**Q**). *Image CL8.14*

Image CL8.12

15. Highlight all of the cleanup frames created on the timeline and right-click **Copy Frames.**

16. Guide and hide the "tail cleanup" layer. We don't need it anymore, but it's best not to delete it yet … just in case.

17. Create a new symbol in the library and call this "ball-tail."

Image CL8.14

18. **Paste Frames** in the "ball-tail" symbol's timeline. Don't worry that it starts with the "squash" key's tail position; we will be moving the ball on the stage later in the exercise.

19. Turn on the Edit Multiple Frames mode. It's in the same area as onion skin mode. Hold the cursor over the icons until you see the correct one. It's used in much the same way except Edit Multiple Frames lets you select many frames at once and move them around. We want the markers to

Image CL8.19

cover the entire timeline currently in use so every frame is visible on screen at once. This is quickly doable by selecting the "Modify Markers" icon under the timeline, resulting in a drop-down menu where you can select "Marker Range All." *Image CL8.19*

20. Using the Selection Tool on stage, highlight all the tail images and drag them so that their tail bases line up with the registration point (+). Before moving on, *deselect* Edit Multiple Frames mode (very important!). *Image CL8.20*

"Shape Tweens And Shape Hints"

Image CL8.20

21. There are gaps in the animation right now. Right-click and select **Create Shape Tween** for each of those gaps which are bookended by keyframes. The last one should end on the "contact stretch" key's tail (the one that is completely stretched out). *Image CL8.21*

Image CL8.21

22. Scroll through and see how the tweening comes along. As long as the tail looks like it's flapping around and the base of the tail never moves, the shape tweens are good. If they are, skip to step 28. If they are not, continue to the next step. *Image CL8.22*

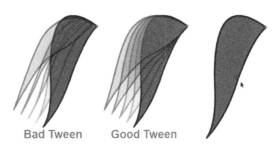

Bad Tween   Good Tween

Image CL8.22   *Image CL8.23*

23. For the tween that morphs around like it doesn't know what to do, we need to help it along. With the tween's *beginning* frame selected, add shape hints either through the menu by **Modify > Shape > Add Shape Hint** or the much quicker and preferred way, the hotkey sequence Cmd/**Ctrl+Shift+H.** Add one for each anchor point (which are also referred to as "vector points") just to be safe, which in this case is four. *Image CL8.23*

24. You'll see red circles with letters pop up in the center of the tail shape ending on the letter "d" (since there are four hints: a, b, c, and d). With the "Snap to Objects" feature *on,* drag the circles to the anchor points starting at the base and going clockwise until all hints are attached. *Image CL8.24*

Image CL8.24

25. Do the same as step 23 on the next keyframe. You'll see the circles turn green if they're attached correctly. *(Note: make absolutely sure that each "letter" hint is attached to the right corresponding anchor point (i.e. the hint connected to the base vector point is also connected to the next keyframe's base vector point).) Image CL8.25*

26. Scroll through to see if the shape is doing what it's supposed to (notice "good tween" from the image that accompanies step 22). If it's not, try rearranging the shape hints by rotating them all clockwise to their next anchor point (don't forget to rearrange the shape hints for *both* keyframes).

Image CL8.25

27. Repeat steps 22–26 as needed for the shapes that don't tween cleanly.

"Adding The Symbol To The Animation"

28. Highlight all frames on the current timeline ("ball-tail" symbol), **Copy Frames and Paste Frames** *after* the end keyframe (meaning do not copy over the existing end keyframe ... they are different), so you now have the same animation looping twice on the timeline. *Image CL8.28*

Image CL8.28

29. Open the "ball-bouncing" symbol from the library and create a new layer. Name it "tail" and put it below the ball layer. *Image CL8.29*

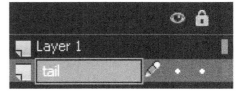

Image CL8.29

30. Make sure you're on the first "squash" frame, create a keyframe on the "tail" layer and drag the "ball-tail" on stage. Line it up so that the base of the tail connects with the right place on the ball and the curve of the tail reaches the lowest point of the ball. Because the contact point would be the ground, the tail needs to start touching. Move the tail's transformation point (seen when the Free Transform Tool is used) to the base of the tail. *Image CL8.30*

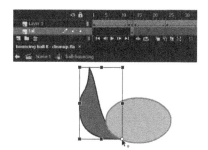

Image CL8.30

31. Create a keyframe (**F6**) on the next "squash" frame so that we keep the same position there as well. *Image CL8.31*

Image CL8.31

32. Scroll ahead to the final "squash" frame and insert a blank keyframe (**F7**) on the "tail" layer, since this frame is where the follow through animation begins. *Image CL8.32*

Image CL8.32

33. Create a keyframe on the first "rebound stretch" frame and move the "ball-tail" symbol up so that the base is meeting the ball at around the same spot *and* the tail still rests on the ground and not below (use onion skin mode to verify with the previous frame if needed). We're setting up for the tweens that will take the tail up and down with the ball. *Image CL8.33*

34. Create a keyframe on the "up" position and move the tail up accordingly. *Image CL8.34*

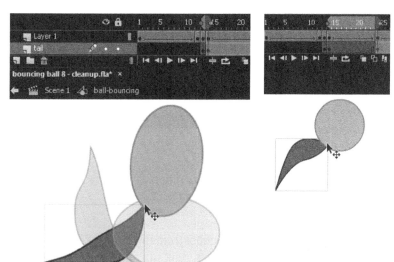

Image CL8.33   *Image CL8.34*

35. Repeat the steps of creating keys and moving the tail where necessary in the timeline ("rebound stretch" and "up") until you arrive at the last contact key.

36. Create a slow out classic tween for when the tail goes up with the ball and a slow in for when it falls. *Image CL8.36*

Image CL8.36

"Adjusting Timing And Slow In/Out"

37. Quick test (**Enter** on the timeline) to see if the timing of the shape tweens *inside* the symbol are doing their work. They probably look a little stiff. This stiffness is because they have no easing themselves. The timing will also be off for the last bounce since it's shorter. In order to properly change the timing, we'll need a timing reference first.

38. Enter the "ball-bouncing" symbol, create a new layer (no need to name it), and insert a keyframe at each of the points where the keyframes are on the tail layer. Highlight this whole layer and **Copy Frames**. You may **Remove Layer** once you've done this as it's not needed anymore. *Image CL8.38*

Image CL8.38

39. Double-click to enter the "ball-tail" symbol and create a new layer. **Paste Frames** from beginning and note how the blank keyframes on this layer match up (or don't) with the shape tween keys for the tail. The second iteration of the tail's movement is longer than what the reference blank keys show in this new layer. *Image CL8.39*

Image CL8.39

40. **Remove Frames** from the two tweens (only on the tail's layer) until the keys ("up" and "contact stretch") match the reference layer's blank keyframes. Now the timing matches the ball's bounce timing, and Animate CC adjusted the inbetweens *for* us! *Image CL8.40*

Image CL8.40

41. Setting the easing of the shape tweens is exactly the same as for a classic tween: from the easing of the tweening area of the Properties panel (although unfortunately there's no Easing Editor for shape tweens as of the writing of this book). Basically the tween will start with

a slow out and end with a slow in, the same way the ball does, but here's a quick list for understanding why the tail needs these various easings of the tweens considering their shape and the fact they're trailing behind the ball:

- First shape tween ("rebound stretch" to "breakdown"): **+100** easing. It will slow out because it's being pulled up quickly. The tail is already outstretched while lying on the ground, so there's nowhere for this drastic change in speed to dissipate. So it whips the tail from horizontal to a vertical angle.
- Second shape tween ("breakdown" to "up"): **−100** easing. It will slow in because it's just coming out of a slow out movement. There's no major change in shape happening. And the ball is in mid-air approaching the apex (top) of the arc, so there's no major change in direction or speed.
- Third shape tween ("up" to "breakdown"): **0** easing. It will have no easing because while the ball is starting to fall faster downward, that speed is being dissipated in effect by the combination of the tail moving down with the ball and the tail being stretched out.
- Fourth shape tween ("breakdown" to "contact stretch"): **+100** easing. It will have a slow out because it's being whipped around the other side of the apex of the arc by the ball's acceleration to the ground.

42. Repeat the previous step for the second iteration of the tail sequence in the "ball-tail" symbol.

Interlude

Let's pause for a moment and recognize in hindsight what symblifying lets us do. If you were to just have shape tweened those tail shapes on the main stage, there would be no way to get a different easing for the change in shape, up-and-down movement, and horizontal velocity. While the ball is jumping up in the air at its fastest speed, the tail has just hit the ground. When the ball is falling to the ground at its fastest speed the tail is just coming out of rounding the top of the arc. In the first case, the ball had a slow out applied to it because it was bouncing up. The tail had a slow out because it was changing shape quickly after being whipped upward. In the second case (falling down), the ball has a slow in applied to it because it is accelerating downward. But this time, the shape tween of the tail still has a slow out because it's at the end of its last major shape change (bent to straight) ... though it is accelerating downward as a whole with the ball because they're connected.

Adjusting the easing may sound complicated because there's a lot going on, but managing the timing and spacing of multiple objects is where it helps to "symblify." By putting a simple animation inside a symbol, and then that inside another, and another, and so on until the needs are met, this complicated motion made up of many different parts can be boiled down to simple subsections. But because of the initial complication, rough animation is needed to get the essentials (keys) of this movement before any of the final tweening can happen. Symblification is Tradigital animation.

In the following (and last) part, we're going to clean up the follow through animation of the tail whipping in front of the ball. This animation was roughed straight ahead, but the cleanup need not follow the same rules, as you'll see.

"Follow Through Cleanup"

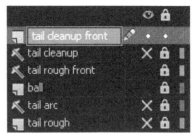

43. We will use each of the drawing methods in this closer look to finish cleanup on this follow through. But first, insert a new layer on the main timeline, name it "tail cleanup front" and make sure it's above every existing layer. *Image CL8.43*

Image CL8.43

44. Insert a keyframe on the "tail cleanup" layer at the frame of the first keyframe on "tail rough front" (that should be frame 55). *Image CL8.44*

Image CL8.44

45. For speed, use the Pencil Tool (**Shift+Y**) to draw over the first follow through rough and the Paint Bucket Tool (**K**) to fill the shape as you did earlier. *Image CL8.45*

46. At the last rough frame, insert a blank keyframe (**F7**) on "tail cleanup" and use the Rectangle Tool (**R**) method, for accuracy and cleanliness, to draw over and clean up the image. *Image CL8.46*

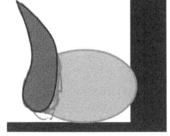

Image CL8.45

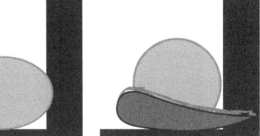

Image CL8.46

47. Insert a blank keyframe a frame after the one on step 44 and copy/paste in place the tail from step 45, here.

48. Drag the anchor points and the lines between them around until it mostly fits the rough that was drawn. *(Note: the reason we're adjusting an existing image is so that the point the tail contacts the ground and the rounded base of the tail don't change much.) Image CL8.48*

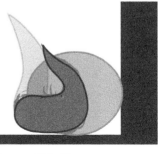

Image CL8.48

49. Repeat the previous two steps for the remaining rough frame to be cleaned up. Use onion skin mode to make sure that the lines you're working with on that frame do not venture outside a path *between* the two keyframes sandwiching it. *Image CL8.49*

Image CL8.49

50. To really complete a nice elastic feeling to the final settle of the tail, we'll have it contract slightly back into a resting place. We'll do this over the next couple of frames. First, insert a keyframe a few frames ahead of the last to start our final span. *Image CL8.50*

Image CL8.50

51. On the second-to-last keyframe, which was the last before we added another in the previous step, use the Free Transform Tool (**Q**) to stretch the tail out farther to the right slightly (in some versions of Flash, CC for instance, you'll need to put the pivot point at the base of the image first or hold the **Alt** key as you drag).

52. Create a shape tween with an easing of 100 (slow

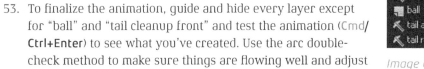
Image CL8.52

out) to this final span, and by doing that the tail lands a little farther outstretched and then slides slightly back to a more "comfortable" position. *Image CL8.52*

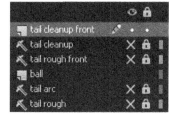
Image CL8.53

53. To finalize the animation, guide and hide every layer except for "ball" and "tail cleanup front" and test the animation (**Cmd/Ctrl+Enter**) to see what you've created. Use the arc double-check method to make sure things are flowing well and adjust where needed. *Image CL8.53*

54. If you notice that the bounce goes off screen on the main stage, use the Edit Multiple Frames option, set the markers to cover the whole timeline (by setting "Marker Range All" as we did before), highlight all, and **Shift+left-arrow** until the ending image is placed back fully into the stage. *Image CL8.54*

In this chapter, you navigated between symbols, shape and motion tweens, guiding and reordering layers, and all through two different methods of rough and cleanup

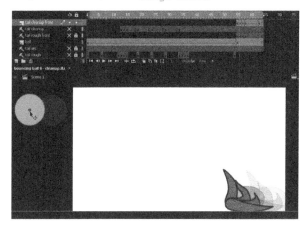
Image CL8.54

animation. Here you were able to see how this layering of animation can be combined to get a great result, especially in parts where heavy overlapping action and follow through are needed. Even though the ball's tail is connected, it's moving semi-independently; "semi" because it's still dictated by the ball's path, only delayed in its execution. This way, separating the two elements into separate symbols makes sense.

Think of animation in symbols as a hierarchy. The "tail" and "ball" symbols are the deepest layer and are separate of one another. We nested animation inside the "tail" symbol but not the "ball" symbol because it didn't need it. At the second level, the "tail" and "ball" symbols are tweened up and down at the same rates inside the same symbol: "ball_bouncing." Nesting makes sure that even though the tail is changing shape on its own, the ball and tail move up and down *as a pair* ... they're connected after all. And finally at the base level, the "ball_bouncing" symbol

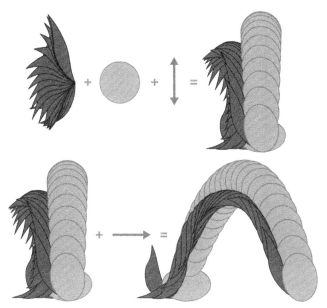

Image 8.4 A representation of symblification—the tail symbol with nested animation and the ball symbol tweened up and down together gave us the "ball_bouncing" symbol's nested animation (top, left to right). The "ball_bouncing" symbol with that nested animation tweened to the right gave us the ball bouncing across the stage with a tail exhibiting overlapping action (bottom, left to right).

itself is moved left to right on stage. There's a level of symbols for the changes in shape, one for the changes in up/down and one for the left/right. Put these all together, and you have a ball bouncing in an arc with a tail trailing behind it in a smooth, wavy motion. After roughing out the overall feel of the piece, you *symblified* the movement to its individual parts and layered them to create a complicated animation.

There are a lot of excellent Tradigitally animated shows, shorts, and movies out there; their prevalence is probably one of the reasons you bought this book. But with each of those, there are variations in style because of the artistic direction, use of the program tools to animate, and application of our 12 Principles. One thing that is common across the board, however, is the use of rough animation.

Image 8.5 The speed of sketching by hand (left) is preferred over the precision of drawing through shape tools (right) for rough animation.

Rough animation preserves the link between our imagination and the image. The path goes something like this for drawing: thought > hand/pencil > image. The path for computer imaging (meaning without drawing by hand) has an added step, however: thought > hand/mouse > program construction tools > image. It's for this reason that we want to use rough animation in traditional animation before cleaning up with the more refined tools of the program. Ultimately, cleanup is not about paving over the personality and implementation of the principles of our rough; it's about improving those two aspects by using the precision of the computer without drowning out the creativity of the artist.

USING FOLLOW THROUGH AND OVERLAPPING ACTION With "Symblification"

Animation is hard. Animation is complicated. Animation is fun. All these statements are true—well at least two out of the three. The third is a tossup based on how much gratification you get from your creation and the process it took to get there (see statements one and two). Animate CC has been instrumental in bringing the ability to create professional grade animation to the personal level. The ability to quick-test animation on the fly alone probably helps more people achieve real and measurable progress in frame-by-frame animation than anything else in recent creation. But one step further than that are the drawing tools, symbols, and tweens. We'll get more into the drawing tools and methods in Chapter 10 "Solid Drawing," but you've already seen what tweening and nesting animation within symbols can do. Those two features help immensely to alleviate the pains of overwhelming complication in some animation.

As mentioned in the last chapter, breaking animation down into its smaller parts before attacking the whole risks losing the vitality and personality of your movement. The example of the walk-cycle being only a series of simple, almost unconscious movements working together to produce a cohesive walk with feeling and personality is probably even more telling now that you have worked through this chapter. Rough animation of this bouncing ball with a tail, or a walk-cycle, or most anything else lets us first stand back and see the forest for the trees. We don't want to get lost in the detail of every fine movement too soon. But once that rough animation is put down, it's time to simplify things … and in Tradigital animation, that usually means symblifying things.

> "Animation is hard. Animation is complicated. Animation is fun. All these statements are true—well at least two out of the three. The third is a tossup based on how much gratification you get from your creation and the process it took to get there (see statements one and two)."

Putting animation inside symbols and then those inside other symbols and so on until you have layered it such that a complex movement emerges is the essence of symblifying. It usually is as simple as noticing that the upper portion of an arm swings back and forth like a pendulum, moves up and down with the body but also has overlapping action. The arm is connected to the body but starts swinging back after the foot has touched the ground and the body starts to drop. You should have already roughed out the walk, so you know how fast you'd like the arm to be moving and when. But to make it easier for you to keep things smooth, you could eliminate having to clean up the three sections of the arm (upper, lower, hand) frame by frame by symblifying the part that connects it to the body. Even just to tween a layered series of nested symbols as reference for the movement and position would be enough to help clean up if you've decided to draw over it.

All symblifying does is let you focus on one particular part of the animation and then break that part up into the motions that make up the whole. A gymnast does a back layout full twist (a flip while moving backward and rotating 360 degrees in the air). Moving backward can easily be accomplished with a tween. The flip is composed of a jump and a rotation, so a rotating symbol inside another symbol which is tweened up and down is needed. Then all that needs to be done is an animation of the person turning around one time, in place (which would probably need to be animated by hand). The hierarchy would look like this (where the last item is the one ultimately on the stage and each previous item is nested in the symbol before it): spin > rotation > jump > horizontal motion. You would still start with rough animation of the whole and then clean it up with symblification and tweens, like we did with the tail.

Breaking down an animation into smaller parts isn't really a new way of thinking about animation, since animators have always taken a closer look at what makes up the parts of a motion when roughing. Many times they would put a few Timing Charts on one paper representing the different spacing assigned to the various moving features needed to get the refined movements. As we discussed in Chapter 2 "Slow In and Slow Out," the easing graph for tweens is basically just a digital Timing Chart. Symblification is just splitting up a larger complicated motion into smaller, more manageable subsections, all of which are usually tweened and adjusted using those easing graphs. No matter if you're writing out multiple Timing Charts for multiple features as in classic animation or using multiple easing graphs for multiple symblified features as in Tradigital animation, the concept is the same.

Image 8.6 The various motions which make up the whole are separated into their own symbols. Example taken from "ch8-examples-gymnast.fla" on the companion website.

Every workflow that differs from another will have a different result on the final product, no matter how slight. But the way of thinking about the animation remains largely the same. Now that you've seen it, look for it in every FLA you can find (including the ones included with this book, obviously). Symblification is the way of Tradigital animation.

REAL-WORLD EXAMPLE
"Whip"

Principles Used

Arcs: The end of a whip acts like a projectile that is periodically redirected by an outside force that's pulling it around, so it will travel in arcs as such. The arm and its parts all move in smooth, organic motions perpetuating the type of arc in the connected features.

Anticipation: There is a lot of windup that happens in a whipping motion. First the whip needs to be raised up and swung back before throwing it forward. That motion (with overlapping action) anticipates the following action by moving back before going front, and shows the audience the relationship between the movement of the arm and that of the whip it's holding.

Slow In/Out: The further down the line of connected joints, the larger the spacing of the slow in and outs will be but not

Image 8.7

necessarily the intensity. For instance, at the moment at the end of the arm's swinging arc to the bottom everything snaps to an end. The sudden stop at the shoulder rotation isn't as intense as the massive snap at the end of the whip because of the difference in distance traveled but they both have similar slow in/out.

Squash and Stretch: As we will see with forward kinematics, when you focus just on a feature of the body and not the whole (or at least without the face), the chances of the movement resulting in a robotic motion is greater. Squashing on the anticipation and stretching at the extension of the whip will do a lot to avoid this pitfall of the cropped view.

Pose to Pose/Straight Ahead: The motion of the arm is known and well-planned for using pose to pose. The whip animation can be planned as well but is usually best worked out through straight ahead because it is a reactionary movement to the arm.

Overlapping Action: A whip might be the quintessential example of Overlapping Action and Follow Through. Think of it like a really, really long tail. The effects of this principle will be big. It will take longer for the motion to cascade down the whip to the end and will require more time to come to a stop even though it's very light, because it's so far away from the base of its movement (the handle).

Setting Up

Open "ch8-real_world-whip.fla" file provided on the companion website. The setup this time is different. There is a "thumbnails" layer which has the major informative poses worked out for you (mostly just to get things going). This was done by visually studying slow-motion footage of whip-cracks, getting a feel for the mechanics of it and then marking the most important points.

As far as what you will be using for cleanup, there is one "arm" symbol which is made up of "bicep" (upper arm) and lower arm symbols, and the lower arm symbol is then made up of the forearm and hand symbols inside it. There is also a line that has been drawn in a neutral position on another layer of the main timeline to represent the whip. What we're going to look at this time is another area of symblification, which will act as a form of forward kinematics. Forward kinematics describes the connectivity of objects through joints which are manipulated individually. For instance, to move an arm setup for forward kinematics you will rotate the shoulder first (which moves the lower arm and hand with it, stiffly), then move the lower arm (which moves the hand with it, but doesn't change the shoulder position) and finally the hand which is linked at the wrist (*Image 8.8*). Imagine how you would pose an action figure, and you'll have an idea of how to

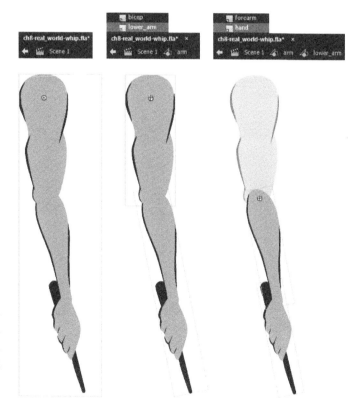

Image 8.8 The setup of the arm is for forward kinematics. From left to right, the arm symbol is made up of a bicep and lower arm and the lower arm is made of a forearm and hand.

approach posing for forward kinematics. We used a bit of this in Chapter 6's real-world exercise with the arms in the golf swing but it wasn't as focused as what we're doing here.

> "Forward kinematics describes the connectivity of objects through joints which are manipulated individually."

In Animate CC, using symblification, we have an added level to this setup wherein we can tween each feature to rotate about the joint using the pivot point of the symbol, and all the tweens can happen at the same time. This series of parental relationships is how robotics works. The parent joint moves (shoulder) at a certain rate at the same time the joints down the chain (elbow and wrist) move at different rates and/or times which culminate in one master movement. It's also how your *arm* works. Move it around right now, and you'll see. We know this type of chained movement already through life experience mostly, but this academic familiarity will help in the application of that knowledge to animating the arm. We're going back to steps for part of this example since forward kinematics is a rather new method of using symblification as presented in this book. But first, we need to rough it out!

"Rough Arm Poses"

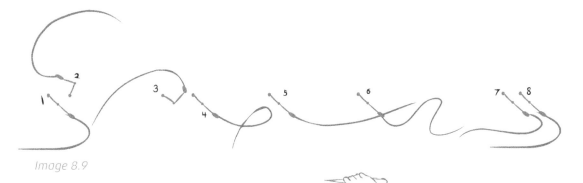

Image 8.9

There isn't much to be said about this process that hasn't been said already. You want to sketch the main keys of the arm motion in first. You can see here I've drawn out some thumbnails of the general poses that we're going for (*Image 8.9*). They are actually playing on the timeline, making these thumbnail poses into an animatic or simple rough animation of sorts. You don't have to copy them directly. Actually you're encouraged to work off your own experience and intuition for this movement, but they're good for reference if you get stuck. Those key poses are the arm at rest, up ready

Image 8.10

to throw forward, and then back to rest (these are extremes—the changes in direction). Then we'll put in the breakdown pose of swinging down toward the resting position (*Image 8.10*). These rough frames are all we need to work the forward kinematics on the arm animation. We will address the resulting overlapping action of the whip after cleaning up the arm movement.

"Forward Kinematics Arm"

1. The shoulder will have the most general movement. It's the least complicated motion because of it being at the base—it's dictating the overall path of the animation: up, down, and back to rest. Place keyframes at each of the roughs you drew (keys and breakdown). For me that was frames 7, 11, and 13 and I will be referring to this timing throughout. *Image W8.1*

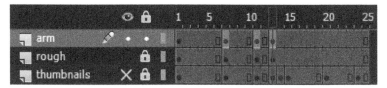

Image W8.1

2. On each of the keyframes created in the previous step and using the Free Transform Tool (Q), rotate the whole arm around the shoulder so that the upper arm lines up with that of the rough. *(Note: do NOT squash/stretch this symbol, because it represents the whole. We want to apply the squash/stretch to the symbols which are only the individual features, which will be done in the next section.) Image W8.2*

3. Now apply classic motion tweens to those spans. Give appropriate easing to each tween to reflect the slow in/out that's needed. I put an "S" curve for the first tween span and then −100 and 100 to the last two, respectively. *Image W8.3*

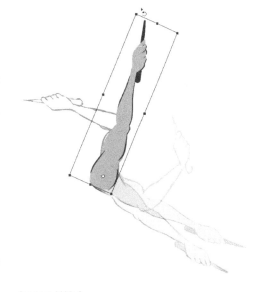

Image W8.2

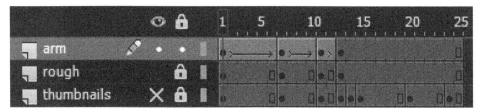

Image W8.3

4. There is going to be some overlapping action with the lower arm's movement compared to the upper. Enter the "arm" symbol from the stage at the up keyframe (frame 7), insert a keyframe (**F6**) a couple frames *after* that (making it frame 9) to account for overlapping action, and position the lower arm (which also contains the hand), to the corresponding pose. *Image W8.4*

5. The final keyframe for the arm (frame 13) is the down position and we want a bit of a snapping effect to the arm which will be mirrored in the whip. So enter the "arm" symbol here, insert a keyframe for the lower arm, and position it to be perfectly in line with the bicep (*not* the resting position, we're extending a little beyond that). *Image W8.5*

6. Since the stretched arm from frame 13 is not the resting position we started with, copy the lower arm's resting position from the first key and paste it a few frames ahead so we can cushion back to it (I chose frame 18 in my timing). *(Note: we're using nested animation with our symblification here so make sure that the looping area of the Properties panel says the "lower_arm" instance is playing from the frame it's on—18.)*

7. When all of the new lower arm positions have been keyframed within the "arm" symbol, tween between the spans with desired easing. Mine were 100, −100 and an "S" curve (for the cushion), respectively. *Image W8.7*

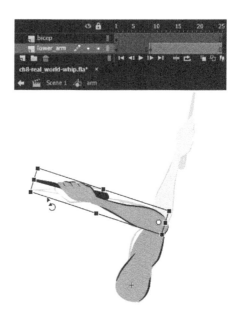

Image W8.4

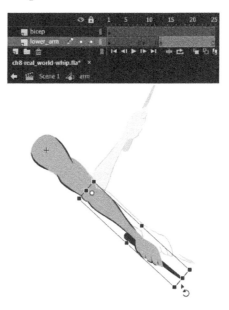

Image W8.5

Image W8.7

8. We want to repeat step 4 for the hand symbol instance inside "lower_arm." Instead of a two frame overlap, I chose one. This made the position with the arm bent back at keyframe 10. *(Note: because you can only double-click to enter a symbol instance on a keyframe and the lower arm keyframe doesn't match the breakdown frame in the rough, those images won't align when you're working through this step on frame 10 inside "lower_arm." Do your best to approximate the angle the hand shows in relation to the forearm.) Image W8.8*

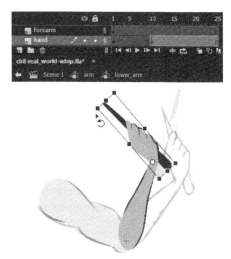

9. The hand's cushion is a little different because while the elbow can't hyperextend, the hand can in this arrangement. First we'll set it up by getting the hand's resting position set in. Go back to the stage at frame 1 and double-click the lower arm twice to return to the "lower_arm" symbol. Insert a keyframe up at frame 13 (which you'll remember as the end key in our rough) and paste in the resting hand position from the first keyframe. Then insert another keyframe at the frame where we ended the lower arm's cushion back to rest (frame 18). *Image W8.9*

Image W8.8

10. Insert a keyframe at frame 15 and rotate the hand to be a little more extended downward than the resting position. This will allow the hand to exhibit some follow through after the arm has snapped into its downward position. *Image W8.10*

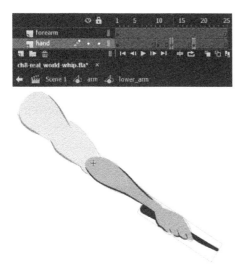

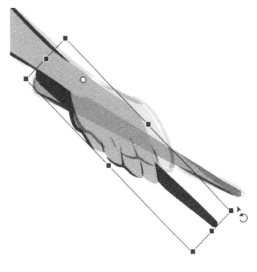

Image W8.9   *Image W8.10*

11. To complete the hand's movement, we're going to tween the spans. But right now that would mean that the first span where the hand is

Image W8.11

bending backward would begin with both the upper and lower arm's movements. The hand should display overlapping action on the lift so insert a keyframe a few frames after the first (I chose frame 6 in my timing) and tween between every keyframe *except* the first and second. This gives us four new tween spans and lets the hand demonstrate overlapping action (for starting the motion late in the beginning) and follow through (for continuing an extension after the arm completes its own). *Image W8.11*

You should now have an arm that moves in smooth arcs with a whipping motion and some cushioning. Without the cushioning, the swinging motion could've come out with a very robotic feeling. The human arm and a robot one with the same joint system will move in similar ways, but the vitality will more likely be missing from the robotic one because it's just plain better at being precise. Humans are generally awful at natural precision no matter how hard we try, and that needs to be reflected in our movement. So even though we didn't work out the rough animation to that level, knowing that we want the arm to overextend just a little past its comfort zone and cushion back to a resting position we can make that happen on the fly.

That isn't to say that working out the cushioning movement via rough animation first wouldn't have been helpful, but that there are many ways to do the same thing in a Tradigital workflow. We applied the same working knowledge of arm-swinging mechanics to the forward kinematics of the arm as we would've done in the rough animation. However, computers are precise. While the arm's movements have more vitality in them because of the cushioning we applied, the overall execution still looks formulaic. The arm's features never change shape and *that* is robotic. The arm doesn't feel fleshy because squash and stretch hasn't been applied yet.

"Squash And Stretch"

12. Enter the "arm" symbol and insert keyframes (**F6**) to the "bicep" layer to *exactly match* the ones on the "lower arm" layer (frames 9, 13, and 18). Though this chapter is on overlapping action, these keyframes need to match because as we apply squash and stretch to the bicep it will move the position of the joint where the lower arm is supposed to look attached. So we're going to need to reposition the lower arm to move with the squashing and stretching of the upper. *Image W8.12*

Image W8.12

13. Apply squash and stretch where appropriate for the bicep *only*. Squash at frame 9 to simulate a flex and stretch at frame 13 to simulate the overextension. *(Note: the accompanying image shows these neutral (left), squashed (middle), and stretched (right) shapes with their frame numbers above them. Notice how the elbow position changes.)* Image W8.13

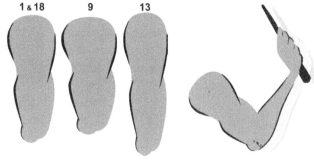

14. Move the lower arm instance at those keyframes (9 and 13) to reconnect with the elbow's position. *Image W8.14*

Image W8.13   Image W8.14

15. Give the empty spans classic motion tweens with the *same easing* that was applied to the lower arm's tweens.

16. Enter the lower arm symbol and repeat steps 12–15 for the "forearm" layer and symbol instance, this time matching with the hand's keyframes (6, 10, 13, and 15). Squash and stretch similarly as the bicep before—this time squash at 10 and stretch at 13. *(Note: since there's only one squash and one stretch moment, we don't need a keyframe at frame 18 because that's only for the hand's cushion.)* Image W8.16

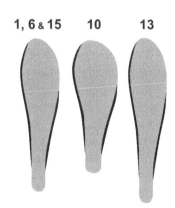

Image W8.16

"The Whip"

We've largely ignored the whip itself, so far. This is because it's a resultant action of the arm's movement. Essentially you were just slowly figuring out how you wanted to swing your own arm in the previous steps, and now you're going to "see" how the whip reacts through straight ahead action. We're going to work through this by section since it's almost all done with frame-by-frame animation and numbered steps would be redundant.

"Rough Out The Movement Straight Ahead"

For this type of work, I like to turn every frame of a new layer into a keyframe by highlighting them all and hitting **F6** or **F7** (since the layer is blank anyway, functionally these keys do the same thing). Then I turn on onion skin mode and set the span to see back about three frames. From here, you just sketch in the frame that you're on and hit the ">" key to move on to the next frame and repeat until you're at the end. It's good to keep in mind the length of the whip (though it can be exaggerated at points for effect) and also the type of motion a whip makes, which was shown to you in the thumbnails. *(Note: in the accompanying image, the "thumbnails" layer is in outline view and there are two layers named "rough" (the highlighted one is for the whip and the "rough" layer below that is the key poses for the arm we did before the numbered steps began.) Image W8.17*

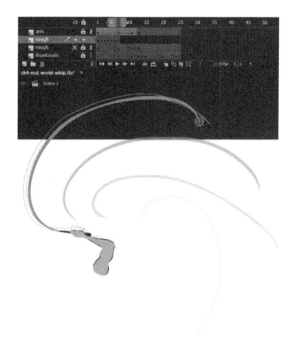

"Analyze The Straight Ahead Work"

Now that the straight ahead rough animation of the whip is done, look back at what you did to see if it could be improved or if there are any areas that could be shape tweened easily (for me, the only real place for an effective shape tween was the very end when it settles back to rest on the ground). Insert another layer and draw in any frames that need to be fixed, replace with the old roughs (after **Save As**, of course), and re-analyze. Keep an eye out for what the whip's keyframes would be if you had done this pose to pose. The accompanying image shows one of these keys which also needed to be fixed (in red). *Image W8.18*

Image W8.17

"Tiedown And Cleanup Using Onion Skin Mode"

To make sure that the whip isn't jittering around when you clean up the final (remember humans are imprecise) draw what would be the key frames you determined from the previous section's analyzing on a separate layer and

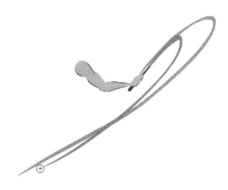

Image W8.18

relate them to the handle of the whip. Next, tie down the whip's movement by working through the sequence the same way you would've in pose to pose (keys, extremes, breakdowns, cushions, and so on), but staying as close as you can to the positioning you liked in the straight ahead rough (*Image W8.19a*). They're not going to line up exactly. Onion skin mode helps you avoid the jittering when doing inbetweening in the tiedown because you can see the points where the whip crosses itself from one frame to the next. If many frames cross over a similar point in space, this is a transition point (or point of reference) for our cascading movement. Take a look at the accompanying image of the first three frames (*Image W8.19b*). While the whip is being picked up, the lines all cross at the

Image W8.19a

same point on stage. If the first and third frames intersected there but the second didn't, the whip would look jittery. The other condition that can make it look jittery is more obvious, and that's if the change in position of the line doesn't look consistent. You'll see these as anomalies in the pattern you see with onion skin mode on. If you're not well versed in it yet, you will be with practice. Finally, when the tiedown is done, clean up the whip motion by positioning the line where and when it's needed and tween where you can (*Image W8.19c*).

Manipulating a line as opposed to drawing in each frame gives more options for tweening where appropriate. It also allows for fine adjustments in the case that a curve doesn't look quite right. The other benefit to cleanup with the line in this case is that because it's so thin, problem areas in the motion will be much more obvious as you work through in onion skin mode (*Image W8.20*). If you don't like the style of the line as the whip, you could

Image W8.19b

always design a more detailed version to be animated frame by frame back over it now that the legwork has been done on the motion.

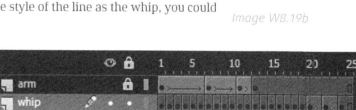

This scene was done in a similar fashion as the

Image W8.19c

previous chapter in that both straight ahead and pose to pose methods were used in one overall movement. There is an organic movement of a human, and an inorganic movement of an object which is connected to it (toilet paper in Chapter 7 and a whip here). They both also employ a significant use of Follow Through and Overlapping Action. The major difference this time was the forward kinematic setup of the arm. This method isn't suggested for too many situations, however, because it has a limited range in its execution. It would be *great* for robotic arms like on an assembly line or one of those claw machine games. A tree swaying in the wind, for example, could also use this setup if you need to see branches moving within it as well. Forward kinematics is a more specific use of symblification. Zoomed in or cropped scenes like this one are helped with forward kinematics mostly because the audience's eye is completely trained on the movement and a level of precision is needed but, as mentioned, rough animation is essential to making sure that precision doesn't run away with the vitality in your animation.

Image W8.20

FINAL WORDS
Follow Through and Overlapping Action

Truth be told, there is not much difference between "normal" animation and that with overlapping action or follow through. This principle is all about shining a light on the fact that not everything moves at the same time or rate even if (and possibly especially because) it's on the same body or object. A dog with floppy ears will have them dragging behind just about everything he does. If he changes directions quickly, those ears will continue on their previous trajectory until they're stretched out and can't move that way anymore and then whip back toward the dog like our tail did to the ball. That's the overlapping action. Follow through is when our dog comes to a sudden stop and the ears keep moving a bit until finally coming to rest (*Image 8.11*). The principles that control the movement of the simple bouncing ball or the dog's wild running are the same as those which dictate the ear's movement with the added caveat of being influenced by the dog's movements such that they trail a frame or two behind.

Overlapping action can also be conscious movement too, though. Boxing comes up a lot in this book, and it does for good reason: it shows a lot of the physics of body mechanics at work. To throw a simple straight punch, the legs push, hips twist, and the shoulders follow while the arm is extending and the hand is rotating. This chain of overlapping events in motion sums up to equal "punch." In real life, if they were to all happen at the same time, that punch wouldn't be as powerful; they *need* to be chained together. In animation, this overlapping action also works to enhance the anticipation of the impact when exaggerated (which we'll get into more in Chapter 11 "Exaggeration").

The subject of the next chapter is Secondary Action, and you'll see a lot of crossover in the concepts of how to approach Overlapping Action and Follow Through there. For now, it's important to remember that while some parts of a whole might be moving at different rates, they are not necessarily independent of each other. They are connected and impact each other by weight or movement. This connection is why it's best to address a shot as one whole piece with rough animation first. Mistakes will most likely be made, but that's why we refine with either a second pass after double-checking arcs and timing or through the cleanup itself. Symblify your Tradigital workflow sounds like nonsense … until you do it.

Image 8.11

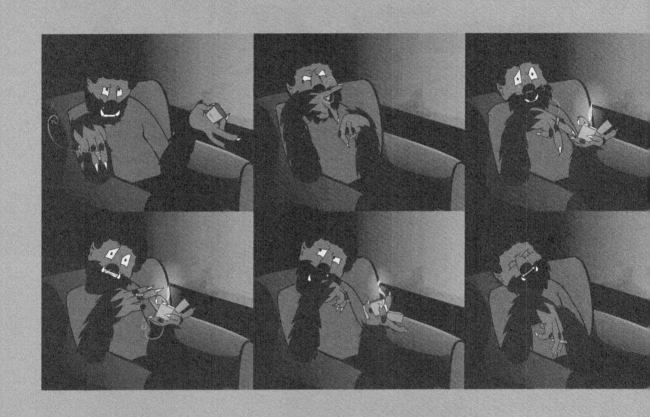

Image 9.0 Three's Horrible: Part I
by Stephen Brooks
(RubberOnion.com).

Chapter 9
SECONDARY ACTION

INTRODUCING
Secondary Action

Let's say you have a chef talking to a subordinate. The chef is very upset but is trying to contain his anger and not yell at the scared, little guy. If you imagine this happening straight, as in our angry chef is talking directly at the employee with a forced grin, it plays out simply, and the audience has to interpret a lot from the way the voice actor delivers the lines and from the expression on our chef's face. Now imagine that while he's subtly chastising his poor assistant, the chef is also chopping up onions with a butcher's knife (if there are any chefs-in-training out there, the fact that it's not the correct knife for the task is part of the joke). "I'm not angry," he says as he slams the knife on the cutting board and forces a smile. "I'm just a *little* disappointed." Slam goes the knife again. This extra level of action is helping to communicate our chef's true feelings better and adds more depth to the acting of the scene. The act of chopping up the onions is the secondary action, as it supports the story point of the primary action: scolding the subordinate with controlled rage.

> "Secondary actions are those that could stand alone as their own set of movements but are used to support the story point of the primary action."

You will notice that Secondary Action differs greatly from the subject of our previous chapter, Overlapping Action and

Follow Through. To reiterate what was mentioned there, examples of overlapping action and follow through would be a scarf dragging behind a boy running in winter, a tail trailing behind a weasel jumping around a field, or the ears of a giant elephant flopping around as it marches. The thing is many people mix these up with the principle in this chapter. The confusion begins because overlapping action and follow through are secondary *motions.* They are motions that are directly impacted and whose paths are defined by the primary one. Secondary actions are those that could stand alone as their own set of movements but are used to support the story point of the primary action. Our chef could chop up an onion with a butcher's knife any number of ways, as a standalone action: happily, sadly in a depressed state, or angrily like in our example. In a different scene, the chopping might be the primary action where the story point is that he's making onion soup for the first time, so the secondary action might be a stream of tears he's crying. A girl talking to her crush twirls her hair. A scientist doing calculations chews on an eraser. A dog trying to walk faster bites the leash and gives a tug. These are all examples of Secondary Action. It's very important to know the distinction.

You can already start to see how much flavor and texture secondary motion gives to a scene, and how many ways you could do it. The bouncing ball exercise for this principle is going to build on what we did in the last chapter, which will also illuminate the differences between the two principles. The tail was added for overlapping action in Chapter 8. This time, we need to choose a story point for our secondary action to support. Since the ball is already bouncing from left to right, we'll make the story point such that "the ball is fearfully running away from something that is chasing it." In order to sell this concept to the audience, we're going to be creating a face for the ball and having it looking over its "shoulder" terrified while it's fleeing. It's not the existence of the face that's the secondary action; the look over the shoulder and the way it's done is. To do this, we'll be exploring more uses of symblification and introducing another feather: masks.

Image 9.1

BOUNCING BALL Secondary Action

Setting Up

Open the "bouncing ball 8 – cleanup" project file and **Save As** "bouncing ball 9 – secondary action." Right away, enter the symbols at play and make sure that there are no layers with rough animation on them; if there are, delete them. Deleting the unnecessary layers is just to keep things clean for yourself and is a good practice to get into as your project files become increasingly complicated with the more sophisticated animations that you'll be doing. If you need them for whatever reason in the future, you can simply copy/paste the frames from a previous project file, so nothing is actually lost or deleted in this way. It's only tidied up.

You are now far enough along that the only idea which really should be reinforced at this point is that we will be approaching the facial expressions and positions by way of pose to pose rough animation. Adding facial expressions after having completed the primary action

Image 9.2 Flash CS6 (left) and Flash CC (right) have different icons for the same pressure sensitivity feature.

is really the most beneficial in this case since a certain beat needs to be hit at a specific time, and coordinating the expressions with the action is where the pose to pose method shines. The Brush Tool (**B**) is always suggested for these roughs. We will go over this feature more in the next chapter ("Solid Drawing"), but if you would like to try using pressure sensitivity (if your graphics tablet allows for that feature), you'll need to find the icon with the Brush Tool selected first. In Flash CC it looks like ripples emanating from the tip of a pen, while in Flash CS6 and before it's a thick-to-thin "swoosh" icon. Regardless of the version of Animate CC you have, with the classic layout the pressure sensitivity icon will be at the bottom of the toolbar and say "Use Pressure" when hovered over. Toggling the pressure sensitivity feature on just allows for the line thickness to be varied based on how hard you press the pen on the tablet.

PART I
"Facial Animation—Expression Keys"

1. There will be three main keys for our face animation: scared looking ahead, very scared looking back, and forcefully closing eyes afraid to look and move. Note the timing of the bounces and where best to put the last two keys (obviously we're starting with the first).

2. Double-click to enter the "ball-bouncing" symbol and again to enter the "ball" symbol.

Image BB9.3

3. Extend the timeline out to the end frame of the main timeline (frame 63). *Image BB9.3*

4. Insert a new layer above all and name it "face rough."

5. Using the Brush Tool (**B**), sketch a simple face looking to the right of the screen (profile view) scared with a partially open mouth. To keep things easy in this example, use an eye with a pupil and a simple shape for the mouth. Adding shapes for the eye, pupil, and mouth to the ball and tail will give us only five shapes to work with ultimately. *Image BB9.5*

Image BB9.5

6. Using the timing noted in step 1, choose a frame where the ball will look over its shoulder, insert a blank keyframe (**F7**), and sketch that image. It should be looking behind (to the left of the screen) with an open, scared mouth position. *Image BB9.6*

Image BB9.6

7. Repeat step 6 for the final key where the ball has come to a stop and its face is looking ahead again (profile view, for us), is squinting its eyes shut and is gritting its teeth. *Image BB9.7*

8. Insert a blank keyframe (**F7**) two frames before the final key and draw a breakdown

Image BB9.7

frame with eyes partially closed and the mouth starting to grit its teeth. *Image BB9.8*

9. Insert a blank keyframe and draw the inbetween on the frame sandwiched by the ones in steps 7 and 8. The eyes should be fully squinted (since they will shut first) and the mouth half closed between the two existing roughs. *Image BB9.9*

Image BB9.8

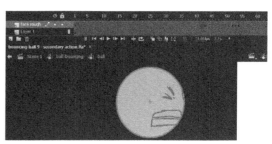

Image BB9.9

10. Step back one level to the "ball-bouncing" symbol (click its name next to "Scene 1" above the stage) and make sure that the "ball" symbol is playing the correct corresponding frames throughout the bounce, including the last keyframe. If it's not, highlight all ball tweens and check "sync" in the Properties panel. Don't forget to set the correct frame for the last keyframe as well (frame 58). *Image BB9.10*

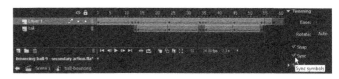

Image BB9.10

11. Re-enter the "ball" symbol through double-click and test the animation with Cmd/**Ctrl+Enter** to see if the timing is working how you imagined it. If not, adjust the keyframe positions until it works the way you'd like.

Interlude

With these three rough expression keys (the other sketches were inbetweens), you have added quite a bit more feeling to the scene. What we want to do next is clean these up, but it must be done in such a way that will allow us to animate the expression changes. You could rough out all the inbetweens yourself frame by frame, but we are going to be continuing a more Tradigital approach by delegating some of this inbetween work to Animate CC by way of shape tweens. Consideration must be made into how we will accomplish our final animation before determining how the cleanup of the image itself will be done. What we want is for the face to be looking ahead and then turn smoothly but quickly to look behind. When the face is looking ahead, half of the mouth and the ball's entire left eye are hidden from view because in a three-dimensional with 3D world they're on the other side of the ball out of view of the audience. When a feature is partially obscured like the mouth is, it makes doing a shape tween for the reveal difficult since the shape is not actually *changing* as much as being *revealed*. This same issue also poses an obvious problem for the previously invisible eye, hidden from the view on the "other side" of the face until the turn. In order to accomplish this revealing of obscured or hidden features, we'll be using masks.

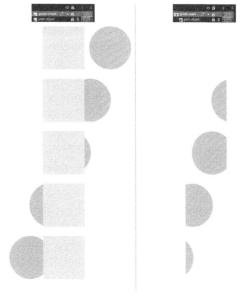

Image 9.3 As two independent layers, the green box obscures the pink circle below it (left). When masked, the green box layer instead serves as a window (right).

The simple explanation of a mask in Animate CC is that it's a shape which acts like a window through which we can see whatever is behind it. In the program's case, "behind" refers to anything that is linked to the layer (like we did for guide layers). So to get the effect of a face turning from partially obstructed view to straight into the "camera," we'll draw a full face and simply create a window (mask) the exact shape of the ball. As the face symbol is moved around, whatever is outside that window (on the other side of the ball) isn't shown. We won't be applying the mask in *this* part of the exercise, but we need to know what we're *going* to do in order to symblify the facial animation correctly as mentioned in the previous sentence. We must clean up the image of the face in full view, put it in a symbol, extend the timeline so that this new symbol's internal timeline matches the length of the main (as it we want it to play in sync), put it back in the "ball" symbol," and move it into position so that the inbetweening can begin.

PART II
"Facial Animation—Cleanup And Symblification"

12. Guide the "face rough" layer and lock all layers.

13. Insert a new layer in the "ball" symbol and name it "face." Clean up the *second* keyframe of the rough (the face looking back but facing the camera). We're starting with this one because it's the only full view of the face we have and will be used to set up for the mask animation. Turn on Object Draw (**J**) mode, use the Oval Tool (**O**) for the eyes and use the Rectangle Tool (**R**) using vector point manipulation that we learned in the previous chapter for the mouth. *Image BB9.13*

Image BB9.13

14. Note which frame number the rough's middle keyframe is on (the one you just cleaned up without creating a new keyframe on the "face" timeline). Highlight the entire image (eyes and mouth) created in the previous step and turn it into a Graphic Symbol (**F8**) named "face" with a registration point in the middle. *Image BB9.14*

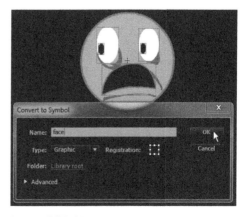

Image BB9.14

15. Enter the newly created "face" symbol and with all the object highlighted, right-click and select **Distribute to Layers** (Cmd/**Ctrl+Shift+D**). You should see five layers created: two eyes, two pupils, and a mouth. However there is one blank layer that's a leftover from the distribute command. Delete that. *Image BB9.15*

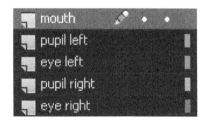

Image BB9.15

16. Name the corresponding layers with the names of their parts. For the eyes, as with all features on a character, name it with the position relative to the character. For instance, "eye right" is the character's right eye, not the one that is rightmost on the screen. *Image BB9.16*

Image BB9.16

17. Extend the timeline out to the length of the main (frame 63). *Image BB9.17*

18. Click and drag downward on the frame noted from step 14 and click F6. Having multiple frames selected like this while inserting a keyframe (with the hotkey F6) creates a keyframe on each of those layers in the highlighted area. *Image BB9.18*

Image BB9.17

Image BB9.18

19. Return to the "ball" symbol and create keyframes on the "face" layer for the first, second, and last keys on the "face rough" layer. *Image BB9.19*

20. The keyframes for the various features will not line up perfectly because the mouth shape is different, but for the first and last keyframes move the "face" symbol to the right until it is in position with the rough on the layer below. *Image BB9.20*

Image BB9.19

Image BB9.20

Interlude

Now that we have everything split up into layers and appropriate symbols, we will apply a mask to see how the effect is coming together, use shape tweens within the "face" symbol to animate the expression changes, and finally add classic motion tweens to it within the "ball" symbol so that the face position itself changes. Everything we did is possible without the rough, but since we have it the guidelines for acting have been set. There isn't much difference at this point between the way we're animating the rest of the face and how we would do it if every frame was drawn as in traditional animation. Even then, there is a mental separation between the features as you animate: "What does the eye do here? How fast does it go? Where does it go in the next frame?" This battery of questions usually happens within the head of an animator drawing each frame so this process is turned into the aforementioned "symblification" and is actually separated within the program. The more complicated the movement, the more this process helps in creation *and* alteration (if needed).

PART III
"Facial Animation—Masking And Tweens"

21. In the "ball" symbol, insert a new layer and name it "mask." *Image BB9.21*

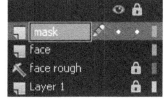

Image BB9.21

22. Since we want only the part of the face inside the ball's space to show up, the mask needs to be the exact size of the ball itself. Unlock the layer with the ball on it, copy the ball and then relock.

23. Paste in place the ball on the "mask" layer. *Image BB9.23*

24. Make sure that the "mask" layer is directly above the "face" layer in the order, then right-click the "mask" layer and select **Mask**. You will notice that the mask layer automatically becomes the parent to the layer below it (meaning the layer below, "face," is now indented under "mask"), and they both get locked. In order to see the mask's effect, *both*

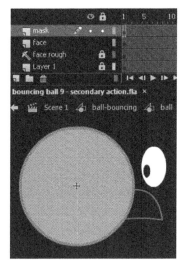

Image BB9.23

240

the mask and layer that it's masking need to be locked. *Image BB9.24*

25. You can see the effect of the mask already on the first and last keyframes. We need to adjust the expressions to fit the roughs. Unlock the "face" layer and turn the Outline view on the "mask" layer so that we can see through it. *Image BB9.25*

26. On the first frame, double-click the symbol on the "face" layer to enter so that we may edit its shape.

27. To work on one feature at a time, hide every layer except for the one you'd like to work on (such as "mouth"). The plan is to adjust the mouth as a whole so that the two halves (one shown and other not) basically match up with one another which makes the shape tween easier for Animate CC to do. Use the vector and line adjustment method to refine this shape tween. *Image BB9.27*

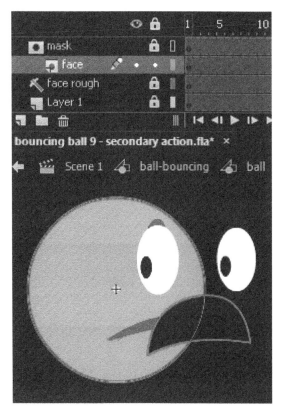

Image BB9.25

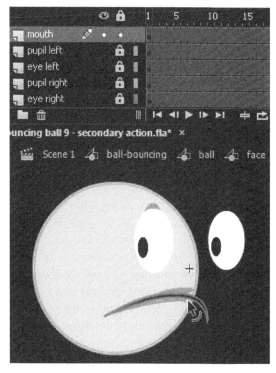

Image BB9.27

28. Change the position of the pupils relative to the surrounding eye so that it's looking to the right as well. *Image BB9.28*

Image BB9.28

29. Back in the "ball" symbol, insert a keyframe (**F6**) a few frames before the "looking back" keyframe in the middle and create a classic motion tween. Use the Easing Editor to give it a nice, smooth slow in and out (remember the "S" curve). *Image BB9.29*

Image BB9.29

30. Repeat step 29 for the last keyframe to return the symbol back to position. *Image BB9.30*

Image BB9.30

31. Because we will need to clean up the final roughs frame by frame, we'll need to turn the tween in step 30 into all keyframes so that we may address each frame individually. Highlight the tween from step 30 and press **F6**. *Image BB9.31*

Image BB9.31

32. Double-click the "face" symbol on the keyframe at the start of the span created in step 29.

33. Create keyframes at this frame for all layers and with them still highlighted, apply a shape tween. *Image BB9.33*

Image BB9.33

34. There is no Custom Easing Editor for shape tweens, so to get the same slow in/out as we did in step 29, we need to apply the easing amount manually. Create keyframes for all layers halfway between the two keyframes in this current shape tween span so that you now have it split into two tweens. Then apply a −100 easing (slow in) to the first and a +100 easing (slow out) to the second tween in the span. Double-check your tweens to make sure it's tweening

well. If not, use shape tweens to fix. *Image BB9.34*

Image BB9.34

35. Return to the "ball" symbol and scroll ahead to the breakdown rough created in step 8.

36. Double-click to enter the "face" symbol, insert blank keyframes (**F7**) for all layers at this frame, and clean up the rough using your current knowledge of drawing in Animate CC. *Image BB9.36*

37. Repeat steps 35 and 36 for the next two rough frames. *Image BB9.37*

Interlude

You should now be seeing the ball bouncing left to right, then looking behind it, and finally squinting its eyes and gritting its teeth as it comes to a stop, worried about what's coming but too scared to continue moving forward. The other thing you'll notice is that while the tail is dragging behind with great overlapping action and comes to a stop with follow through, the face is sitting mostly stationary in its place. When the ball is bouncing upward the face should trail behind a bit, looking down for a couple frames before following the upward motion. This same overlapping action is basically what your head does in little movements when you run. Every time a step is made, the force of that impact stops

Image BB 9.36

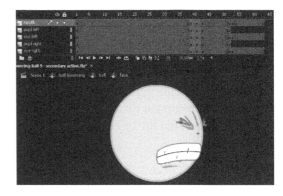

Image BB 9.37

the body/spine. But the head can still rotate a little, so it's up/down motion overlaps a little with the body.

The way that we can fix and improve this shot is to take everything we did in the cleanup, put it inside another symbol, assign the pivot point to the center of the ball, and rotate the face up/down a couple frames after the squash and up keys of the main bouncing ball. If we were to draw all the roughs before animating this scene, the overlapping action of the face would be included in them. But since we're adding the feature in order to learn the application of a principle, our roughs were finetuned to just the face and limited to just the expressions—leaving the overlapping action to be applied separately.

38. In the "ball" symbol, click the "face" layer to highlight all its frames on the timeline. Right-click these and **Copy Frames**.

39. Create a new Graphic Symbol (Cmd/Ctrl+F8), name it "face overlap," and right-click **Paste Frames** on its timeline.

40. Return to the "ball" symbol, click the "face" layer and insert a new layer above it (so that it's also attached to the "mask" layer), and name it "face overlap."

41. Drag the "face overlap" symbol from the library onto frame 1 so that it lines up with the same image on the layer below ("face"). *Image BB9.41*

42. Delete the "face" layer.

43. Click the "face overlap" symbol and, with the Free Transform Tool (**Q**) selected, drag the pivot point (white dot) to the *ball's* center (not the face's center). *Image BB9.43*

44. Return to the main timeline (click "Scene 1" above the stage) and create a new layer.

45. Scrolling along the timeline, insert a blank keyframe (**F7**) at every "up" and "squash" key. *(Pro-tip: you can actually add labels on keyframes like these by typing in a label in the "Label" section of the properties Panel when the desired keyframe is selected.) Image BB9.45*

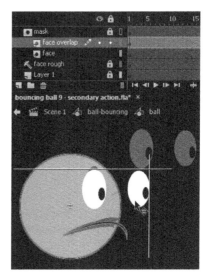

Image BB9.41

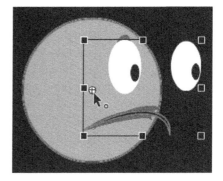

Image BB9.43

Image BB9.45

46. Click the timeline created in step 44, **Copy Frames** and **Delete Layer**.

Image BB9.48

47. Enter the "ball" symbol, create new layer and **Paste Frames** (on frame 1). This layer is your reference layer, so you can see the frames that all the relevant keys are on.

48. Create a keyframe (**F6**) on the "face overlap" layer four frames after the final blank keyframe on the reference layer. This frame is the final resting position. *Image BB9.48*

49. On frame 1, with the Free Transform Tool, rotate the face counter-clockwise so that the face is looking up slightly. *Image BB9.49*

50. Insert keyframes (**F6**) on the "face overlap" layer two frames after every *other* blank keyframe shown in the reference layer. These are your "up" key positions, remember, since we start on an "up." *Image BB9.50*

51. Insert keyframes on the "face overlap" layer two frames after all the remaining blank reference keyframes and rotate the face clockwise so that it's looking down slightly. *Image BB9.51*

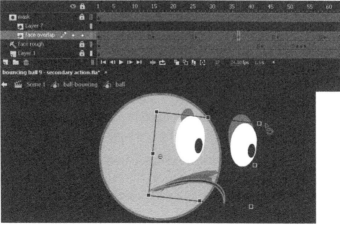

Image BB9.49

Image BB9.50

Image BB9.51

52. Highlight all the spaces between the existing keyframes on the "face overlap" layer and create a motion tween. Use the Easing Editor to give it a nice slow in and out graph (the "S" curve). *Image BB9.52*

Image BB9.52

Image BB9.53

53. If you test now, you'll notice that one tween seems off. When the ball is looking back, its head is cocked to the side. Select this keyframe and rotate it back to normal (with no rotation) to remove this strange effect. To still get the "head tipping back" effect, move the face up on the ball a bit. *Image BB9.53*

54. Enter the "ball-bouncing" symbol and scroll ahead to where the face looks behind the ball.

55. Click the tail (unlock the "tail" layer if it's currently locked) and move it to the right so that it looks like it is further behind the ball. Adjusting the tail position in this way will better sell the look of the ball turning around mid-bounce. *Image BB9.55*

Image BB9.55

You should now have a ball bouncing away from something, looking behind it, and then falling to a stop while closing its eyes fearfully—all while a tail and face demonstrate the dragging motion of overlapping action and complete with a follow through. The designs are rudimentary, the scene simple, but the principles have all been applied and a plethora of tools are now known as well as their hotkeys. As mentioned before, when approaching a scene like this in an animated short, or under any real-world scenario, you would rarely want to create it the way we did in these exercises (adding onto an animation bit by bit from the start). If the story point of the scene is a ball runs away from something and is scared, you would sketch a rough animation first and *then* figure out how to approach the cleanup using your knowledge of the tools at hand.

Doing it the way we did in these bouncing ball exercises, however, building step by step and chapter by chapter, aids in the understanding of the principles and tools at our disposal so that this focused work can be merged together to function as one on any future standalone animated shot—which will be covered more in the last of the principles: Appeal. That's not to say that you won't ever add something to a previously "finished" animation ... it happens all the time; but usually it's altering something that already exists in the scene, like an expression change, clothing feature, or anything else in the overlapping/secondary action categories. They spice up a scene and are built off of a base, so these are the target of alterations when a scene is done. If the main, primary action of a shot needs to be altered, you're essentially scrapping it. That's why it's so important to know the story point and nail down the basic movements first.

Let's think for a second that instead of a bouncing ball with a tail, we're animating a man in a trench coat. With our story point the same as in this exercise, it would be easier to just animate a loop of a character running from left to right. But by adding secondary action of our running man turning to look over his shoulder as he's running away like we did to the bouncing ball, the texture is so much richer. The animation is more interesting to look at. You don't need to stop there, though, you could add a little trip as he turns around to look. Not enough to fall, just enough to show he's running at his limit and at any moment could come crashing down, allowing whatever he's running from to catch up to him.

Image 9.4

"Exploration is the great secret of creation. Very rarely do you know, from the start, exactly what to do or how to do it—it's something that you constantly discover every time out."

Working out your concept is where thumbnailing helps, as well. Drawing those small, sketchy images quickly will let you explore these acting choices to see which works well. Then you can rough the scene out and make sure it works in movement the way you imagined in your thumbnails. Pablo Picasso is supposed to have said (translated from Spanish), "if you know exactly what you're going to do, then what's the point in doing it?" In a world of misattributed quotes, this could very well be one—but the sentiment remains. Exploration is the great secret of creation. Very rarely do you know, from the start, exactly what to do or how to do it—it's something that you constantly discover every time out. Secondary action goes hand in hand with this concept because while there are many ways to approach the primary acting of a scene, things get more complicated for the animator to predict and perform when adding in another layer to that performance. This added texture to the acting is worth the added time it takes to simply sketch out a few more drawings and explore the best options.

247

Much like the breakdown frame (which is in between two keyframes, showing the transitional position/expression), secondary action can make *or* break a scene. Secondary action is always in support of the main animation and story point. Examples could be acting out a similar sentiment as the primary action (as in our bouncing ball exercise where it's running away scared and looking back scared) or an opposite attitude (as in the angry chef example where he's trying not to look angry in the primary action but the chopping of the onion is giving his true emotions away in the secondary action). Sometimes, you can change the tone of an entire scene just by altering the secondary action, which is what we're going to be looking at in this section.

Right now, the ball glances back with a scared look on its face. We're going to simply add a happy/excited expression after that, making the scared face essentially a breakdown frame on its way to being happy. So now the feeling is not so much scared for its life as scared it's going to get caught in a game of tag which is fun. Juxtaposing scared and happy makes a kind of gray area in what the story point could be called now, because in this case the ball is bouncing away happy-scared. Fundamentally, the ball (playing a game of tag) is scared; it's simply a different kind of scared. However, if you were to see images of kids playing a game of tag out of context, it might look like they're legitimately terrified and maybe in danger. A scene like that without sufficient context would be ambiguous to the viewer, with them not being able to easily determine the emotional state of the character.

> "A chain is anything which links together a series of expressions or movements to demonstrate depth in acting."

This problem falls under a failure of staging. Even though the point is that our bouncing ball is scared it's going to get caught in tag and is running away because of that, the acting is not succeeding in communicating the deeper meaning behind the story point—that overall it's happily thrilled that it's experiencing this fear of getting caught in a game. So by having the secondary action be a look behind which starts with a scared look and "morphs" into a happy expression, the scene turns from almost a horror movie clip into something more innocent. Linking these expressions together to tell the complicated emotional story of our esteemed bouncing ball is appropriately called an "expression chain." A chain is anything which links together a series of expressions or movements to demonstrate depth in acting. Let's do that! Don't forget to **Save As** with the suffix "closer look" so that we don't lose work.

"Expression Chain"

1. Enter the "ball-bouncing" symbol.

2. Scrub through the timeline until you see the closest keyframe to the expression change (which should be an "up" key at frame 45) and enter the "ball" symbol. *Image CL9.2*

Image CL9.2

3. Scrub ahead until you get to the next keyframe on the "face overlap" layer and enter the "face overlap" symbol from there. *Image CL9.3*

4. From the current frame, enter the "face" symbol. Above the stage you should see "Scene 1 > ball-bouncing > ball > face overlap > face." This hierarchy is a perfect visual representation of symblification: multiple symbols with nested animations layered within each other. *Image CL9.4*

5. Insert a keyframe (**F6**) on the "mouth" layer at the current frame.

Image CL9.3

6. Using what you've learned about shape manipulation, turn the mouth shape into a very wide, happy

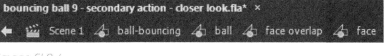

Image CL9.4

one. *(Pro-tip: you might need to add a vector point by holding Cmd/Ctrl when click-dragging with the Selection Tool in the middle of the line on the bottom to get the curve right. To aid in the shape tweening, you can ostensibly "remove" the point by making the curves on either side become a singular curve and with "snap to objects" enabled dragging the point up or down until it snaps.) Image CL9.6*

Image CL9.6

7. Create a shape tween in the space before the keyframe created in step 5. If needed, use shape hints (Cmd/Ctrl+Shift+H) to get the tween working correctly. *Image CL9.7*

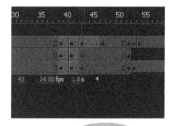 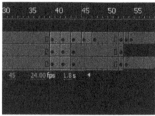

8. Insert keyframe (F6) at the halfway point in the shape tween, reattach the shape hints created in step 7, and check the second tween to see if it's working smoothly. If not, use shape hints to fix. *Image CL9.8*

Image CL9.7   *Image CL9.8*

9. Give a −100 easing (slow in) for the first tween and 100 (slow out) for the second in the set created in step 8.

10. Right-click the keyframe created in step 8 and **Copy Frames**.

11. **Paste Frames** one frame before the final straight ahead span where the mouth ends up closed and gritting teeth. *Image CL9.11*

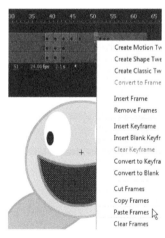

Image CL9.11

12. Insert a keyframe two frames before the key created in step 11 and give it a shape tween with a slow in (easing −100). Don't forget the shape hints if they're needed. *Image CL9.12*

Image CL9.12

You've now basically hijacked the symbol with the facial animation, altered the expression, and kept all the other movements the same. Quick editing like this is something you've seen quite a few times in this book. Animate CC, and using it for Tradigital animation in particular, is outstanding with pin-point alterations. There's no need to draw in and replace a bunch of frames every time a change is made. Notice how the entire mood of the scene has been updated to reflect a completely different emotional state. You could do this all day long. If you alter the easing of the bounce to give a hard slow in/out, increase the squash and stretches, and bump up the amount of overlap shown in the face, you could make the action more "cartoony." Then if you were to take that same cartoony-style bouncing and shorten the timing within the symbols, it would make that cartoony effect more intense. Of course, changing the timing across each symbol individually would take some extra time, but not much extra effort. You could edit it even further by reverting the expression to one without a smile, which would turn it from a cartoony tone to a more desperate and intense one.

What if there's no fear whatsoever? Let's say our bouncing ball is just traveling along minding its own business without a care in the world. What might be a good way to show that? Whistling, blowing bubble gum, having a stupid-happy smile on its face all work. Let's go with blowing a bubble from gum. We'll accomplish this change by simply wiping clear the facial animation we created and replacing it with this new secondary action. Don't forget to **Save As** with another suffix (for instance "bouncing ball 9 – secondary action – closer look II") so as not to lose work.

"Bubble Gum"

13. On frame 1 from the main stage, double-click the face on the bouncing ball until you get to the "face-overlap" symbol, highlight every frame except for the first, and right-click **Clear Keyframe** (we won't be needing this movement since the ball isn't turning around). *Image CL9.13*

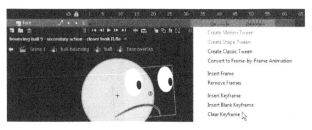

Image CL9.13

14. Enter the "face" symbol and guide (and hide) every layer except for the ones which contain the right eye's features (eye and pupil).

15. Highlight every keyframe except those on frame 1, right-click and **Clear Keyframe**. *Image CL9.15*

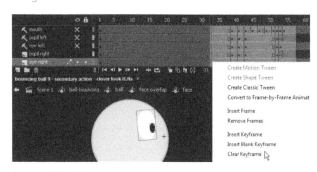

Image CL9.15

16. Let's give the eye a nonchalant, half-closed lid look. To create an eyelid quickly, draw a line (to be the bottom of the top lid) across the eye using the Pencil Tool (**Shift+Y**) and then use the Paint Bucket Tool (**K**) to fill in the now enclosed top portion of the eye with a similar color as the body of the ball. Don't forget to remove the overlapping lines. *Image CL9.16*

Image CL9.16

17. Insert a new layer and name it "bubble gum."

18. Select good stroke and fill colors that will represent bubble gum well and use the Oval Tool (**O**) to draw a circle on the stage to represent a fully blown-up bubble and move it to the bouncing ball so that it looks like it has just been blown up from the lips (that can't be seen). *Image CL9.18*

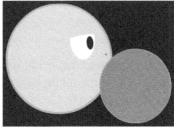

Image CL9.18

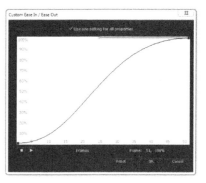

Image CL9.19

19. Highlight the image created in step 6, and convert it to a Graphic Symbol (**F8**) with the name "bubble." *Image CL9.19*

20. Using the Free Transform Tool (**Q**), move the pivot point (white dot) to the left of the ball where the "lips" would connect and Insert Keyframe (**F6**) toward the end of the timeline (I chose frame 51). *Image CL9.20a and CL9.20b*

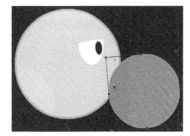

Image CL9.20a

Image CL9.20b

21. Back on frame 1, shrink the size of the bubble down to an appropriate start size (small). *Image CL9.21*

22. Create a motion tween between the two bubble keys with a slight slow in into a harder slow out (which will look like an "S" with a shorter beginning curve). *Image CL9.22*

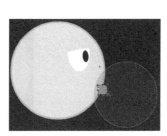

Image CL9.21

Image CL9.22

252

23. Using **F7** to insert blank frames, the Pencil Tool (**Shift+Y**) to use the bubble's stroke color, and onion skin mode, straight ahead about four frames at the end of the timeline showing the bubble popping. *(Note: special effect animation is an entire sub-branch of animation and is a specialty skill. Don't feel bad if it doesn't come out looking great. Effects animation will require a lot of practice and study. The good news is that Animate CC makes it easy to explore these techniques and refine through practice.) Image CL9.23*

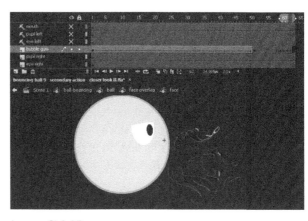

Image CL9.23

24. Remember that with the current mask applied, anything outside of the bouncing ball's shape won't be shown. But in the bubble gum's case we actually want the opposite effect: to see everything except that which is overlapped by the shape of the ball. To move the bubble gum so that it's *not* affected by the mask, we need to put the bubble gum animation on a layer *below* the ball layer. To do this we're going to need to nest the bubble gum's animation sequence in its own symbol. Start by selecting the "bubble gum" layer so that all the frames are highlighted and right-click **Copy Frames**. *Image CL9.24*

Image CL9.24

25. Guide the "bubble gum" layer so that it won't show up in the animation and we don't have to delete it. It's good practice to use this feature while working in case you need the layer in question later for some reason. *Image CL9.25*

Image CL9.25

26. Create a new Graphic Symbol (**Cmd/Ctrl+Shift+F8**), name it "bubble-blow" and right-click **Paste Frames** so that the animation is now nested in this new symbol. *(Note: if the layer has pasted in as a guide layer, then you may have completed step 13 before step 12. Toggle the Guide option back off to fix it.) Image CL9.26*

Image CL9.26

27. Re-enter the "ball" symbol, insert another layer *under* everything, and name it "bubble-blow."

28. Drag the "bubble-blow" symbol onto the stage in the position you would like and with the Free Transform Tool (**Q**) selected move the pivot point (white dot) to the center of the ball. *(Pro-tip: look for the registration point, +, since that should be at the exact center of the ball. Snap to Objects will lock the pivot point to this area.) Image CL9.28*

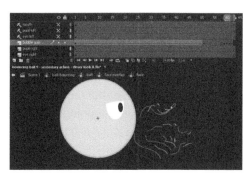

Image CL9.28

29. Test the movie (**Cmd/Ctrl+Enter**). Notice that while the eye (representing the face, solely, now) is showing overlapping action, the bubble is not. Every time there's a joint, the overlapping action is kind of "reset" such that it will drag later than what's before it. The connection between the bubble and the face represents a joint, so the bubble will overlap *after* the face's movement.

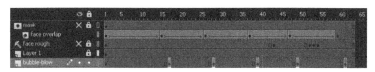

Image CL9.30

30. Still working with the "ball" symbol, insert keyframe (**F6**) on the "bubble-blow" layer two frames after the keyframes on the "face" layer except for the first. We'll do that later. *Image CL9.30*

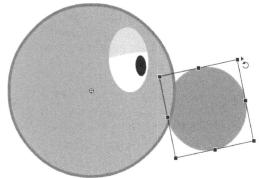

Image CL9.31

31. Rotate each keyframe (including the first) clockwise or counter, corresponding to the face's movement. Make sure to have the counter-clockwise rotation be more than the clockwise since the ground will limit the bubble's movement downward on and just after contact, but there's nothing preventing the bubble from stretching up more as it falls. *(Note: the final keyframe doesn't need a rotation.) Image CL9.31*

32. Insert a keyframe two frames after the first (now that the rotation has been applied). *Image CL9.32*

Image CL9.32

33. Highlight every span between the second and last keyframes and apply a motion tween to all, simultaneously with a slow in/out easing ("S" curve). *Image CL9.33*

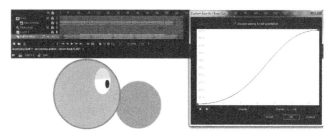

Image CL9.33

Look at how enormously different the three scenes created in this chapter are. Granted, we've changed the story point for this last "bubble gum" exercise, but that was to help you see across all three scenarios how changes, fixes, and even complete reworkings of scenes can be done rather simply (or at least a bit simpler than in fully traditional animation) with the assistance of Animate's tools. Let's be clear on something: you don't usually create high art when learning. This last sequence is a bouncing ball with an eye, a tail, and some bubble gum. Who even knows *what* that is? Whereas in animation you need to keep the story point in mind as you work and everything must support that concept, learning animation itself has a point: learning. Each chapter in this book has a point: the program working for the principle. Making pretty things is not yet on the roster—nor should it be.

There's nothing beautiful about this last sequence other than the representation of your increasing knowledge. Because of that, there's nothing that says you can't **Save As** another file name and just start messing with it—playing around with it. You're not worried about ruining a great piece of art. You can use this detachment to continue your learning, for instance, by going back to the other chapters' bouncing ball exercise files and seeing if you can add more principles in the shots. Or you could try to add some anticipation to this scene. Use squash and stretch to its full acting potential and try to make the ball shimmy across the stage instead of bouncing. Learn and explore. This is creation.

Another quote high on the misattribution scale (like the Picasso one, earlier) is the writers' expression, "kill your darlings." Widely credited to William Faulkner, it actually seems to come from Arthur Quiller-Couch who said "whenever you feel an impulse to perpetrate a piece of exceptionally fine writing … delete it before sending your manuscript to press. Murder your darlings." Step aside the unsettling discussion of killing and murdering for a second and replace "writing" with "animation," and you'll start to see why this is being brought up. The idea is that if this exceptionally fine work of art you've just created—

Image 9.5 Artist rendition, looking for the point.

however brilliant in isolation—doesn't serve the greater story or concept, it should be removed. Earlier in that same quote he says "style … is not … extraneous ornament," which in itself is pretty ornamental language. But it means that just because something is decorated, fancy, or even well put together technically, it doesn't necessarily indicate "style." For creatives, they relate (rather morbidly and hyperbolically) this destruction of well-done work to the killing of someone they love ... killing their darlings. It just serves to remind artists to critically look at their creations as they're finished to determine if they work within the overall piece. For instance, if you've animated the most amazing dance sequence but the rest of your animation is limited and bare, it will look out of place and in turn will drag your audience out of the film with it. If that's the point (for irony or self-reflection), then leave it in; if not, it should be removed. Editing yourself is a difficult lesson to learn, even for experienced artists. That's why the bouncing ball is such a great exercise. There's no risk of it becoming a "darling." You're free to explore and, if necessary, to kill.

Using Secondary Action With "Multitasking"

Secondary Action is essentially multitasking; not just for the character, but also for the animator. When you're animating a character, simply completing one action is difficult enough, so it can often feel daunting to add another action to the goals of a shot. Because of the complexity of animating multiple actions, a lot of animators might end up convincing themselves into thinking that these secondary actions aren't necessary. Let's cut this idea off at the head. They're not necessary. As a matter of fact, nothing in art is really *necessary*. Food, water, air, shelter ... these are all requisites for life. In engineering as long as a building stands, it has fulfilled its purpose. But it's in the architectural design that the style emerges. This example is representative of art as a whole: the unnecessary spice of life. With art, we can entertain, challenge, inform, confuse, distract, please, support, alienate (and loads of other descriptor words both positive and negative). Secondary Action is a true "acting" principle. It's what adds to the scene in order to color the character's actions and motivations in a certain way. This added visual information is what will heighten the quality of your animation and open up so many avenues for comedy, drama, and everything in between. So no, it's not technically necessary—but it can be.

> "Secondary Action is essentially multitasking; not just for the character, but also for the animator."

Let's take as an example, a classic bad guy scene. Our hero is cornered in a room on all sides; there is no way out. The villain is calmly sitting in a chair "monologuing" about what an understanding businessman he is, but if you cross him ... he'll have to be *less* understanding. This setup is another version of the angry chef scene we described earlier. He's saying one thing but thinking another. If it's just the villain talking to the hero, it's all down to the expressions and voice acting to sell this idea that he's a dangerous guy, but the point is that he's trying to intimidate through a quiet conversation. Now imagine that the villain is eating an apple with a knife and cutting off piece after piece. The cutting is the secondary action. The presence of the knife in his hands carving up an object to devour, even though it's just an apple, adds so much depth and presence to the scene. It becomes much more viscerally threatening because now you have a physical representation of what he's really thinking (*Image 9.6*). It's these touches which reel the audience in and make them invested in what's happening while never being taken out of the moment long enough to notice that these are just drawings. Secondary Action is a powerful ally.

One of my favorite examples of Secondary Action in use (actually, this movie has a *lot* of them) is the alien brain movie scene from *The Iron Giant* (*Image 9.7*). In it, Hogarth is watching a late-night, sci-fi creature feature on TV. He's not supposed to be up late watching scary movies so naturally he goes all out with a blanket fort, toy ray-gun, and Twinkie with whipped cream and popcorn for snacks. Hogarth barely takes his eyes off the screen, and when he does it's only to dip his head with an exasperated groan at the hint of a romantic storyline—he wants to see monster attacks! He starts the scene by filling a Twinkie with whipped cream, eating it, and licking the excess whipped cream off his thumb. He also holds the ray-gun in his hand with the other helping him eat a bowl of popcorn. All of those actions are secondary to him watching the movie. The point of the scene wouldn't change if you removed them, but

Image 9.6

Image 9.7 The Iron Giant (1999) Warner Bros./Kobal/ Art Resource.

it is supported heavily by them. We're completely drawn into the moment because Hogarth is and we relate to him. There's hardly a better example which demonstrates what exactly Secondary Action is, at a fundamental level.

You *could* get the point across with just the shot of Hogarth watching TV; the secondary action isn't *needed* in that sense. But after watching that sequence in *The Iron Giant*, it's hard to imagine it without the "extra" actions. After seeing a scene with proper secondary action applied, the audience should barely be aware of it but unable to see it any other way. They should be thinking, without hesitation, "it needed to be that way." Would Heath Ledger's heralded performance as the Joker in *The Dark Knight* be as charismatically maniacal if he wasn't constantly licking his stretched and painted lips as he spoke? This one constant quirk (secondary action) combined with the shaggy hair and constantly lowered head reminds us, visually, of a wolf—wild, untamed, dangerous—ready to attack without notice. It adds to the character and provides depth. Try to think of the "they will never take our freedom" speech from *Braveheart*. William Wallace (at least in the cinematic version) is riding back and forth on a horse as he passionately gives a pre-battle speech to his wary soldiers. Throughout the speech, the horse is getting more and more rambunctious while the scene crescendos to a final war cry of "freedom" and the horse runs across the front line so that William Wallace can see, and be seen by, all his riled-up warriors. What if he were, you know ... just standing there? Not as interesting, right? It wouldn't be nearly as emotional.

> "Secondary action is ... the co-star of the main action—there to support and not distract."

It's true that secondary action is just that: secondary. It's the co-star of the main action—there to support and not distract. Just because it's secondary, there is a tendency, as mentioned, to think of it as unnecessary. But also, it's just as often simply looked at as altogether unimportant. Secondary Action is an animation principle for a reason. It can add enormous value and depth to a scene. That's not to say that it can't be overdone; anything can, but consideration should always be given to this principle and whether it can bring anything to a sequence to make it clearer and more interesting. It can be small and confined like the cracking of knuckles or a full body expression like shifting in a chair—whatever helps to better communicate the point of the scene. Try roughing out a scene with only the primary action in mind, *then* think about some secondary action and re-rough. You can build up to your own multitasking, but it should look mostly spontaneous for the character you're animating. It's all part of giving it the illusion of life.

REAL-WORLD EXAMPLE
"Roll-Tapping Fingers"

Principles Used

Overlapping Action: The action of "roll-tapping" your fingers (a term I just made up) is inherently made up of overlapping action. With your wrist on the table and fingers bent up in the air, first you tap the pinky, then the ring finger, followed by the middle and index fingers. Each finger is doing the same action (tapping the table) but is doing it with offset starting times and rates.

Slow In/Out: The individual finger taps will slow in on the way down and have a slow in and out on the way up.

Timing: The effect that timing has on a secondary action like the tapping fingers in this example is huge. It's like in a *pas de deux* (dance duet) when one dancer is being highlighted by the choreography, the other is supporting these actions (primary) with their own (secondary). When an action is done it's very important to a scene because it can mean the difference between a graceful dance of acting and a harsh fight for attention.

Image 9.8

Solid Drawing: The makeup of the human hand is something everyone can notice if it's drawn wrong, but very few could say why, other than "it looks weird." Talk to any traditional animator, and I bet you could get them to talk a lot about their problems in effectively drawing hands. The fact that the hand is pointing toward the camera, but angled slightly away, with the fingers bent in, means that it's incredibly important to maintain a sense of volume and solid form in order to make sure the audience is being sucked into the scene because of the secondary action and not taken out of it by thinking that this hand "looks weird."

Secondary Action: The finger tapping isn't the primary action in the scene; the annoyed dialog is. The story point, however, is that the character is annoyed so to *support* the primary action, the finger tapping is employed as a secondary action at the right time.

Setting Up

For the final standalone real-world example (the following chapters inform and enhance the ones already listed), open the file titled "ch9-real_world-finger_tapping.fla" from the companion website. In this one, you'll notice that there is actually already a completed scene. "What is there left to do, then?" Right now, there's nothing but the expression on our character's face and the words he's saying to truly convey the feeling of annoyance that we want to get across to the audience in this scene. It needs something more to support this story point. We need to add secondary action (which is serendipitous, being that this is the topic of the chapter).

In this case, the goal is to add to our scene like you had finished it, decided that you wanted a more well-rounded performance from the character, and are now going back to fix it. This scenario of adding to a scene will happen a lot in any type of animation you do (well, stop-motion to a lesser extent because of the nature of the medium). What we'll be doing is creating rough animation (of course) over the scene for a singular feature (the hand). Then we'll clean that up inside of a symbol which can be set to play once any time we want the action to repeat like we did with the blinking animation in Chapter 1's real-world exercise. There won't be a numbered step-by-step guide for this example, but there's nothing in here that you haven't seen already. Let's get to it.

"Rough Fix"

Insert a new layer named "rough" and sketch out some rough animation of an annoyed finger "roll-tap" (*Image RT9.1a*). Make sure that the layer is turned into a guide layer so that it won't show up on the final. I did this rough animation "on twos" (one drawing every two frames) to match the lip-sync which is also on twos. Because it's a self-contained action, you can highlight the sequence of frames and drag them forward or backward on the timeline to fit in best with the acting of the scene. The scene could use a couple more of these, so you can copy/paste the exact sequence where you want or draw in a new timing or configuration of the tap (obviously, if you draw something different, you'll need to clean this up as well, as opposed to

Image RT9.1a

playing the same sequence again). Finally, you can end the scene with a subtle hand gesture to really put a period at the end of the action (*Image RT9.1b*). The ending is at your discretion since you're the director and acting coach for the character. Let him know what you want from him.

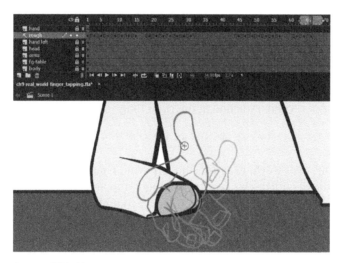

Image RT9.1b

"Cleanup"

Image RT9.2a

Copy the entire timeline of the rough, double-click into the hand symbol, and paste those rough frames on a new layer. They won't be in the same position but you can fix this like you've done before with the bouncing ball's tail from Chapter 8 by using Edit Multiple Frames. With the rough animation aligned, you're free to tackle the cleanup (*Image RT9.2a*). You could essentially trace the rough frame by frame (or every other frame in my case since I animated on twos), treating the whole hand as one image or addressing one finger at a time. But since we're learning about the program and the various ways you can use it for Tradigital animation, you could also clean up only the up-and-down movements of each finger individually and put them in their own separate symbols, like I did.

In the completed example on the companion website, each of the finger symbols I made has five keyframes: down, breakdown, up, breakdown, and down. To create the roll-tap then, I set only the pinky at frame 1 to Play Once while the rest are single frame and each time a finger moves the next one in the line gets set to Play Once (*Image RT9.2b*). Making each finger its own self-contained symbol also lets you whip up new movements like a quick double-tap with only the index finger by just playing the index finger nested animation twice without the other fingers moving (which you can also see in the example I did). This compartmentalized symbol makeup for the hand takes a bit longer at first, but once you get used to seeing a feature's construction in terms of a symbol pack the process won't be much different than simply cleaning up directly on one timeline.

When the roll-tapping sequence has been animated, you can either copy/paste that sequence further down the hand symbol's own timeline where the rough animation has dictated (call that option "A") or delete the timeline in the hand symbol down to show only a single roll-tapping

Image RT9.2b

sequence (again, see timeline at the top of *Image RT9.2b*) and use the "Play Once" looping feature of the symbol on the main timeline to play it whenever it's needed (option "B"). If you choose option "A," you simply clean up the rough animation within the same hand symbol you've been working in. If you choose option "B," to clean up the final hand gesture animation you can insert a keyframe (**F6**) on the main timeline at the start of the final hand gesture sequence, right-click the hand symbol and select **Duplicate Symbol**, copy/paste the last sequence's rough animation into the new symbol, and just clean up as before. The obvious benefit to option "A" is that it's easy to keep things organized— all the hand animation is in the "hand" symbol … simple. The benefit to option "B," though, is that because each sequence is nested in its own symbol, these can be repeated and moved around at will throughout the scene or reused easily in other scenes (*Image RT9.2c*). I chose option "B" in the example on the companion website to demonstrate this quality. You'll notice I ended up with three symbols: one for the roll-tap, one for an index finger double-tap (which reused the index finger), and one for the final hand gesture.

Image RT9.2c The first two keyframes on the "hand" layer are Play Once symbols of the roll-tap. The second two, in order, are an index finger double-tap which replaces the roll-tap in the rough and the final gesture animation.

"Continuing With Secondary Action"

There are so many ways you can add to a scene with secondary action. What else might we add to this one? How about an eye roll? What if our character kind of shuffles slightly in his seat like he's uncomfortable and getting resituated? And after you do these rough animations comes the big question: how might you go about applying these to the final animation? The eye roll, for instance, would need to be added to the existing symblified facial animation (*Image RT9.3*). But the character shifting a bit in his seat could be done with subtle tweens to the whole body (and maybe some overlapping tweens to the head and hand for good measure).

There are two places where the internal actor of the animator lives: the breakdown frames and the secondary action. The breakdowns determine how you will get from one important frame to the other.

Image RT9.3

For instance when moving from a smile to a frightened expression, will the breakdown be anxiety or dumbfounded surprise? That decision will determine a lot about the content of that sequence. The feeling and flavor rests on how you approach that breakdown frame. There are some major acting choices to make there. Likewise, secondary action can confirm or contradict the primary (while still supporting the story point). If a character is smiling at the camera, what the audience interprets from that expression can change greatly if the secondary action is petting a kitten or breaking a pencil in half with a thumb. One confirms the happy expression, and the other contradicts it—but that's because the story points are different for both scenes. It's the acting choices that have been made in the secondary (and primary, obviously) action that lead to a rich expression of character in the scene. This type of depth in acting is what you want to achieve, and Animate CC can make these types of additions easy to implement when elements and actions are split up into symbols and can be focused on individually.

FINAL WORDS
Secondary Action

Jiminy Cricket swinging his umbrella around while he's talking is a clear example of secondary action. Bugs Bunny chewing on a carrot is absolutely secondary action. The site gag of Bugs and the carrot came from a scene in *It Happened One Night* in which Clark Gable was eating a carrot, which is *also* secondary action (*Image 9.9*). Those actions are never the point of the scene, but they've become inseparable parts of their character's persona. Having a character always chewing on a toothpick is also a secondary action (as long as it's not the point of the scene). These are all visual representations of a demeanor or outlook on life and are constant traits, like the Joker licking his lips. Earlier in this chapter we've had examples of momentary displays (a chef chopping onions while angry, a dog biting at its leash, etc.), and we explored in the bouncing ball exercises how expression chains can add proper context within the secondary action itself (in that case, looking behind itself). There are endless ways to tackle a particular scene, and this principle reminds you that when you're done with the primary points to see if you can add a bit more depth and clarity to the animation. It might just be the most "acting"-heavy principle—constantly asking you to be aware of the actual character of your ... character.

These principles can be pretty heady, and their application is not always entirely straightforward. Nested animation and using it with symblification are two of the clearer ways to apply Secondary Action. Remember that all the methods you apply to your main animation need to also be used with this principle, since the idea is that they could be their own standalone actions but are instead being used to prop up the story point of the primary one in the scene. In other words, while the smaller versions of certain secondary actions (chewing a toothpick or licking lips constantly) can almost be quarantined in their own symbols, larger actions which affect the whole body (like

Image 9.9 Clark Gable eating a carrot from It Happened One Night *(1934) inspired this same habit given to Bugs Bunny. Columbia/Kobal/Art Resource.*

William Wallace pacing with a horse during his speech in *Braveheart*) need to be approached together with the primary action as a single entity. This combination is the multitasking at work.

> "The Tradigital process of roughing everything out until all the motions look like they work well in concert and *then* cleaning up the animation with symblification rides a beautiful line between traditional planning, creative spontaneity, and digital accuracy."

All actions can be thought of in terms of a hierarchy. And in the case of Tradigital animation, they should absolutely be thought of in this way. The face is on the head. The head is on the neck, which is on the body, which balances on the feet. This entire person moves around in a 3D space. Symblifying the person keeps things organized enough to focus on specific parts when necessary as well as larger groups of features. You will absolutely be multitasking motions in your animation; it's almost impossible to avoid. The Tradigital process of roughing everything out until all the motions look like they work well in concert and *then* cleaning up the animation with symblification rides a beautiful line between traditional planning, creative spontaneity, and digital accuracy. But we still have not illustrated anything other than a few simple shapes. That all changes in the next chapter, "Solid Drawing." That chapter is where you will see your application of knowledge take a massive increase, and you will reap the benefits of the slow and steady building of these principles and tactics.

Image 10.0 Dragon character pack and the gestures, poses, and expressions achieved with it. Example from Wingaroo online game created by Alexandru Craciun. Character design by Jennifer Adkins Smith (flash-fox.com). Animation by Stephen Brooks (RubberOnion.com).

Chapter 10
SOLID DRAWING

INTRODUCING
Solid Drawing

The order of the principles in Frank Thomas and Ollie Johnston's book *The Illusion of Life* is often debated: was it purposeful or not? I tend to think that it wasn't in order of importance, but rather in an order which made it easier for them to explain in series. The reason that order is being brought up now is that Solid Drawing is second to last on their list. Illustrators, character designers, and simply those with a talent or penchant for solid draftsmanship take umbrage at the idea that their priorities aren't reflected with the same importance they put on them. Make no mistake, Solid Drawing is a principle of utmost importance in animation. It's really the basis for a lot of the work that we do; so why is it, again, at the end on the list of the 12 Principles of Animation?

> "Solid Drawing in animation refers to the well-defined formwork in traditional illustration that through efficiency in design only suggests the more complicated details, which otherwise would make frame-by-frame animation nearly impossible."

You might have a little *déjà vu* with the statement that the principle of Solid Drawing is the basis of much of our work, since a similar thing was said in our first chapter on Timing. Both sentiments are true. It was mentioned in Chapter 6, "Staging," that we live in a 3D world. To be more accurate, in our perceivable world, we live in four dimensions; the fourth is time. We simply started this book with all of the principles which emphasize that particular dimension of movement (except Staging, where we talked about setting). Now we're looking at the way our objects and characters inhabit the other three dimensions: length, width, and height. Even that description is a bit of an oversimplification, but trying to explain all of the facets that go into Solid Drawing is what makes this principle so difficult to really discuss. We started with the "movement" principles because it was important to see what could be done with the simplest of creations and how to work within the program. Now we need to see what it looks like to bring illustration into the mix and what the subtle differences are between a static image and design for movement.

"What Is Solid Drawing?"

"Does your drawing have weight, depth, and balance?" Frank and Ollie recollect this infamous sign in the trainee area of the Disney studios with the follow-up statement, "Men had devoted their whole lives to the mastery of these elusive principles, and here was this sign about as pretentious as one that said, 'Buy Savings Bonds,' or pointed to the nearest exit." It's an important perspective on the fact that animation has an added dimension to the work of static artistry—it's an extension of this already loaded field of art. That's not to diminish static art in any way; vaudevillian standards of acting were artistry in their own right before film with sound came into the picture (pun intended). Even stage acting is a different type of mastery than acting in film. What seem like subtle distinctions in creative fields are still differences, and with them come new complications and a reordering of the priorities of one's skills. Sculpture is to stop-motion animation as illustration is to hand-drawn animation—all four fields have their

Image 10.1 Timeline showing animation "on ones" (top) and "on twos" (bottom).

various relations to one another but are completely unique in the way mastery is developed and perceived.

The meaning behind Solid Drawing comes from more traditional, static, illustrative arts where the principles of form were developed, but it's focused with animation in mind. Traditional character animation was usually animated at 24 or 12fps (12fps means they were animating "on twos," which is holding a drawing for two frames to save on work without sacrificing the look of normal movement). Animating at that rate means that they needed to illustrate that character 12 to 24 times for every single second of animation (*Image 10.1*). A balance needed to be made in order to simplify the sheer *amount* of representations of solid drawing to keep track of during their animation. For example, look at MGM's "Tom and Jerry" cartoons before 1942 (they started in 1940). That was a time before Tex Avery made the jump over to the studio from its rival, Warner Bros. Tom Cat looked more complicated than I bet you remember, with spikes representing his hair all over his body. All of these many individual hair points were *incredibly* difficult to keep track of for the animator. When Tex came in, though not working directly on the shorts, he helped the artists simplify the design to suggest the hair rather than actually specifically show it (*Image 10.2*). This simplification resulted in not only a smoother-looking character in design, but also propagated to smoother animation since the animators now had far less to keep track of frame to frame and could devote more focus to the movement itself. This finely tuned way of looking at design is what we're going to talk about. Solid Drawing in animation refers to the well-defined formwork in traditional illustration that through efficiency in design only suggests the more complicated details, which otherwise would make frame-by-frame animation nearly impossible.

Solid does not mean rigid in this case. It refers to strength of form, meaning that you believe if it existed in the real world, it could stand and move the way it does. It should show that it has

Image 10.2 Before Tex Avery's soft redesign of Tom and Jerry (left, Puss Gets the Boot, *1940) and after (right,* The Lonesome Mouse, *1943).*

volume, weight, and the ability to retain its own shape—you don't want it looking too "gooey." Disney animators referred to this balance between stability and also being flexible enough to show cartoon exaggeration like squash and stretch as being "plastic." It's not talking about the material, but rather the adjective of a substance that is easily shaped or molded—pliable. The fact is there are just too many facets of solid drawing to cover in one chapter. This is a long-term pursuit of all animators. There are, however, a few things to keep in mind as we go forward into the exercises.

"Essence Of Solid Drawing Crash Course"

Composition: Drawing for animation means that construction is a necessity to keep consistent. A body is made up of simple shapes: rectangles, ovals, and triangles. These simple shapes combine together to make 3D shapes. For instance, six squares make a box (a rectangle); two circles make a cylinder; four triangles and a rectangle make a pyramid; and a triangle and an oval make a cone. There are many other shapes that are created this way. These 3D shapes can be distorted to make interesting shapes. Imagine how a box can distort to look like an overfilled grocery bag or a cone warping to look like a horn. These interesting shapes combine together to make virtually anything. *Image CC10.1*

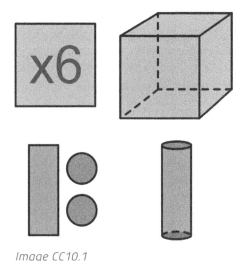

Image CC10.1

Don't Twin: Twinning is where one side of a body mirrors the pose or action of the other. It has a flattening effect on a drawing and can really take the audience out of the moment by reminding them that these are just drawings after all. Think of a cardboard cut-out of a person. If they are standing straight up with their hands on their hips in exactly the same way, you won't be fooled for a second; that's obviously a cut-out. But if that same person were to be standing at an angle, even in the same pose, it wouldn't look as flat and might actually trick your brain for a second as you walk by it in the store. The pose is the same, but by making the simple adjustment of turning the body in perspective the silhouette of the form isn't perfectly mirrored (or "twinned") on both sides. Twinning makes an image flat, rigid, boring, and other similarly themed descriptor words—so even though this tip is called "don't twin," if you *want* to make your audience feel those things about a character at a particular moment that's when you break this general no-twinning rule. *Image CC10.2*

Keep Proportions: In animation, we play a lot with form by exaggerating poses and squashing/stretching throughout movement. But through these poses, proportions of features still need to be accounted for. The size and position of the eyes relative to the nose, for instance, shouldn't ever change on a person at rest. This change would affect the entire design. Even when you apply squashing and stretching, consideration of the proportions is necessary to know how and when something gets the distortion treatment. Knowing the rules is key to breaking the rules because if something goes wrong and doesn't look right and you don't know the rule you're breaking, you'll have no idea how to fix it. Construction is key to maintaining proper proportions as you animate.

Image CC10.2

Turnaround: Part of character design is creating model sheets. One type of these model sheets is the turnaround wherein a character with the same pose and expression is spun around from front to back at 45 degree intervals (front, 3/4, profile, 5/4 and back views). They are all drawn next to each other with horizontal lines extending through them all (which is why the "turnaround" is also called the "line sheet," along with other less frequently used terms) representing the various features so that it is assured they all are in the same spots relative to the previous image. We don't want the nose to suddenly jump up a couple of inches on the face when a character turns to look at something. The most difficult of these is the profile (side) view. Sometimes it can be hard to imagine how features that look great from the front would look from the side in a 3D world. It's important to work this view out ahead of time, because even though we're working in 2D drawings, the illusion of depth and volume must be maintained (see *Image TP7.1* from Chapter 7's real-world exercise section).

Line of Action: The line of action is an imaginary line (sometimes drawn by the animator during a thumbnail or gesture drawing such as the red one in the accompanying image) through the character to show the general flow of the pose. The uses and their effect on the poses are mostly obvious: angles are sharp, curves are fluid, and straight lines are strong. The difference between a character with a strong thrust in fencing and a thief reaching to pick up something delicate surrounded by alarms would be a curve. The line is pointing in the same direction (let's say, bottom left to top right), but the fencer is straight (strong, deliberate) and the thief is curved (gentle, careful not to set off an alarm). Knowing the line of action also helps to formulate a pleasing string of poses in your animation so that they're not too similar. A lot of interest and dynamism is achieved through opposites. So if you know a character is leaning forward in one shot, the line of action in the anticipation key would be the opposite of that. Purposeful drawing is a part of Solid Drawing. *Image CC10.5*

Image CC10.5

Straights and Curves: This idea of opposites being more interesting comes up a lot in every aspect of creation (story, music, color). The same can be said in forms. A straight line opposite a curved one creates an imbalance, and that imbalance insinuates a flow. An arm flexing its bicep is made up of two straight lines on one side and two curves meeting at a spot, pointing at the angle made by the straight lines. This simple series of lines makes you immediately see which side is flexible, which is hard, and the squeeze and constriction of the situation. When viewed from the side, the upper leg is curved in the front while straight in the back and the opposite for the lower leg (shin is straight, calf is curved). This combination creates an "S" curve which feels dynamic even when the leg is standing still. When used in conjunction with the "line of action," your keys will burst at the seams with interesting forms. We'll get into these results in our last chapter, "Appeal," but this interest is important for charming the audience into wanting to see more. In short, it's not boring. *Image CC10.6*

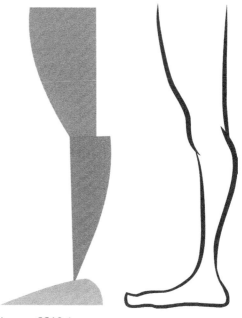

Image CC10.6

Balance: The center of mass is the point where all the forces acting on a body are canceled out. For someone standing up straight and balanced, it's around their belly button; the weight of their upper body is supported by the force of their legs standing up. If they were to lean forward, the center of mass would actually leave their body to exist in front of their belly button, and if they don't put their foot out for support they will fall over. A straight stick has basically uniform mass over the entire length, so if you throw it, it'll just spin in the air as you would imagine—rotating around its center.

A hammer has one heavy end and one light end, so the center of mass is actually up by the head. If you were to throw it, the hammer would rotate around that point. This same point on both examples is where you could balance it on your finger. Human anatomy is more complicated than that, however, so careful consideration of weight and balance must be kept. Knowing or approximating where the center of mass would be in a pose can help greatly.

All of these techniques help with the parts of Solid Drawing that are most applicable to the movement aspects of animation specifically. If a character is unbalanced in an illustration, it'll look strange and someone might catch it; but that same character animated off balance will look *very* wrong, and *anyone* will see it. Straights and curves make the images much more pleasing to look at in a single image but add to the flow of motion when animated. Compositions help us keep proportions, turnarounds help those proportions be realized in 3D so that the character can move well in space, and fostering good lines of action while avoiding twinning keeps the gestures more interesting.

> "Solid Drawing is as much about 'good' drawing as it is about consistency and believability."

You should always be drawing. Study anatomy, dynamic forms, different styles like realism and minimalism, caricatures ... even architectural drawing can help with not only background design but also the use of character composition. There are so many aspects of great and pleasing drawing that can be explored and used. Repeating shapes, for instance, is a good way to infuse instant appeal into your character. Illustration is a deeper field than you can probably imagine right now. Solid Drawing is as much about "good" drawing as it is about consistency and believability. So having great illustrative and drafting prowess isn't as entirely necessary as doing what you *can* do well and steadily. You set up the rules of your own character models and movement and stick to them. The principles help you to lay the groundwork of those rules, but ultimately you're the creator of this world you're drawing. Whatever style and approach you choose, Solid Drawing can be applied by keeping the above tips in mind.

EXERCISES Solid Drawing

You can already see that Solid Drawing is a very heavy principle, but for the purposes of how Animate CC can best be used with this principle we're going to be focusing on the cleanup. As was discussed in Chapter 7, "Straight Ahead Action and Pose to Pose," just about everything starts (or should start) with a sketch. In animation, however, you usually have to also know your character design before you even start sketching. Creating a character design is the other part of what we're focusing on in this chapter's exercises. When designing a character, you ultimately want to work up to a model sheet which shows the proper proportions, colors, and style (see "turnaround" in the crash course in the previous section). To make a model sheet, before you ever even get to the cleanup phase, the process looks like this:

"General Design Process"

1. *Sketch* ... a lot. Draw and explore what you would like your character to look like.

2. *Analyze.* When you've gotten a few sketches that you like, look at what about them appeals to you.

3. *Refine.* Take what you liked and put those aspects together into a final, complete form that you're pleased with.

4. *Breakdown* the form into simple shapes. Look at the 3D shapes (box) and determine what simple shapes (square) can easily represent it. Simplifying the form into primitives is what you use to "build" the character from the ground up, with consistency and within proper proportions without relying on just drawing skill (see again *Image CC10.1* from earlier in this chapter).

5. *Model sheets* will force you to take the form and show it turning around in 3D space to explore the full makeup of your character's features. After making that turnaround, you could duplicate any pose in any angle (hypothetically ... skill does play a part in the more difficult poses, of course).

6. *Understand the needs of the model* you've created to give the movement you desire. The range of motion it has will determine how you ultimately want to approach the animation of the character. A robot with limited range could easily be tweened symbols split up into each part, while a character in the "rubber hose" animation style (see *Image 12.6* in Chapter 12) might have larger groupings of features to be animated by hand.

7. *Cleanup.* No matter what sketch of the character you create now, because of the construction knowledge you have from the model sheets and the desired movement knowledge you have from understanding the needs of the model, the cleanup process will be expedited.

What we're going to be doing in these exercises is following along in cleaning up character sketches using various methods within Animate CC. The closer look section will show how their parts are split up to make the best use of their forms in animation with symblification. Learning the tools and overall methods of digital draftsmanship will give you the insight you need to make your own wonderful

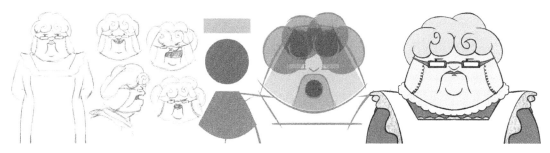

Image 10.3 General design work flow described above from left to right.

works of art as you gain more knowledge in the impossibly deep field of illustration. And the more you practice animating in Animate CC, the more obvious the choices will be on how to use your design best. For this chapter, when we get into splitting the character's features into subsections to prepare it for animating, you'll see how the decisions of what gets simplified (and what doesn't need to be) are made. Just like Tex Avery did with Tom Cat, design choices must reflect the needs of the animation *and* the animator; this exercise isn't a perfect blueprint of how to create every character just as the rest of this book's exercises aren't to be copied exactly every time their respective principles need to be applied. As always, it's important to pay attention to *why* something is being done as much as how, so you can apply these best to your own character designs.

"The Tools"

There are a few drawing tools in Animate CC which you've already seen. There is a good way to look at them, however, which might help you decide which ones to use. They are placed in three categories relating to how they work: drawing, cutting, and building.

Drawing—uses the Pencil (**Shift+Y**), Paint Brush (**Y**), and Brush (**B**) which you've already been introduced to.

Cutting—refers to the stop-motion style of cut-out animation where figures were made up of cutup paper and animated by moving around on a surface one frame at a time. The closest in feel to cutting out shapes using a utility knife is the freedom of the Lasso (**L**) and precision of the Pen (**P**) Tools.

Building—much like playing with Play-Doh, this category is about taking simple shapes, pushing and pulling them to morph into something different, and then combining those into more complicated and sophisticated forms. We use the Rectangle (**R**) and Oval (**O**) Tools mainly for building, but also the Line (**N**) Tool (leftmost in the accompanying image) for closing off sub-shapes.

We will be using each of these methods for cleaning up different features of the head/face design. Everyone has a preferred method for creation in the cleanup phase. Sometimes an artist draws so much and their style is more iconic that they prefer to build the characters up from simpler shapes when cleaning up—which almost feels to them like they're working in a completely different medium like clay when it's still 2D animation. Other times precision is what they're after, so they prefer to use the Pen Tool and cut out perfectly-formed shapes to "glue" together ... a very arts-and-crafts approach. I prefer to draw. To each their own. Regardless of the illustration style, the medium is ultimately the same: 2D digital vector graphics.

> "2D animation is on a sliding scale between 'cut-out' and 'full' animation, and 'Tradigital' falls somewhere between the two of them."

2D animation is on a sliding scale between "cut-out" and "full" animation, and "Tradigital" falls somewhere between the two of them. Where exactly it sits within this spectrum depends on the design and what the scene is asking for. With this example, we're going to be riding a line right dead in the center. The head and protruding features (like ears) will be made of shapes, the features on the face will be drawn in, the hair will be formed using the "cutting" style of the Pen Tool and finally it will all be colored and textured (in various places). Because we're splitting up the design this way instead of drawing everything directly on top of each other (which would mean we'd have to do it again on each new frame), when animating from this design we get the chance to move the features around in subtle or even major ways to accomplish some smooth movements in a quick fashion. This type of preparation pays dividends in the end due to the amount of time it saves and the quality of animation we can achieve when utilizing it with the 12 Principles.

We're starting with a sketch already completed (*Image 10.4*). The image could have easily been drawn directly into Animate CC, but I opted to sketch this out on paper so that I could do it at the park … any chance to get outside. The "ch10-solid_drawing-head_sketch.jpg" file is on the companion website. It wasn't even scanned; just a picture taken with a cell phone of a sketch on paper. It's important to point that out because

Image 10.4 Character head design sketched on paper which we will import and cleanup within Animate CC.

there are many people who just don't sketch on paper because they "don't have a scanner." Thanks to camera phones, it's not as big an issue as it once was. Open a new Animate CC file and name it "ch10-solid_drawing-1." We're including the "1" because you'll want to **Save As** with incrementally increasing numbers so that you don't lose any work now that things are getting a bit more exploratory. You can bring in the JPG by either dragging and dropping it onto the stage from the folder (which might not put it on the stage, depending on your version of Animate CC, but will *always* show up in the library) or going to **File > Import > Import to Stage** or by way of the hotkey sequence **Cmd/Ctrl+R**. When you have the sketch on the stage, name the layer "sketch," lock it, and insert another layer above it (we'll name it later). Now let's get started!

PART I
"Head and Protruding Features— Shape Tools"

1. We start by choosing a skin tone for the head (which can be changed later). We won't be having outlines for anything that is not a same color overlapping itself (such as the nose) like

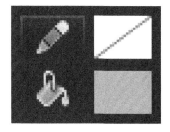

Image T10.1

you see in Mickey Mouse's form or on the show *Samurai Jack* (for an extreme example of this, look at the silhouetted figure in *Image 9.5* toward the end of Chapter 9's closer look section). So after choosing a fill color make sure there is no stroke color. *Image T10.1*

2. Select the Oval Tool (**O**), turn on Object Draw mode (**J**), and drag an oval the approximate size of the head. Drag the ends of the shape around until it fills the head. *Image T10.2*

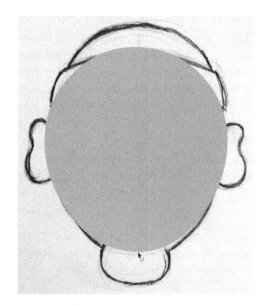

3. Toggle on the outline view on the layer and repeat step 2 to create the chin and the ears. The shapes will overlap, and that's fine since they're the same color. It will end up looking like one shape but one in which the head, chin, and ears can be moved independently of one another. Toggle off the outline view momentarily to double-check the shape of the head as a whole still works well. *Image T10.3*

Image T10.2

4. If things are getting too cluttered to look at, Insert Frame (**F5**) on frame 2 *only* on the layer we're working on and turn on onion skin mode. You should now be able to still see the image we imported to the "sketch" layer, but faded and tinted blue. *Image T10.4*

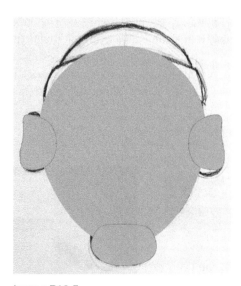

Image T10.3

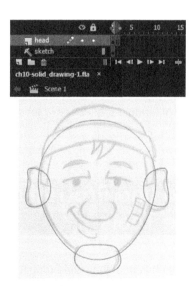

Image T10.4

5. Change the fill color to a hair color and using the Rectangle Tool (**R**) create the base hairline for our character. The tufts of hair will be done later. *Image T10.5*

Interlude

The general shape has been created and the groundwork laid for the other features. This process is reminiscent of painting wherein the base tones are placed in first and are added to bit by bit. Keeping each shape in its own object makes it very easy to adjust its position and shape if necessary. The fun thing about Object Draw mode is also that you can change the color of each shape as well, individually. Simply selecting the object and choosing a color will change it live on stage. You can select multiple objects by either dragging across them with the Selection Tool (**V**) or individually selecting many by holding **Shift** while clicking them. For all intents and purposes,

Image T10.5

they are uniquely separate shapes even though they look cohesive. Again, bringing up the example of *Samurai Jack*, this type of style relies on and fosters a better appreciation for good staging. Incidentally,

Foster's Home for Imaginary Friends also uses the no-outline style often. Next, we're going to draw in the topical features like the nose, eyes, and tufts of hair.

"Next Up …"

Not much needs to be said about the Brush Tool, since we've worked with this quite a bit already and it's the most intuitive of the tools. The main points are that when it is selected in the toolbar, the sub-options located at the bottom display things like brush shape, size, and "use pressure," which with certain tablets allows for a thicker line to be drawn the harder the pen is pushed on the surface. There is another feature which allows you to paint as normal, inside fills and with other options. These are really best explored by the user (*Image 10.5*). They're rather

Image 10.5

self-explanatory and have such specific-use features that some will find them endlessly useful while others will never find a need for them. Most importantly, though, is what's hidden in the Properties panel when the Brush Tool is selected. Look for the "smoothing" area. The higher the number, the more Animate CC will smooth and flatten the nuances of the lines you draw. Predictably, the lower numbers have less interference, which will almost always lead to a jagged line (*Image 10.6*). Many Tradigital animators use a setting between 20 and 50 in Animate CC. It's really the Pen Tool that needs to be explained, though.

In the field of stop-motion animation, there existed one style called "cut-out." If you have ever seen Terry Gilliam's animation in *Monty Python* or the ever popular *South Park* by Trey Parker and Matt Stone, you will have seen cut-out-style animation. JibJab, the company founded by Evan and Gregg Spiridellis which produces its own original content for the web is another great example of this technique. Each example uses different tools but employs the same basic method. My intention here isn't to discuss the method of animation as much as the procedure it takes to create the assets. When done using physical paper cut into the shape of whatever they need (torso, hat, etc.), a utility knife is usually used (scissors are less common) to cut around the paper as if tracing a shape. This process is essentially the same mentality when drawing with the Pen Tool. You create a point at each place on the shape you're drawing that needs a change in curve, and once a vector point is created you are given handle bars like in the Easing Editor that allow you to change the severity of the curve leading in and out of the point. It's very precise but is a tool designed for a certain mindset if it is to be used a lot. We will use its precise nature to create the hair tufts which, because we can control the number of vector points created, will make shape tweening easier for Animate CC to do.

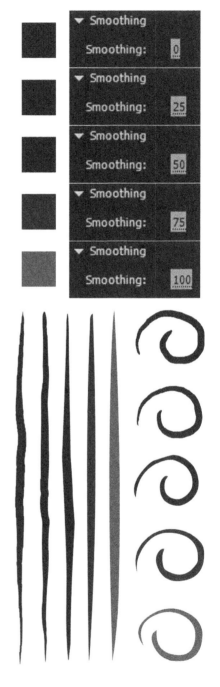

Image 10.6 Color-coded representation of a slowly drawn line and quick swirl with various brush smoothing settings.

6. Insert a layer above the rest and name it "face." Go back to the unnamed layer, call it "head," lock it, and hide it. You could have named this layer in the first place, but it's rare that a plan is perfect from the outset. As the form takes shape, the method for splitting it up will become more apparent. Having this type of flexibility is why Object Draw (J) is so important to have on; it keeps the future of your creation versatile and ready to be taken in any direction. *Image T10.6*

Image T10.6

7. We hid the "head" layer (instead of turning on outline view) so that we could draw in the features of the face without having to clutter up the stage with outlines that aren't being used. Choose the Brush Tool (**B**) and black for the fill color.

8. Draw a scribble. Hold Cmd/**Ctrl** to get the Quick Selection Tool and double-click to enter the scribble object you just created. Still holding Cmd/**Ctrl**, highlight the scribble, release the Cmd/**Ctrl** key, and press **Delete** (or **Backspace**). Now press the **J** key on your keyboard to turn Object Draw off. What you've just done is create an object with nothing in it so that you can draw freely within it without having to do it all in one stroke. This whole step is also a *pro-tip* as this is the method I use to draw almost everything in Animate CC. *Image T10.8*

9. Draw the nose. If you have pressure sensitivity enabled and it works with your tablet, you can get some great thick-to-thin lines, called "weighted" lines (most of the illustrations in this book have them). If you do not have a pressure-sensitive tablet,

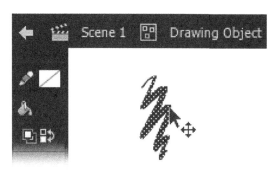

Image 10.8 Scribble with Object Draw on (top) then double-click to enter (bottom), delete scribble, and turn Object Draw mode off.

draw a stroke as normal and then use the Quick Selection Tool method to drag the stroke into a good painterly "weighted" one. When done, return to the main timeline by clicking "Scene 1" above the stage. *Image T10.9*

10. Use the same Object Drawing method outlined in the previous two steps to draw the mouth and then the eyelids (one at a time, each in their own object). With the eyelids, however, use the Line Tool (**N**) without Object Draw mode to close off the shape and mimic the full eyelid volume, fill in the enclosed area with the flesh color, and delete the lines. *Image T10.10*

11. Double-click to enter one of the eyelids. With Object Draw *off* but Snap to Objects *on*, use the Line Tool (**N**) to close the shape by connecting the two ends; then use the Paint Bucket Tool (**K**) to fill in the head's flesh color. Finally, select the line (by double-clicking) and **Delete** it—it's not needed anymore now that the fill has been made. Exit the object and repeat this same step for the other eyelid. *Image T10.11*

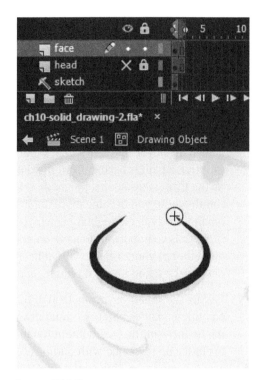

Image T10.9

12. With Object Draw mode (**J**) back on, finish off the eyes by using the Oval Tool (**O**) to create the pupils and *then* the whites of the eyes; if you do it the other way around, you won't

Image T10.11

Image T10.10

be able to see the pupil size from the sketch through the white oval you created. This way, however, you won't be able to see the pupils after the white eyeballs are drawn … we'll fix that in the next step. *Image T10.12*

Image T10.12

13. Multi-select the two white ovals representing the eyeballs (not the pupils) using **Shift** while clicking on each with the Selection Tool (if using quick select, you'll simply hold down Cmd/**Ctrl+Shift** while clicking) and then step them back behind the pupils by pressing Cmd/**Ctrl+down-arrow** until the whites are behind both the pupils and eyelids. *Image T10.13*

Image T10.13

14. Repeat step 10 to draw the eyebrows with a black fill color. *(Note: you can, indeed, use the Rectangle Tool (R) or Line Tool (N) for this cleanup as we did for the bouncing ball's tail in Chapter 8, although I used the Brush Tool (B). In truth, there are many ways to make the same illustrations; it all comes down to choice.) Image T10.14*

15. When we create the hair tufts, we want to clearly see the sketch and know where we made our hairline. Insert a new layer, name it "hair," hide the "face" layer and then unhide the "head" layer.

16. First we need the colors of the hair. Use the Eyedropper Tool (I) and click the hair color to import it as the fill color (which until now was black).

17. To select a similar outline color to the fill, click the stroke color in the toolbar which activates the eyedropper as well, and then click the color currently selected for the fill for quick access (sometimes the popup can obscure the fill box, in which case you can also sample the color of the hair on stage since they're the same). Open the Color panel (Cmd/**Ctrl+Shift+F9**) and click the pencil icon which indicates you want to edit the stroke color. On

Image T10.14

the right, there is a vertical sliding bar which increases/ decreases the brightness of the color selected. Drag the marker down a little to get a slightly darker color than we previously had—this new shade is our hair outline. *Image T10.17*

18. Select outline view for the "head" layer, select the "hair" layer to draw on, and choose the Pen Tool (**P**) to create the hair tufts. Treat each tuft as its own shape. Click and hold wherever a point is needed to change the curve and drag the handles around as necessary to line the curve up with the sketch. To close the shape, click on the point you started with and then fill it in with the Paint Bucket Tool (**K**). Using the Pen Tool takes some practice to get used to, but it can create excellent curves with minimal vector (anchor) points, ideal for shape tweening. *(Note: in order to get a sharp end point, you'll need to create an anchor point before that so for this shape we enter a single point for the base, curved point halfway down the tuft length, single point for the end, curved point halfway back up the other side, and then two final points for the base and to close the shape.) Image T10.18*

Image T10.17

Image T10.18

Interlude

The hair tufts probably look a little messy right now with their overlapping lines, but we're going to hide the tops under the hat. The fact that these need to be hidden is something that was known going into the cleanup of the sketch and honestly probably even *during* the sketch, because I am intimately aware of the drawing tools Animate CC has to offer and what their benefits are. Obviously in the beginning, efficiency is probably not going to come naturally; it's an attribute that's learned over time. Remember that what this book aims to accomplish is combining the 12 Principles of Animation with the program Adobe Animate. The exact way that the program will be used by you is different from the way others will use it. The same could be said for your animation. Just as you won't learn trigonometry after following along with one homework assignment, you'll need to practice and explore much more with Animate CC until creating within a workflow you're comfortable with becomes virtually second nature. A key to Tradigital animation is simply knowing what options you have in front of you and choosing the path of least resistance as long as the result employs the principles needed.

"Next Up …"

We've taken a look at gradients in the closer look section of Chapter 5 on "Arcs" with the wrecking ball (which was a radial gradient) and Chapter 6 on "Staging" with the receding stage (which was a linear gradient). Here, we'll use both of these to give a little extra touch to the nose and hair tufts, respectively. The only truly new part here will be importing an image to use as a texture for the bandage and hat, which have yet to be created (*Image 10.7*). It should be noted that these can be considered flourishes of style, not actually needed to reinforce the principle of Solid Drawing, but the same can be said for a lot of things in illustration. We aim to remind the audience through subtle ways that the character inhabits a 3D world which has textures that are soft and rough, objects which are pliable and stiff, and any other visceral feeling that can be conveyed.

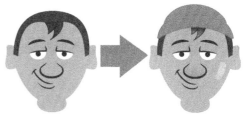

Image 10.7

The use of gradient on the nose will add a slight feeling of depth, but will also suggest the type and "quality" of the skin since what we're doing is making it slightly more red on the end of the nose. Maybe he's cold or sick. Maybe it's allergy season or he's had a glass or two of wine. Or he could just simply have a chronically reddish nose. Whatever the case, it adds to the "story" of the character. The gradient in the hair adds a slight sense of realism without much work, since many people have hair that is lighter at the ends than the roots. The texture in the hat and bandage will set them apart on the face as being uniquely non-organic materials to what surrounds them.

The "Animate" Difference: TAGGED COLOR SWATCHES

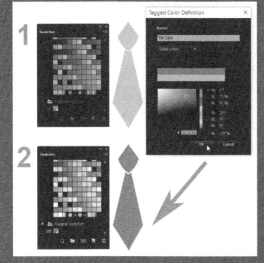

Image AD5

For larger productions, there is an attractive feature in Adobe Animate where you can create tagged swatches in the Color Panel that update globally whenever they're changed. For instance, if you create a tagged swatch for a character's tie color to red you can do it easily by changing the tagged color swatch itself to red. Think of the tagged color swatch as a symbol and wherever that swatch is used is like a symbol instance. If you change the source color by editing the tagged color swatch, it will instantly update everywhere that it's referenced. To create a tagged swatch, select a color from the Color Swatches panel (Cmd/Ctrl+F9) and click the "Convert to Tagged Swatch" button at the bottom 🔲. All tagged swatches can be easily distinguished by a white triangle on the bottom right corner of the swatch. You can name the tagged swatches, organize them into palettes ⊞ and folders, and edit via double-click.

19. We're going to create the hat and bandage. Start by inserting a new layer above all, name it "acc" (short for accessories) and make sure that this and the "sketch" layer are the only two visible. *Image T10.19*

T10.19

20. You may use whichever method you prefer best so far to create the two images, but I'm going to show you two more methods for your repertoire: changing the rectangle corner radius (step 21) and the Free Transform Tool's Envelope option (step 23). First image we'll create is the bandage so choose a good tan color for it and make sure there is *no stroke* selected.

21. With the Rectangle Tool (**R**) selected, locate the "Rectangle Options" area of the Properties panel. There are four areas where numbers are shown (right now they probably all say 0). These are the rectangle corner radius values. There is also a slider bar which changes the value of the four corners on your rectangle. The higher the number, the more curved the corners are. For our bandage I used values of 15. Drag the size of the bandage on the stage horizontally (it won't line up, so just approximate the size you need). *Image T10.21*

22. Double-click to enter the object and select it with the Free Transform Tool (**Q**). Drag it up to the position of the bandage in the sketch and rotate it to the correct angle. Do *NOT* deselect the shape or the next step will not work (while rotating a shape rotates the transform box with it, reselecting the shape would orient the transform box back to be aligned with the stage and not the object). *Image T10.22*

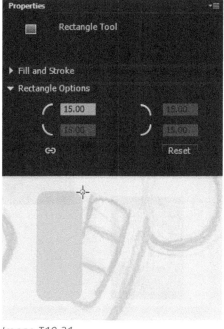

Image T10.21

23. In the toolbar at the bottom, select the "Envelope" option. A bunch of points show up around the shape. Drag the middle point of the longest lines in the bandage shape to show it curving around the head. Use the handles on the

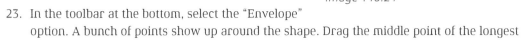

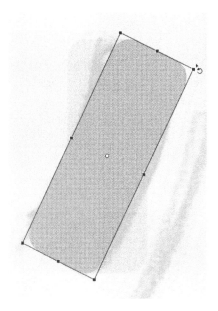

Image T10.22

Image T10.23a

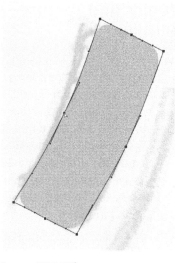

Image T10.23b

corners to make the edges curve to match the new arch in the bandage. *Image T10.23a and T10.23b*

24. Repeat the previous four steps to create the fold of the hat, except this time you'll also want to have a black outline (which will get tinted later, so don't worry if it looks a little odd right now). *(Note: the fill color will ultimately be replaced with the texture, but it's good to choose one now to help determine what hue you will ultimately change the texture to and also to select a good stroke color to go with it.) Image T10.24*

Image T10.24

25. Finish the top of the hat by using the Rectangle Tool (**R**) back at a curve setting of 0 in the Rectangle Options in the Properties panel or use the Oval Tool (**O**). When finished, place this object behind the fold of the hat using the method you learned earlier in this series of exercises (Cmd/**Ctrl+down-arrow**). *Image T10.25*

Image T10.25

"Color And Texture—Gradients and Bitmap Fill"

26. We're starting with using a bitmap fill to create texture. Insert a new layer, name it "ref" (short for reference. You should get in the habit of having your own shorthand for names; you'd be surprised how much time it ultimately saves). Import the texture image "ch10-solid_drawing-texture.jpg" the way you did at the start of this entire exercise. With it selected, break it apart with the hotkey sequence Cmd/Ctrl+B. *Image T10.26*

Image T10.26

27. Use the Eyedropper Tool (I) to select the texture. You'll notice it being placed into the fill color window of the toolbar. Hide the "ref" layer.

28. With the Paint Bucket Tool (K), fill in the folded up bottom part of the hat. Notice how even though it's contained within an object, you can fill it with a color (and make other alterations). You can't do this with symbols and groups. You'll notice that the colors don't match anymore, and that's OK. We will get to that. *Image T10.28*

Image T10.28

29. Use the Gradient Transform Tool (F) to rotate and stretch the texture to match the angle the hat is in until it looks good to you. *Image T10.29*

30. Select the object with the texture and make it a Graphic Symbol (F8) named "character-head-hat_fold" (it's part of your character on the head and is a hat, but it's only the fold of it).

Image T10.29

31. With the hat's fold symbol selected on the stage, locate the "Color Effect" in the Properties panel. In the Style drop-down menu, select "Tint." There is a box with a color in it. Click that swatch (which engages the eyedropper) and select the fill color in the top of the hat. The slider bar labeled (appropriately) "Tint" goes by percentage. Drag it around until it looks to best match

the color we selected for the bandage
before. I chose 80%. *Image T10.31*

32. Repeat the previous steps for the
    top of the hat. I chose 90% for the
    Tint percentage here to distinguish
    between the outer hat's color and that
    of the underside (which is what you
    see with the hat flipped up like that).

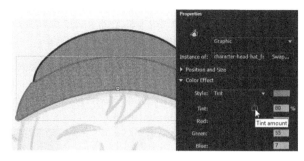

Image T10.31

33. As for the bandage, there's one thing
    we didn't do when drawing it in the
    first place—there is no center gauze as
    there is in the sketch. You'll see why we saved that step for
    later soon, but first turn the existing bandage object into a
    Graphic Symbol named "character-head-bandage."

34. Double-click the newly created symbol and insert a new
    layer above the existing one. Highlight the bandage object
    then copy (Cmd/**Ctrl+C**) and paste-in-place (Cmd/**Ctrl+Shift+V**)
    onto this new layer above.

35. Now that they're on separate layers, you may Break Apart
    (Cmd/**Ctrl+B**) the two identical objects. Using the Line Tool (**N**)
    without Object Draw mode on, draw two parallel lines on the
    top layer which are perpendicular to the bandage like you're
    sectioning off the gauze. Now delete the outer parts of the
    bandage shape and the two lines. *(Note: if you momentarily
    hide the bottom layer you'll see that
    what you did on the top layer just now
    left a small rectangle to represent the
    gauze.) Image T10.35*

Image T10.35

36. Rename the top layer "gauze" and hide
    it. We want to fill the bandage base
    with our bitmap texture so from the
    Color panel (Cmd/**Ctrl+Shift+F9**) choose
    "Bitmap fill" from the drop-down
    menu and our texture should be there
    in a little swatch. Click that swatch
    to select it, and with the Paint Bucket
    Tool (**K**) fill in the bandage object.
    Adjust as necessary the way you did
    before. *(Note: you might see more than*

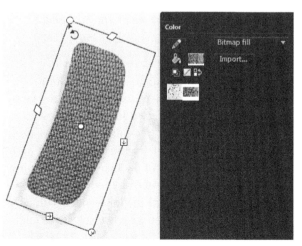

Image T10.36

one bitmap swatch. For instance, in the accompanying image there are two—one of them is the sketch which was imported.) Image T10.36

37. Next, we want to save the color of our bandage to use it for our tint color back on the main stage. Unhide the "gauze" layer and select its color with the Eyedropper Tool (I). Now open an as-of-yet unexplored panel called the Swatches panel (Cmd/**Ctrl+F9**). The icons at the bottom of the panel look similar to the library's and work in the same way: the folder icon creates a new custom folder where you can save your own color swatches and the paper icon creates a new color swatch. Click the paper icon to create a new swatch from the color you picked with the Eyedropper Tool earlier. *Image T10.37*

Image T10.37

38. Return to the main stage, highlight the bandage symbol instance, and choose Tint from the Color Effect area of the Properties panel. This time you should be able to pick the bandage color from the bottom row of swatches. I chose 75% for the Tint value percentage. *(Note: because there wasn't another color selected between these steps you can just as easily choose the one shown in the fill color box in the toolbar, but now you have a method of saving color swatches so you can return to them on the fly without having to reselect from a source every time.) Image T10.38*

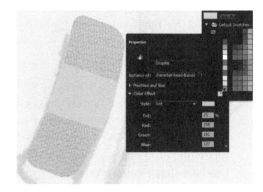

Image T10.38

39. With the bitmap textures done, we want to give a gradient to the nose. First, though, we're going to give it a fill color to alter. Hide every layer except for "head" (which should be locked) and "face" (unlocked). Use the Eyedropper Tool (I) to select the color of the head, enter the nose object, and use the same method we used for the eyelids to close off the nose space with a line and fill it with the color we selected. Don't forget to delete the line afterward. *(Note: you may choose to start collecting swatches for this*

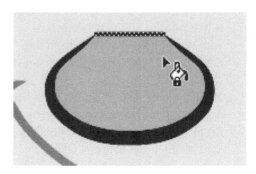

Image T10.39

character in a new swatch folder or add them to the default folder.) Image T10.39

40. In the Color Window (Cmd/**Ctrl+Shift+F9**) click the paint bucket which selects the fill color we're going to edit and choose "Radial Gradient" from the drop-down menu. The left marker on the spectrum is the center of the fill, and the right one is the outer edge it radiates to. For instance, if the left is black and right is white then within a circle this fill would be black in the center and white on the outside of the circle.

41. Double-click the left marker and choose the nose/head color. Do the same for the right marker. Single-click on the left marker to select for editing and drag the "hue" slider (the rainbow-colored vertical bar) to get a little closer to red than where it is now. *Image T10.41*

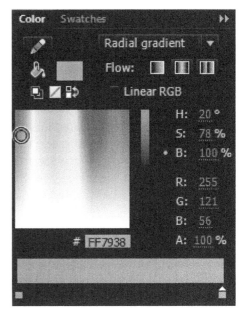

Image T10.41

42. With the Paint Bucket Tool (**K**), wherever you click is where the center will default to. Click the tip of the nose. *(Note: in some versions of Animate CC, a click-and-drag will allow you to live-preview where the center of the gradient will go.)*

43. Use the Gradient Transform Tool (**F**) to adjust the gradient so that the end of it (the head's flesh color) stops at or before where the fill does, so the transition between the nose's gradient and the head's solid color is seamless. The handles work much the same way as they did way back in Chapters 5 and 6, but there are new points. You know the outer box stretches the gradient and the outer circle rotates it. For radial gradients, the inner circle moves the origin point, and the outer circle with the arrow-out increases the overall size of the gradient, evenly. *Image T10.43*

Image T10.43

44. Now that the more complicated gradient is out of the way, apply a subtle *linear* gradient to the hair tufts where the ends have a slightly lighter tint than the base color. This process should be a piece of cake now relative to what you did earlier in this exercise! *Image T10.44*

The texture and quality of material in animation is important to consider. If you look at Simba from *The Lion King*, you know what he would feel like to pet. Of course, he's a lion and those exist, but even if you've never petted a lion you still probably know what it would feel like. There are experiences your brain brings to the equation when imagining tactile qualities like that. The way the mane flows when he's moving quickly but stays in relative position when at rest gives you an idea of the consistency. The fur on the rest of the body is clearly short—short enough to barely be drawn, only colored in so that it probably feels like the body of a horse or Labrador. There is no comparison possible with Stitch from *Lilo and Stitch* (because it's an alien), but you probably also have an idea of what he would feel like; the same goes for Mike Wazowski from *Monsters, Inc.* and Mushu the Dragon from *Mulan*. The feel and relative solidity of an object or feature can be shown through the type of patterns used to show it, the gradient or series of colors that fill it or a more realistic texture applied over the top of it—and that's all before the actual movement is applied.

Image T10.44

Another great example of implied texture in design is the Beast from *Beauty and the Beast*. There are at least three distinct types of hair on his body all displayed with different levels of sharp or curved ends. This type of textural layering in the design makes you *feel* the character, though it is still only a 2D drawing. The addition of a cape evokes the feeling of a Phantom-of-the-Opera-type character living in the shadows while simultaneously providing a great opportunity for overlapping action in his movement. Consequently, Batman evokes the same type of feeling as the Phantom. In his case, however, the sharp "ears" and rock-solid look of the body design makes for an interesting duality: moves like a ghost but hits like a sledgehammer. As long as we're talking about Batman, notice that his silhouette is made up of two rectangles (body/cape and head) and two triangles (bat ears on the costume). It's a simple design—iconic—which speaks volumes about the character before you ever hear him talk. This ability to represent concepts and character traits in an easily understood form is what we strive for in solid drawing. So long as the audience feels like this character lives in a

3D world, moves convincingly according to that design, and can easily imagine what they might feel like, you will have succeeded. As far as the movement goes, we have yet to tackle it. That's what's coming up in the closer look section; we will split this character up into parts ready to animate and start to examine how that might work.

CLOSER LOOK
Preparing For Animation

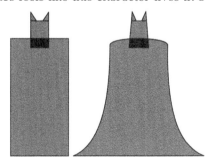

Image 10.8 Simple shapes make up the general design (left) while slight alterations give it a more organic form (right).

Now that the face has been cleaned up using a variety of techniques, we need to separate the features and put them into subsections, ready to animate. Before you start, you need to understand what the demands of the scene are and what particular qualities are presented in the design you've created. In our case, we wanted our face to be able to make simple turns through tweening and it is also set up for quick lip-sync for dialog. Nothing in what we're going to do in this setup locks you into working this way. If you want to animate a head turn frame by frame because you need special control over a particular breakdown, you can absolutely do that. Again, it must be reiterated that Animate CC is a tool and this particular Tradigital workflow is one of many that can be employed. It's all about knowing what you want to do, being familiar with the tools and what they do, and using these together with principles of animation to make a workflow that best represents you as an artist. We're going to split up the various parts of our design into various symbols, all packed within one master symbol. Don't forget to **Save As** with a "closer look" suffix in the title.

"Symbolizing The Design"

1. We have four layers which together contain the entire design for the character's head: "head," "face," "hair," and "acc." In order to split these up in the quickest way, we first need to group the features on each layer that will be within their own symbols. *(Note: you may still have a "ref" layer with the texture image on it left over from the previous section which is no longer needed—you may delete this layer.)*

2. Hide every layer except for "head" (it may still be locked from the previous section and if so, unlock it). Just look at what's here. There's a basic head shape, hairline shape, a chin, and ears. If we were to try to animate the head as it were turning in three dimensions, the chin and ears would move side to side but not need to morph their shapes much other than in size. These are best moved as symbols. The head and hairline, however, will change shapes as they turn, so it's best to use shape tweens when moving the head (and the hairline we want the audience to think is "attached") around as though it were in 3D space. Currently everything is split up in proper sections, ready to animate ... mostly. First we need to turn the chin and ear objects into symbols.

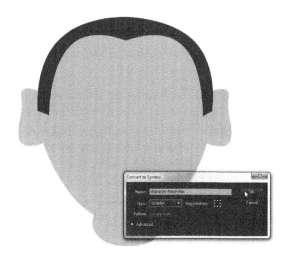

Image CL 10.3

3. Highlight the chin object and turn it into a Graphic Symbol (**F8**) with the name "character-head-chin" (the chin is part of the head which helps make up the design of "character"—this is a fairly common naming convention

in projects with large teams because it's easily readable and hierarchical). *Image CL 10.3*

4. With one of the ears selected, turn it into a Graphic Symbol with the name "character-head-ear." Even though they're two ears, they are identical—so we only need one symbol for them. After the symbol is created, copy, paste in place, and then **Modify > Transform > Flip Horizontal**. Then simply **Shift** click-and-drag it to the other side of the head and delete the ear that was there. (Remember you can put the symbol behind the other ear object by hitting Cmd/**Ctrl+down-arrow** on the keyboard as many times as it takes.) *Image CL 10.4*

Image 10.4 Both highlighted figures are instances of the same ear symbol, only flipped.

5. Hide every layer except "face." Nothing here can be shape tweened consistently, so they all need to be put into symbols (symbolized). The nose should be "character-head-nose," the mouth should be "character-head-mouth," and the same process in the previous step should be used for the eyebrows with a similar naming structure. That leaves the eyes for the next step. *Image CL 10.5*

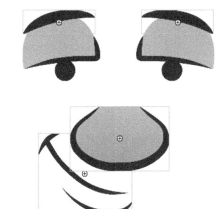

Image CL 10.5

6. Eyes are an interesting and complicated feature. Knowing how they work and how they will be animated determines how they will be split up. Analyze the design. In the design we've created, there are essentially two independently moving parts: the pupils and the eyelids (the white "eyeball" stays the same shape and would only distort in proportion to the rest of the eye). The eyelids are mirror images of themselves, and while they don't *have* to move together, they often do. We can always frame-by-frame eyelids if they need to move independently, but for the times they're doing the same thing (blinking, for instance) it's helpful to have whatever animation is created on one eyelid to be mirrored on the other. Therefore, we need to symbolize one pupil and one eyelid. This step was about analyzing the structure. We will symbolize those features in the next step.

7. The eye should work as one unit. If anything gets misaligned during animation, we need it to go back to a perfect lineup. This is why it's important that the registration of every symbol

needs to be in the same spot. To make sure of this, highlight the character's entire right eye and group it (Cmd/**Ctrl+G**). Then copy and paste in place twice. Now there are three identical eye groupings on top of one another. Click the top one and turn it into a Graphic Symbol (**F8**) with a registration point in the center and name it "character-head-eye-pupil." Double-click inside the newly created symbol, highlight the group, break it apart (Cmd/**Ctrl+B**), and delete the eyelid and white of the eye so that only the pupil is left. *Image CL 10.7*

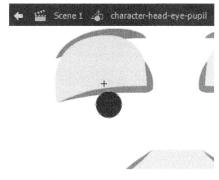

Image CL 10.7

8. Return to the main timeline and repeat the previous step to create "character-head-eye-eyelid" (this time deleting everything in the new symbol except for the eyelid). *(Note: do not click on the pupil shape to create this new symbol since the pupil shape on top is the symbol we created in the previous step.)*

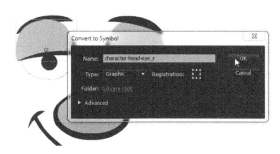

Image CL 10.9

9. Return to the main timeline again and highlight the *entire* eye (that includes the remaining group in the back and the two new symbols, "... eyelid" and "... pupil"), and turn it into a Graphic Symbol named "character-head-eye_r" (the "r" is for right). Enter that symbol. *Image CL 10.9*

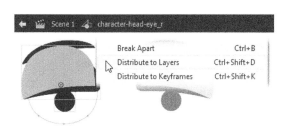

10. Highlight everything within the symbol, right-click, and select **Distribute to Layers**. *Image CL 10.10*

Image CL 10.10

11. Hide the top two layers (the eyelid and pupil), break apart the group that's left, and delete the eyelid and pupil objects, leaving only the eyeball object (white oval). To verify that the white oval shape is actually there you can turn on outline view for the layer like I did in the accompanying image. *(Note: there is a blank layer created when the layer distribution action happens (shown in the accompanying image) which you may delete now.) Image CL 10.11*

12. Unhide the pupil layer, highlight both the eyeball object and pupil symbol instance, and hit **F8** to create yet *another* symbol named "character-head-eye-eyeball." Enter this symbol, **Distribute to Layers** and return to the main timeline. If you don't know why we created this symbol yet, it will make sense after we've finished setting up the left eye. *Image CL 10.12*

Chapter 10 SOLID DRAWING

291

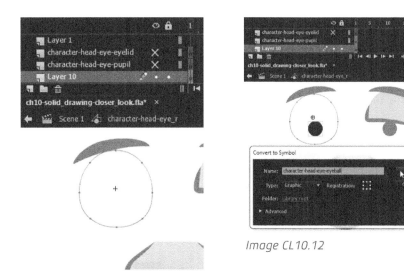

Image CL10.11

Image CL10.12

13. On the main timeline, copy the newly created eye symbol, paste in place and move it over to the left eye's position and delete the existing eye of all its objects. There should now only be two symbols representing the eyes. But one is flipped the wrong way. We'll fix that and finalize the eye setup.

14. With the copied symbol created in the previous step, right-click, select **Duplicate Symbol** and name it "character-head-eye_l." Enter the symbol. *Image CL10.14*

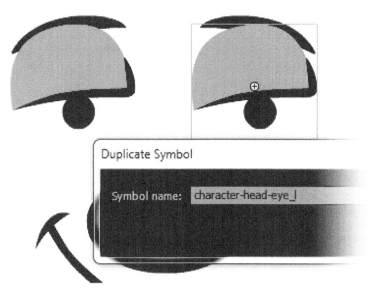

Image CL10.14

15. The eyelid layer is probably still hidden as a result of the previous steps so you'll need to unhide that layer. Click the eyelid instance in the newly created "character-head-eye_l" symbol and flip it using **Modify > Transform > Flip Horizontal**. Realign if necessary. Return to the main timeline and step them back behind the eyebrows using the **Shift+down-arrow** method. You've just set up the eyes, one of

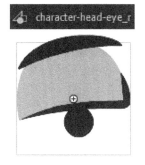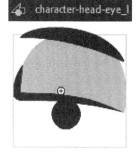

Image CL10.15

the more complicated features, for digital animation that's both easy and versatile. You will nest animation in the eyelid symbol to blink, and that animation will simultaneously play and be mirrored to the other side (though when you do this, make sure the looping option for the eyelid instances are set to Single Frame and use Play Once when you want the blink). The pupil being paired with the white of the eye is for a similar reason. Anytime you move the pupil in one eye it will move the pupil in the other eye to the *same direction* since the instances aren't mirrored like the eyelid. Because of the layer order, the pupil will always remain under the eyelid. And because the pupil is a symbol it's easily moved through classic tweens with the added benefit of using the Easing Editor for a more sophisticated movement. *(Note: you can add a further layer of finesse to the setup by creating a mask layer above the pupil and copy/paste in place the eyeball shape there, so the pupil will self-crop if its shape goes outside the eyeball zone. See the setup I did for this in the FLA provided on the companion website.) Image CL10.15*

16. Hide every layer except "acc." Analyze the features on this layer to determine if any more work needs to be done on them. The hat is made of simple shapes inside symbols. The top part can be classically tweened as is, but the folded-up section at the bottom of the hat will need to have some nested animation in the form of shape tweens to turn the head. This just means that when it comes time to animate, you'll want to duplicate the instance of the lower part of the hat and extend the timeline to sync with the main and just animate as normal. The bandage can move as one and distort where necessary for most movements so it's great as the symbol it already is. *(Note: the hair tufts on the "hair" layer are going to be shape tweened and are already in self-contained objects so there was no need to alter them or the layer.)*

17. Unhide everything except the sketch layer so that you can see the entire design now. Highlight everything you see on stage and turn it into a Graphic Symbol (**F8**) named "character-head" and then double-click to enter it.

18. Right off the bat, highlight everything and drag it up until the registration point (+) sits around where the neck would meet the head (not the very bottom, but a little bit up in the head shape where a neck might meet the base of this head). *Image CL10.18*

19. With everything still highlighted, right-click and select **Distribute to Layers**. This distributing action is why we separated everything the way we did. Now every feature that will end up being individually animated is on its own layer. Go through the layers and clean up the names so that they're simpler (for instance turn "character-head-eye_l" to just "eye left") or just straight name the layers that only have objects on them (such as "head" and "hat fold" and hat top"). *Image CL 10.19*

Interlude

Now everything is split up according to the design and ready to be animated with simple movements. Anything more than 45-degree turns will require more frame-by-frame animation because, let's face it, Animate CC can only do so much interpreting. But honestly you wouldn't want to do more than that. For bigger movement, the control you have from creating your own individual frames is unmatched. It's the accuracy of the tools and the ease of alterations that make Animate CC such a friend to animation. **Duplicate Symbol** is a feature you're going to want to get very familiar with. If you are animating a scene which is 50 frames long, each symbol which can have animation in it (for instance, the eye symbols) should also have their timelines 50 frames long. Animation that is nested within the symbols will be tailored for that scene. For another scene which is 40 frames long, you will want *another set* of animation with each symbol being that long, 40 frames. The easiest way to replicate the same design with different internal nested animation possibilities without editing what's already been created would be to simply take the master symbol from the previous scene, duplicate it, and then duplicate all the symbols inside it. A good practice when duplicating symbols is that for each scene, a suffix should be added to any symbol with animation in it with something representing the scene number (like "character-head-eye-eyelid-sc1" ... or you could go the other way, depending

Image CL 10.18

Image CL 10.19

on your preferences, and add a prefix as "sc1-character-head-eye-eyelid"). This method means that you're able to work off of a previously created set of symbols, making it easy to stay on model.

"Animating a character talking is appropriately called "lip-sync" since you're essentially synchronizing the lip (or mouth) movements of your character with prerecorded audio."

"OK, we have a character's face, but how do I make him talk?" Animating a character talking is appropriately called "lip-sync" since you're essentially synchronizing the lip (or mouth) movements of your character with prerecorded audio. This term comes from live musical performances where a singer must move their lips to the lyrics of a song which they are not actually singing (like at the Super Bowl, usually). That's why many people mistakenly confuse this term for "lip-singing," which isn't a thing. So when you're animating a character talking, it's a lot like what you do when you're pretending to be Cyndi Lauper or Michael Jackson (or more current performers) mock-singing in the mirror into a hairbrush.

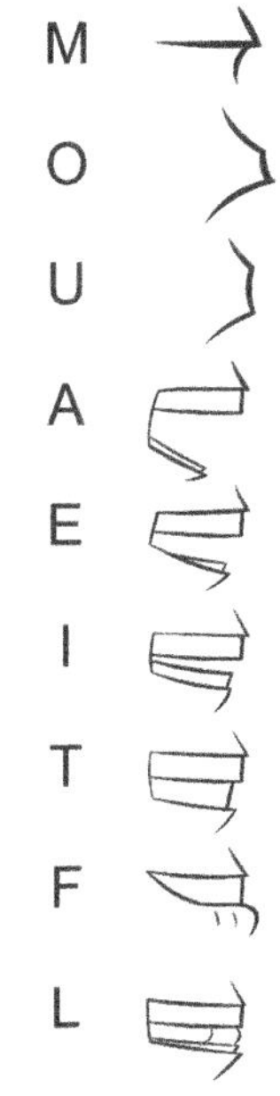

To create the lip-sync, there is a method that has become very popular for its ease of use, called "mouth comp." A *comp,* in design, is short for "comprehensive." Mouth comp is a method using a comprehensive collection of mouth shapes that are nested within a symbol which can then be used to display and swap out whichever shape is desired at any given time. For instance, a popular collection of mouth shapes looks like this: M, O, U, A, E, I, T, F, L (*Image 10.9*). That might look like nonsense, but it becomes clearer when you know that M is the mouth shape for saying the sound that the letter "m" makes. It also doubles for the letter "P" and a normal closed mouth position (which is why it's first). O (which is really the "oo" sound in this list), U ("uh"), A ("ah"), E ("eh"), I ("ee") basically sound out the word "why" since that word is made up of all the vowel sounds. T doubles as D, J, N, S, Z, and diphthongs like "ch" and "sh." You can imagine that there are other mouth shapes which can represent many different sounds. People sometimes will put in more mouth shapes or use less (look at older Anime TV series), and even make collections of the same shapes as if they were happy, sad, and other emotional states.

M
O
U
A
E
I
T
F
L

Image 10.9

"Mouth comp is a method using a comprehensive collection of mouth shapes that are nested within a symbol which can then be used to display and swap out whichever shape is desired at any given time."

We will be making these shapes, but the 12 Principles demand something a bit more of us in the quality of our lip-sync, which we will discuss after the setup is done. For now, keep in mind one thing: comprehensive is an unfortunate word to have been used to describe this system. Part of the interesting visual texture classic animation can bring to the table are interesting mouth shapes, unique to the acting of the scene. Just like 2D animation as a whole, lip-synching is on a sliding scale between simple replacement of shapes to full-blown frame-by-frame animation. We aim for something in the middle for most of our Tradigital work to make the best use of time-saving techniques while not losing the quality to simple efficiency. The fact that this system has even been shortened to "mouth comp" is a testament to the amount of corners animators sometimes cut in the pursuit of getting something done. The constant threat of using increasingly efficient tools is that the allure to use them to make things easier on us is so great, when sometimes the easier way out actually sacrifices the caliber of animation we *could* create by inconveniencing ourselves just a little bit. That is essentially the crossroads we live on—the tightrope we walk—in Tradigital animation. With this duplicity in mind, let's see how to first make things easy on ourselves.

"Lip-sync"

20. From the stage, double-click the master "character-head" symbol and then the mouth to get into "character-head-mouth."

21. You already have the closed mouth position (or "M" or "P"... however you'd like to look at it). We need to create the other mouth shapes. To start, we should do rough sketches just as with everything else. To set ourselves up for rough animation here, insert a new layer *below* the current and name it "rough." Name the other layer with the mouth on it appropriately "mouth."

22. Insert a blank keyframe (**F7**) on frame 2 of the "rough" layer and turn on onion skin mode. *Image CL 10.22*

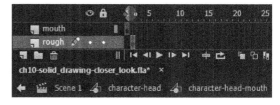

Image CL 10.22

23. With a good rough color selected like blue, sketch an "O" mouth shape. Remember that for our purposes "O" makes an "oo" sound. *Image CL 10.23*

24. Repeat the previous two steps with increasing frame numbers for the rest of the mouth shapes: U, A, E, I, T, F, L. Refer to the previous section for pronunciation explanations. Keep in mind that the upper teeth are connected to the skull and *do not* move up and down. You could

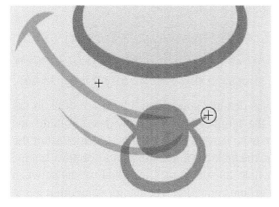

Image CL 10.23

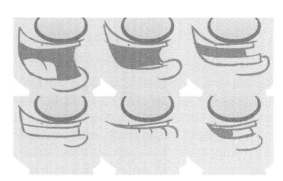

Image CL 10.24

decide not to follow a design point like this but to break a rule you first have to know it … so let's follow the human-teeth-are-not-retractable one for now during the learning process. *Image CL 10.24*

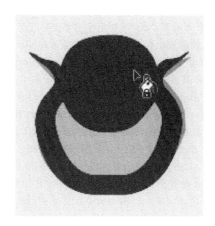

25. Lock the "rough" layer and turn off onion skin mode. On the "mouth" layer, insert a blank keyframe on the second frame and clean up the mouth shape you sketched in the rough. *Image CL 10.25*

26. Insert blank keyframes and cleanup each of the next frames' roughs until you've reached the end. *(Pro-tip: to keep the upper teeth in the right position, you can keep them in their own object and copy/paste in place for each cleanup frame that shows the upper teeth. If they extend beyond the lips you've drawn, you can use the Eraser Tool to crop it or simply draw the lips in their own object in the first place and fill around them with the flesh color the way we did for the nose by closing off the shape with the Line Tool. I prefer this second method.) Image CL 10.26*

Image CL 10.25

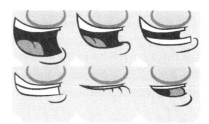

Image CL 10.26

27. Guide the "rough" layer so that it won't show up when on the stage and step back one symbol level to "character-head."

28. Click the "character-head-mouth" symbol and in the Properties panel set its looping setting to Single Frame. (It should be set on frame 1 by default.) *Image CL 10.28*

29. To see how this looping works, change the number in the looping settings to anything between 1 and 9 (the number of frames in your mouth symbol) and watch the mouth shape change. In order to lip-sync, just put down a keyframe and change the number where needed. *(Pro-tip: there are plenty of independently created extensions for Animate CC that make this mouth comping system easier by either giving you a slider which updates the symbol frame in real time or by showing each frame as a thumbnail you can click.) Image CL 10.29*

Image CL 10.28

You are now set up to lip-sync. Animate CC uses the WAV and MP3 sound files well. Import the audio file you wish to use to the library (**File > Import > Import to Library**), create a unique layer, name it "audio" (or whatever you'd like ... "dialog" maybe) and then just drag that audio file from the library onto the stage. You won't see anything on stage, but you will see the previously blank frame on your "audio" layer show an audio spectrum visualization starting from there and playing the length of the timeline or until the next keyframe (*Image 10.10*). With that frame selected, make sure the Properties panel has it set to "stream" (which locks the audio file to the timeline, synched to each frame). Now it's easy to insert a new layer called "lip-sync ref" and drag the mouth comp instance from the library to the stage and change the frame displayed to whichever mouth is needed for each frame (it's best to do every other frame because a mouth change on every frame is usually too quick

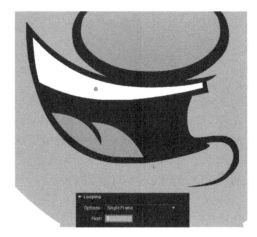

Image CL10.29

for the eye to see well at 24fps). After that's done, you just copy all those frames with the mouth on the "lip-sync ref" layer, paste them in the head symbol, and using Edit Multiple Frames mode, move the mouths into proper position. Alternatively, you could have originally copied the mouth frame (the keyframe, not the symbol) from within the head symbol first and pasted *that* to the timeline on the "lip-sync ref" layer—which makes sure that after the lip-sync animation is done and you copy all those frames to put back into the head symbol, they will paste immediately into the proper position. That's the essence of lip-sync animation using the mouth comp system. But we should go a step beyond that.

Image 10.10 View of the timeline after dragging audio file on to Animate CC stage from the library.

It's good to have done the above steps because you have lip-sync mouth shapes at least listed out. Before Animate CC this process would need to have been done using an x-sheet (short for "exposure sheet" because animators love their shorthands). An x-sheet would basically list out the sounds (with letters) that would be made on any given frame, show how long it would be held and usually have notes on what type of easing it would most likely require. With the mouth comp method, we skip the listing of the sounds and their frame numbers and replace that with pre-made mouth shapes (which represent the written lists of the sounds) actually placed on their corresponding frames. These can be tested and retested until the lip-sync looks right, in essence. One could stop there, but if we use this mouth comp animation as *reference*, it makes animating frame by frame so much more attainable ... and quick! Let's say we have a character saying "I don't *think* it should make a difference. But maybe ..." where the "think" is a beat where his face is squashed up, teeth are gritting, eyes are closed, and the "maybe" finishes with a serious, dead-pan look. You'll want to control the way the lip-sync works around "think" leading up to and falling out of it, so you can change the mouth shapes on the keyframes which make up "think" by drawing new ones in objects and then deleting the (now unused) symbols. The mouth comp animation would be kept for the ending, though, because a non-emoting face is what you're going for as the character finishes speaking. That speedy flexibility is Tradigital animation at its best.

USING SOLID DRAWING With "Object Drawing"

Drawing within Animate CC is versatile, which can sometimes mean "difficult to choose which of the dozens of known ways to do something." As outlined, it helps to think of the tools and the methods they inspire in terms of drawing, cutting, or building. If you can determine which of these feels the most "right" to you, it will help greatly in knowing which way you want to take a design. It's like a "Choose Your Own Adventure" book in that way. One thing that remains between the methods, however, is the Object Draw mode. This wonderful little feature allows us to create uniquely separated items in order to layer onto one another without cluttering up the timeline or library and *still* be able to edit directly from the stage (something that, which has been said a few times before, cannot be done with groups or symbols). My favorite process involves the "scribble, double-click, delete, J" maneuver to create and enter a blank object and then turn off Object Draw so that I can sketch in this special container at whim. That little sequence takes about 2 seconds. Think about animating an arm movement frame by frame. You could draw the whole thing as one. But if you draw the hand in its own object, you have the option of tweaking the position ever so slightly if the arc doesn't look right without doing much to change the overall look of the frame. *And* you save a ton of time.

> "The simple versatility of Object Draw is just the kind of 'help or get out of the way' feature that we look for in Tradigital animation."

Another great feature is the ability to draw multiple things (such as features on a face, or plates on a Triceratops) and then **Distribute to Layers** to get each of these items on their own layer *after* the drawing is done. When trying to draw something across multiple layers the first time out, the chances that you could accidentally click something on a layer other than the one you're working on and suddenly start drawing on *that* layer is pretty high. Drawing between multiple layers can get confusing very quickly. That's why using Object Draw on one layer and **Distribute to Layers** after the design is finished is so helpful; it's a great way to sidestep a lot of those problems. Finally, objects (as well as groups and symbols) can be arranged on a single layer to be either above or below one

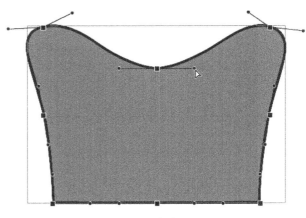

Image 10.11 Object Draw mode keeps images separate on the same layer while still being directly editable.

another using the Cmd/**Ctrl+up-arrow** or **+down-arrow.** That is a small feature you will find yourself using more and more on increasingly complicated designs. Overall, the simple versatility of Object Draw is just the kind of "help or get out of the way" feature that we look for in Tradigital animation.

We didn't even mention the fact that, because objects are independently editable, they can be reshaped and resized directly from the stage using everything from pulling points with the Selection Tool to even the Envelope feature in the Free Transform Tool (*Image 10.11*). Object Draw mode is an excellent middle ground between sketching and the final symblification of the cleanup. A great workflow is to do rough animation with the Brush Tool using either the pose to pose or straight ahead methods, then clean up the drawings using Objects, and finally separate or group objects into proper symbols that get nested within one another (symblification) to be ready for animation. Object Draw also helps for drawing different mouth shapes in a series. For instance, in anatomy the upper teeth don't move because they're attached to the skull. The bottom teeth move with the jaw. The lips move over the top of both of them. This positioning is pretty clear, but sometimes when drawing individual images straight ahead, you may lose track of the exact position of the upper row of teeth. They may be close, but when jumping around between frames as you will using the mouth comp lip-synching method, any small difference in the upper teeth will look like they're jittering around (usually). Having both sets of teeth in their own objects as you draw makes the creation of the standard mouth shapes very quick. You can, of course, have them on their own layers if you're working within a symbol too. There are many ways to accomplish the same or similar things, and it helps to familiarize yourself with as many as you can. But Object Draw, specifically, is often overlooked and should be given special attention.

A Word to The Beginners …

If you were an absolute beginner with Animate CC and were following along exclusively with the bouncing ball exercise but skipping the real-world sections, now would be a great time to go back and revisit the chapters for that added level of practice. The tools needed to be understood and shown in order to get to solid drawing. The way solid drawing is represented most distinctly within Animate CC is through the creation of character packs by using objects and symbols to keep your character on-model as well as making it easier to alter any pose precisely (and reversibly). Up to this chapter, you have bounced a ball with easing, arcs, and squash and stretch; understood the methods used in the rough animation to plot that out; had a working knowledge of staging; and discovered what the added spice of overlapping action, follow through, and secondary action bring to the table. It was the perfect time to explore the drawing methods and real-world development of Tradigital character packs. Going back at this point and working through the real-world examples starting at Chapter 1 will absolutely nail in the concepts and how to use them in the program. It may feel like a step back, but this is 100 percent a huge step forward.

> "The way solid drawing is represented most distinctly within Animate CC is through the creation of character packs by using objects and symbols to keep your character on-model as well as making it easier to alter any pose precisely (and reversibly)."

The next two chapters are "Exaggeration" and "Appeal," respectively. Obviously, we'll get into it deeper in those chapters, but basically the principle of Exaggeration is about pushing the character models you can create thanks to this chapter for effect as well as situationally using Staging or Anticipation. It's about pulling in all the knowledge from the previous chapters and pushing them beyond their own confines for effect. Similarly, the principle of Appeal is basically using all of the other principles to their best effect to make what is happening on screen something that the audience wants to see more of. That is to say, the last two principles in this book are the most far-reaching and all-encompassing of the 12. There are no more bouncing ball exercises. It's all "real-world" work from here on out. If you haven't worked through the real-world sections of the previous chapters because you have been following the path I set out for you in the Introduction of this book, now's the time to go back and work through them. Slow and steady practice is the best way to learn animation in any of its capacities, and that's how the book is set up.

FINAL WORDS
Solid Drawing

This principle reminds us to keep improving. Even if you're a fantastic illustrator already, there's always something else to learn. Drawing is the basis to classic animation, and because of that there are many people who start out animating today without much of an appreciation for this ability and what it can do for their animation. If you break any of the "rules" within these principles, it should be a conscious choice not an inability to follow through. While this book aims to bring the principles into the program and make it accessible for beginners as well, the subsections implied in certain principles are not something that can be explored deeply without creating the world's largest published work. For Solid Drawing, you should be improving your draftsmanship (drawing skills). The "crash course" I gave earlier in this chapter is about the specific attributes that are most applicable to movement: staying consistent, having interesting and telling poses, etc. To truly apply this principle into your work, however, you need to draw ... a lot. It's right there in the name.

Milt Kahl, one of Disney's Nine Old Men, is known as one of the finest draftsmen to ever have been in the animation profession. Shere Khan (*The Jungle Book*), Merlin (*The Sword in the Stone*), and Pinocchio are all completely different designs with drastically differing movement requirements. They also all hide very complicated solid drawing problems to solve, and were all animated either fully or in part by Milt Kahl. Shere Khan demonstrates wonderful anatomy and a perfect blend of menacing and charismatic facial features; however, the camouflage stripes are a challenge to keep track of while animating. Merlin is an old man almost entirely hidden behind the biggest beard and cloak imaginable, which makes posing him a challenge because you always have to be aware of what is happening *under* all that covering. He also needs to morph into other creatures and objects and still retain his "Merlin-ness," but despite these challenges he has a brilliant silhouette. Pinocchio is a walking, talking marionette, so you need to believe he's made of wooden parts, not flesh and bone,

Image 10.12

but still be able to relate to him as a living creature. All of these design requirements are a part of solid drawing, but so are the animation difficulties. In Chapter 12 "Appeal," we will look at the "I've Got No Strings" dance sequence in *Pinocchio* shot by shot. But if you own the movie and can play it right now, I encourage you to watch that scene for not only a singular demonstration of the difficulties present in the design and movement *requirements* of the character, but also the masterful execution in fulfilling them through solid drawing. (Also, while you're at it, see how many other principles you can find at work—and keep an eye out for the "twinning" as well, and ask yourself "so why does that work *here*?" Hint: remember that he's made of wood.)

Milt Kahl also animated another tiger (Tigger) in *The Many Adventures of Winnie the Pooh*. Except this time, notice how different the design and movements are. The features are the same, but the specifics of the anatomy are different. The stripes are still there and still difficult to keep track of, but the way they're laid out on the body makes it easier for the animator to track than if they were more real (just as with Shere Khan). If you step frame by frame through the scene where Tigger wakes Pooh, you'll see just how solid the solid drawing is. You can believe that he (and Pooh for that matter) exist in a 3D world. The angular drawing style that Milt employed, inspired (among others) by Picasso, is still present in all of these designs, but each design is specific to the needs of the character and story. Ludwig Von Drake (*Walt Disney's Wonderful World of Color*), who was animated by Milt but also by Ward Kimball, is probably my favorite example of a similar design style being tailored to a specific character. Ludwig looks to be very similar to Donald Duck (he's supposedly Donald's uncle), but with the hair of Larry Fine (*The Three Stooges*), a voice emulating Albert Einstein, and the coat and glasses reminding us of classic educational lecture videos, he's clearly a different character. But honestly, if it wasn't for solid drawing, all the clothes, hairpieces, and voices in the world wouldn't make us think he wasn't just Donald in disguise. His head to body proportions, neck and arm thickness, and distinguishing wrinkles on his face are all uniquely different to Donald's. If these aren't maintained on every frame, the illusion would be lost to our association with the more well-known and similar design of Donald Duck. The fact that you know it's Ludwig without question is the subtle genius of solid drawing at work.

Don't be distraught in thinking that this is going to be difficult to do because you're right. It comes easier for some. It's one of the perks of talent, but almost no one is excellent at something out of the box. Animation is about progression: step by step, frame by frame, all on the way to creating something that wasn't there before. The 12 Principles of Animation are a way for us to get close to a standard curriculum for learning this incredibly deep field. To say "draw better" might be an oversimplification, but it's hard to deny that it's a part of being better in a field heavy in drawing. What Animate CC does, however, is make it easier to keep a wonderful drawing as close to how you drew it as possible while making subtle movements as well as always having an easy reference for proportions on any new drawings. If a wolf's eyes need to grow huge and burst out of his head in excitement (via Exaggeration, next chapter's principle) à la *Red Hot Riding Hood* by Tex Avery (a master in exaggeration), you only need to draw and change the eyes and their immediate parts affected like the surrounding eyebrow area; everything else can remain in the same proportion or stretched slightly. Animate CC makes changes like this very easy and easier to go back to the "normal" state when needed. This ability will be no more apparent than when applying momentary exaggeration, which is the topic of the next chapter.

Image 11.0 Frames from Pencilmation #34: A Hole New World by Ross Bollinger (pencilmation.com).

Chapter 11

EXAGGERATION

INTRODUCING
Exaggeration

The meaning of "exaggeration" is well known. What this means in animation however, as with many of the 12 Principles, is a bit more abstract and general. Many people immediately think that this just means to exaggerate an expression or movement, but it can and should be extended to concepts, situations, settings, and just about every other area. You shouldn't exaggerate everything all the time, but rather everything *can* be exaggerated for effect. Let's try to understand this concept a bit more without using the word exaggerate. "Pushing" something is a common way for directors to ask for this principle to be applied, and appropriately so. Where a simple smile might work, pushing for more of a smile could work better. The perspective on an environment might convey depth well, but pushing that effect further would make the depth more obvious. Sometimes it's like your scene is teetering on the edge of a bungee-jump but too scared to really get into it—it's just standing on the edge of something interesting and exciting. In that case, your scene might just need a little ... push.

Another way to think of exaggeration, especially in terms of its more abstract interpretations, is "hyperbole." An old common cartoon trope when a male character saw a hot woman was for his head to turn into a fire alarm horn "aoogah!" ... because she's hot like a fire, get it? Turning the colloquial concept "hot" into a literal demonstration of something that indicates its presence might be the most high-brow and unfunny way to explain a joke, ever, but that's what's going on behind the scenes of wild Tex Avery-esque moments like that. It may be instinctual for the artist, but there is a decision being made nonetheless: how many times can we go *this* crazy before overwhelming our audience? The amount you utilize exaggeration and in what ways will depend on whether you're going for a more realistic or caricatured style. It would seem out of place for Cinderella, herself, to be making wacky expressions and visual puns, but Gus the mouse (or "Gus-Gus" or Octavius for the trivia fanatics) is perfect to take on this roll. He and Jaq don't overpower the film with their antics, not just because they're mice and small, but because they allow a balance for the audience. The premise of Cinderella is a bit unbelievable in the first place, and Jaq and Gus, the mice sidekicks, are a conduit for the audience to get their fill of fun and exaggerated premises so that the main story can feel more grounded and Cinderella less like a fantasy and more like a person in a fantastical situation.

"The amount you utilize exaggeration and in what ways will depend on whether you're going for a more realistic or caricatured style."

Early Daffy Duck is a wonderful representation of exaggeration by premise at work. Take the short *To Duck or Not to Duck* (1943) as an example. Directed by Chuck Jones, it's no secret now that there will be some heavy exaggeration going on. Every single moment in this short is oozing with exaggerated expressions, poses, situations, premises, puns, actions, and so on. After listing off all the weapons and assets that Elmer Fudd has to kill him, simultaneously swiping them all away including his clothes, Daffy says, "What protection have *I* got? A bulletproof *vest* I suppose!" He opens his feathery plumage to show that he's actually wearing a bulletproof vest, and then shyly closes his mock feather/clothing, "How did that get there?" This reaction is all after an excellent sequence of maniacal laughing at the idea of Elmer the hunter being a "sportsman," which also featured exaggerated poses and opposing action lines. These sequences lead directly into the completely ridiculous premise of Daffy dragging Elmer into a fair fight (since he's such a "sportsman," says Daffy) in a boxing ring surrounded by ducks.

The joke is that the hunter has all the advantages, so what might that look like the other way around in a common sport? As unfunny as it is to explain a joke, seeing the difference in the makeup of the two scenarios and how they handle exaggeration in their own way (one realistic fantasy, *Cinderella*, and the other a pure caricature, *To Duck or Not to Duck*) shows that Exaggeration is not just a "make funny drawings" principle, but one which has many uses through a wide array of situations.

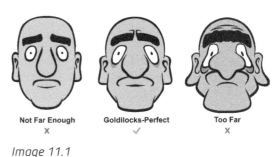

Not Far Enough X Goldilocks-Perfect ✓ Too Far X

Image 11.1

In this chapter, we're going to be pushing the work that was explored in our real-world examples. Exaggeration is a flourish, some extra *frou-frou* on a scene but, like with Secondary Action, when it's done right it will be hard for the viewer to imagine it any other way. If something hits, make it hit harder. If it has overlapping action, overlap more. When showing a character under pressure, you can go ahead and just turn him or her into a pressure cooker whistle-screaming. Exploring options and seeing how much you can push a shot is really the only way to know for sure how far is too far—or how far is Goldilocks-perfect. Walt Disney wanted realistic animation, but it was the interpretation of that movement as filtered through a person's mind or experiences which made it that way. Exaggeration is very much a part of that same pursuit of realistic movement. Sometimes you have to push something past reality to make it *feel* more real and identifiable, while other times you want to go beyond that wall of interpreted realism into the realm of pure, zany caricatures.

EXERCISES Exaggeration

In this chapter, we're going to be examining a couple of the real-world exercises from chapters past and seeing how we can push the principles' use further and utilize Exaggeration better. Notice the use of the word "better." Unless you're tracing frames of footage from real life (called "rotoscoping"), you're almost always exaggerating the motion in some way. As mentioned, though Walt Disney wanted the animation his company made to have the sense of being real, he also was pushing for a more heightened version of it when needed. Behold, exhibit A to Z (because nothing else needs to be said): *Mickey's Trailer*. Every inch of that short is exaggerated, from the premises to the actions. And it gets progressively pushed further and further as the short continues through its run-time of 8 tight minutes. And that was in 1938, the very, very beginning of Disney's "golden age."

The two previous real-world exercises we'll be working with are the "chewing" scene from Chapter 3 "Squash and Stretch," and "Pitching a Bomb" from Chapter 4 "Anticipation." First we'll look at "chewing" and how we can improve it.

Exercise 1 "Exaggerating 'Chewing'"

Image EC11.0 The visual beats will still be the same between the original (top) and exaggerated (bottom) versions of this real-world exercise.

In this real-world exercise, we made a character take a bite, chew, and swallow some food. This animation was done by using a couple of different methods of showing squash and stretch and making use of the "loop" feature of a Graphic Symbol for the chew cycle. The shot we ended up with was a good example of one which already had some exaggeration in it without really trying. The goal this time is to make it obvious that this is clearly a caricatured version of the action. To take the bite, his mouth will grow in size and open further than humanly possible (like a snake dislocating its jaw to swallow its prey whole) to show the audience what the meaning of this scene really is—the gluttonous way our character is devouring his enormous meal, happy as can be with the challenge. During the final swallow, his neck will outstretch more like an ostrich with his head squashing, seemingly to squeeze the mouthful down his neck, and come stretching back to position like a rubber band. Before starting, open the file "ch3-real_world-chew.fla," or whatever the corresponding largest version number you saved is, and save it as "ch11-real_world-exaggerated_chew."

1. First we need to re-rough some of the shots to push them further. First, delete the "rough animation" folder left over from the work we did in Chapter 3, then create a new layer above the cleanup folder, turn it into a guide, and name it "rough-exaggeration." This should be the only unlocked layer. *Image EC11.1*

Image EC11.1

2. On the keys with the fully open mouth, the bite, both up-and-down chew points in the cycle, and the final up-and-down swallowing keys, insert blank keyframes (**F7**) and sketch out a more exaggerated version of these poses and expressions. You can use my sketches for reference, but feel free to play with your own style. *Image EC11.2*

3. Look at the animation you completed in Chapter 3 and remember how we split up the head animation into three symbols ("head" is the first bite while "head-chew_loop" and "head-swallow" are self-explanatory) and when on the timeline those instances were swapped for another. You can highlight an instance on stage and look at the Properties panel for "Instance of:" to determine which keyframe on the "head" layer is which instance.

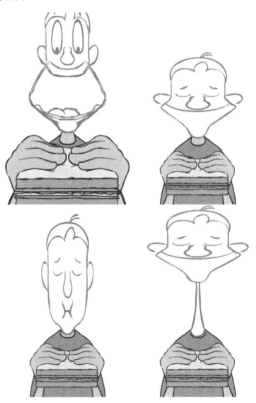

Image EC11.2

4. Now that you've determined which symbols contain each part of the animation, for each individual section you'll need to highlight the new rough key sketches, **Copy Frames**, and then **Paste Frames** inside the head symbol (whichever version needs those keys) on a new, separate layer. Let's start by copying in the first head symbol's animation key sketches. Take the time when pasting in the frames to line up the sketches to the existing cleanup so you can get right to the alterations in the next steps. *Image EC11.4*

5. Since there are three head symbols with animation nested inside you'll need to clean up within each symbol. To reiterate, in these steps we're starting on the first head symbol with the bite. Within the "head" symbol and seeing the rough keys you pasted in on the previous step, adjust the size and/or makeup of the shapes and symbol instances to match the new rough. Notice in the accompanying image that the mouth and cheek line layers are hidden and locked since the mouth is animated frame by frame and the cheek lines are tweened to that movement (if possible, otherwise they too would need to be animated frame by frame). *Image EC11.5*

Image EC11.4

6. Reapply or add any shape hints which may be necessary at this point (such as for the jaw shape tween which is what the accompanying image shows). *Image EC11.6*

7. Now that the tweens are finished, go ahead and finish the sequence by cleaning up the frame-by-frame animation of the mouth. Do this the same way you did in the real-world exercise in Chapter 3 by sketching rough inbetweens on a new layer and then cleaning them up on the feature's layer. *Image EC11.7*

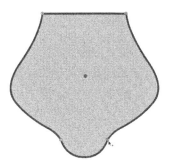

Image EC11.5

Image EC11.6

8. Once all the rough keys and the animation between them are cleaned up in the head symbol we were working in (with the first bite), highlight all the keyframes which make up the last post (the closed mouth bite on frame 26) and **Copy Frames**. This is because we need this exact pose to start the chew cycle, which is the next symbol we're cleaning up. *Image EC11.8*

The following methods works for any version of Flash but Adobe introduced a feature called "Paste and Overwrite Frames" in Animate which replaces steps 9–13! Check out "The Animate Difference" section for this feature which is just before Exercise 2.

Image EC11.7

Image EC11.8

9. Enter the "head-chew_loop" symbol, create a new layer above all the rest, right-click the first blank keyframe there and **Paste Frames**. The image which accompanies this step shows what you'll see after those actions. The blank layer you inserted became the top layer which was pasted ("nose") and is the only one which is extended the length of the internal timeline. The rest of the pasted frames and layers are below it and only have the first keyframe. *Image EC11.9*

10. To make sure that the timeline doesn't get too complicated, before moving forward we're going to tidy it up a bit. Remember that the chew loop is made up of two poses (an up-and-down version of the mouth closed and chewing). The starting pose is the down version of the chew and so is the end, which leaves the middle keyframe (at frame 7) to be the up version of the chew pose. The other two sets of keyframes (on frames 4 and 10) are

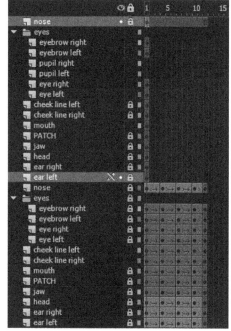

Image EC11.9

breakdowns which were used to give a slow in and out for the tweens. We only want the keys on frames 1, 7, and 12 so highlight both sets of breakdown keyframes including part of the tween spans before and after them (as shown in the accompanying image). Then right-click **Clear Keyframe** and again to select **Remove Tween**. *Image EC11.10*

11. Looking back up at the frames and layers you pasted in on step 9, you'll notice that they're in the exact same order as what was already in this symbol before that step except the pupil layers are missing. Highlight all the keyframes under the blank pupil layers down to the last pasted-in layer (which was "ear left") and then drag these keyframes down to corresponding layers below in order to replace the old keyframes with these new ones. *Image EC11.11*

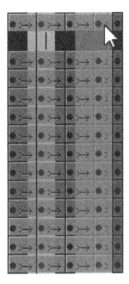

Image EC11.10

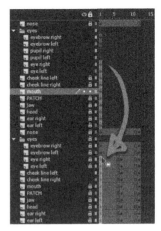

Image EC11.11

12. Repeat the previous step for the last of the layers *above* the blank pupil layers (the nose and eyebrow layer keyframes) and then delete all of the pasted in layers from step 9.

13. You have now replaced the existing starting pose for the chew cycle with the new exaggerated one. Since the final keyframe in this sequence is the same pose, highlight one frame from every layer between the first and second keyframes and drag that forward on the timeline to replace the final keyframe with these. *Image EC11.13*

14. Repeat steps 4–13 (paste in the rough keys and align, adjust the features that are being tweened, frame-by-frame the rest) to complete the rest of the chew cycle animation and again for the swallow symbol. Don't forget to paste in the cleanup keyframes from the poses needed into the swallow symbol—it starts with the first cleanup pose of the chew cycle and ends with the first cleanup pose in the main "head" symbol from the beginning.

15. The exaggerated expressions and the animation to and from them is finished within the head symbols themselves,

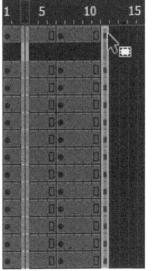

Image EC11.13

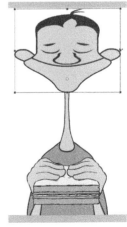

Image EC11.15

but now we should add some more
extreme movement of the symbol
instances on the main timeline. This
is where you adjust things like if the
head lifts up high, push it higher. If the
head squashes down, drop it lower and
add more squash to the instance itself.
Image EC11.15

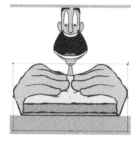

Image EC11.16

16. Add in any extra exaggeration which
    assists the expression and head
    movement changes such as increasing the size of the hand and
    sandwich symbol while shrinking the size of the head to make
    it look like the character is leaning far back while holding the
    sandwich outstretched. *Image EC11.16*

17. The last thing we'll do is exaggerate the final settle into position
    by extending the timeline out a few frames (such as to frame 86
    like I did), inserting a keyframe there on the head layer, lowering
    the head and stretching it at the previous keyframe (frame 81),
    and finishing it up with a classic tween between these last two
    keyframes with an "S" curve. *Image EC11.17*

Image EC11.17

The "Animate" Difference: PASTE AND OVERWRITE FRAMES

Image AD6

One of the most subtly helpful features given
to Animate CC which didn't exist in Flash was
the ability to paste frames from multiple layers
on the timeline while replacing what was there
instead of creating all new layers. The method
shown in steps 9-13 in Exercise 1 of this chapter
was the quickest and most secure way to
accomplish the same feat (there are actually
two methods shown there so you learned both
— those are the copy/paste and drag-and-drop
methods). Now you can accomplish this much
quicker. Image AD6 shows how you can now
use Paste and Overwrite Frames to do the same
thing we did in steps 9–13 in Exercise 1 of this
chapter but in a much more expedient way. The
feature in the right-click drop-down menu from
the timeline and will push the existing frames
froward (notice frame number 2 in the image).
Simple use Clear Frames (from right-click) on
those which were pushed froward and re-apply
the appropriate tweens to the frames you pasted
earlier.

Exercise 2 "Exaggerating 'Pitching a Bomb'"

With the principle of Anticipation, it's all about building to some payoff. In the case of our pitcher, the baseball had been replaced with a bomb and the wick was slowly getting shorter and shorter. The feeling of anticipation was, knowing that the bomb could go off at any second, "would he throw it away in time?" The answer was ... no. Because in a cartoon, that's funny. This time, we're going to exaggerate the length of the wick but still have it burn off slowly—this way there is still plenty of wick left when he winds-up for the pitch. The audience should be wondering what the payoff will be if there's still plenty of time before the bomb goes off. But instead of having it explode in his hand, we're going to adjust the existing payoff gag to have him get hit by a random lightning strike. It's a bait-and-switch type payoff. This happened to Wile E. Coyote all the time in his cartoons with his foil, the Road Runner, by Chuck Jones at Warner Bros.—not to mention just about every scheme Donald Duck cooked up over at Disney.

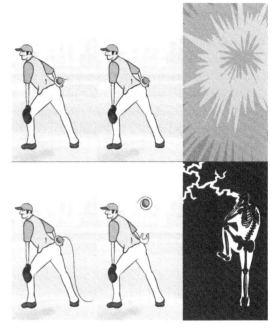

Image EB 11.0 Original (top) and the exaggerated version (bottom) differ also in timing.

To accentuate the comically long bomb wick, we're going to add a little secondary action. There's already some in the form of a head shake/nod (added for extra effect in step 45), but we're adding tossing the bomb casually which will show the extra-long wick spinning around. The principles of Slow In/Out, Arcs, and Overlapping Action and Follow Through are also in the forefront and when roughing out the actions we're using both Pose To Pose and Straight Ahead Action. As always, you can look at the provided FLA for reference, inspiration, or something to copy. Copying and deconstructing is a completely valid learning tool. Study stuff you respect and admire. Sometimes drawing it over yourself is the only real way you can fully understand and appreciate how a technique was accomplished. It's all part of learning. Monkey see, monkey do. Open the "ch4-real_world-pitcher.fla" (or latest version number) and **Save As** "ch11-real_world-exaggerated_pitcher."

1. Just as in the previous exercise (exaggerating chewing), we want to rough out the new parameters of the scene. We should still have the rough layers that were provided for you to create the scene in the first place so hide everything except for the folder with the rough layers. *(Note: if you don't still have a rough animation folder in your latest file because you deleted it to clean up the timeline, open one of the earlier versions of the base file ("ch4-real_world-pitcher"), and copy/paste the layers to our new file for this chapter ("ch11-real_world-exaggerated_pitcher").)*

2. The first thing to address is the wick length. Redraw a comically long wick on the layer with the existing wick rough and delete the old one. *Image EB11.2*

Image EB11.2

3. Scroll ahead to the point where the pitcher starts his windup sequence (should be frame 161) and create a wick length there to represent how much had been burned away. This will help you keep the wick burning consistent when we get to the secondary action of the toss. You should now highlight the preceding three keyframes on the "wick burning" layer and **Clear Keyframe** since those were indicating the timing of the old wick-burning rough. *Image EB11.3*

4. Now we need to adjust the timing to account for the secondary action we're going to add in. Scroll back to the beginning, hit **Enter** on your keyboard to start playing the rough animation, and after the baseball is replaced with the bomb, look away. Visualize how much time is needed to casually toss and catch the bomb behind his back and wait for the wick to burn down a bit before you want the windup to happen—then hit **Enter** again and note where you stopped it. I stopped mine at frame 253 which leaves about 7 seconds for the bomb toss and watching the wick burn. Adjust your timing for the rough animation layers only by inserting frames (**F5**) during that waiting period span.

Image EB11.3

5. Repeat the previous step to determine where you want the secondary action to start. Then insert keyframes and sketch in the rough animation on the pitcher and wick-burning layers to achieve this secondary action. The bomb should rotate in the air to better remind the audience how long the wick is by having it stretch, then coil around the spin and finally fall back down after the catch. I chose frame 156, which is around the halfway point in the anticipation beat we extended in the previous step. *Image EB11.5*

6. Scroll ahead to the part where the windup sequence is just beginning in the rough and using the straight ahead action method sketch in the wick for the frames that match the pitcher's rough animation timing. The wick will display Overlapping Action. This particular sequence should be familiar to you because of doing similar work in the real-world exercises in Chapters 7 and 8. *(Note: we want the wick to ultimately be hidden behind the pitcher so the*

Image EB11.5

audience momentarily forgets about that setup when the lightning strikes.)

7. Now let's address the new payoff: the lightning strike. Because this is an unexpected payoff we want this comedic beat to hit before the original bomb-exploding one. I chose to have the lightning strike about 0.5 seconds after the windup sequence ends so drag the keyframe with the existing bomb explosion image back to this new timing and delete the existing image. Sketch in the lightning strike image. We're going for standard cartoon electrocution-style visuals. The lightning bolt will appear instantly and our character will be a silhouette and you'll see his skeleton underneath. For the actual effect, we'll add a flicker during cleanup but for the rough, one image is enough. *Image EB11.7*

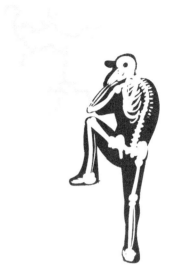

Image EB11.7

8. Drag the keyframe with the charred image of the pitcher back to a point after the lightning strike. I use the same hit-**Enter**-visualize-then-hit-**Enter**-again method to determine quick timing for shots like this.

9. To start the cleanup/fixes/alterations, move the existing cleanup frames forward during the anticipation sequence the way you did in the rough. The only symbol with nested animation is the hand, so make sure you change the Play Once frame number to match the new frames (this goes for each keyframe of the hand symbol—remember there's one layer in front of the body and one behind).

10. The final anticipation cushioning tween as well as the pitcher-go-boom image keyframe (with the smoke layer if you added that from step 45 in Chapter 4's real-world exercise) need to be brought back to match the new, quicker timing of the lightning strike payoff. The explosion cleanup layer isn't needed anymore and can be deleted.

11. What we need to address now is the wick. The main place to start would be the starting wick length so scroll to the first time we see it in the rough animation but after the mystery arm leaves (so we don't get confused about which symbol is which) and double-click to enter the pitcher's hand symbol and then the bomb symbol within that. You should remember the setup from when we worked on it in Chapter 4. Clear every keyframe except for the ones on the first frame for "bomb," "spark," and "wick." *Image EB11.11*

Image EB11.11

12. Hide every layer except for "bomb" and "wick," delete the existing wick image, and create a new one with the Line Tool (**N**) to match the rough. *Image EB11.12*

13. Unhide the "spark" layer and drag the instance to the bottom tip of the wick, remembering to have it actually positioned on the wick line (you'll most likely need Snap to Objects toggled on for this).

14. Extend the timeline for the "bomb" symbol out, at least to cover the length of the timing we worked out back in step 4 (remember that mine was about 7 seconds so I extended the timeline out to frame 200).

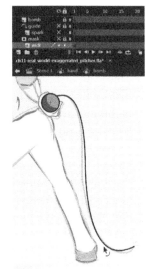

15. The next thing we want to do is add in the wick-burning animation so scroll ahead to the start of the windup animation where we had drawn how much wick would be burned away in the rough animation. Provided that you adjusted the Play Once frame number of the hand symbol at this keyframe mentioned in step 9, double-click to enter to the "bomb" symbol like in step 11 and insert a keyframe (**F6**) at that frame on the "spark" layer.

Image EB11.12

16. Drag the spark instance up to the point the wick ends in the rough animation and snap it to the wick line like in step 13. *Image EB11.16*

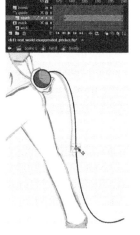

17. Copy the only keyframe on the "wick" layer, paste it on the guide layer, and then create a classic tween between the two keyframes on the "spark" layer. The spark should now be traveling along the wick. *Image EB11.17*

18. The mask animation we need to use this time will be a bit different. Since the wick is longer and has more of a curvy path, a straight shape tween on the mask won't work like last time. Unlock and unhide the "mask" layer and

Image EB11.16   *Image EB11.17*

then start by setting up the mask shape the same way as we did in Chapter 4: create a rectangle which covers the entire length of the wick on frame 1 with its rightmost edge just ending at the wick. *(Note: remember that using a fill color with an alpha less than 100% will allow you to see through the mask shape to what is below it, which is what will*

ultimately be shown to the audience.)
Image EB11.18

19. In the wick that I drew, the spark first needs to travel a downward path to the bottommost curve of the wick. Insert a keyframe at this extreme and adjust the mask shape to have its rightmost edge end at the spark. *Image EB11.19*

20. Now the spark is starting to travel upward but is still traveling left at a faster rate than we need to allow for the mask shape to adjust in-kind with the curve. So at the frame where the spark reaches a point relatively opposite the initial end of the wick and where it's starting to travel upward more than left, insert a keyframe on the mask layer and adjust the shape so that the bottom-right *corner* is matching the spark's position. Holding Option/**Alt** when dragging with the Free Transform Tool (**Q**) works beautifully for this step. *Image EB11.20*

21. Now that the spark is basically moving directly upward, simply move ahead to the frame with the ending keyframe in the spark animation span, insert a keyframe on the mask layer, and drag the bottom of the mask rectangle up to meet the spark position. Create a shape tween between all the keyframes created in the last three steps. Now when you lock both the "mask" and "wick" layers you should see the spark traveling along the wick line while the wick is disappearing as it's being burned away ... just like we did in Chapter 4's real-world exercise.

22. If you go back to the main stage now you'll see that when the mystery arm comes out, the wick is moving around very stiffly before the hand-off. What we're going to need to do here is not anything you haven't seen thus far so this will be done quickly. First enter the "mystery_arm-hand" symbol and scroll forward to the first place you see the bomb appear in the hand, right-click the bomb, **Duplicate Symbol**, and name it "bomb-no_wick." Then enter this new symbol and delete everything except for the bomb layer (note that this part of the step isn't shown in the accompanying image because when you're done you shouldn't see the wick or spark anymore). *Image EB11.22*

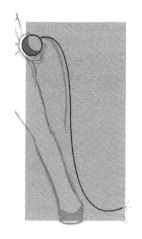
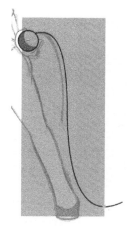

Image EB11.18   Image EB11.19

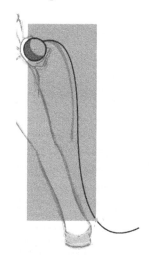

Image EB11.20

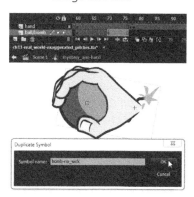

Image EB11.22

23. Return to the main timeline, insert a new layer, and frame-by-frame and/or shape tween the wick entering the screen convincingly with the mystery arm (obviously the wick image on the main timeline is only for a few frames, being replaced by the wick within the pitcher's hand symbol). Add the "bomb-spark" symbol as needed. *Image EB11.23*

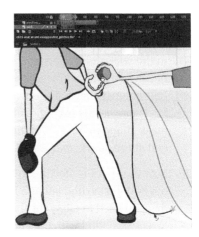

Image EB11.23

24. We'll come back to the secondary action bomb toss at the end. For now go to the beginning of the windup and repeat the process in the previous two steps to make sure the wick is not stiffly rotating with the bomb during the windup and instead matches the rough animation you did earlier. *(Note: this time you don't need to duplicate the bomb symbol to get one with no wick since it's already been created. You can swap symbols. Also don't forget to insert a keyframe at the beginning of the windup sequence in the hand symbol to replace the bomb.)*

25. Next, scroll ahead to the lightning strike. We'll do a little FX work here. The lightning bolt will come in fully formed as a yellow bolt the frame before the rough that you drew. On the following frame, the background turns black and all you see is the lightning bolt and the skeleton. Then it's just a matter of flipping the black and white colors for a few more frames and ending on the final burnt keyframe with the

Image EB11.25a

Image EB11.25b

smoke coming off him (if you added this effect at the end of the real-world exercise in Chapter 4, that is). You could've created a Graphic Symbol with just those two inverse color frames and looped it on-stage for the flashing effect as well, but it wasn't necessary for a shot as short as this. *(Pro-tip: when drawing the lightning bolt, to get jagged edges you can use one of the other brush shapes such as the square which I used.) Image EB11.25a and EB11.25b*

26. With the easier changes out of the way, we need to address the secondary action of the behind the back ball toss. First we'll address the hand animation since it's going to dictate the bomb's tween timing. To clean up the hand animation, go to each key in the rough animation on the main timeline and enter the hand symbol from there to complete that image. Finish the

hand animation cleanup by inbetweening the spans between those keyframes. *Image EB11.26*

27. You'll remember that the nested bomb animation we made initially in Chapter 4 (and edited here) doesn't have its internal frames in sync with the main timeline, so to keep the bomb's wick burning synchronized before and after the toss insert a keyframe (**F6**) at the end of the span when the bomb is back at rest.

28. Replace the symbol instance of the bomb with the wick to one without a wick at the beginning of this secondary action toss sequence. To clean up this motion, insert keyframes and manually position the ball frame by frame for the initial movement until it leaves the hand and then classic tween the bomb up and down the way we have for many chapters with the bouncing ball. Finalize the ball animation by animating it back to rest in the same frame-by-frame way as the way you started this sequence. *Image EB11.28*

29. Now that you've done the process animating the wick on the stage, this part doesn't need to be explained as much. Just try to match the length of the wick to the starting and ending lengths. You'll most likely be able to shape tween the beginning and ending of this sequence when the wick shape isn't changing as rapidly due to overlapping action, but the rest will need to be animated frame by frame using straight ahead action and the Pencil Tool (**Shift+Y**). You can manually move the spark instance around for those frame-by-frame parts of the sequence but will need to tween it on its own layer during those parts where you've decided to shape tween the wick. *Image EB11.29*

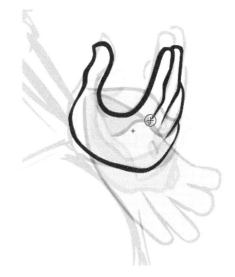

Image EB11.26

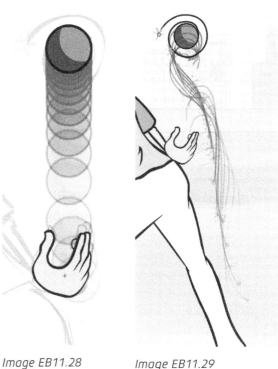

Image EB11.28   *Image EB11.29*

Notice how much more the anticipation of the moment reads with the alteration of the timing, changing the punchline to being less straightforward and expected, and the extra secondary action.

The secondary action, specifically, not only fills in some of the visual stagnation of the longer anticipation moment, but also directs focus to the bomb, which is an example of the use of staging. Not only can everything clearly be seen, but the story point of the moment is never forgotten or overshadowed. The audience can be drawn into the moment because it's waiting for what's going to happen next (anticipation), but to facilitate that the secondary action and the payoff needed to be there. In this example, you've used every single principle covered thus far in one scene.

Precise Tools, Exaggerated Use

Giotto, an Italian painter in the late Middle Ages, was asked by the Pope (well, a messenger he sent anyway) around the year 1300 AD to draw something to prove his skill, to which Giotto responded by painting a single perfect circle. If you've ever tried to do that, it is almost incomparably difficult. As a matter of fact, many artists (myself included) warm up in the morning by drawing dozens, if not hundreds, of circles over and over on paper as a way to kind of calibrate the senses before starting work. The extreme freehanded precision that Giotto showed in making that perfect circle spoke volumes at the time as to the level of skill and mastery the painter had. Today, you can hold **Shift** and drag out a perfect circle using the Oval Tool (**O**) in Animate CC (*Image 11.2*). Of course, while the drafting compass was

Image 11.2 Art.

officially invented in the mid-1500s, you could replicate what a compass does by holding a brush to a string which freely rotates around a rod in the center, but the story is too good to nitpick. And it illuminates a point really well, which is that with all the precise tools at her fingertips, an artist is often tempted to stay within the boundaries of exact proportions it allows one to create. Just as an animator can be dragged into some wild directions by drawing freehand without tools or construction sketches, using more tools can also lead to working in solely impressive but boring accuracy.

> **"The introduction of new technology doesn't have to mean the rejection of traditionally established principles and techniques."**

Often, as an artist grows in skill and knowledge they will become more stagnant for fear of losing whatever technical ability they have. "Don't rock the boat" is a phrase that comes to mind. Fear of experimentation is a dangerous place for any artist because exploration is key to creative endeavors, and when that stops playing a part, things get ... boring. This fear can manifest itself, many times strangely enough, in established artists not being entirely receptive to new technology. Though it's new and needs to be "explored," the addition of more precise (and numerous) tools can be seen as a threat to the creative process because it seems like the soul of creation is being taken away. This criticism isn't wrong. But what really happens is that in the early days of a new tech's inclusion into a medium, trailblazing artists are finding the right balance of its use into their existing workflow. What incorporating new technology or techniques has to do with the principle of Exaggeration is that the same tools that are used to keep your character on model (symbols, objects, shape tools, etc.)

can hold you back from exploring the more playful side of animation because "hey, the character's already drawn—why draw it again?" In truth, this could be said for every one of the principles and is the core reason this book exists—to counter that reasoning. The introduction of new technology doesn't have to mean the rejection of traditionally established principles and techniques.

REAL-WORLD EXAMPLES
Exaggeration

Example 1: *Rabbit Punch*

In Chuck Jones' *Rabbit Punch* (1948), Bugs Bunny fights Battling McGook. The latter's introduction has him flexing, during which the brute's muscles, as dictated by normal human anatomy, enlarge. But just to show that this guy is no ordinary foe, many more muscles just start showing up until he literally shows biceps atop biceps. This use of exaggeration isn't just making something bigger; it's adding more features to his actual design. If asked to make a character "flex so much that he looked impossibly strong" (which would be the story point of the shot), many people when starting to use Animate CC would probably make each muscle group a symbol and just grow them in size—or possibly even use shape tweens to morph the muscles. This approach would be

Image 11.3 Rabbit Punch
(1948). Licensed by Warner Bros.
Entertainment Inc. All rights reserved.

evidence of linear thinking. When given a set of tools, there is a sense that they must be utilized at all times to achieve an end goal. In the case of the flexing *uberman*, you could have the same effect as the final in *Rabbit Punch* by drawing in different muscle groups and tweening those in to appear in series. The problem is that you might not have even come up with the idea had you not stepped away from thinking of the scene in terms of only the tools you have. Of the many wonderful things about animation, the ability to show anything you want might be the most valuable—and the scariest to lose.

Example 2: *Donald's Snow Fight*

About 1 minute into Disney's animated short *Donald's Snow Fight* (1942), Donald goes to get his overcoat because it's cold outside. What he comes back with is an absolutely huge fur coat that makes him look like a walking church bell. The animators even call out to that fact by having him finish his rendition of "Jingle Bells" by swinging from a tree acting like a musical bell. The concept is exaggerated. In movement, the coat actually makes him waddle more than he usually does—and he's a duck. Exaggeration. They actually draw attention to this absurdity with Huey, Dewey, and Louie making fun of their uncle Donald and his ridiculously sized coat by building a similarly sized snowman around a rock—which ultimately takes the coat out of the equation. The joke has run its course and the use of exaggeration was just right so there's no reason to continue it. It's time to move on to the next bits. We see snow and icicles fall on Donald to make him look like a rhino in a cage. He bowls a snowball into Huey, Dewey, and Louie when they look like bowling pins from the snow packed around them. There are ice mortars, snow bombs with mouse traps in them, and flaming arrows that melt everything around them. The situation progresses steadily until ultimately getting to a point of such exaggerated premise that it's hard to believe anyone would have survived if that happened in the real world.

Like *Mickey's Trailer*, it's the slow increase in the use of exaggeration that brings the audience in and along for the ride. To use an example from live-action film as a relative sample of this technique in a different genre, Steven Spielberg's *Jaws* (1975) starts with a very scientific and realistic premise: a large shark is swimming in waters where it is unexpected and is killing swimmers. Rogue shark attacks have happened, though rarely, so it's not a crazy idea. But the movie steadily ratchets up the unbelievability factor until the final scene is just simply ... impossible. The reason it works is because the audience has been sucked into the story and slowly introduced to increasingly unlikely events with expert direction of acting, cinematography, and editing so that by the time they get to the end, the impossible is completely believable and even relatable. This example just illuminates the versatility of exaggeration as a concept and is a helpful way to think about its use in broader terms. In both of the examples, *Rabbit Punch* and *Donald's Snow*

Image 11.4 Donald's Snow Fight (1942).

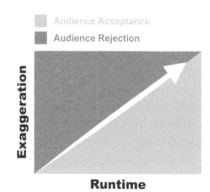

Image 11.5

Fight, the use of exaggeration is different. Events and premises are often exaggerated for effect; that, they have in common. But the varied use of exaggeration in movement and design shows what a difference its application makes in the end style of a project. In *Donald's Snow Fight*, it's clear how Animate CC can be used to apply this type of exaggeration since it's more or less represented in the events unfolding on screen, which would be the more conceptual use of this principle and less about the tools. You would mostly just animate the way you always would. But on closer inspection, you can see the exaggerated use of squash and stretch and character form in the breakdown frames which would call out the use of the Free Transform Tool, shape tweens, and other Animate CC features.

"Disney's History of Technological Innovation"

Thumbnailing, sketching, roughing ... these are all important connections to the traditional way of animating where these principles originally came from. Disney Studios pioneered not only ideas and methods like the 12 Principles and storyboarding, but also animation technology. The multiplane camera, optical camera (to merge live action with animation), xerography, C.A.P.S. (Computer Animation Production System), and Deep Canvas are just a few of the many innovations that were used. And it's not like these were created in vacuums of one another; C.A.P.S. actually eliminated the need for the multiplane camera and xerography by digitally doing the same jobs. Technology, tools, and methods all march forward together. No matter the tools, the principles of movement remain mostly the same. The new technology means that existing methods will merge with new ways of animating and form new workflows; that leaves us on the Tradigital doorstep. You've seen how the tools can aid in the application of the other principles, and even when we got into methods and some concepts (like pose to pose, follow through, secondary action, etc.), it was still clear that the tools could easily help facilitate them. Exaggeration is a bit of a different principle than the rest because it's almost more about breaking the rules/principles a little bit for effect (or "pushing" to the breaking point), and that can be at odds with the newly learned ways

Image 11.6 Walt Disney standing in front of the multiplane camera.

of precisely executing the principles. The bottom line: if something can be done easily, it might be the tools hypnotizing you into complacency. Use the principle of Exaggeration to push yourself and your animation out of any possible pit of contentment, and keep exploring the world around you.

CLOSER LOOK
Using Exaggeration or "Knowing When *Not* To Use Exaggeration"

In our chewing example, we had two very exaggerated moments where the form was pushed into "wacky" territory: the bite and the swallow. These moments were accents of absurdity which helped the viewer to digest the story point of the scene better and with more vibrancy. Had we gone farther than that, the scene would've become more about the absurdities and less about what's being done. We tempered our use of exaggeration in that example. But this is a rule made to be broken. Tex Avery, and the aforementioned Chuck Jones, made a habit of shattering it at every turn. It became a style for Tex to have the wild expressions, pushed poses, and heightened timing. It can be overused if the exaggeration is without purpose, and truth be told, that's very easy to do. All of Goofy's actions are exaggerated more than other characters. For one, his name is "Goofy"—he's going to be goofy. But more than that, his character even moves the way you would expect a lanky person to move ... just enhanced. Exaggeration plays a key part in his personality.

In Disney's *Beauty and the Beast*, we know that Gaston has to battle the Beast in the end. They set us up to expect that payoff very early on in the film. His obsession with Belle can only mean that he's on a collision course with her soon-to-be protector. But if you've seen the Beast, you know he's monstrous—he's huge! How exactly are you to believe that a human male could go toe to toe with a magically mutated monster of destruction? Exaggeration comes into play here through his

Image 11.7 Northwest Hounded Police *(1946),* directed by Tex Avery, shows two expression extremes of exaggeration.

famous song "Gaston." The whole scene is basically a series of hyperbolic lyrics and displays of strength to show him as an intimidating specimen "roughly the size of a barge." They even go as far as pointing out that he bites in fights to subversively make you relate to him closer to a "beast" and simultaneously show him fighting dirty. This song and dance sequence isn't a throwaway scene just for fun; it's setting you up so that when the ending comes it will make the most sense. It may seem silly—it's exaggerated—but if that number wasn't in the movie, the final fight might not make much sense, especially not the way it happens. Exaggeration isn't just situational in his animation, it's also used in his design. Gaston is drawn as a caricatured "strong man" in his proportions. Also, his expressions are mostly pushed just beyond "normal" in the movie, the way someone's face seems to give away their lies as they try to overcompensate. Happy becomes ecstatic, sad becomes dreadfully morose, angry becomes enraged, and so on. He's basically overacting. The trick for the supervising animator, Andreas Deja, was to let you know that Gaston is not as courageous as everyone says he is—and he may not even believe it himself—but also keep him a real and credible threat. He's a villain after all. That balance is an incredibly fine line to walk, and exaggeration was used just enough to walk it.

"Knowing when or when not to use a principle is just as important, if not more so, as how to use it. Exaggeration is the best example of that notion."

Knowing when to use a principle is just as important, if not more so, as how to use it. Exaggeration is the best example of that notion. *The Simpsons* parodied exaggeration in cartoons with its cartoon within the cartoon: *The Itchy and Scratchy Show*. While it satirized the casual use of violence in cartoons and people's general apathy toward it, it also (knowingly or unknowingly) parodied the use of exaggeration to display that violence. Itchy and Scratchy are visually modeled after Tom and Jerry and Herman and Catnip, but could be stand-ins for any number of cartoon duos like the oft-mentioned Wile E. Coyote and Road Runner. *The Simpsons* itself is full of exaggerated comedy. It's fun seeing what an incredibly exaggerated cartoon within an already exaggerated animated sitcom would look like. What happens when exaggeration goes too far: *The Itchy and Scratchy Show*.

FINAL WORDS
Exaggeration

As straightforward as it sounds, Exaggeration is a heady concept, and it's very easy to do poorly. It's not enough to simply make something bigger, sillier, or more pronounced; it has to be done the right way to get an effect that won't overshadow the rest of what's being done. On top of that, proper use is more about knowing what effect it will have on the presentation of whatever idea you're going for and what type of exaggeration is needed: premise, movement, design, etc. Mostly everyone exaggerates naturally. Exaggeration is a pretty intuitive concept but its inclusion in the 12 Principles was important to make sure the animator always kept it in mind throughout their work. It really is in a place apart from the rest, however, because it's simultaneously trying to push you past where you normally might go and trying to remind you not to go too far but without necessarily telling you what either of those two things mean. You just have to discover them for yourself with careful consideration of what exactly it is you're doing. Keep the concept in mind and push your work until it goes too far. It's really the only way you can know if you've gone far enough.

> **"Keep the concept in mind and push your work until it goes too far. It's really the only way you can know if you've gone far enough."**

Watch animated films, shorts, and series that you love and respect. Analyze them and work them over in your mind. Step through frame by frame and see what your idols have created and how. Explore your own concepts of what is funny, dramatic, thrilling, or whatever sense you want to go for and keep pushing them into new areas. Having a style, after all, doesn't mean that your work needs to remain stagnant. The next, and last, principle is Appeal. Where Exaggeration was about pushing things forward, Appeal is kind of about making sure they stay together when you do. We will be looking at more examples of it at work and discussing its meaning and how we can bring it into our work. The step-by-step work is done in this

Image 11.8 Norm & Cory *by Andrew Kaiko (youtube.com/andrewkful).*

book—the attention now needs to shift to what these conceptual principles mean for our work within Animate CC Even if you're familiar with the principles, it's important to relax on the technical side of things and refresh the meaning and use of the principles so that you can revisit them with fresh eyes along with your new knowledge of work within the program. Now, let's see how to really make our animation appealing!

Image 12.0 Orbis Park by Andrew Kaiko (youtube.com/andrewkful).

INTRODUCING
Appeal

If you're working in a visual medium, you want your audience to *want* to see what you've made. This is a generally accepted starting point. So where does that leave you when you need to create, say, an evil character in animation? They need to command attention from the viewers just like your other main characters. It's good to start off with this example for appeal to separate the soft definition many people have of "likeable" to how we're going to use it. Appeal in animation is related closest to an actor's charisma; despite what they're doing, you always want to see more.

As Frank and Ollie pointed out, if something's "ugly and repulsive [it might have] shock value, but no story strength." This quote gets more to the core of how Appeal relates to solid drawing than it does to standards of beauty. For instance, in Disney's first animated feature film, *Snow White and the Seven Dwarfs* (1937), one of the most iconic characters is the Witch who gives Snow White the apple. Those who haven't seen the movie in a while (or at all) might not entirely remember that the witch is a disguised form of the actual antagonist of the film, The Evil Queen. The queen's goal is to be the "fairest of them all," and when she finds out that Snow White is the more fair (pretty), the Evil Queen sets out to remove her from the competition. This character is the perfect embodiment of the principle of Appeal since she's charismatic in both forms but in different ways (*Image 12.1*). As the second prettiest in all the land, the Evil Queen has more standards of beauty than the Witch does, and they even move differently. They're ostensibly two different characters (though voiced by the same actress). However, in both forms, one "pretty" and one "ugly," you still want to see more of her and what she's going to do. Appeal, regardless of the representations of standards of beauty, is what makes this character such a presence to watch.

Image 12.1 The Witch (left) and the Queen (right) both demonstrate appeal in different ways, though being the same person.

Madam Mim (*The Sword and the Stone*), Madame Medusa (*The Rescuers*), Ursula (*The Little Mermaid*), and Cruella de Vil (*101 Dalmatians*) might not win any beauty contests, but they are some of the most captivating characters on screen. Appeal goes beyond what they look like; it encapsulates how they act and sound as well as how their form is presented. It would be easy to make any of these characters completely unappealing simply by failing at solid drawing or presentation of forms—but also by having them overstep boundaries of charm. If you don't want to see what they're going to do or say next, they would be dead weight. The reason the focus is on villains is because they're the most complex. A hero is usually the "everyman," someone that the audience can use as a proxy to place themselves into that position in the fantasy of the movie. It's a delicate balance, to be sure, because the exaggeration at use usually needs to be really subdued—which is difficult to do and keep the characters appealing. But the villain is someone the audience should actively hate, if not at least simply disagree with, but still want to watch. Ultimately, we want to see the villain fail, but at some level you want to see *how* they were winning until that point—for that, they need appeal.

> "Appeal in animation is related closest to an actor's charisma; despite what they're doing, you always want to see more."

Essentially, Appeal is all about taking every one of the principles—indeed everything you know about art and animation—and putting it all together in harmony to create something that people will want to watch. It's as simple as that to say, not so much to do. How does this relate directly to Animate CC? It doesn't, necessarily. Animate CC is a tool, and in a principle that at its core is asking you to take everything you know and make it all work together, the way to use that tool is every single way you know how. What we're going to be doing in this chapter is similar to what was done in the previous chapter on Exaggeration. We'll look at examples of good use of appeal, break down the principles at use, see how that impacts the overall character's presentation, and determine what this means for your work within Animate CC (i.e. how to replicate it). Then you will be given exercises to work through completely on your own aside from some guidelines in step-by-step form. This part of the book is where the plane has picked up enough speed on the runway to where the wheels start to lift off the tarmac and take flight. You know the tools, you know the methods, and now it's time to put it all to use for a purpose. Let's get into it!

"Appeal is all about taking every one of the principles—indeed everything you know about art and animation—and putting it all together in harmony to create something that people will want to watch."

REAL-WORLD EXAMPLES
Appeal

Few things are as important as a character's introduction to the audience. In film, novels, comic books, and TV, memorable introductions stand out almost more than any other facet of storytelling. The first time you see Darth Vader he's walking, leading a boarding party, choking a rebel, with an immediately intimidating design (the helmet, the breathing sound, the deep voice, the all-black attire with cape against his simply armored and contrasting white colored soldiers). The way he walks in is so purposeful and determined; at first sight you know this guy is not going to stop until he gets what he's after. You know what he's all about from his first lines, and that's all you need to know to want to see more. What is he going to do?

Conversely, Willy Wonka's entrance is much different. The clothes he's wearing, the audience's collective apnea at his sight convinces us that this is a momentous occasion, and finally the reveal that he has just played with that mysterious perception to pull a prank on the very people who've come to see him all say that this guy is quirky and you're never quite going to know where he's coming from. There's so much depth in his character from the outset, so many places the storytellers could go from there, and that makes you want to see more of him.

You can continue to analyze other great live-action introductions even when they're not technically the first time a character is seen. Throughout the opening escapade, Indiana Jones (from *Raiders of the Lost Ark*) is set up as a smart and physically capable adventurer with a goal of preserving artifacts in museums for academic (and monetary) purposes, and it gives us two of the most recognizable moments in film: measuring the sand and fleeing the boulder.

Technically the second time he's seen in the film, Bela Lugosi's turn as Dracula (1931) is full of mysterious and charming flare as he regally walks down a dark, imperial staircase holding a single candle saying, "I am Dracula … I bid you welcome." Then he shows his strange love for the wolves' howling, calling them "children of the night" and walking back up the stairs for our hapless guest to only then realize that Dracula has walked through a wall of spider webs and left them untouched. Creepy.

These are all examples of great introductions and masterful use of Appeal in setting, action, and character design (costumes, makeup, posture, etc.) but all in live-action film. Observation is paramount in any art, and this skill is especially applicable to animation. Because we're creating illustrated characters who act as though they're in a 3D world, analyzing how the charismatic and magnetic depictions of characters in live-action are achieved and the actors and directors who made them possible directly helps us know how to control our own animated worlds to best effect. For our first example, we're going to look at one of the greatest character introductions in animated film history.

Example 1: "Scar's Introduction from Disney's *The Lion King*"

The Lion King, in general, has outstanding introductions. Almost every character has a memorable one, and even the introduction to the movie itself is amazing and iconic. The villain, Scar, however is unique, even among the long history of antagonists in animated film. He's not physically imposing, or really even outright threatening to the main characters. His introduction balances a tightrope between showing you how relatively pitiful he is and where his power will ultimately show up. He's a schemer, a plotter, and he knows which fights he can win and which he can't. He chooses his path selfishly but wisely. The movie has been out for a while, but I'm against ruining an ending to a great film for anyone for any reason. So all I will say is that even the factor that leads to his eventual downfall is shown in the introduction. All of these decisions are made at the script and storyboard phase. How can we give the audience what they need to know to understand this character? What we're mostly going to look at is all of the representations of Appeal that show up in Scar's design and movement

Image 12.2

throughout the scene to see how this idea brings together all of the other 11 remaining principles. They're broken down into moments and numbered/named accordingly.

1. *The mouse*—an unanthropomorphized mouse emerges from a cave and starts scurrying around. The **timing** of the mouse's quick movements and long breaks for cleaning or sniffing are used to create **anticipation** until …

2. *The capture*—Scar's paw slams down on top of the mouse (**squash and stretch**). There's a pause of a little over 1 second (**anticipation**) before it picks the little creature up slowly. There's a very gentle **slow-in** to this move and **overlapping action** in the paw having to straighten out before following the rest of the leg (or "arm" in this semi-anthropomorphized example).

3. *The first words*—these are very telling. "Life's not fair, is it?" He's toying with his meal, seemingly empathizing, but the contradiction between Scar's comparably enormous size compared to the mouse just feels like he's picking on the little guy. The arm is even raised up high so that he doesn't have to lower his head in order to talk to it (**staging**) and there's a good sense of volume in the "fingers" of his paw and dimension in his face as his head turns (**solid drawing** and **secondary action**). The facial expression is priceless as his eyes are barely open at first but it then turns to a kind of fake concern. The mouse this whole time and throughout the rest of the scene is swinging back and forth (**arcs**, **timing**, and **slow in/out**) and struggling to get away, which is another example of **secondary action**.

4. *"I will never be king"*—he says "I" twice, and with two different expressions. In the first, he's still messing with the little mouse. But the second expression is like he's annoyed at the thought, like he's heard these words said to him a hundred times. It's his "yea, I know … I get it, thanks" expression, looking away from his poor meal for a second. So when Scar turns back to the mouse to finish with "will never be king," he pulls off a mocking, head-rocking motion which pays tribute to a similar move made famous by Milt Kahl. It's a kind of "nanny nanny boo boo" or "blah blah blah" maneuver. With this little sequence, he's demonstrating that it's pretty common knowledge that he'll never be king, he wants it, and that frustration is going to be released on the mouse. This whole part is oozing with **secondary action** on Scar himself— wonderful acting.

5. *"And you …"*—Scar lets the mouse out of his grip for a moment, and it starts trying to escape by running across his paw. As he extends his fingers and rotates his paw; Scar is just showing contempt and complete domination over his prey (more **secondary action**). The entire shot is now in a close-up of this event, so you're not even seeing Scar. You're focusing on the mouse. You, as the audience, are realizing that you sympathize more with the mouse in this moment and the whole thing is **staged** well to show that the mouse, no matter how hard it tries, isn't getting out of this situation, which increases the **anticipation**.

6. *Last words*—"… shall never see the light of another day." Scar says this line with glee, almost giddy at the notion of what he's going to do. There's no respect, the fake empathy is now openly admitted, and he really seems terrible. His head rotates with a very smooth **slow in/ out** to look back at the mouse, now back in his clutches and struggling to get away. Scar laughs

with another head wobble—he giggles really. He's quite pleased with himself. There's a lot of **anticipation** here and plenty more **secondary action**, which is all revealing more of his character. Really, the whole scene is one big buildup to ...

7. "*Adieu*"—this word is said simply and softly with a slight head tilt. His mind is made up. He's done with this game, and now it's time to eat. He opens his mouth, and the tongue rolls out with great **overlapping action**. The dimension in his face and volume retained throughout, including now seeing the cavernous, gaping jaws, demonstrate-excellent **solid drawing** and subtle **exaggeration** (pushing the pose just a little further to accentuate the big, menacing jaws that the mouse, who the audience has now imprinted themselves on, sees).

This entire scene happens in 30 seconds! The only principle that wasn't called out was Straight Ahead Action and Pose to Pose. The pose to pose method was almost certainly used for the acting performance of Scar. It's not just the best way to get that result, but it may be the only reliable way to achieve acting that nuanced in an animated character. The animation for the mouse was most likely done with straight ahead action, but the fact is that there's no surefire way to know unless one were to ask the animator, Andreas Deja. All tallied up, every principle is here. There are many more uses of each principle in the sections, but they were just too numerous to list. For instance, squash and stretch are applied to Scar's face when he's speaking. These slight contortions of his face beyond his normal anatomy allow for more acting range and add to appeal. The length and thinness of his face make it easier to form a triangular configuration, which is a subtle cue in design that this is the bad guy. He even has a goatee to enhance this look. Compare him with his brother Mufasa, whose chin is more square (design for power) and mane is fuller (symbol of health), and there's no mistaking who they want you to think is the villain.

> "Analyzing others' works is a gateway to understanding how to evaluate and improve your own."

All of the principles are working with each other to form a complete picture of who Scar is, what he's about, what he wants, and how you should feel about him. Ultimately, this harmonic use of the principles builds the appeal of the character, giving him a magnetic charm. Just as solid drawing is something that artists of all types continue to work on throughout their career appeal is hard to quantify and teach, but it can be achieved through constant work and honest critiquing. Analyzing others' works is a gateway to understanding how to evaluate and improve your own. We've looked at an antagonist (villain), so now it's time to look at a protagonist: a puppet who just wants to be a real boy.

Example 2: "Pinocchio's Song 'I've Got No Strings'"

In 1940, Disney released *Pinocchio*, a story about a living puppet who dreams of becoming a real boy and is aided by his conscience Jiminy, a cricket in a top hat. In the original story, Pinocchio was a pretty hateful character, so he had to be updated for Walt Disney's vision. When test animations were being done by Frank Thomas and Ollie Johnston, Pinocchio looked more like a real wooden doll, complete with a pointed nose and wooden hands. It was agreed that the character needed more appeal so that the audience could relate to him more, so Fred Moore came in and redesigned the character to this end but kept the wooden doll aspect as a starting point—that is, after all, what Pinocchio is. It wasn't until Milt Kahl suggested that they abandon the wooden doll design aesthetic completely and just design an innocent, little boy that Pinocchio, as we know him today, was born (*Image 12.3*). Milt redesigned the character as a

Image 12.3 The design progression of Pinocchio, from left to right.

human child (which garners immediate appeal to the audience because of familiar relation), and then he added mechanical joints and a wooden button nose after the fact onto the existing human figure to sell the idea of his being a puppet. When Walt signed off on this new design, he directed the story team to refit the script to represent Pinocchio's updated naïve personality.

But due to this adjustment, Pinocchio was too easily fooled, so they repurposed a minor character (a cricket), who originally is smashed under a hammer by Pinocchio himself and comes back as a ghost, to be the deuteragonist (second most important character) and act as Pinocchio's conscience. Following in the way Milt approached the design of Pinocchio, Ward Kimball created this new cricket character, now named Jiminy, in a similar way – more human/anthropomorphic features first and flourishes second. However, even the serrated legs and antennae were left off the design because, according to Ward, it looked disgusting and detracted from his appeal. Ward Kimball is quoted as saying, "The only thing that makes him a cricket is because we call him one." He was given gloves, a cane, and a top hat to go with his mature role as guide in the film, and another iconic character was born.

This team effort shows how the early Disney crew was still working out how they would achieve appeal in its full theatrical form, and almost acts as an external representation of what you must go through to develop your own character's design and personality. We know, though, that there's another factor, movement aesthetic, which plays into the character's appeal which will become more apparent after we break down the scene. Pinocchio in the "I've Got No Strings" number was animated by Frank Thomas, and the sequence director was Wilfred Jackson.

1. *Standing in strings*—we start with a long shot of Pinocchio alone on the stage after Stromboli's introduction, with a spotlight on him atop a large staircase (**staging**). This shot is *the* iconic image of Pinocchio. His pose is a fantastic representation of his personality, completely summing up his innocent attitude. He almost looks proud to be up there with his chest pointed up slightly but also nervous with his chin tucked in (**solid drawing**). He looks around slowly at the audience (**timing** and **slow in/out**) and starts to smile from the applause (**secondary action**). "This is going to be great!" he's thinking.

2. *Pinocchio sings*—with his new-found confidence, Pinocchio starts marching in place to the beat of the music (**timing**) with a **slow in and out** applied to each up-and-down movement,

Image 12.4

like he's bobbing. Notice the fantastic **overlapping action** of his hair tuft in the front and his bowtie. Now supremely excited, he **stretches** back far while putting his hand on his chest and belting out "I." Notice the great **staging** of his pose to clearly see where the other arm is in his silhouette.

3. *"Got No Strings"*—he marches down the stairs, ready to take on this musical number with every fiber (wooden pun intended) of his being. The strings he leaves behind swing in **arcs** like pendulums that have been disturbed. The march Pinocchio does down the stairs, including the initial step, utilizes every single principle. Can you pick them all out?

4. *"... to hold me dow-"*—this part gets me every time. I can't help but laugh. When he falls, there is absolutely *no* **anticipation**. The absence of anticipation is still a use of the principle because it's only in the decision to remove any hint that it's coming that makes Pinocchio's trip so funny to the audience. Not only do we not know it's coming, neither does *he*! The expression

on his face as he tumbles is clearly readable (**staging**) and the comedic **timing** is spot on throughout.

5. *The fall*—the final moment that he launches up and falls nose-first into the hole has clear use of **arcs** and **slow in/out** as well as **anticipation** in the fact that there is a small beat as Pinocchio **squashes** at the bottom of the stairs before **stretching** up into the final motion. After the impact, his feet nail down the humor of the scene with wonderful **follow through.** You might miss the **overlapping action, follow through,** and **squash and stretch** of the hat on first viewings, but it adds a lot to the scene whether you notice or not. If you look frame by frame, you can also see that while his feet are still in the air, they bend (**squash**) and then extend (**stretch**), which adds to the feeling of sudden impact.

6. *Pinocchio's stuck*—right after the impact, there's a subtle beat where he does nothing, which adds to the **anticipation**. "Is he OK? Am I a terrible person for laughing?" you may be thinking. He slowly brings his hands close to his chest in "push up" position. With some great attention to varying **slow in/out,** it's clearly shown that it's harder for him to push up the farther his head is lifted. The final pose is a great example of **solid drawing** and **staging**. You can clearly see everything, you know where his body parts are in relation to each other and the environment, and there is a real sense of depth. The actual expression is priceless. "Did I just mess everything up? What do I do now?" he seems to be thinking.

7. *The reaction*—from here, after a quick comment by Jiminy from the peanut gallery, it's Stromboli's show (animated by the excellent Bill Tytla). This villain is so boisterous and emotional with large, expressive gestures that you might miss one of the finer moments in Pinocchio's acting. As Stromboli is freaking out, Pinocchio can be seen trying to push up a couple times and get his nose unstuck. Stromboli then slams his hand down on the piece of wood, popping Pinocchio's nose out of the hole. There is a short beat where Pinocchio recognizes that he's not stuck anymore and smiles so innocently with his eyes still fixed downward to the board. Stromboli actually has to pick him up and shake the living puppet to communicate just how angry he is. That short moment where Pinocchio smiles and looks genuinely happy that this little problem has been solved, not recognizing how much trouble he could be in, is such an amazing moment. Stromboli's anger is the primary point of the shot, so Pinocchio's acting could be considered the secondary action in the frame. The acting is so real and strong that Pinocchio still has his moment of honesty and innocence around all of Stromboli's fury.

This entire scene happens in 25 seconds (including Jiminy's shot). You could go shot by shot through the entire musical number and see just how diverse the acting is to give appeal to the character; but there are a couple things of note in particular that need to be pointed out to really drive the idea home. When Pinocchio actually goes back to singing the number, he's now already taken a tumble and been chastised by Stromboli in front of the entire audience. Because he's so naïve and innocent, however, he's able to go right back into performing, if a bit timidly. Frank Thomas wanted to animate the gestures Pinocchio does to be a bit out of sync with the music so that it seems amateurish. The idea was that he had never really practiced the song and dance number; he's just been thrown into it and so is figuring it out on the fly. So when the spotlight turns back on, it startles him. When he starts to sing "I've got no strings," he almost misses the moment, jumping (using a stretch preceded by an anticipation squash) into the first word. "To hold me down" should be accented by a point to the ground, but the gesture comes in late. He's trying to remember the steps he never practiced and perform at the same time. Apparently, when Frank Thomas told Milt Kahl of his plan to have the movements be off-beat as an insight into Pinocchio's mood and character, Frank says that Milt told him, "That's the lousiest idea I've heard anywhere!"

Milt Kahl's vision is what improved Pinocchio's design from the one that Frank Thomas (and Ollie Johnston) were working on to what we see today. But it was Frank's vision of the "I've Got No Strings" song and dance sequence which differed from Milt's that ended up endearing the character with that wonderful appeal we saw in the finished product. Different animators approach acting and design in unique ways, and ultimately it's the vision of the director to merge all of these sequences together into one. Wilfred Jackson might have been the sequence director on this example, but Walt Disney was an extremely hands-on feature director for the entirety of *Pinocchio*. That vision is what comes through with the input of the animators charged with acting the scenes and story points out on screen. Appeal is so much more than something that looks nice. It's the difference between a film you have on in the background while you clean the living room and one that captures your attention through each minute of the runtime.

There's one more thing about this scene which should be pointed out. As Pinocchio continues the song, he's figuring out the dance steps as he goes. There's a fun leg-kicking motion that he uses to hop across the stage. The first to stage right (the left of the screen, also known as "house left") has a lot of bounce to it with overlapping action and squash and stretch. The second sequence of this leg-kick step to stage left has almost no up-and-down motion on the part of his head—it looks like a refined movement. He's figured it out on the first sequence, and now he's got it down pat. This success can be seen in his expression. But the most notable part is after that sequence, where his confidence is growing and he experiments with more dance moves, Pinocchio swings his lower leg (shin and foot) around in circles rotating around the joint at his "knee." If you look closely at the type of joint, this move is technically impossible! If he were to try that in real life, his shin would knock up against his upper leg and not be able to pass through. The only way that the leg could make this spin is if it were offset—if the shin were connected on the outer part of the upper leg. That isn't how the leg

Image 12.5 The "impossible" leg-swing progression.

joint is shown (*Image 12.5*). The fact is, you don't notice it, not just because it happens so quickly but because the move fits the character. This move feels like a natural progression of his dance in relation to his personality and offers more insight into his character, which we gladly accept as the audience. It shouldn't really be able to happen, but it's very appealing. You have to know what the rules are before you can break them correctly.

Using Appeal Where "Every Principle Plays its Part"

Appeal is a dance among the other principles. They need to work together for a common cause. A hero should be appealing, but so should the sidekick. Villains should be appealing. Environments, tertiary characters, and even objects should demonstrate appeal. What happens if in Disney's *Sword in the Stone* (1963) you don't like looking at the area where the actual sword sits in the stone? The entire moment when Arthur grabs the sword and does what none before him could do becomes just a scene where something happens, but you can't ... quite ... remember what it was. Something with a knife, maybe? The staging is important to set the scene, but solid drawing applies to environmental elements as well, especially those which impact the story.

Those two together help the actor (the animated Arthur) to build the requisite anticipation in the scene by way of the other principles of design and motion, all of which leads to an appealing character in an appealing scene. It may seem like a lot to keep in mind, but really it's just about being aware of what you want the audience to feel and how to go about doing that. The 12 Principles of Animation came from that motivation.

Image 12.6 Music video in a 1920s rubber-hose animation style, My Flea Has Dogs *by Mukpuddy Animation (mukpuddy.com).*

There is no single, magic tool within Animate CC to help facilitate the application of this principle. Analyzing animation videos frame by frame can go a long way in helping you learn to create by way of deconstruction, but ultimately the buck stops with you—the animator. After a while, the principles and their deeper meanings will become second nature to you as well as how to apply them, but for now, as a quick reference guide, here are things to keep in mind through each shot you animate:

- **Timing**—determines the pace and rhythm of the action.
- **Slow In/Out**—provides the presence and intensity of a cushion to the movement in the timing.
- **Squash and Stretch**—emphasizes impacts, quick movements, and uncomfortable poses.
- **Anticipation**—is made up of beats where action is withheld or is an action that insinuates another.

- **Arcs**—are organic and help the eye track a movement as natural.

- **Staging**—directs the eye to what you want the audience to pay attention to.

- **Straight Ahead Action and Pose to Pose**—two methods for animating which are spontaneous and structured, respectively.

- **Overlapping Action and Follow Through**—add dimension through movement. When motions on (or related to) a body happen at different rates, they overlap. Follow through is when a body stops moving and other parts keep going.

- **Secondary Action**—is an independent action which helps to support the story point of the main action.

- **Solid Drawing**—facilitates the illusion that the character, though simplified, exists in a 3D world with volume and weight.

- **Exaggeration**—pushes any of the previously mentioned principles beyond "normal" physics or anatomy to accentuate the moment or character.

- **Appeal**—pulls all the other principles together in harmony to captivate the audience.

Think of your character as a living breathing creature; one with dreams, fears, desires, quirks, opinions, and everything that fills out a personality. This will help you to block out the actions in a sequence better and be more true to your character. Push the sketches a little further to see if that helps add more feeling to the poses, and if it doesn't that's OK. You can always pull it right back. Make sure that you've considered the staging of the poses and gestures to best demonstrate the action and use the straight ahead and pose to pose methods to rough out what you have decided; during these decisions is also when you're nailing down the timing of the acting. Consider if anticipation might be needed in broad strokes and try to reflect that idea in the timing, and if not, disregard. Keeping the other movement principles in mind (Slow In/Out, Squash and Stretch, Arcs, and Overlapping Action and Follow Through), continue roughing out the scene. If you haven't worked it into your sketches already and before you go too much further, try to see if some secondary action might improve the audience's ability to read the emotions or intentions on screen better. Finish roughing out the animation and then double check your arcs. Now look at what you've done and determine which of Animate's features would best accomplish the scene you have in front of you: which features can be symbols, and which of those should be nested within another? Clean up the images using solid drawing and then symblify the character for animation. Finally, using Animate's set of tools, animate what you can through nested animation and tweens (limited

Image 12.7 Saving Christmas by Stephen Brooks (RubberOnion.com).

dimension movement) or animate frame by frame when appropriate (large changes in perspective or distortions of the model). This process is animating in Animate CC, the Tradigital way.

You should always ask yourself, "Is this really something the character would do?" Another question that would be good to add to some of your decisions is, "Am I taking this approach just because it's easier?" and follow that up with, "Could my approach be improved?" The reason these questions are important is because when you have hundreds and thousands of images to sketch or at least account for, it can become easy to fall into a workman's groove, where it becomes more about getting it done than getting it done right. Maintaining focus on the story point of whatever scene you're working on and the personality of the character you're animating are steps 1 to 1000. After that are the technical aspects of making the motion come out looking the best so that your character is acting and not just committing a series of movements. It's getting repeated again: Animate CC is a tool. It exists to aid in your creation. And as with all tools, you have to know what you want to do first before you use it. The principles are there to focus your attention on the most significant points in order to make those important decisions. Appeal is the one principle whose consideration is a part of every step of the process—which is why it's both last in this list and, I believe, in Frank and Ollie's original listing.

> "When you have hundreds and thousands of images to sketch or at least account for, it can become easy to fall into a workman's groove, where it becomes more about getting it done than getting it done right."

FINAL WORDS
Appeal

Animation, the way we're doing it, is the communication of simple and complicated emotions, ideas, and actions by way of lines and shapes. To accomplish this goal, it's usually the most direct attitudes that make the most readable drawings. Delicate and nuanced images often come across as ambiguous. These simplified drawings make great conduits for pantomimed action and dialog, but as Dave Hand said sometime in 1938, features like "the face begins to flatten out when you get too close on it." For *Pinocchio*, avoiding that flattening meant that a lot of work needed to be done on the Blue Fairy for her close-ups to get more dimension out of her face (*Image 12.8*).

Image 12.8 The Blue Fairy from Pinocchio *(1940).*

With the help of Adobe Animate, gradients have gotten easier to apply consistently, the application of a texture has been reduced from a large hassle, lines scale with their size on stage without having to redraw, and even having shapes with no outlines is so easy it seems surprising to newer artists that animating without outlines was once a difficult issue to overcome. Despite the list of limitations of the past being shortened, our knowledge of the fundamentals of movement, design, and character acting shouldn't change. And unfortunately, that's exactly what seems to happen. They say that "necessity is the mother of invention," but nobody follows up the saying with, "And after that invention, completely abandon everything you know." Appeal is usually the first principle to vanish whenever attention drifts away from the 12 Principles of Animation as a whole, and it's arguably the most important. Think of what the original masters of animation had to do in order to create a feature-length or short film with as much heart and character as they did. They were artists in every sense of the word. Does anyone really think that they wouldn't have used every tool at their disposal to further the expression of their art form? It can be assured, however, that no matter what new tool or feature they would use, the art would come first.

I would like to leave off with this parting thought, since it's the very last thing mentioned in the 12 Principles of Animation section of Frank Thomas and Ollie Johnston's *The Illusion of Life*.

> "In the mid-thirties, we wished for shading, for textures, for areas with no outlines, but they were not practical. We had to find other ways of putting over the points in the scenes, and in so doing developed character animation into a communicative art that astounded the world. But at the time there was neither glory nor pride in our efforts, only the nagging limitations. As we passed each other in the hall, we shook our heads and shared the thought, 'It's a crude medium.'"

Those limitations are largely gone, but the principles developed while creating the "communicative art that astounded the world" *due* to those limitations remain. This point underlines the entire purpose of this book. For the beginner in any facet, it's important to remember how these principles were developed and why, so as to see the true benefits that are at your fingertips right now. By bringing all of the principles into your

Image 12.9 Frank Thomas (left) and Ollie Johnston (right) at Stanford University in 1932.

work within Animate CC—merging the traditional with the digital—you are an extension of the great animation history we all know. All art grows and adapts to what's new around it, and clearly animation isn't (and shouldn't be) any different. It's a remarkably flexible and diverse field of expression and storytelling, rivaling that of any other medium. This inherent flexibility in the face of new technology has led to the rise of Tradigital animation of which you are a part. The bottom line: appeal *is* animation. And animation in any form can be appealing. It's up to you to make it so.

Index

Page numbers in italics refer to figures.